The
Critical Response
to
Chester Himes

The
Critical Response
to
Chester Himes

Edited by
Charles L. P. Silet

Critical Responses in Arts and Letters, Number 34
Cameron Northouse, Series Adviser

GREENWOOD PRESS
Westport, Connecticut • London

Library of Congress Cataloging-in-Publication Data

The critical response to Chester Himes / edited by Charles L. P. Silet.
    p.   cm.—(Critical responses in arts and letters, ISSN
1057–0993 ; no. 34)
    Includes bibliographical references and index.
    ISBN 0–313–29941–2 (alk. paper)
    1. Himes, Chester B., 1909– —Criticism and interpretation.
2. Detective and mystery stories, American—History and criticism.
3. Harlem (New York, N.Y.)—In literature.   4. Afro-American police
in literature.   5. Afro-Americans in literature.   I. Silet, Charles
L. P.   II. Series.
PS3515.I713Z6   1999
813'.54—dc21   99–16098

British Library Cataloguing in Publication Data is available.

Library of Congress Catalog Card Number: 99–16098
ISBN: 0–313–29941–2
ISSN: 1057–0993

First published in 1999

Greenwood Press, 88 Post Road West, Westport, CT 06881
An imprint of Greenwood Publishing Group, Inc.
www.greenwood.com

Printed in the United States of America

The paper used in this book complies with the
Permanent Paper Standard issued by the National
Information Standards Organization (Z39.48–1984).

10 9 8 7 6 5 4 3 2 1

Copyright Acknowledgments

Claude Julien, "Space and Civil Rights Ideology: The Example of Chester Himes's *The Third Generation*," *Sociocriticism,* Nos. 4–5 (1986–1987), 143–152. Reprinted with permission from *Sociocriticism.*

Aribert Schroeder, "Toni Morrison's Variations on Chester Himes," *AFRAM Newsletter*, No 29 (July 1989), 20–25. Reprinted with permission from *AFRAM Newsletter* and the author.

Robert E. Skinner, "The Black Man in the Literature of Labor: The Early Novels of Chester Himes," *Labor's Heritage*, 1 (July 1989), 51–65. Reprinted with permission from *Labor's Heritage* and author.

Wendy W. Walters, "Limited Options: Strategic Maneuverings in Himes's Harlem," *African American Review*, 28:4 (1994), 615–631. Reprinted with permission from the author.

Steven J. Rosen, "African American Anti-Semitism and Himes's *Lonely Crusade*," *MELUS*, 20:2 (Summer 1995), 47–68. Reprinted with permission from *MELUS.*

Gary Storhoff, "Slaying the Fathers: The Autobiography of Chester Himes," From *a/b: Auto/Biography Studies*, 11:1 (Spring 1996), 38–55. Copyright © by the Joyce and Elizabeth Hall Center for the Humanities at the University of Kansas. Used by permission of the publisher.

Gwendoline Lewis Roget, "Chester Himes—The Ethics of Ambiguity: An Interview with Joseph Sandy Himes, Jr.," *Xavier Review*, 14:1 (Spring 1994), 1–18. Reprinted with permission of the author.

John A. Williams, "My Man Himes," in *Amistad 1: Writings on Black Literature and Culture*. Edited by John A. Williams and Charles F. Harris. New York: Vintage, 1970. Pp. 25–93. Quotations reprinted with permission of the author.

John W. Roberts, *From Trickster to Badman: The Black Folk Hero in Slavery and Freedom*. Philadelphia: University of Pennsylvania Press, 1989. Quotations reprinted with permission of the University of Pennsylvania Press.

All quotations from the works of Chester Himes in this volume are reprinted by permission of Roslyn Targ, Roslyn Targ Literary Agency, 105 West 13th Street, New York, NY 10011.

Thunder Mouth Press:

All Shot Up, (c)1960, 1996 by Chester Himes

"A Nigger" in *The Collected Stories of Chester Himes*, (c)1990 in this anthology by Lesley Himes

Lonely Crusade, (c)1986 by the Estate of Chester Himes

My Life of Absurdity, (c)1976 by Chester Himes

Contents

Essays

Contents   xi

An Interview

Series Foreword

Critical Responses in Arts and Letters is designed to present a documentary history of highlights in the critical reception to the body of work of writers and artists and to individual works that are generally considered to be of major importance. The focus of each volume in this series is basically historical. The introductions to each volume are themselves brief histories of the critical response an author, artist, or individual work has received. This response is then further illustrated by reprinting a strong representation of the major critical reviews and articles that have collectively produced the author's, artist's, or work's critical reputation.

The scope of *Critical Responses in Arts and Letters* knows no chronological or geographical boundaries. Volumes under preparation include studies of individuals from around the world and in both contemporary and historical periods.

Each volume is the work of an individual editor, who surveys the entire body of criticism on a single author, artist, or work. The editor then selects the best material to depict the critical response received by an author or artist over his/her entire career. Documents produced by the author or artist may also be included when the editor finds that they are necessary to a full understanding of the materials at hand. In circumstances where previous, isolated volumes of criticism on a particular individual or work exist, the editor carefully selects material that better reflects the nature and directions of the critical response over time.

In addition to the introduction and the documentary section, the editor of each volume is free to solicit new essays on areas that may not have been adequately dealt with in previous criticism. Also, for volumes on living writers and artists, new interviews may be included, again at the discretion of the volume's editor. The volumes also provide a supplementary bibliography and are fully indexed.

While each volume in *Critical Responses in Arts and Letters* is unique, it is also hoped that in combination they form a useful, documentary history of the critical response to the arts, and one that can be easily and profitably employed by students and scholars.

Cameron Northouse

Acknowledgments

Every project such as this one relies on the cooperation of many people. I would like to thank all those who generously allowed me to reprint their original work.

My gratitude also goes to Thomas Kent, Chair, Department of English, Iowa State University for his financial support for photo duplication and research assistance.

I also want to thank Sarah Brown and Deb Amenson, who provided much good work on this project as my research assistants, Anna Hoevelkamp, who remained calm while typing the index, and Sheryl Kamps, whose wizardry with the computer put the manuscript into its present form.

Finally, as always, I want to thank my wife, Kay, whose constant encouragement has made this project, as well as all my other publications, possible.

Ames, Iowa
June, 1998

Introduction

As the title of the recent biography suggests, Chester Himes led several lives during the seventy-five years of his troublesome career. Chester was the youngest son in a rising African-American family who made its way into the black middle-class only to fall back as the result of a series of unfortunate reversals. He spent his twenties as an inmate in the Ohio correctional system, and there he learned the craft of writing that would bring him fame and heartbreak and a modest living during his adult years. After his release from prison Himes was a writer of angry and violent protest novels and over the next twenty years he became, along with Richard Wright and Ralph Ellison, one of the more celebrated black writers in America. From the mid-fifties until his death in Spain thirty years later, he was an expatriate and a tangential member of the community of black artists, which included Wright and James Baldwin, who fled American racism to settle in Europe during the period after the Second World War. In his later years, Himes wrote a revealing and uncompromising two-volume autobiography and a series of masterful crime novels, the "Harlem Domestic" books—for which he is probably best remembered today—which brought him a measure of fame and a more steady income. In all of these "lives" Chester Himes struggled to come to grips with the racist American society into which he was born and lived and to realize his place in that society as a black man and an artist.

Life

Chester Bomar Himes was born on July 29, 1909 in Jefferson City, Missouri to Joseph Sandy Himes and Estelle Bomar Himes. He was the youngest of three sons. Joseph Himes was a teacher of industrial arts and spent the years of Chester's youth as a faculty member at several black institutions predominantly in the south. The Himes's family moved frequently and Chester's education was spotty but obviously adequate. Not only did Chester become a writer but his brother Joseph, Jr. earned a doctorate in sociology at Ohio State

University and later became a professor at North Carolina State College in Durham. By the time Chester was in his teens the family had settled in Cleveland and after his graduation from Glenville High School, he entered Ohio State University in the fall of 1926. However, his university career was short lived, and at the end of the spring quarter 1927 he was asked to leave for poor grades and participating in a speakeasy fight.

Back in Cleveland Chester worked as a bellboy at the Gilsy Hotel and slipped into a life on the edges of the city's crime world, where he became engaged in hustling, drinking, and gambling. Eventually he ran a whisky joint in the back of Bunch Boy's gambling club with his future wife Jean Johnson. In 1928 he burglarized the YMCA, and although he was arrested, his mother pleaded for clemency and the judge suspended his sentence. Shortly thereafter, he was arrested again, for writing bad checks, and this time his father persuaded the authorities to give him a two-year suspended sentence. In November 1928 he was caught for robbery, convicted, and sentenced from twenty to twenty-five years in the Ohio State Penitentiary.

For the next seven and a half years Himes served time, and in the enforced discipline of prison life he began to write fiction. His first publication, "His Last Day," appeared in *Abbott's Monthly* in November 1932 and his story, "Crazy in Stir," was published in *Esquire* in August 1934. It was the first of several stories which he wrote in prison that would appear in the magazine, and they brought him to the attention of the wider literary world. Chester was paroled on April 1, 1936, and he returned to his family in Cleveland where he continued to work on his writing. In August 1937 he married Jean Johnson. The years immediately after his prison experience were lean ones and Chester accepted a number of menial jobs, finally working for the Ohio Writer's Project where he compiled the official history of Cleveland. During this time he completed the early drafts of his first novel, a prison story originally called *Black Sheep* which was eventually published as *Cast the First Stone* in 1952.

After a short stay at Louis Bromfield's Malabar Farm, where he worked as a butler, in 1942 Jean and Chester followed Bromfield to Los Angeles to find industrial work. Over the next three years Chester held some twenty jobs, most of them in defense plants, and he contributed articles and fiction to *Opportunity* and *Crisis* and finished his second novel *If He Hollers Let Him Go* on a Rosenwald Fellowship. In 1945 the novel was published by Doubleday and Chester began work on *Lonely Crusade* which Knopf brought out in 1947. In spite of his limited literary success, the Himeses live a precarious life, and Chester continued to take menial jobs where and when he could find them.

On April 3, 1953 Himes embarked for Europe and excepting for several return trips of various duration to the United States, he would remain an exile for the rest of his life. In Paris he was introduced into the expatriate black community, largely through the efforts of Richard Wright. While he lived abroad both *The Third Generation* (1954) and *The Primitive* (1955) were published in America. Aside from his *A Case of Rape* (1963), released in a French translation, a collection of essays, stories, and a play, *Black on Black: "Baby Sister" and Selected Writings* (1973) and his two volumes of autobiography, *The Quality of Hurt* (1972) and *My Life of Absurdity* (1976), for the remainder of his life Himes's writing career was devoted mainly to his detective series featuring the two Harlem detectives Grave Digger Jones and Coffin Ed Johnson.

In January of 1957 Himes met Marcel Duhamel who contracted him to write a novel for the French publisher Gallimard's "La Série Noire," a notable collection of crime fiction which Duhamel was then editing. The first, *For Love of Imabelle* (1957), was published in English in the United States then by Gallimard in translation and later reissued, again in English, under the title of *A Rage in Harlem* (1965). The rest of the series appeared initially in French translation and later in English. Himes described the books as his "Harlem Domestic" novels. The second, *Il pleut des coups durs* (*The Real Cool Killers*) won in 1958 the prestigious *Grand prix de la littérature policiére* for best crime novel published in France. The series eventually attracted a new audience in America for Himes which encouraged the reissue of his earlier, non-crime fiction.

Throughout his years in Europe Himes traveled extensively. He had been separated from Jean since 1952 and in 1959 he began a relationship with Lesley Packard, whom he married in 1978. Himes finally settled down in Alicante, Spain in 1968 where he and Lesley built a house. In 1963 Chester suffered a stoke and in his later years experienced various other health problems. The house in Spain proved to be his haven during the remainder of his life. Although his reputation continued to grow both in the United States and abroad and his books were increasingly reprinted, Himes remained strapped for money, and his final years were spent quietly, mostly at his home. Chester Bomar Himes died on November 13, 1984 in Benissa, Spain.

Critical Reception

From the publication of his first novel, *If He Hollers Let Him Go*, Chester Himes confounded the critics, and they never quite got a handle on his work. Was his fiction too violent or was it merely reflecting the realities of American racism? Was he sexist or just reflecting the tensions inherent in a community where Afro-American males were desperately searching for a sense of self? Did he sell out to the publishing world dominated by white editors when he wrote his "Harlem domestic" series or were these hard-hitting yet more mainstream crime novels an extension of his more "artistic" but less popular protest novels? Did the "protest" books reflect the real Himes and were the crime books a diminished afterthought? Was his two-volume autobiography a self-serving complaint against the slights and failures of his life or an uncompromising, albeit refracted, view of one black man's struggle against a racist society? Through the years in various reviews and articles the critics wrestled with these questions. Perhaps in the end it is because of such contradictions that Chester Himes retains a fascination for us today and through our mixed, often confused, responses to them that he achieved his measure of importance, not just as a "black" writer but as an American writer, one who captured something of the truth of our society and of our literature in the last half of this, the "American" century.

James Baldwin, who later came to know Himes as a fellow expatriate in Paris, wrote one of the more interesting and substantial commentaries of Himes's early career. In his review of *Lonely Crusade* he summed up his response to the central character of the novel this way: "... we are faced with a black man as many faceted as we ourselves are, as individual, with our ambivalence and insecurities and our struggles to be loved. He is now an American and we cannot change that: it is our attitudes which must change both towards ourselves and him." Unfortunately Baldwin's grasp of what we would now perceive as the essence of Himes's fiction remained a minority voice. All too many of the reviewers of Himes's early "protest" fiction either criticized the violence of the books or apologized for it or merely complained about what they saw as his awkwardness of style. Most reviews simply dismissed the books with a brief description of the plot. Some reviewers acknowledged that his portrayal of American racism was accurate; many deplored his lack of any constructive suggestions for its amelioration.

Even when Himes received a certain measure of fame through the republication of his detective novels in this country, after they were first released in translation in France, the notices with few exceptions remained slight. In part this was due to the fact that the critics were reviewing what they thought of as "crime" fiction, at best a bastard genre, and certainly not "literary." Although the reception of his two volumes of autobiography fared better, primarily it remained for literary scholars and academic critics, who had the leisure and the historical perspective and the space, to extensively explore the complexities of both the "protest" and "detective" novels—terms Himes himself disliked and thought demeaning categories for his work. This serious critical attention began in the early 1970s, and shows no sign of letting up.

Himes's literary reputation in France probably affected his reception in the United States and the growing popularity of his crime fiction which had been re-issued beginning in the 1960s both contributed to Himes becoming not only increasingly better-known and better-read but also more seriously regarded by the literary establishment here, a position which Himes might have found curious and perhaps a bit amusing. As a result of this increased attention most of his earlier novels have come back into print, often with informative introductions, and two of the books, *The Primitive* and *Cast the First Stone* have recently been published in the form Himes originally intended with the editorial excisions restored. A volume of his collected stories also appeared in 1990 both here and in Great Britain, and his unfinished novel, *Plan B*, was published posthumously both in French and English.

There have appeared several full-length critical studies of his work, a comprehensive bibliography of both primary and secondary materials, a collection of his interviews, and most recently the first biography of his life. In addition other scholarly works have included chapters on Himes and articles about him now appear with regularity in the quarterlies and scholarly journals. Short of a collection of his correspondence and a collection of his non-fiction, almost everything he wrote is now available for study. An indication of Himes's expanded reputation is evident by the inclusion of *The Real Cool Killers* in the recent Library of America's *Crime Noir: American Noir of the*

1950s which is now available along with standard sets of Ralph Waldo Emerson, Henry James, and Mark Twain.

Himes once believed that in American letters there was room at the top for only one black writer at a time and therefore black writers were always competing for that coveted spot. He felt that he always came in second, initially behind Richard Wright and then behind James Baldwin. Perhaps one of the reasons he often spoke slightingly of his Harlem Domestic books was that he felt that writing crime fiction was not helping him in the contest. It is somewhat ironic that the fame brought to him by the Coffin Ed and Grave Digger Jones series not only helped to break the color-barrier in American crime fiction, but also attracted readers who later discovered his earlier, more "literary" works and spurred interest in him as a serious American writer.

Certainly no one any longer believes that there is only one top place for black writers on the contemporary literary scene. There is a healthy tradition now developing in crime writing for Afro-Americans led by the phenomenal success of Walter Mosley's Easy Rawlins books. The proliferation of novels, drama, and poetry by such authors as Toni Morrison, Ernest J. Gaines. Gloria Naylor, Derek Walcott, Maya Angelou, Alice Walker and others would suggest that whatever constraints Himes felt as an exiled black writer seems to be loosening. It is heartening that Chester Himes is now being accorded a place beside Wright, Baldwin, and Ellison, the writers of his generation who opened the way for the current wave of Afro-American writers, writers who can now be accepted not only as creators of ethnic literature but full-fledged American writers, a part of the native grain.

Note on the text

In choosing the selections for this book I have tried to include only those items that were of some importance. Most of the reviews of Himes's books did not fit into this category; those that I have included were among the more interesting and substantive. I also picked one interview: the very interesting and informative one conducted by Gwendoline Lewis Roget, because it modifies some of the mis-perceptions of the essays which were included. It also does not appear in Michel Fabre and Robert E. Skinner, *Conversations with Chester Himes* (Jackson: University Press of Mississippi, 1995), an informative collection of interviews with Himes himself.

Originally I had intended to divide the articles into those which dealt with the so-called "protest novels" from those on Himes's "crime" writings. Because the line is often blurred between the two and because many of the essays discuss both types, I finally decided to intermix the two. The current chronological arrangement also provides a sense of the growth of Himes scholarship in a sequential ordering.

Most significantly, I chose only those writings about Chester Himes which have appeared in English. There is another entire tradition of writing about Himes and his fiction in French, but I did not feel comfortable including translations in this collection. It is tradition better left for others to explore. I have retained this approach in the bibliography appended to the end of the

volume as well by only listing items published in the English language. As I
state in the headnote to that section, those wishing to explore material about
Himes in other languages should consult the comprehensive bibliography by
Michel Fabre, Robert E. Skinner, and Lester Sullivan.

Finally, I silently made a few, minor corrections in some of the essays, but
for the most part I did not want to edit wholesale the selections I made. So there
are some repetitions, especially of biographical materials, in a few of the essays
which I retained. I did not want to violate the integrity of the individual articles,
and because such anthologies as this one are usually read piecemeal, to remove
the biographical sections would greatly reduce the meaning for individual
readings of some of the selections.

Chronology

1909   Chester Bomar Himes is born on 29 July in Jefferson City, Missouri to Joseph Sandy Himes and Estelle Bomar Himes. He is the youngest of three children. His father teaches at the Lincoln Institute.

1913   The family moves to Cleveland, Ohio.

1913   They move again this time to Lorman, Mississippi where Chester's father is chairman of the Mechanical Arts Department at Alcorn A & M College.

1917   Estelle assumes a teaching post in Cheraw, South Carolina where she moves with Chester and Joseph leaving her husband and son Edward behind. After a few months they move again, this time to Augusta, Georgia.

1918   Estelle and the boys return to Alcorn where they enroll in Alcorn College. Edward, seven years older then Chester, leaves for Atlanta University. He has little contact with the family after this.

1919   Chester's father resigned his position and the family moves to St. Louis.

1919–1923   Joseph takes a job with the Branch Normal School in Pine Bluff, Arkansas where the children attend classes. Chester's brother, Joseph, is blinded in a chemistry experiment at school and the family moves to St. Louis so that he can receive treatment for his eyes.

1923–1925   The family lives in St. Louis.

1925   The Himes' family returns to Cleveland.

1926   Chester graduates from Cleveland's Glenville High School in
             January. While working as a busboy at Wade Park Manor Hotel
             he falls down an open elevator shaft, is gravely injured, and is
             awarded a $75 a month disability income by the Ohio Labor
             Industrial Board.

1926–1928   Chester enrolls at Ohio State University in September 1926 but
             is asked to leave at the end of the spring quarter 1927 because of
             his involvement in a speakeasy fight and his poor grades. He
             works as a bellboy at the Gilsy Hotel, Cleveland and becomes
             involved in hustling, drinking, and gambling. Himes runs a
             whisky joint in the back of Bunch Boy's gambling club on
             Cedar Avenue with future wife Jean Johnson. With his friend
             Benny he burglarizes the YMCA on Cedar Avenue. They both
             are arrested, but his mother pleads for clemency and the judge
             suspends his sentence. In September Chester is arrested again,
             this time for writing bad checks in Columbus. His father
             persuades the judge to give him a two-year suspended sentence.
             Finally, Chester is arrested in November for robbery, and on
             December 27th he is convicted and sentenced to from twenty to
             twenty-five years at hard labor in the Ohio State Penitentiary.

1928–1936   Himes serves seven and a half years in the Ohio State prison
             system: five years in Columbus and two and a half years on a
             prison farm. He begins to write fiction probably in late 1931.
             Himes publishes his first short story in *Abbott's Monthly and
             Illustrated News* in 1932. More fiction and articles appear in
             Abbott's as well as the *Atlanta Daily World, Bronzeman*, and
             The Pittsburgh Courier. In April 1934 "Crazy in Stir" appears
             in *Esquire*, and it is followed by other stories. His *Esquire*
             pieces bring him to the notice of the larger literary world.

1936   Himes is paroled from prison on April 1 and returns to live
             with his family in Cleveland. He continues to sell fiction to
             Esquire and *Coronet*.

1937   Chester marries Jean Lucinda Johnson on August 13th in
             Cleveland, Ohio. He writes the first version of his prison novel,
             Black Sheep, which is later re-titled *Cast the First Stone*, but it
             is not published until 1952.

1937–1941   Himes is employed as a laborer by the Works Progress
             Administration; later he works as a research assistant at the
             Cleveland Public Library. While assigned to the Ohio Writer's

Project he writes the official history of Cleveland. Chester contributes an unsigned column "This Cleveland" to the *Cleveland Daily News*. He is courted by the Communist Party. Later, he serves as a butler on Louis Bromfield's Malabar Farm.

1941–1944   When Bromfield leaves for Hollywood, Chester and his wife follow him to Los Angeles to find industrial work. Over the next three years he holds over twenty jobs, mostly in the shipyards, and writes fiction and essays for *Opportunity* and *Crisis*. His wartime experience in the defense plants provides material for his second novel, *If He Hollers Let Him Go*, which he begins at this time. Himes receives a Rosenwald Fellowship which allows him to finish *If He Hollers Let Him Go*. He and Jean move to New York City

1945   *If He Hollers Let Him Go* is published by Doubleday.

1946   Chester and Jean move back to northern California. They live in rural Susanville on property owned by Jean's brother while Chester works on his next novel *Lonely Crusade*. Estelle Bomar Himes dies. *Hollers* loses out for a George Washington Carver prize. They return to New York City.

1947   Chester's second novel *Lonely Crusade* is published by Alfred Knopf.

1948   Chester spends the late spring at the Yaddo Writer's Colony, Sarasota Springs, New York, working on another novel. He delivers his talk, "The Dilemma of the Negro Writer," at the University of Chicago.

1949   Himes works at a variety of menial jobs, mostly as a caretaker at estates, country clubs, and resorts.

1950   He continues a variety of jobs and in June conducts a creative writing seminar at North Carolina College arranged by his brother who had accepted a faculty appointment there.

1951   Chester and Jean move to Bridgeport, Connecticut where he works on his writing then back to New York where he is employed at a number of menial jobs.

1952   Separates from Jean in April.

1953   *Cast the First Stone* is published in January. The corrected version is published as *Yesterday Will Make You Cry* by W. W. Norton in 1998. On April 3rd Himes leaves for Europe. In Paris he associates with the expatriate Negro community, most notably Richard Wright. Himes moves to Arcachon, on the Bay of Biscay and later visits London.

1954   *The Third Generation* is published by World Publishing. Himes moves to Mallorca.

1955   After a visit of several months to New York, Himes returns to Paris in December.

1956   *The Primitive* is published by New American Library. The unabridged version titled *The End of a Primitive*, with a brief introduction by Lesley Himes, was published by W. W. Norton in 1997.

1956   Visits the United States.

1957   In January back in Paris Himes meets Marcel Duhamel who hires him to write a crime novel for the Gallimard's "Série Noire," thus inaugurating the "Harlem Domestic" series. *For Love of Imabelle* is published in English by Fawcett World Library. It is the first of the Grave Digger/Coffin Ed crime books. The novel later was issued by Gallimard under the title of *La Reine des pommes* in 1958. It also appeared in 1965 under the title *A Rage in Harlem* by Avon. Himes tries living for part of the year in Denmark.

1958   *Il pleut des coups durs* is published by Gallimard. Avon publishes the novel in 1959 as *The Real Cool Killers*. *La Reine des pommes* wins the *Grand prix de la litérature policière* for best crime novel in France.

1959   Along with *The Real Cool Killers* Avon publishes *The Crazy Kill*. Gallimard also issues the novel under the title of *Couché dans le pain*. *Tout pour plaire* is issued as *The Big Gold Dream* by Avon in 1960. Gallimard also publishes *Dare-dare*. As *Run Man Run* the book is later published by Putnam in 1966. Chester begins a relationship with Lesley Packard.

1960   *Imbroglio négro* is published by Gallimard. As *All Shot Up* it is published by Avon who also brings out *The Big Gold Dream*. Richard Wright dies in Paris.

1961   *Ne nous énervons pas!* is published by Gallimard and as *The Heat's On* by Putnam. In 1972 Berkley Books reprinted the novel under the title *Come Back, Charleston Blue*, after the title of a film adapted from the novel. *Pinktoes* is published in English by the Olympia Press, Paris and by Putnam/Stein &

Day. Himes writes a screenplay, "Baby Sister," but final production is canceled.

1962   Returns to the United States to do a film documentary on Harlem for *France-Soir.*

1963   *Une Affaire de viol* published by Editions Les Yeux Ouverts. It is reprinted as *Affair de viol* by Editions des Autres with an introduction by Michel Fabre in 1979 and under the title *A Case of Rape* by Targ Editions 1980. Himes has a stroke in Sisal, Mexico and returns to France.

1964   *Retour en Afrique* is published by Plon in Paris. and is reprinted as *Le Cassis de l'Oncle Tom* by Plon in 1971, and as *Cotton Comes to Harlem* by Putnam in 1965. Himes has second stroke. Visits Egypt.

1965   *Cotton Comes to Harlem* is published by Putnam and *For Love of Imabelle* is published under the title of *A Rage in Harlem* by Avon.

1965–1966   *Run Man Run* is published by Putnam. Himes lives in southern France at La Ciorat. Also travels to Denmark, Spain, and Sweden.

1968–1969   Chester and Lesley move to Alicante, Spain where they build a house in Moraira. *Blind Man with a Pistol* is published by Morrow in 1969, and later is reprinted as *Hot Day, Hot Night* by Dell in 1970.

1970   *Blind Man with a Pistol* is published under the title of *Hot Day, Hot Night* by Dell. The film version of *Cotton Comes to Harlem*, starring Godfrey Cambridge and Raymond St. Jacques is released.

1972   The first volume of Himes' autobiography *The Quality of Hurt* is published by Doubleday, and *The Heat's On* is republished under the title *Come Back, Charleston Blue* by Berkley Books. Himes goes to New York to be recognized by the Carnegie Endowment for International Peace.

1973   *Black on Black: "Baby Sister" and Selected Writings* is published by Doubleday.

1974   *Come Back, Charleston Blue*, the film version of *The Heat's On*, again with Godfrey Cambridge and Raymond St. Jacques, is released.

1976   The second volume of Himes's autobiography *My Life of Absurdity* is published by Doubleday. A condensation of both volumes was issued as *Regrets sans repentir* by Gallimard, Paris, in 1979.

1978   Himes marries Lesley Packard.

1980   *A Case of Rape* is published by Targ.

1982   *Le Manteau de rêve,* a collection of stories, is published by Editions Lieu Commun, Paris.

1983   *Plan B* is published by Lieu Commun, Paris. It is later issued as *Plan B* by the University Press of Mississippi in 1993.

1984   Chester Bomar Himes dies on November 13th in Benissa, Spain.

1986   *Faut être négre our faire ça,* a collection of five stories, is published in Paris by Lieu Commun.

1987   *"Baby Sister"; "Joue, Gabriel, joue!"; "Naturellement le négre ... ",* a collection of two stories and a play, is published with a Preface by Michel Fabre by Editions de l'Instant, Paris.

1988   *Une Joli coup de lune* (originally titled "The Lunatic Fringe") is published by Lieu Commun, Paris.

1990   *The Collected Stories of Chester Himes* is published by Allison & Busby, London and is republished in the United States by Thunder's Mouth Press in 1991.

1997   *The End of a Primitive*, the expanded version of *The Primitive*, is published by W. W. Norton.

1998   *Yesterday Will Make You Cry*, the original version of *Cast the First Stone*, is published by W. W. Norton.

The Writings of Chester Himes

Anyone working on Chester Himes owes a large debt to Michel Fabre, Robert E. Skinner, and Lester Sullivan who compiled the first comprehensive bibliography of Chester Himes's work in their *Chester Himes: An Annotated Primary and Secondary Bibliography* (Westport, Connecticut: Greenwood Press, 1992). The following list is based their pioneering work as well as the additional bibliographic information in Edward Margolies & Michel Fabre *The Several Lives of Chester Himes* (Jackson: University Press of Mississippi, 1997). The list below is arranged chronologically by the first American editions but also includes mention of French translations if they were published before the American edition. The Chronology to this volume lists the publication of Himes's books in the order in which they first appeared.

If He Hollers Let Him Go. Garden City, New York: Doubleday, 1945. Rpt. New York: New American Library (Signet Book), 1949.

Lonely Crusade. New York: Alfred A. Knopf, 1947. Rpt. Chatham, New Jersey: Chatham Bookseller, 1973.

Cast the First Stone. New York: Coward-McCann, 1952. Rpt. New York: New American Library (Signet Book), 1956. [See *Yesterday Will Make You Cry*, 1998].

The Third Generation. Cleveland: World Publishers, 1954. Rpt. New York: New American Library (Signet Book), 1956.

The Primitive. New York: New American Library (Signet Book), 1956. Rpt. New York: New American Library (Signet Book), 1965. [See *End of a Primitive*, 1997].

For Love of Imabelle. Greenwich, Connecticut: Fawcett World Library (Gold Metal Book), 1957. Rpt as *A Rage in Harlem*. New York: Avon (Avon Book), 1965 and New York: New American Library (Signet Book), 1974. First published as *La Reine des pommes* (translated by Minnie Danzas). Paris: Gallimard (Série Noire), 1958. Original manuscript title: "The Five Cornered Hat."

Real Cool Killers. New York: Avon (Avon Original), 1959. Rpt New York: Berkley Books (Berkley Medallion Books), 1966. First published as *Il pleut des coups durs* (translated by C. Wourgraf). Paris: Gallimard (Série Noire), 1958. Original manuscript title: "If Trouble Was Money."

The Crazy Kill. New York: Avon Books (Avon Original), 1959. Rpt New York: Berkley (Berkley Medallion Book), 1966. First published as *Couché dans le pain* (translated by Janine Hérisson and Henri Robillot). Paris: Gallimard (Série Noire), 1959. Original manuscript title: "A Jealous Man Can't Win."

The Big Gold Dream. New York: Avon Books (Avon Original). 1960. Rpt. New York: Berkley (Berkley Medallion Book), 1966. First published as *Tout pour plaire* (translated by Yves Malartic). Paris: Gallimard (Série Noire), 1959. Original manuscript title: "The Big Gold Dream."

All Shot Up. New York: Avon Books (Avon Original), 1960. Rpt. New York: Berkley (Medallion Book), 1960. First published as *Imbrolio négro* (translated by Jeanne Fillion). Paris: Gallimard (Série Noire), 1960. Original manuscript title: "Don't Play with Death."

Cotton Comes to Harlem. New York: G. P. Putnam's Sons, 1965. Rpt. New York: Dell (Dell Books), 1966. First published as *Retour en Afrique* (translated by Pierre Sergent). Paris: Plon (*Collection Actualitiés*), 1964. Original manuscript title: "Back to Africa."

Pinktoes. New York: G. P. Putnam's Sons/Stein & Day, 1965. Rpt. New York: Dell (Dell Book), 1966. First published as *Pinktoes*. Paris: Olympia Press (Traveler's Companion), 1961.

The Heat's On. New York: G. P. Putnam, 1966. Rpt. New York: Dell (Dell Book), 1966. Republished as *Come Back, Charleston Blue*. New York: Berkley (Berkley Medallion Book), 1972. First published as *Ne nous énervons pas!* (translated by Jeanne Fillion). Paris: Gallimard (Série Noire), 1961. Original manuscript title: "Be Calm."

Run Man Run. New York: G. P. Putnam's, 1966. Rpt. New York: Dell (Dell Book), 1966 and New York: Berkley (Berkley Medallion Book), 1966. First published as *Dare-dare* (translated by Pierre Verrier). Paris: Gallimard (Série Noire), 1959. Original manuscript title: "Run, Man, Run."

Blind Man with a Pistol. New York: William Morrow, 1969. Republished as *Hot Day, Hot Night.* New York: Dell (Dell Book), 1970 and New York: New American Library (Signet Books), 1975.

The Quality of Hurt. New York: Doubleday. 1972. Rpt. New York: Thunder's Mouth Press, 1972.

Black on Black: "Baby Sister" and Selected Writings. New York: Doubleday, 1973.

My Life of Absurdity. New York: Doubleday, 1976. Rpt. New York: Paragon House, 1976.

A Case of Rape. New York: Targ Editions, 1980. Rpt. Washington, D. C.: Howard University Press, 1985. First published as *Une Affaire de viol* (translated by André Mathieu). Paris: Editions Les Yeux Ouverts (Collection Actualitiés), 1963.

Plan B. Jackson: University Press of Mississippi, 1985. First published as *Plan B* (translated by Hélène Devaux-Minié). Paris: Lieu Commun, 1983. Original manuscript title: "Plan B."

The Collected Stories of Chester Himes. New York: Thunder's Mouth Press, 1991. First published as *The Collected Stories of Chester Himes.* London: Allison & Busby, 1990.

The End of a Primitive. New York: W. W. Norton & Company, 1997. [Original version of *The Primitive*].

Yesterday Will Make You Cry. New York: Old School/W. W. Norton, 1998. [Original version of *Cast the First Stone*].

REVIEWS

History as Nightmare
James Baldwin

In *If He Hollers Let Him Go*, published in 1945, Chester Himes studied, with rage and sometimes with disturbing perception, the struggle and defeat of one Negro war-worker on the West Coast, our native tensions intensified by war and the protagonists' relationships with his upper-class mulatto girl and the sexual tensions between himself and a female white war-worker. It was one of those books for which it is difficult to find any satisfactory classification: not a good novel but more than a tract, relentlessly honest, and carried by the fury and the pain of the man who wrote it. It seemed to me then one of the few books written by either whites or Negroes about Negroes which considered the enormous role which white guilt and tension play in what has been most accurately called the American dilemma.

Lonely Crusade can almost be considered an expansion of the earlier novel. Much of the rage is gone and with it the impact, and the book is written in what is probably the most uninteresting and awkward prose I have read in recent years. Yet the book is not entirely without an effect and is likely to have an importance out of all proportion to its intrinsic merit. For, just as the earlier book was carried by rage, this book is carried by what seems to be a desperate, implacable determination to find out the truth, please God, or die.

In less than four hundred pages Mr. Himes undertakes to consider the ever-present subjective and subconscious terror of a Negro, a dislocation which borders on paranoia; the political morality of American Communists; the psychology of union politics; Uncle Tomism; Jews and Negroes; the vast sexual implications of our racial heritage; the difficulty faced by any Negro in his relationships with both light people and dark; and the position of the American white female in the whole unlovely structure. This is a tall order and if we give Mr. Himes an A for ambition—and a rather awe-stricken gasp for effort—we are forced also to realize that the book's considerable burden never really gets shoulder high. It is written almost as though the author were determined within one book, regardless of style or ultimate effect, to say all of the things he wanted to say about the American republic and the position of the Negro in it. Part of the failure of the book certainly lies in this fact, that far too much is attempted; and the story never really gets under way because of a complete lack of integration. Any one of its elements, perceptively studied, would make an impressive novel; and, further, because of the crudity of the story structure, the climax—the murder of a bigoted white man by his Negro stooge, an incident valid in itself and with terrible implications—fails of its effect and seems almost an afterthought; and the resolution—the holding aloft, of the union banner—leaves one with that same embarrassed rage produced by a reading of *Invictus*. The book, nevertheless, has flashes of power and insight—the handling of the white girls' relation to Lee, for example, and Lee's sexual relationship with his wife; and one of the subsidiary characters, the Uncle Tom named Luther, is handled and seen so accurately that no white man, ever again, should dare to turn his back on any Negro he feels that he has bought and conquered.

I have already indicated that Mr. Himes seems capable of some of the worst writing on this side of the Atlantic, but his integrity has actually the cumulative effect of making him seem far wiser and more skillful than he is. The value of his book lies in its earnest effort to understand the psychology of oppressed and oppressor and their relationship to each other. It fails to raise his book to the level of *A Passage To India* but it does lend it an historical importance, not unlike that accorded to *Uncle Tom's Cabin* or, more recently, to *Native Son*. For, of all the spate of recent novels concerning racial oppression not one has exhibited any genuine understanding of its historical genesis or contemporary necessity or its psychological toll. One might over-simplify our racial heritage sufficiently to observe, and not at all flippantly, that its essentials would seem to be contained in the tableau of a black and white man facing each other and that the root of our trouble is between their legs. More and more it is impossible to discuss the Negro in America without also discussing American customs, morals and fears. *Lonely Crusade* is an ugly story but the story of American Negroes and white America's relation to them is a far uglier story and with more sinister implications than have yet found their way into print. It is no longer just a Negro's story, we have no longer the convenient symbol of a minstrel man and his wild guitar, of the Negro rapist, or the brave, black college student battling upward against all odds. Time moves too fast, human beings are too complex, yesterday's benevolence is more dangerous than a time bomb now. On that low ground where Negroes live something is happening: something which can be measured in decades and generations and which may spell our doom as a republic and almost certainly implies a cataclysm. Unlike Bigger Thomas, gone to his death cell, inarticulate and destroyed by his need for identification and for revenge, and with only the faintest intimation in that twilight of what had destroyed him and of what his life might have been, Mr. Himes' protagonist, Lee Gordon, sees what has happened and what is happening and watches helplessly the progress of his own disease. *And there is no path out.* In a group so pressed down, terrified and at bay and carrying generations of constricted, subterranean hostility, no real group identification is possible. Nor is there a Negro tradition to cling to in the sense that Jews may be said to have a tradition; this was left in Africa long ago and no-one remembers it now. Lee Gordon is forced back on himself, not even bitterness can serve him as a weapon any more. The impact of rejection and continual indignity on his personality is a personal one and this impact, multiplied, can destroy, not only himself, but an entire nation.

The minstrel man is gone and Uncle Tom is no longer to be trusted. Even Bigger Thomas is becoming irrelevant; we are faced with a black man as many faceted as we ourselves are, as individual, with our ambivalences and insecurities and our struggles to be loved. He is now an American and we cannot change that; it is our attitudes which must change both towards ourselves and him. "History," says Joyce, "is a nightmare from which I am struggling to awaken." We have all heard what happened to those who slept too long.

"History as Nightmare: Review of Lonely Crusade," *The New Leader*, October 25, 1946, pp. 11, 15.

No Thrills in Harlem

Kofi Akainyah

On one level, the black American Chester Himes was simply a brilliant writer of thrillers. The patch he made his own was Harlem which, having lost touch with its golden years, had by the 1950s gradually slid from "sugar to shit". It had become a place where prowling muggers cased pedestrians like hyenas watching lions at feast, squares ended up in holes and even the hip met sudden death. Pressed down into its fetid darkness the losers in the American dream fed upon themselves.

It was a nightmare world and in it Himes implanted two black detectives. They were tough: Coffin Ed Johnson could kill a rock and Grave Digger Jones, his partner, would bury it. They operated in a locality in which "colored folks didn't respect colored cops", where Christians were full of larceny and the underworld paid tribute only to the gun. To keep the law they shot first and questioned the bodies afterwards. "This is a violent city", says the Chief of Police in *A Rage in Harlem*. Himes's art is a match for it. It is smooth yet savage.

The best thriller writers are tense and immediate. The reader craves for instant accessibility, the excitement given an added kick by each twist in the tale. The thriller is a literary roller-coaster, powerful because it is transient. Writers such as Agatha Christie, Leslie Charteris and Ian Fleming have stood out because they succeeded in creating characters more enduring than their ephemeral stories. In creating Coffin Ed and Grace Digger, Himes also transcended the limitations of the genre. But he did more. Only he and Raymond Chandler have been able so vividly to evoke the texture and taste of a locality.

A Rage in Harlem was originally issued in 1957 as *For The Love of Imabelle* and is a gem sparkling with wit. Himes's perception of detail is acute and his strokes are deft and economical:

> The waitress came over and stood beside their table, looking off in another direction.
> "Are you waiting on us or just waiting on us to get up and leave?" Gus asked.
> She gave him a scornful look. "Just state your order and we'll fill it."
> Gus looked her over, beginning at her feet.
> "Bring us some steaks, girlie, and be sure they're not as tough as you are ..."

Jackson, the hapless character in the story, reels from crisis to crisis. Duped by a gang into an attempt to turn $10 bills into $100 bills he is caught by a marshal. In order to avoid punishment he offers to bribe the marshal. To get the money to pay the bribe he has to steal it from his employer. Having stolen it he gambles with some of the money in order to be able to replace what he has stolen. In gambling he loses his stake. Only the marshal gets his bribe. "Let this be a lesson", he says to Jackson, "crime does not pay." The rub is that the marshal is a fake, a wanted murderer and a member of the sting. The dénouement leaves a litter of bodies and Coffin Ed with acid on his face. Jackson's twin brother, a man who sells tickets to heaven dressed as a nun is only one star in an unwholesome cast. It is a satisfying read but Harlem does not hold many thrills for its residents.

The other reissue, *The Real Cool Killers*, first published in 1958, is one of Himes's best known thrillers. Black people in Harlem did not shoot whites in cold blood. But a big Greek is shot dead for no apparent reason. The police and Grave Digger are unleashed in the search for the killer. It becomes clear that the Greek was a pervert, sweet on little black girls and into flagellation. The case against each suspect disappears. Sugartit, Coffin Ed's daughter is apparently involved and so also are The Real Cool Moslems, a gang of black youths. Once again a lot of blood is spilled before the case is closed.

However, in the creation of Sheik, the leader of the Moslems, Himes jumps the gun on Greenlee. This nigger was a spook who, having rejected the slave role now used its protective dissimulation for his own purposes. Sheik's command to his men while awaiting a search by white policemen is instructive.

> They believe spooks are crazy anyway ... just act kind of simpleminded. They gonna to swallow it like it's chocolate ice cream. They ain't going to do nothing but kick you in the ass and laugh like hell about how crazy spooks are ...

He almost succeeded, and so also did *The Spook Who Sat by the Door*.

In the 1970s there was a crop of black films such as *Shaft, Superfly* and *Across 110th Street*. They were thrillers and together with the works of writers such as Mickey Spillane, should be distanced from Himes. For another level Himes was a political writer. The thriller was merely a vehicle for his politics and it is this dimension which sets him apart. Indeed, his first book *If He Hollers Let Him Go* dealt with racial oppression and was derived from his wartime experience of working in the shipyards on the west coast of America. The violence of his thrillers is a violence of which he had experience. Forced to drop out of Ohio State University he ran a racket for a notorious gambler before, aged 19, he was gaoled for robbery. That the violence did not destroy him was, in part, because he knew its cause. With communist antecedents, it is not surprising that in 1953 he left America for France, a place of refuge for other black Americans. His thrillers should be read in the knowledge that just below the skin, sheathed in irony, lies the message, "I'm just a cop", says Grave Digger in *The Real Cool Killers*, "if you white people insist on coming up to Harlem where you force colored people to live in vice-and-crime-ridden slums, it's my job to see that you are safe."

Himes died in Spain in November 1984 aged 75 and still an exile from his native land.

West Africa, September 23, 1985, pp. 1973–1974.

The Crazy Kill and *If He Hollers Let Him Go*

Sally Cragin

If you prefer your *romans* to be *noir*, and have already worked your way through Black Lizard Press's laudable reissues of the works of classic crime novelists (among them Jim Thompson), plan a visit with another vivid, irresistible chronicler of the bas-monde, Chester Himes. The late, great Himes, who died in Spain in 1984, lived much of his life on the Continent but set many of his novels in post-war Harlem. Today, he's best remembered for a droll, laconic pair of detectives, Coffin Ed Johnson and Grave Digger Jones, a duo that pilots through a sea of sordid and occasionally ludicrous crimes (mostly of passion) with a cool that would freeze the Thin Man's martinis. *Cotton Comes to Harlem* is the most famous Coffin Ed/Grave Digger opus (it was fashioned into a successful blaxploitation flick in 1970), but the others are equally intoxicating, among them *Blind Man with a Pistol* and *The Crazy Kill*, both recently reissued by Vintage Crime. Against the anarchic backdrop of Harlem, where "folks do things for reasons nobody else in the world would think of," in Grave Digger's words, Himes shows Harlem as a simmering cauldron in which the lives and habits of grifters and their gals, clergy and criminals alike, collide in a heady, invariably explosive brew.

In *The Crazy Kill* (originally published in 1959), the MacGuffin is the body of a kindly ne'er-do-well named Val, who's found stabbed in a bread cart near a tenement where a rollicking wake is in full swing. Trouble is, a Holy Roller preacher named Reverend Short had either fallen or been pushed from a third-story window shortly before. All the evidence seems to point to a big-time gambler, Four Ace Johnny Perry, who drives a Cadillac convertible customized with playing cards on the doors. Johnny has made the fatal error of being too much in love with his wife, a gorgeous juicer named Dulcy, whose connections with the deceased are among the many mysteries the intrepid gumshoes must unravel.

Of course, getting the guy is just the gravy—the fun is in the chase. What sets Himes and *The Crazy Kill* apart from so many true-crime pulps of the period is the author's relish for the crucial details—psychological, behavioral, sartorial—that distinguish a dizzying array of flamboyant characters. Himes's gifts also include a penchant for the almost artless digression, which gives his carnival world a gritty comedic dimension. Take this police-dossier item describing Coffin Ed and Grave Digger making their rounds: "First they'd had a foot race with a young man peddling skinned cats for rabbits. An old lady customer had asked for the feet, had become suspicious and called the police when told that they were nub-legged rabbits."

That comic edge is disturbingly absent from Himes's wartime novel *If He Hollers Let Him Go*, a relentless psychodrama about a young defense-industry mechanic named Bob Jones. In the four pivotal days of *If He Hollers*, Jones teeters on an abyss of self-destructiveness goaded by the unslaked prejudice he and his fellow workers encounter in Los Angeles. Unlike the black New Yorkers of busy, built-up Harlem, who have one another for company and consolation, Jones is very much estranged in a strange land. He ricochets through a landscape saturated with "hard, bright California sunshine," where the whites who rule are, under Himes's unswerving pen, genially bigoted. The moments of transcendent joy for Jones are brief indeed. Gazing at the construction site where his presence as a boss for a black crew is needed, he reflects: "I'd never given a damn one way or the other about the war excepting wanting to keep out of it; and at first when I wanted the Japanese to win. And now ... I was stirred as I had been when I was a little boy watching a parade. I had never felt included before. It was a wonderful feeling."

Unfortunately for Jones, that moment of unity is short-lived. Before long, he's been cheated of his position, and in the aftermath decides to humiliate his wealthy black girlfriend by taking her to a restaurant where he knows they'll be treated badly. The episode is the catalyst for Jones to embark on an odyssey of boozing and brawling with a vicious, atavistic passion. Jones begins as a brute with integrity and is reduced to a mere brute. His tragedy (and society's) is that he knows what he needs to do to get along, but, like Spike Lee's seething Mookie in last year's *Do the Right Thing*, soon has his fill, and can take no more. The ugly truths captured in *If He Hollers*, first published in 1945, continue to resonate with dismaying cacophony. There are no answers, and no absolutions. Shortly thereafter, Himes invented the brilliant Coffin Ed and Grave Digger Jones and began to spin his tales about domestic crime in Harlem. No wonder—justice must be served somewhere.

"Brief Reviews: The Crazy Kill and If He Hollers Let Him Go," *Boston Phoenix Literary Section*, February 1990, p. 3.

The Best Black American Novelist Writing Today

Shane Stevens

For some years now, I have had the strong belief that Chester Himes is the best black American novelist writing today. While others have received most of the acclaim, Himes has been steadily producing a body of work that is an extraordinary literary achievement. Extraordinary in its output, now numbering some fifteen novels; in its faithful depiction of an authentic American life style; and in its sheer narrative skill and power. Indeed, Himes may well be the best contemporary American practitioner of the lost art of narration.

I first came upon Himes when I was still living in Harlem and roaming its streets. The name of the book was *If He Hollers Let Him Go*; later I was to learn it was his first novel, published in the 1940s. In reading it, I had what one could only call a whole series of Joycean epiphanies wherein I saw, for fleeting moments, the interconnection of all our activities, the precise inevitability of each meaningless incident acting and reacting upon countless others. It was a mind-blower and the best of all possible trips for a young novelist seeking the questions of life. I remember I was at the very beginnings of my own first novel, and I alternated between elation at my discovery of this man's talent and despair because he seemed to have said it all. After *If He Hollers Let Him Go*, it was on to *The Primitive*, *Pinktoes*, *A Rage in Harlem* and the others.

It soon became apparent that Himes was creating a world of interlocking people every bit as fully formed as William Faulkner's world in his imaginative Yoknapatawpha County. With each succeeding work more flesh was added, more development, more delineation. Yet unlike Faulkner's creation, Himes's Harlem was real; real in a way white men had never known it because they did not want to. It lived, laughed, cried and died and gave birth all over again to hope and despair. It was the Harlem of a half-million people of color, many of whom hated the white man with a passion. And Chester Himes was telling it like it is. But even more, he was carving out of his skull a vision of epic proportions: a vision of race warfare that was to prove all too prophetic.

Today, after some twenty years, Himes's vision is still operative and, tragically, even more realistic. If he is today more bitter than he was in those earlier years, if the specter of death in his recent works is even more pronounced, it is surely a reflection of this man's essential honesty in the face of the terrible chasm that exists in contemporary America. Yet once all of this has been said, as it must, there remains the central fact of Himes's great talent; his total humanity, the wit and compassion with which he details the everyday existence of his people.

This purposeful honesty I speak of, this essential compassion and originality of wit in the struggle for life are readily apparent in Himes's latest novel, *Blind Man With a Pistol*. Here we are confronted with a kaleidoscopic view of a big-city ghetto. Harlem. Where an ancient black Mormon, living in absolute squalor with eleven wives, seeks a twelfth; where a homosexual white man, looking for black soul mates, is brutally murdered; where an old man, who wants his youth restored so that he can marry a teen-ager, causes a family slaughter; where a half-crazed blind man, who wants no one to know he's blind, is goaded into killing and being killed; and where black power, brotherhood and visions of glory, auctioned off by dream merchants of death for the price of a life, fan the flames of riot. It's all there: the good and the bad, the sane the insane, the fearful and the fearfully angry. And through all of it, across a night and day of unspeakable agony in a jungle of despair, moves an all-too-human parade of people, black and white, trying to communicate with one another. Trying with violence, money, love and hate, to bridge the awful gap between them.

That very few of them succeed is not an indictment of the book or of life itself, but what living has come to be for so many of us. Himes has let it be known that he considers *Blind Man With a Pistol* his most important work. I suspect this is because he has put into this novel, more than in any of the others, much of his feeling about what is happening here in America. Yet he has not let this interfere with his telling of a story.

I for one am thankful that Himes is alive and writing. In this age when agit-prop scribblings are assuming the veneer of literature, it is comforting to know that there is still an authentic voice describing for all of us the universality of pain. Of all the black American writers now working the vein of imagination, Chester Himes alone seems to have carved out for himself an area of confrontation that is applicable—and meaningful—effective social protest and effective art.

Among the others, there are James Baldwin and Ralph Ellison, both of whom have adapted the pose of the disaffected liberal. Their middle-class, aesthetic viewpoint is readily apparent in their desire to be free of all limitations of race and national tradition. This is not to condemn, of course, but to suggest that this viewpoint does have its own built-in limitation: that of cutting oneself off from one's native experience. At the opposite extreme are the racist-oriented works of such men as LeRoi Jones. Here the disaffection from reality, from the perspective of the bad *and* good in all of us, from the complexity of human nature, is complete and the result is mere caricature.

Chester Himes' style of attack may well be different, but the long shadow of Richard Wright—who I sometimes suspect knew where it *all* was at—grows more evident in each succeeding book.

Washington Post Book World, April 27, 1969, Section 9, pp. 4–5.

Rhythms of Black Experience
George E. Kent

Chester Himes' *Black on Black* contains 17 short stories, 5 essays, and a scenario, and covers a period in Himes' writing extending from 1937 to 1969. Himes, himself, as explorer of black experience represents a considerably alienated sensibility, a fact which is only partly obscured for *Black on Black* by the sheer quantity of alienated black writing produced in the 1960's and 1970's. In addition, Himes is extremely individual, a writer of many parts although frequently all parts do not come together in a single piece. Yet his examination of black experience in America has created a place of its own. Lately, he also stuck to his own path in the first volume of his autobiography, *The Quality of Hurt* (Doubleday, 1972) and there is little doubt that his detective stories, notably *Cotton Comes to Harlem* which was made into film, provided some inspiration for the current spate of hardboiled black movies.

In his confrontation with the black experience, it is tempting to see his hardboiled approach (toughed often with sentiment underneath) as his strongest strain. He seems to incorporate both the James M. Cain type fiction with the rebellious hero, made famous by Richard Wright in the novel *Native Son* (1940). In *If He Hollers Let Him Go* (1945), his first novel, Himes pitted a tough but frustrated hero of black middle class status against relentless racism of a war-time shipyard. In *Lonely Crusade* (1947), he involves the same general type of hero in a struggle with Communist ideology, interracial sex, and racial discrimination. In *Cast the First Stone* (1952), he took advantage of a knowledge of prison gained from serving 7 1/2 years of a 25 year sentence for armed robbery; however, the book is about white characters. In *Third Generation* (1954) he gave an often tender and searching exploration of his own pathos filled family background, and in *The Primitive* (1955) he explores again the high tensioned and frustrated black hero of middle class status, in relationship to general suffering, violence, sex. Afterward come a long spate of detective stories in the hard-boiled vein.

The contents of *Black on Black* thus represent the shorter pieces which Himes was also doing. His stand-out pieces often reveal a gutted black life, although he ranges into lugubrious humor, the whimsical, the satirical, and the character study. There is no illusion about a black life wired in as moral beneficiary of the larger society. "Baby Sister," the scenario which he wrote at the instigation of European producers "who thought the American film *Raisin in the Sun* was a failure," give the starkest picture. Himes says, "As the story of Baby Sister unfolded in my mind I was moved to tears. When not crying I was singing at the top of my voice: *What did I do to be so black and blue?*" The following statements probably epitomize much of his sense of black experience in America:

And in The Valley [where Baby Sister's family and other Blacks live] there is no good shepherd. Only the will of the community can save her [Baby Sister] from the wolves. But the inhabitants of this community, restricted, exploited, prostituted, violated and violent, timid and vicious, living in their rat-ridden hotbox, stinking flats, are either the hungry wolves themselves, or are struggling desperately to save themselves from the hungry wolves. And it is perfectly reasonable and natural these people should be hungry, the wolves and the sheep alike. If your own food—food for the soul and food for the spirit as well as food for the stomach—had been held just out of your reach for three hundred years, or longer, you would be hungry too. And one way to keep from starving in this land of plenty when you have no food is to eat your baby sister.

Himes reports that the French critics who read *Baby Sister* called it a Greek tragedy. The scenario has no gods, no suggestion of the viability of transcendent values. What it has is *inevitability* and *fate*. Given the sex bait Baby Sister in such a spiritually low-ceilinged environment, her mere existence means that she will provoke violence and be sold by one of the wolves: the pimp Slick, an anonymous pick-up, a downtown house of prostitution in New York, the police, her brother Susie, to name a few. For those around her, she may mean death at any moment. There is only a kind of destiny known as "Chances go round." As might be expected the scenario explodes eventually in a terrible violence, just when it seems that Baby Sister may escape.

To make his point, Himes has stripped the resources from the black experience—perhaps a bit further than warranted. The religious mother is completely ineffectual. Her little brother would save her, but cannot rise above the role of nuisance, for all the touching quality of his aspirations. The minister's name speaks for itself—Reverend Converted Sinner, who at one point attempts to rape Baby Sister who has taken refuge in his bed. Baby Sister herself enjoys and is repelled by her sensational attraction, and in the simple survival sense is by no means helpless. At the end of the play, she still has her vitality but Himes makes it difficult to imagine her escape.

Perhaps in an acted version, the scenario would reveal moments of poetry. Read, it confines itself to naturalistic shocks which further violate the humanity of the black experience. Although one can see the advantage of keeping Baby Sister relatively inarticulate regarding her yearnings, it would seem that the author could give her more mental suggestiveness than the statement in which she wishes people would stop looking at her as if she had no clothes on.

Along the same line of his hard-boiled approach are such stories as "A Nigger," "The Night's for Cryin'," and "Tang," but a bit more of the human dimension of the characters' values is apparent. Sometimes, as in "Tang" and "A Nigger," a kind of insane humor breaks forth with the terror. Such stories as "Heaven Has Changed" and "Cotton Gonna Kill Me Yet" have the virtues of the tall, satirical tale. "Prediction" catches up with the deadend emotions which fostered the radical movement of black literature during the 1960s. "Mama's Missionary Money" is a story of childhood high-jinks of a boy and his friends at the expense of money saved up to do good for the heathens. And there's more. All in all, they show considerable range and skill on Himes' part, but do not give the definitive evidence of the range of emotion, feeling, and search which the novels afford. The novels remain indispensable for a full understanding of Himes' talent.

About the essays there is little to be said. They are clearly dated pieces, which contributed more to the quantity than to the quality of the book. At its most perceptive, Himes' is the completely alienated sensibility, responding to the stern logic of the American experience.

Chicago Review, 25:3 (1973), 76–78.

Chester Himes—"Alien" in Exile

Loyle Hairston

Among the several pictures in the second volume of Chester Himes' autobiography,* there is a photograph of the author Himes surrounded by a group of young black writers. On another page we see him in Nikki Giovanni's apartment with the well-known poet. I wonder if any of these people would have sought him out ten years ago when he was living and struggling in obscurity (from Americans) in Europe? In point of fact, no one did. But thanks to one of his detective novel, *Cotton Comes to Harlem,* he was suddenly catapulted into fame and (a little) fortune, not because of the success of the novel, however—like most of Himes' fiction with the possible exception of *If He Hollers, Cotton* was simply reviewed and forgotten by those who acclaim him now—but because a screenplay based on the novel became the first of a spate of exotic black films produced by Hollywood to placate the restless ghetto "natives."

Thus Chester Himes was "discovered" by members of the Black literati who tend to confuse making it in the establishment with "changing the system." (They can be found at any bourgeois "soul" party, Afroed, corn rolled and dashikied in costumes of "black awareness," denouncing "white folks" between tiresome dissertations on the role of the "black artists" in promoting the "black revolution." All of this while indulging in the worst social vulgarities of the hated white middle-class!)

Since recognition by the white establishment is the basis for the Black literati's stamp of approval, Chester Himes (like Alex Haley, author of *Roots,* more recently) has now qualified for their acclaim. According to the second volume of his autobiography, Himes has lived an equally absurd life abroad. But since posturing and affectations are vices one could never accuse Chester

Himes of, his candor and caustic temperament would probably make his current admirers cringe to the roots of their petty bourgeois hairs.

These are the people who crowned Chester Himes the "dean of Black American writers" without having read his books! Such is the shallowness (and opportunism) of some Black intellectuals whose values mirror those of the white society that systematically undermines their humanity and sense of integrity. I mention this because, however Himes might feel about such people, he is in some respects their counterpart from another generation. In the two volumes of his autobiography, Himes confines his criticism of U.S. society to wrist-slapping the "racist white folks" with little apparent understanding of the society which promotes racism and class antagonism for definite ends—to maintain a system of privilege, wealth and power for the privileged, rich and powerful.

Not only has he adopted the values of the "white folks," but the life he is now living in Europe indicates an uncritical endorsement of the narrow, individualistic outlook. His complaint against America seems largely a personal grievance! What is somewhat puzzling about this is the fact that, while not an intellectual, Himes is a far more sophisticated man than many of his current admirers; and unlike them, he has some hard knowledge of the social currents that corrode the moral and spiritual landscape, often leaving us adrift in wastelands of confusion and despair.

In a certain sense, this is what his autobiography is about—the futility of being a serious person in a society hostile to a critical sensibility; about being trapped in a culture that is unresponsive to the people's real needs and distorts the way they perceive the world; about an attempt to rescue a sensitive spirit from a social experience immersed in the backwaters of racism and the consequent illusions to which that sensitive spirit succumbed. Not that Himes consciously acknowledges being so victimized or admits to despair, but the weariness of a disillusioned spirit pervades the autobiography.

My Life of Absurdity reveals how exile compelled the author to dissipate a fine intelligence, sensitivity and talent in the drudgery of maintaining himself while he clawed and scratched his way to some kind of success. But since acceptance and acclaim only come with money success, what chance did an exiled Black writer of fiction have? Even a good writer whose work didn't even sell in his own country. And Chester Himes is a good writer with a creative mind and an incisive grasp of the stresses that provoke tragic personality conflicts. *If He Hollers, The Third Generation,* and *The Primitive* are novels that belong to the mainstream of U.S. fiction as much as any American writer's work. In a less hypocritical country he probably would have gotten the recognition he believed he earned on the literary quality of his earlier work.

But America had no interest in entertaining Chester Himes' wishes. After all, the country already had its celebrated Black novelist in Richard Wright; and one at a time was the rule of the liberal game. So much for American egalitarianism! Frustrated, dismayed, Himes fled to Europe. But since there is little in *My Life of Absurdity* to show that he has recovered from the "hurt" of America, he either fled too late in life or didn't flee far enough. Unlike Richard Wright whose exile resulted from deep philosophical, psychological conflicts in a stifling anti-intellectual cultural atmosphere, Himes fled for very different reasons. He went to Europe to achieve what America had denied him—recognition and success.

My Life of Absurdity is a deceptive book, though written simply and without seemingly any prearranged attempt to make any specific points about his life except as he lived it. On one level I found it difficult to take Chester Himes seriously; became annoyed with his inanities and preoccupation with an endless stream of simple-minded incidents and banalities. Written in the fast-paced style of a potboiler, the narrative is indeed a novelized catalog of absurdities, some as vulgar as they are entertaining, as pointless as they are amusing, as stupid as they are interesting. But on another level I began to feel the bitterness underneath the lively, seemingly light-hearted narrative, giving off an overall impact of documented despair. This is the autobiography of a man disillusioned with his fellow creatures and weary from the struggle to win acceptance from those he has grown to despise. The problem, however, is that Himes has been consumed in the process, though he achieved at least a measure of his ambition in the twilight years of his life.

The author of *Absurdity* is, by his own account, far from a pleasant man but he makes no apologies for his boorishness and cynicism. Instead he is defiant, satisfied with his open contempt for the world that rejected him so long as a writer. The sentiment underlying the easy but hard-boiled tone of the book, the child-like candor with which he "tells all" in such lively detail reveal an anguish that has left a hollow ring in his late-coming success. But it is also Chester Himes' way of telling America to "kiss my ass"!

While his disenchantment with the U.S. is understandable even through his rather self-centered reasoning, his bitterness does not help him to understand his country any better or to examine his inability to break the cultural umbilical cord to the mother country. This paradox goes unresolved throughout Chester Himes' self-imposed exile. But despite these contradictions, he remains a writer dedicated to his work, with a kind of single-minded passion to make his mark as a Writer. This is admirable, sometimes even heroic, given the circumstances he had to combat as a foreigner with few connections abroad and no knowledge of the French language and culture.

A resourceful, feisty little man, Himes somehow managed to turn these handicaps into advantages, as they freed him to be himself more openly, without fear of being put-down or scolded by his peers or society. And being anonymous to the point of ground-level zero in France, his very circumstance compelled him to call upon his full mettle as a writer in order to survive. The way he managed this is a tribute to his courage, intelligence, self-confidence and audacity because he, in fact, saw far more lean days in Europe—including days when he found himself flat broke—than he enjoyed even relative comfort.

His other passion was women, ostensibly because of an insatiable sex drive. But it becomes more apparent in the autobiography as a need for a strong relationship with a woman to shelter him from the cold, alienated isolation in which he lived. But with a couple of exceptions he seemed incapable of feeling strongly about anyone but himself and his needs at a given moment. And yet in his own way he was loyal to the few women who became close to him.

Himes is a disgusting male chauvinist with seemingly a special disdain for Black women who rarely (whenever he chanced to encounter them abroad) appealed to him even as objects of lust! (I wonder how the female members of his Black literati admirers cope with that.) In point of fact, Himes shows a distinct preference for white people, which is not surprising given the kinds of racial confusion often manifested in the Afro-American consciousness once it has fallen under the influence of white middle-class values. Himes speaks well enough of Black people, denouncing racism whenever it touches him frontally, but exile and the lack of a realistic political awareness leave him with a disturbing ignorance of his own people.

As I said earlier, Himes' resentment of the U.S. is more of a personal grievance than an attempt to understand that this country treats not only Chester Himes but 30 million Black people with similar contempt and rejection, whatever their endeavors. At one time or another many of us have been driven into some kind of "exile" to recover from the unrelenting hostility of a society that defines human worth as *white*. I think Himes fled to Europe because his survival as a writer demanded it. It was as necessary to his ambition as Gaugin's desire to paint compelled him to give up his respectability for the harsh, frustrating world of a struggling artist. But there was an additional burden to Himes' ordeal—a society hostile to his very existence as both man and writer. But in exile he failed to grow intellectually and spiritually, lapsing instead into a destructive life style that eventually granted him a modicum of hollow personal success at the expense of his potential as a serious writer.

Here, I think, lies the tragedy, not only of Chester Himes who is probably satisfied with the way he had conducted his life (though I doubt it), but also of too many young Blacks whose sensibilities are eventually eroded in the pursuit of establishment recognition. I don't think Himes is satisfied with being remembered as a writer of detective fiction.

He called this volume of his autobiography *My Life of Absurdity* because it is the way he views his life. Moreover, it is the way he sums up the life of man in society—as a protracted ordeal of absurdities. This is something of an existential view which attempts to posit a truism upon a narrow evaluation of human experience. Himes ascribes a similar outlook to William Faulkner, the writer he admires most, but the disclaimer is Faulkner's work itself which attempts an exhaustive portrayal of the capricious tendencies of men and women in conflict with a world out of harmony with simple needs.

And finally, I too am a Chester Himes fan and have been ever since I read *If He Hollers* several years ago; and because I empathize with the man who wrote movingly in *The Third Generation* of the family and social experiences that shaped him as a man. I know something of the loneliness that is the writer's lot, a necessary imposition of the creative process. But creativity itself comes also from without, from being in keen, perceptive communication with the world around you. The world is not a private place, and the whirl of life has little time for private complaints unless they relate to a larger framework of existence. In short, though a writer thinks and works in privacy, spiritual isolation from the affairs of the world is fatal to his efforts.

Chester Himes' exile seems to have set him adrift in spiritual isolation....

Freedomways, 7:1 (1977), 14–18.

A Case of Rape
Michel Fabre

"Not only does this novel shed light on racism in France ... it also allows us to better understand how (Himes) manages to transform historical events into imaginary episodes"

Published in 1963 as *Une Affaire de Viol*, Chester Himes's *A Case of Rape* remains without a doubt his most mysterious novel. The success of his "Série Noire" detective stories, after *La Reine des Pommes* (*For Love of Imabelle*) was awarded the *Grand Prix de la Littérature Policière* in 1957, led to the reissuing of most of his fiction in the United States, but this did not include *A Case of Rape*. Now a collector's item after having been remaindered by the publisher, the novel is still virtually unknown to the American reader. Not that it passed unnoticed in Paris: novelist Christiane de Rochefort wrote a well-meaning but strangely pro-feminist afterword for it, and several French critics hailed it as a denunciation of racist myths. But at the time, the Birmingham (Alabama) police were busy unleashing their dogs against civil rights demonstrators, and the news of Himes's ironic contribution to the demystification of race relations was lost in the fray.

Nevertheless, this narrative contains quite a few profitable areas of study. Primarily, it is strikingly different from the rest of Himes's fiction. His first two novels, for example, explored the American race and labor scene in the semi-naturalistic tradition of the Forties. *Cast the First Stone* (1952), coming next, was one of the best prison novels ever written but did not transcend the limits of that *genre;* and *The Third Generation* and *The Primitive* were highly autobiographical, the latter blending surrealistic and obsessive patterns quite successfully into what may well be the author's most profound novel. The Harlem thrillers developed along a humorous line, at times becoming truly

Rabelaisian, as if the only possible response to an absurd situation was a self-protective burst of laughter. When Himes somewhat modified the *genre* with *Blind Man With a Pistol* (1969), it was by injecting into it more political and social comment.

A Case of Rape reminds one at times of all these works, yet it is patently something else: it could have been a thriller since it revolves around a criminal plot, but the suspense and the drama characteristic of detective fiction are left out; it could have been an outspoken criticism of the judiciary, like *Cast the First Stone,* but Himes devotes only one short chapter to that matter. It is close to *The Primitive* in its treatment of the Black man/white woman relationship, but it does not really develop into a psychological study; it is as strongly personal as *The Third Generation,* yet Himes stops short of any overtly autobiographical treatment. And above all, *A Case of Rape* is thematically and stylistically baffling because, while it remains close to a case study, when one tries to construe it as a *roman à cléf* one is immediately shunted back from actual events into the world of fiction. This explains much of the fascination of the work: not only does this novel shed light on racism in France and on the lives of Black expatriates in Paris in the Fifties, but it also allows us to grasp some essential motifs in Himes's work and to better understand how he manages to transform historical events into imaginary episodes.

We are able to observe this transformation more fully in *A Case of Rape* than in other novels because it never reached a final stage. Although structurally complete, including all the characterizations outlined in great detail, it lacks, to some degree, dialogues and dramatic scenes. When Himes wrote it in 1956–57, he was planning a long, Dostoievskian work, possibly consisting of several volumes. The alleged "rape" was only to be considered the unifying episode out of which would have evolved the complex life histories of the major characters and, ultimately, an ironic exploration of American identity along with a definition of the American nationality. On November 28, 1957, in a letter to his friend and translator Yves Malartic, who was helping him sell the project to a French publisher, Himes explicitly called the work "my synopsis of *A Case of Rape.*" The project failed and the full-scale narrative was never carried out. The shorter version, however, was sold to a small French publishing house in 1961, and ultimately published two years later by another publisher.

As we have it, the novel includes 15 sections whose individual titles suggest a dispassionate, clinical exposé of the case. The view of the prosecution, the counsel for the defense, the pleas, the verdict, the sentencing, the reactions of the international press: all of this is disposed of in 44 pages. A slightly larger space is devoted to the background of Roger Garrison, who looks into the case, and to the limitations and errors in his investigation. Lastly, the author delves into the victim's past life, retraces a love affair between her and one of the accused, explains how racial fears distorted everyone's reactions, and ends by posing the question: would the narration of the whole truth have convinced a jury of the innocence of the four Black men?

So that the reader may be able to grasp its most illuminating aspects, let us summarize this fictional "case of rape." On September 8, 1956, Mrs. Elizabeth Hancock Brissaud, a white American woman married to a Belgian, was apparently seen fighting with four American Negroes in a Paris hotel room.

The police were called and found her dead on the bed. The autopsy revealed that she had had repeated sexual intercourse the previous day and that she had died from a heart attack caused by over-exertion and the ingestion of cantharidis (Spanish Fly), a potent aphrodisiac. The counsel for the defense disclosed that the victim had been the lover of Scott Hamilton, one of the accused, the year before when they had collaborated on the writing of a novel. The novel had been accepted under Mrs. Hancock's name and she had sent Hamilton half of the advance on royalties; later, however, made aware of their collaboration by an anonymous letter, the publisher had threatened to cancel the contract. Mrs. Hancock needed a statement from Hamilton that he had not collaborated with her, which Hamilton was prepared to grant. Furthermore, in order to dispel her suspicion that he was the author of the letter, he had invited her to his room where his friends could help convince her of his innocence. After some talking and drinking, Mrs. Hancock had fallen asleep, and, on awakening, had mistakenly drunk from a sherry bottle containing the aphrodisiac. Hence her nervous crisis which the accused were trying to subdue when seen by the neighbors, and her subsequent, accidental death. At the end of the novel, we learn the following facts not disclosed during the trial: The night before her death, Mrs. Hancock had been approached by her husband who had long ago completely subjugated her sexually, and whom she was trying to divorce; he had given her Spanish Fly and they had made love several times. In addition, one of the Black men, Ted Elkins, had seen her take the wrong bottle when she woke up, but, believing she despised him because he was darker-skinned than the others, had not warned her because he was anxious to see this "lady" act in a disorderly fashion. *He* was certainly guilty, yet his friends had not even attempted to establish these facts, convinced as they were that the jury would not believe them. All four were found guilty of administering aphrodisiacs to the victim in order to rape her and sentenced to life imprisonment.

A Black writer living in Paris, Roger Garrison, had begun investigating the case. He considered the verdict a perfect example of a conscious racial policy in which the condemnation of Black men for raping white women was used to prove the entire race inferior. Considering the upsurge of racism in France due to the Algerian war and the aborted Suez invasion, he thought he could prove the international character of such tactics. Thus, he did not even attempt to discover the factual innocence or guilt of the accused; he sought merely to show that, in terms of their individual life histories, they were incapable of such a crime. This device, of course, enables Himes to scrutinize the past of Cesar Gee, Sheldon Edward Russell, Theodore Elkins, and Scott Hamilton, and to probe their family histories, all typically American in their often startlingly mixed economic careers and mixtures of races and nationalities. Yet Garrison's investigation led him no where: "In order to convince the whole white race that these four Black men were not inferior, he should have given evident proof of their superiority as men, which he could not do" (p. 104).[1] Nor could he establish any clear relationship between the sentence and "any preconceived plan which could have explained how his literary failure had been engineered for the benefit of the racists" (p. 106)

Thus Garrison's mistakes are plainly obvious: He considered himself too important in the French political game; he underestimated the fact that the

French believed the accused were guilty of rape, and he sought the political reasons, only for the verdict; he left unexamined the relationships among the four men, as well as what actually happened in the hotel room. The question was not to establish whether Mrs. Hancock had been raped but why a white lady could have agreed to come to a hotel room with four Black men, and Garrison did not reflect that "the desperate fight waged by whites to enforce racial supremacy could leave white women more and more vulnerable ... to persecution by Black men and just as defenseless as the Blacks were in front of white oppression" (p. 111). After thus demonstrating the limitations of Garrison's approach and his motives, the novelist further enlightens us by providing additional psycho-social background, and by analyzing the affair between Mrs. Hancock and Hamilton, and also the complex relationships among the accused.

The description of these relationships helps recapture the atmosphere of Black expatriate life in Paris in the mid-Fifties. Although we must to careful to allow for the free play of Himes's "poetic imagination," the setting of *A Case of Rape* can be recreated from the following scene outlined by the novelist for a contemporary magazine piece:

The American colony in the Latin Quarter is dominated by the bustling, confident personality of the "now" Richard Wright who holds court for his neophytes in a little café, the Monaco, just back of the Odéon and Boulevard Saint-Germain and down rue Monsieur le Prince, a block from where he lives with his wife and two lovely daughters. The Monaco is a hangout for English-speaking, student-artist types, Americans mostly, some British, a few Scandinavians, a few African colonials. It is a gossipy little bistro and if one wants to know the lowdown on any compatriot in the quarter one has only to sit there for an hour or so and keep out of the line of fire. Wright stops by once or twice a day and talks of world politics, the American dilemma, the nature of Communism and the pitfalls of creative writing. Most listen and perhaps a few agree.... William Gardner Smith, who maintains his individuality by avoiding the Monaco, is holding his own court, smaller and less wild-eyed, but perhaps better informed than Wright's in the café Tournon.[2]

At this point, it is probably best not to attempt to identify any of Himes's fictional characters with real life people that he knew. Even if he often made use of a few actual episodes and traits pertaining to real persons, he never in tended to write a *roman à cléf* on the Black writers whom *Time* magazine would soon be reproaching with living "Amid the Alien Corn." The characterization of Roger Garrison, for instance, is entirely fictional even though Richard Wright at one time thought that it could apply to him.[3] *A Case of Rape* was written, Himes states, "In order to emphasize the preconceptions and humiliations that Black Americans were subjected to in Paris during the Algerian war."[4] In that sense, we could say that this work is to Himes what *Giovanni's Room* is to Baldwin, the unpublished "Island of Hallucinations" is to Wright, *The Stone Face* is to William Gardner Smith, and *Speak Now* is to Frank Yerby: the expatriate novel. Within this group, *A Case of Rape* stands closer to "Island of Hallucinations," since this work revolves around in-group relationships, and to Smith's condemnation of French racism in *The Stone Face*. Yerby is concerned with interracial love, as is Himes, whereas Baldwin limits himself in this novel at least to a white homosexual affair.

The story of the aphrodisiacs, however far-fetched it may seem, is not purely fictional: when Himes sent Yves Malartic the typescript of *A Case of Rape,* the letter immediately recalled a similar incident in *Cast the First Stone;* which he felt might serve to authenticate the later novel in the eyes of the French public. In response to this suggestion, Himes said in January, 1958:

As to using the page from *Cast the First Stone* to authenticate the story, I have no objection, but *Cast the First Stone* is fiction and I doubt it would serve the purpose. However, the case is that of a Professor Snooks of Ohio State University in Columbus, Ohio. The crime occurred, as near as I can remember, in 1929 and Professor Snooks was executed in 1930. The case should be found in some collection of famous U.S. murder cases.[5]

As related in Chapter 12 of *Cast the First Stone,* the story of Professor Snooks (renamed Snodgrass) does not take more than a few paragraphs, as the protagonist catches a glimpse of the murderer on his way to the electric chair:

He was a well-known surgeon from Springfield, out of a socially prominent family. The girl, whom he had killed by knocking her on the head with a hammer, then severing some important arteries by sticking a knife blade up her ears and reaming them out, was a college student. He had given her Spanish Fly during the period of their intimacy in order to teach her various manners of sex degeneracy and they had smoked marijuana weed together, and blown their tops during their sex-maddened tea-jags; and he had finally, 'in order to obtain complete satisfaction, utterly debased himself before her, receiving the exultation of his sensation from the stimulation of his utter debasement'—that's what the little pamphlets said, which sold for 25 cents and which were very frank about the matter. (p. 113)

In *A Case of Rape,* Professor Snooks becomes André Brissaud, the sadistic husband who forces cantharidis on his wife to enslave her sexually. On the other hand, Scott and his friends, although they possess Spanish Fly, are utterly innocent of artificial sex practices. Elizabeth discovers sensuality with Scott in Paris, and she holds more attraction for him than any other woman before, but this is all very natural. Obviously, Himes deals with rape and aphrodisiacs because, in exploring a miscarriage of justice in order to denounce the pervasive evils of racism, he is able to exploit the strongest possible taboo—sexual relationships between the Black male and the white female—to show how prone white society is to jump to the conclusion of rape.

Insofar as it is a condemnation of racism, the technical aspects of the work become even more interesting if we place it in the context of Himes's career and changing perspective. *A Case of Rape* was written after *The Primitive,* just after the first draft of *Mamie Mason (Pinktoes)* had been completed, but before Himes had begun writing his detective stories. Thus the book partakes of both Himes's "earlier" style—more bitter, more violent, and more explicit in its denunciation (although his condemnation of the system is already more restrained and clinical than it was in If *He Hollers Let Him Go* or *Lonely*

Crusade)—and of his "later" style, more humorous than satirical, often surrealistic, dealing in caricature and laughter as an answer to absurdity.

From this perspective, *The Primitive* would represent the last stage of the "earlier style." Its theme is close to that of *A Case of Rape*. It was written

without hope of its earning any money and little hope of its being published. Believing that this cultured woman with whom I lived and this other white woman of whom I wrote were more primitive than I, it amused me to write this book and it still amuses me to read it.... We [Black people] always know what white people are doing to us and what they are thinking while doing it. We are amused in a masochistic sort of way by their various justifications and rationalizations.[6]

As we can see, satire and denunciation are not unmixed with self-criticism. But there is one element in *The Primitive* which seems to be unnecessary in *A Case of Rape:* the use of autobiography as catharsis. Looking back on the composition of *The Primitive* some 13 years later, Himes adds: "Being largely autobiographical (I did not kill the white woman, however gladly I might have), the book acted as a catharsis, purging me of all the mental and emotional inhibitions that restricted my writing."[7] In *A Case of Rape,* things are already different: the surrealism and buffoonery of the final episodes of *The Primitive* (in which, for example, a chimpanzee appears on television) come to the fore even more often, finally becoming quite persistent in *Mamie Mason* and in the later Harlem thrillers. Himes often seems to let his imagination roam when creating the characters of *A Case of Rape:* Cesar Gee, for example, with his coal-black face and Attilla-like mustache and goatee, is more than a little Rabelaisian. His love of luxury is provocative—he lives at the Hotel George V and parades in a yellow Cadillac until the day the Duchess of Windsor happens to cast an inquisitive and despising eye on him in the middle of a traffic jam. After this traumatic encounter, he resorts to startling Parisians by promenading with a high-pedigree, snow-white borzoi dog. In other words, he is in several respects reminiscent of the Black *bourgeoisie* friends of Mamie Mason; in the same way, the foibles and ludicrous features of other characters in *A Case of Rape* foreshadow the anticlimactic treatment of drama in the Harlem thrillers.

Yet there is a more serious, maybe even more sentimental, vein that pervades *A Case of Rape* and makes it a moving book. Perhaps this is because Scott Hamilton is in many ways Chester Himes. The resemblance lies beneath the surface of both men, although their ages, physical appearances and family backgrounds do offer points of similarity. Hamilton does not like Paris: "indeed, he had never found a place fit for him anywhere and there was a good chance he'd never find one" (p. 87). Himes confessed the same difficulty in a 1954 letter to Carl Van Vechten; the city not only shattered the youthful and quixotic dreams one might entertain, but it also crushed in people prone to dream the very faculty of dreaming.

In Paris, nothing meant anything anymore; everything was changed or distorted, or else, everything had already assumed its true shape or received its true meaning, which was equally destructive. Love had become sexuality, and aspirations had become mere ambition. (p. 88)

   Behind Himes's stance as hardboiled writer, despite his often vitriolic satire
of American mores and his pitiless handling of certain characters, one often
feels that his attitude towards life is that of a warm-hearted, humane, though
sometimes despairing, moralist. He is concerned with the basic qualities and
values of human experience: personal honesty, group solidarity, coping with
the debasement of feelings inherent in prison life, racial oppression, and any
type of human social structure. This is in part why the love story of *A Case of
Rape* emerges not only as moving but as exemplary. It is used to demonstrate
how "the loves of Scott and Elizabeth" come to bear "strange fruits of fear." In
the eyes of moralist Himes, the failure of a civilization appears nowhere more
patently than in the way it distorts and thwarts such an essential human bond
as the man-woman relationship. From the late nineteenth-century to LeRoi
Jones's *Dutchman* or Eldridge Cleaver's "The Primeval Mitosis," many Afro-
American writers have insisted on the white woman/Black man relationship
because they are complementary victims of the racial system (which is not to
say, of course, that the Black woman was not also victimized). Isn't this
precisely what Himes is trying to show here, when he states that "the most
important phenomenon in this liaison between Scott and Lisbeth was not that
it had taken place, nor how, nor why, but simply that it *could* have taken
place"—and quite naturally and understandably so, since the characters were
brought together by their education, religious beliefs, traditions, moral outlook
and "a common disillusionment regarding God and goodness"? The other
notable point is that such a love, in which tenderness, trust and true feeling
blossomed for a while, should have been doomed in the racist/materialistic
context of Western culture.

   Himes has long considered the American Black as "one of the most
sophisticated people in the history of mankind"—sophisticated and subtle
because deprived of original simplicity by the culture of the oppressor. When
writing *The Primitive* so "full of dynamite," he was consciously writing about
more than the so-called Negro problem:

It is the story of the United States' complete incapacity to face up to its human
problem. In that tiny flat of tragedy, the words "Negro" and "Negro problem" sound
like the ravings of idiots. All these people are caught—the white men and women,
the Negro men and women—in the same trap; all victims of the same big overgrown
idiot of a nation with the underdeveloped brain. The sons of bitches brush their
teeth, chew laxatives, take cold showers and buy big automobiles as a cure for
sterility, infidelity, the poll-tax, McCarthy, segregation, the Cold War; and then
build hydrogen bombs and horror stories to scare themselves into screaming
nightmares. They say to me, 'Boy, why don't you write about how great we are—we,
the biggest and the baddest and we got the mostest.'

   Such were Himes's thoughts when he wrote Yves Malartic on July 29,
1954. To such absurdity, the only answer was the one provided by the blues or
by Himes's own bitter humor. "Don't cry, son, it's really funny. You just try to
get the handle of the joke," he had Jessie Robinson say at the end of *The
Primitive*. In a similar fashion, *A Case of Rape* is the chronicle of a love
destroyed, absurdly made impossible by the social and cultural odds against it. It
is the record of the shattering of one of the fond dreams of Himes—the dreamer,

and the unrelenting condemnation of the killers of the dream. In his final
"Hypothesis," the novelist infers that, had the missing proof been found,

the conscience of men would have been forced to contend with the charitable element
of doubt and no one would have dared point an accusing finger at the four Black men,
branding them as potentially guilty of rape. And no one would have wondered which
is the greater crime—rape or the condemnation for rape of an innocent man. Maybe
the trial of all men, of men of all races, would thus have made some progress for
there is an everlasting trial in progress, that of the men guilty of the greatest crime
against man: man's inhumanity to man. And we are guilty of it, all of us. (pp. 166–
67)

Such was Himes's comment on the human condition 16 years ago. *A Case
of Rape* therefore deserves more than the passing glance it is usually accorded:
an often scathing evocation of the prejudices encountered by Black exiles in
Paris, the moving evocation of an impossible love, it constitutes a meditation
that leads Himes-the-humanist to another level of awareness in his lifelong
fight against man's inhumanity to man.

NOTES

1. All references are to the French edition, *Une Affaire de Viol*, Paris, *Les Yeux
Ouverts*, 1963, the translation being mine.
2. From an unpublished piece for EBONY Magazine in the Carl Van Vechten
collection at Yale University, communicated by Miss Nina Kressner and quoted by
permission of Chester Himes.
3. In an April 1960 letter to Margrit de Sablomere.
4. September 15, 1971, letter to Michel Fabre.
5. Quoted by permission of Yves Malartic, to whom I am indebted for calling
my attention to that point, and Chester Himes.
6. New York Times Book Review, June 4, 1967.
7. *Ibid.*

"Dissecting Western Pathology: A Critique of A Case of Rape" *Black World*, 21
(March 1972), 39–48.

The Chester Himes Mystique

Gwendoline Lewis Roget

... she had expected Lee to be hurt, dreading it and yet convinced that it would happen, because she did not see how he could live in the society of America and escape being hurt. (Himes, *Lonely Crusade*)

Albert Camus once said that racism is absurd. Racism introduces absurdity into the human condition. Not only does racism express the absurdity of the racists, but it generates absurdity in the victims.... If one lives in a country where racism is held valid and practiced in all ways of life, eventually, no matter whether one is a racist or a victim, one comes to feel the absurdity of life. (Himes, *My Life of Absurdity*)

Chester Himes's decision to write his autobiography was prompted by a number of exigencies, among them the need for self-validation, the need for self-knowledge and the need for self-liberation. The untimely death of his lifelong friend Richard Wright in 1960 caused Himes to become preoccupied with his own morality. After suffering strokes in 1963 and 1964, he felt impelled to get his life on record, before it was too late. Exhibiting immense candor as well as courage, Himes, in his two-volume autobiography *The Quality of Hurt* and *My Life of Absurdity*, reviews the events of his life within the socio-cultural context of his time. He uses his autobiography to chronicle the hurt that he suffered from psychological abuse, racial discrimination, and the rejection he experienced as a writer in America.

In spite of his need to confess, Himes had an uncanny propensity for mystification which he sustains in his autobiography through the effective use of paradox, ambiguities, racial inversions, and inconsistencies. His unique ability to mystify, shock, and raise the consciousness of his reader through the use of satire and "existential contraries" was commented on by Richard Wright, who commended Himes's "rare genius" as a writer "to describe murder as personal redemption, to speak of love in terms of hate, and to use sex as a symbol of race pride." In *The Quality of Hurt* and *My Life of Absurdity*, Himes the iconoclast comes through, defiant of society's taboos and restrictions, creating his own rules in both his life and his writings, contradicting himself, and being consistent only in his inconsistency. Although he reveals his feelings and opinions on a broad range of subjects and incidents that shaped his life, the authentic Chester Himes still eludes the reader.

The autobiography's three focal points—women, writing, and racism—are couched in paradox, ambiguities, and contradictions. Himes devoted his life to exposing "the viciousness and demoralizing consequences of racism." His diatribes against racial bigotry spared no particular group. He attacked blacks as well as whites. Although Himes was committed to social change and entente between all people, he confesses that he felt like "a pariah" among Caucasians.

This revelation is puzzling when one considers that the majority of his romantic relationships were with white women. Jean Johnson, Himes's first wife, is the only African-American woman with whom he is amorously linked in the autobiography. In his relationships with women, further contradictions and inconsistencies emerge. In *The Quality of Hurt* he postulates, "I must have been a puritan all my life.... I consider the sexual act private. I do not want my sexual experience to be made public." Having come to this level of understanding, he then proceeds to recount in bawdy and graphic language his sexual conquests. That the women in his life played a dominant role is substantiated by his decision to center his European experiences in the autobiography on three women in his life.

Painstakingly, Himes retraces every nuance of his feelings about being denigrated as a writer and having his works misunderstood, misinterpreted, and/or rejected in America. No matter what direction his writings took, as A. Robert Lee has astutely observed, Himes was criticized. When he wrote on black themes, as he did in *If He Hollers Let Him Go* and *Lonely Crusade*, he was criticized for being "too narrow" or "insufficiently universal." When he put race aside and used whites as his subject, as in *Cast The First Stone*, he was accused of "turning his back on his heritage." When Himes wrote on the problems facing the black middle class from within, as he did in *The Third Generation*, he was maligned as "selling out the race." When he wrote *Pinktoes* and the detective novels, he was vilified as "pandering to the tastes of the depraved." In Europe, where he would emerge as an internationally recognized writer, Himes felt immensely vindicated. Yet, while he exulted over his success and acceptance abroad, he expressed contempt for the American critics who passed over him—only to lament, "It hurt me more than I care to admit to be rejected by the American press."

Himes's journey back through his writings not only highlights the critical response to his works, but also informs readers of the genesis of his writings. He reveals how each of his major books came into being, where he was, and what he was doing during that period of his life. In this regard, *The Quality of Hurt* and *My Life of Absurdity* are invaluable complements to his semi-autobiographical novels *The Third Generation*, *Cast the First Stone*, *The Primitive*, and *Une Affaire de Viol*.

The Quality of Hurt chronicles Himes's early years, from his birth in 1909 up to 1954 in Europe. *My Life of Absurdity* picks up the threads of his life in 1954 to follow his transcontinental experiences up to 1972. The unifying themes of the autobiography are hurt and absurdity. Although Himes states in *The Quality of Hurt* that he does not like to exhibit his wounds, in the three books that make up the volume, and in the twenty-four chapters which compromise volume two, he does just that, as he recalls the hurt of both personal and professional experiences.

Chester Himes's autobiography offers invaluable literary witness to the multi-faceted black experience in America and abroad. As long as he was physically able to do so, Himes continued to write. *The Quality of Hurt* and *My Life of Absurdity* help validate the author's self-image as an author first and foremost. His prolific output bears witness to the fact that he mastered the craft of writing. His one self-imposed exigency was that his novels should "swing." He liked to write, he said, "the way a bird sings." Yet even his style of writing was marked by his contrary personality. He could ascend to the heights of nobility, and sink to an abyss of baseness. His writing could be fastidiously rigorous or trippingly clumsy. With the stroke of a pen, he could alter his tone from lyrical to acerbic. He could reason with the cold, discerning eye of a realist, and yet emote with the maudlin sensitivity of a romantic.

Although he was outspoken on the subject of African-Americans, he took umbrage at being called "a race spokesman." In a 1972 interview with journalist Michael Mok, Himes commented that African-Americans "aren't looking for any spokesman. They can speak for themselves. The best a black writer can do is deal with subjects which are personal; so he can tell how it was for him." In his autobiography, Himes followed his own advice. His narrative continues the excellent tradition of African-American autobiography that had its inception with the slave narratives. *The Quality of Hurt* and *My Life of Absurdity* are testament to Himes's re-telling his life "in his own way." In the final lines of the autobiography he exultantly states, "For all its inconsistencies, its contradictions, its humiliations, its triumphs, its failures, its tragedies, its hurts, its ecstasies and its absurdities; that's my life—the third generation out of slavery." It is incumbent upon this generation to establish Chester Himes in his rightful place as a member of the pantheon of great writers. The recently released Paragon House paperback edition of Himes's *The Quality of Hurt* and *My Life of Absurdity*, by making available his autobiography once again to the American public, is a step in that direction.

African American Review 26:3 (1992), 521–523.

Policiers Noirs

Fred Pfeil

In the summer of 1948, Chester Himes' delivered an address titled "The Dilemma of the Negro Novelist in the United States" to a mainly white audience at the University of Chicago. Himes was 39: he had worked as a bellhop, day laborer, small-time hustler, gambler and crook; served more than seven years of a twenty-to-twenty-five-year sentence for armed robbery; and published numerous short stories and two novels, *If He Hollers Let Him Go* in 1945 and *Lonely Crusade* in 1947. The first novel was acclaimed as an honest and effective work of "social protest," still a reviewer's category in 1945. The second, despite its implausibly affirmative ending, contained within its sprawling canvas enough portraits of racist and/or fascist whites, psychopathetic and/or Tomish blacks and unscrupulous and/or double agent Communists to offend everyone—black and Communist reviewers as well as white establishment ones. In 1948, Himes's wounds from the flaying *Lonely Crusade* had received were still fresh; even so, on that summer afternoon in Chicago he hoped his words might yet be taken seriously in his native land.

Himes had three main points to make that afternoon. Any one or perhaps even two of them might have secured his reputation within either the black community or the white establishment. The three of them together, however, made a mess which still sends most people, white and black, scampering for the exits. To begin with, Himes proclaimed that his "negro novelist" and indeed all American blacks were *Americans*: "the face may be the face of Africa, but the heart has the beat of Wall Street." He next insisted that, given white racism, all American blacks "must, of necessity, hate white people ... at some time.... [There] are no exceptions. It could not possibly be otherwise." And finally, he argued that any honest exploration of the condition of the black American psyche would have to admit to and describe the damage at its core.

If this plumbing for the truth reveals within the Negro personality homicidal mania, lust for white women, a pathetic sense of inferiority, paradoxical anti-Semitism, arrogance, Uncle Tomism, hate and fear and self-hate, this then is the effect of oppression on the human personality. These are the daily horrors, the daily realities, the daily experiences of an oppressed minority.

The reaction to such total honesty was utter silence, in response to which Himes stayed drunk for the better part of the next five years. During this time two more novels were accepted for publication: *Cast the First Stone*, a prison novel for which Himes resentfully supplied his publishers with a white protagonist; and *The Third Generation*, a thinly fictionalized account of Himes's family history and early life. Still, his literary reputation continued to fade; he was once again supporting himself mostly as a porter, janitor and bellhop; his marriage fell apart; and he entered into a ruinously self-destructive affair with an equally troubled white woman from the New York literary world.

Yet Himes was finally able to pull himself out of the depths to which his rage, fear and despair had brought him. At what one feels must have been the eleventh hour, he found the cash to leave the country. Like Richard Wright before him, Himes discovered a literary reputation awaited him in Paris. It was in Paris, too, that Himes's French publisher, Marcel Duhamel, first suggested Himes knock out some detective fiction to make a little money. The first such book, *For Love of Imabelle* (republished as *A Rage in Harlem*) won Himes the 1958 Grand Prix Policier; the eleventh and last, *Blind Man With a Pistol*, appeared in 1969 to a flurry of favorable publicity in the United States and abroad. Indeed, it is not too much to say that Himes's reputation today (he died in 1984) rests mainly on these slim, commercial *policiers noirs*.

We know by now, or ought to know, that what gets us off as entertainment is rarely simple and never innocent. All the more so, then, when the subgenre in question is concerned with illegal versus official violence; when the scene is Harlem, and both the criminals and good guys are black; and when the author is a black man with an analysis of white racism's power to provoke within blacks not only an answering hatred but paranoia, self-doubt and self-contempt. Reading the five Harlem thrillers recently republished is, properly undertaken, something like submitting to a special kind of Rorschach test: your reactions to the lurid images, actions and characters they hurl forth reveal at least as much about you as about Harlem or Himes.

Take, for example, the opening sequence of *The Crazy Kill*, which flaunts its energy and virtuosity as brazenly as the first long take of any Orson Welles film. Our attention is turned from a small-time thief stealing a bag of change from a Plymouth double-parked outside an A&P to a man leaning out of the window overhead watching the ensuing chase, leaning so out that he falls from the window, landing on a soft, warm pile of newly baked bread stacked outside the store. Cut back to the apartment from which the man has just fallen—a raucous, bleary wake is under way, attended by a cast of characters with enough lust for power, money and sex to fuel the next five seasons of *Dynasty*:

in walks the man who fell from the window, now revealed as one Reverend Short. Short recounts in slightly crazed terms his brush with death, his salvation in and through the basket of bread; the other characters run to the window to look down; and there in the basket below lies another friend of the family—only this one has a knife in his chest.

Likewise in *Cotton Comes to Harlem*, a con man's back-to-Africa barbecue and rally is ripped off by two white men in a meat delivery truck which in turn is chased at breakneck speed by the con man and his two guards through a spray of machine-gun bullets; in *The Real Cool Killers*, a large, greasy white man, who has been attacked in a bar by a drunken black man with a knife (subsequently literally disarmed by an ax-wielding bartender), is chased through the Harlem streets by a hopped-up hipster firing blanks from a pistol, then shot dead in mid-stride by someone else in the gawking, leering crowd. If it is almost always steamingly hot in these novels, that is because Himes's Harlem is a volcano in constant eruption, a desperate, sordid *Walpurgisnacht* without end:

An effluvium of hot stinks arose from the frying pan and hung in the hot motionless air, no higher than the rooftops—the smell of sizzling barbecue, fried hair, exhaust fumes, rotting garbage, cheap perfumes, unwashed bodies, decayed buildings, dog-rat-and-cat offal, whiskey and vomit, and all the old dried-up odors of poverty.

. . .

It was too hot to sleep. Everyone was too evil to love…. The night was filled with the blare of countless radios, the frenetic blasting of spasm cats playing in the streets, hysterical laughter, automobile horns, strident curses, loudmouthed arguments, the screams of knife fights.   (*The Heat's On*)

Against such a landscape, the violent opening of each novel constitutes less a crime to be solved than an overture promising more mayhem to come. If you wanted to be trendy, you could say that the "hermeneutic" function of the standard crime novel is systematically downplayed in these books in favor of such regular moments of "semic excess" as the following:

One slug caught Sister Heavenly in the left side below the ribs and lodged in the side of her spine; the other went wild. She fell sideways to the pavement and was powerless to move, but her mind was still active and her vision was clear. She saw Benny Mason slide quickly across the seat, leap to the sidewalk, and aim the pistol at her head.
    Well now, ain't this lovely? she thought just before the bullet entered her brain.
                                                                                  (*The Heat's On*)

. . .

He slapped her with such savage violence it spun her out of the chair to land in a grotesque splay-legged posture on her belly on the floor, the red dress hiked so high it showed the black nylon panties she wore.
    "And that ain't all," he said.
                                                                                  (*A Rage in Harlem*)

Only those Postmodernists most fully loosed from "the tyranny of the referent" will be able to savor without qualm the *jouissance* such passages offer. On the other hand, especially when they are placed in their helter-skelter context, it is hard to deny completely the appeal of their twisted energy. It is not incidental that Himes's detectives are named Grave Digger Jones and Coffin Ed Johnson; or that the latter's acid-scarred face is frequently compared to a zombie's; or that they contribute at least as much shocking violence to these narratives as they prevent. Grave Digger and Coffin Ed are in fact not so much crime-solvers as priests of violence; the swirling, brutal action over which they preside and to which they contribute is a voodoo celebration of black America, a black mass indeed.

And then there is the problem of Himes's women. In the Harlem novels there is almost always one grotesquely fetishized compound of male desire and dread like Imabelle of *A Rage in Harlem*: "She was a cushion-lipped, hot bodied, banana-skin chick with the speckled brown eyes of a teaser and the high-arched, ball-bearing hips of a natural-born *amante*." This *femme fatale*, who will before the story's end get slapped around by one or both of our detectives, is also invariably "high yellow," and for more than one reason. She is yellow because she is a blend of the two mythic women that black shipworker Bob Jones oscillates between in Himes's first novel, *If He Hollers Let Him Go*: his fiancée, the beautiful black-bourgeois Alice, and Madge, a blond redneck co-worker who "looked ... rife but not quite rotten," and whose alarm and excitement at the sight of him fill Bob with an angry lust "like an electric shock." And she is yellow-skinned because so was Himes's mother, Anna [sic] Bomar Himes, a woman whose neurotic love and rage overwhelmed his early years. Himes's mother doted on him for his own light skin; she oiled and brushed his hair every night to straighten it, and let him brush her hair and file her nails; she was morbidly sensitive to racial slights from whites and to the encroachment of those blacker in color or manner than she, including her husband, whom she viewed with resent and disgust.

Not surprisingly, then, throughout *If He Hollers Let Him Go* Bob Jones treats most of his fellow blacks with a contempt almost equal to his fury at white people; his single, obsessive concern is to stand tall as a black *man*. Thus too the gross sexist sadism of the Harlem novels. Yet the male hysteria that pervades Himes' work, and the Oedipal pathology behind it, are themselves just two more symptoms of the widespread violence wrought by a racist culture, intertwining love and aggression, rage and fear, hatred and self-hatred in the soul of the oppressed. In an interview conducted relatively late in his life, Himes told fellow black novelist John A. Williams, "I would like to see produced a novel that just drains a person's subconscious of all his attitudes and reactions to everything.... Since [the black writer's] reactions and thoughts will obviously be different from that of the white community, this should create an entirely different structure of the novel." And, from the same interview: "That's one of the saddest parts about the black man in America—that he is being used to titillate the emotions of the white community.... I want these people to take me seriously. I don't care if they think I'm a barbarian, a savage, or what they think; just think I'm a serious savage." The first quote tells us how, intentionally or not, he wrote his Harlem novels; the second, how we ought to read Himes.

The Nation, November 15, 1986, pp. 523–525.

Chester Himes:
The Collected Stories
James Robert Payne

After attending Ohio State University, Chester Himes involved himself with gang activity until his eight-year imprisonment. His first publication, a piece about a prison fire, appeared in *Esquire* in 1932, when the gifted African-American prose stylist and poet was in his early twenties. Like many creators of American culture, Himes has achieved substantially greater critical recognition in France than in his own country. He emigrated to France in 1953. Although Himes's best work has been stylistically compared with Hemingway, and compared with Baldwin, Hurston, and Welty for its insight, his fiction has still not received the extensive critical attention it merits. I think, however, that we are now on the verge of a clearer and fairer recognition of his achievements.

American critics and scholars are at present learning to read better and respond more sensitively to our varied texts representing the drama and ironies of race, class, and gender. Himes's fiction, effectively focused from the beginning to the end of his prolific career on race, class, and gender themes, should prove irresistibly attractive to many scholars attuned to the new approaches. General readers, now more and more drawn to black artistry through the work of such writers as Alice Walker, Toni Morrison, and Charles Johnson, will, I believe, continue to turn to Himes, a popular writer of the previous generation whose fiction has undergone successful film adaptation since the early 1970s. The generously conceived and readable *Collected Stories* will facilitate fuller critical response to Himes, and it should enhance his appeal to general readers.

The collection opens with a brief but helpful foreword by Calvin Hernton and a very useful chronology of Himes's short fiction. It presents both his previously published works and a number of very interesting hitherto unpublished pieces, for an overall total of sixty short stories. Though a few of the stories are marked by a sketchy, inadequate development that suggests hasty composition, riches and pleasures abound.

Pleasures of course will vary from reader to reader. By having the chance to read it in the full context of his other late-1930s-to-early-1940s short fiction, I especially enjoyed an increased understanding of Himes's classic 1937 story "Headwaiter" (originally published as "Salute to the Passing"), a work which epitomizes Himes's superb mastery of nuances of class and race among black men. With stories like "Strictly Business" (1942) and "Tang" (1967) the collection allows us to see, in retrospect, how Himes rivals Nelson Algren as a fictionist of the great American urban underclass, black and white. Long respected for his fiction of prison life, crime, and detection, Himes also demonstrates considerable power as a fictionist of black military experience, in which antagonists, as in the painful "Christmas Gift" (1944) and "All He Needs Is Feet" (1945), tend not to be foreign enemies but rather fellow Americans. Stories such as "A Nigger" (1937) reveal impressive insights on male-female relationships across the color line and are especially notable for their candid and sensitive representation of complex feelings of black men. Most of Himes's stories are in a straightforward, realist-naturalist mode, with some exceptions, including the somewhat technically innovative "Prison Mass" (1933). *The Collected Stories* is graced with fine cover art, a portrait of Himes by Denese Morden.

"(Review of) The Collected Stories of Chester Himes" *World Literature Today*, 66 (Autumn 1992), 722–723.

The Best of Himes,
the Worst of Himes

Ishmael Reed

Life in the United States was hard for a man like Chester Himes, a proud, nonconformist rebel and mulatto whose mother, often mistaken for white, demanded respect even to the point of armed combat. There's that great scene in his book "The Third Generation" in which his mother, passenger in a car whose student driver is threatened by a white farmer, pulls a gun on the farmer.

James Baldwin, another proud and temperamental genius, said that if he hadn't left the United states he would have killed someone. The same could be said of Chester Himes, the intellectual and gangster who left the United States for Europe in the 1950s. He achieved fame abroad with his Harlem detective series, which are remarkable for their macabre comic sense and wicked and nasty wit so brilliantly captured in Bill Duke's "A Rage in Harlem."

The black male characters in these stories either rage against the assaults upon their dignity and self-worth by American society or channel this rage, the strategy used by the dignified Dick Small, the deferential headwaiter in the story "Headwaiter," a virtuoso performance that shows Himes' gift for scene, speech and characterization was evident as early as 1937.

Most of the men in the book spend their time "on the muscle," that is, in a constant state of anxiety and depression. In "All God's Chillun Got Pride," Keith Richards has a "tightfaced scowl ... high shouldered air of disdain ... a hot, challenging stare ... uncalled-for and out-of-place defiance, and a lack of civility and rudeness." As a result of his pride, his career ends in the Army's guardhouse.

Another character's pride almost results in his murder by the landlady of a prostitute he's sharing with a rich white john named Mr. Shelton. When the wealthy Mr. Shelton visits his paramour unexpectedly, Joe Wolf hides in the closet, where he is discovered by Shelton. Shelton refuses to notice him.

"All of a sudden it hit him that Mr. Shelton had opened the door deliberately, knowing he was there, and after having satisfied himself that he was right, had refused to acknowledge Joe's existence. Why he had not only refused to recognize him as a rival, not even as an intruder, why the son of a bitch looked at him as if he was another garment he had bought for her."

Insulted and humiliated, Wolf attacks the prostitute until the landlady "Miss Lou burst into the room pointing a long-barreled .38." Wolfe has to run for his life and swallow his "innate pride, his manhood, his honor."

James (Happy) Trent, an exconvict, returns to civilian life, only to find his mother and brother experiencing hard times. An old ragged overcoat cast off by his brother symbolizes his failure and misery. He steals a new coat and is murdered by a policeman while trying to escape.

The condition of these brooding, troubled characters is so bleak that they spend a good deal of the time dreaming. Some of these stories were written while Himes was serving time in prison.

In "The Meanest Cop in the World," Jack fantasizes that he is a college freshman in love with a co-ed named Violet, "a brunette with a tinge of gold in the bronze of her skin and nice curves beneath her simple little dress," whose demeanor causes a "flip-flop" in his heart. He awakens in jail. "Suddenly Jack realized that he wasn't in love with a pretty girl called Violet, that he didn't even know such a girl, that he was just convict number 100012 in a dark, chilly cell."

Another character slips into a daydream after he reads of a Mississippi trial of two white men accused of murdering a "Negro youth for making a pass at a white woman." His dream locates him at the scene of the trial where, using a variety of weapons, he slaughters every "peckerwood" in sight.

American ethnic literature might be divided between the missionary tradition, that which espouses assimilation and preaches adherence to what one newspaper critic of black behavior calls "white mainstream values" (whatever that might mean), and the satirical comic "trickster" tradition that undercuts and even mocks the writing of assimilation.

Charles Fanning, in his "The Irish Voice in America," argues that the satirical tradition is the one employed by the underdog: "The power of words is a great offensive weapon, a potent and public act of comic aggression that fortifies one against one's enemies." The "serious" and "earnest" writing in this collection often falls flat, especially the love stories in which, typically, a man is involved with a woman of a higher class than his own. Himes, however, is highly successful when he uses "comic aggression" to puncture the social and political daydreams of his times.

The daydream that if blacks prove their valor by sacrificing themselves for whites or by fighting against their enemies, American society would embrace them as dark brothers is treated in "Two Soldiers," about a black private who displays his bravery on the battlefield on behalf of Joshua Crabtree, who goes "berserk" at the very sight of a black man in uniform. "'Set me down, white brother, and save you'self,' George whispered through blood-flecked lips." As in "Glory" and "Home of the Brave," only then does the white character recognize the black's humanity. Calvin Hernton is right in his excellent introduction when he asserts that some of these stories, though written in the '30s and '40s, address contemporary issues.

Feminist revisionist theory, promoted in such plays as "The Straw Woman," that white women in the South suffered as much as the blacks who were often lynched and maimed, is a daydream exploded by Himes's story "A Penny for Your Thoughts": A white woman assaults a man who is trying to calm a mob bent on lynching a black man accused of rape. "'Why, you nigger-lovin' bastard, what's Texas comin' to when a white woman ...' She drew back and slapped him across the mouth with the barrel of her gun." To add to the irony, the intended victim is a black veteran.

Himes' America is alive and well, and racism, that ugly social parasite, has found a host in parts other than the South, and festers in the speeches of politicians who know they can gain votes by "running against the nigger" as politicians used to say in the old South.

After an hour's flight during which I was red-lining sections of this book, one of those "aberrational" events that happen to the black men, including those in Himes' book, frequently, happened to me.

While approaching the parking lot accompanied by a black professor and a white student who'd come to pick me up for an engagement at the California Institute of the Arts, I was stopped by three white men who identified themselves as Burbank Airport Narcotics Security. The one who did all of the talking was obviously high on testosterone. He wanted to know why I exited from the terminal instead of choosing the exit in front of the baggage claim, as my fellow passengers had. (I hadn't checked any bags.)

I could imagine Chester Himes, for whom living in a racist society was a situation of absurdity, doubling over from laughter. I thought of a dozen smart answers that I could have given to such a stupid question. But I know my America like a book. The wrong answer would have given me the same fate as a character named Black Boy in "The Night's for Cryin'":

"The cops took him down to the station and beat his head into an open, bloody wound from his bulging eyes clear to the base of his skull."

As evidence that the same experiential gap between blacks and whites that existed when Himes wrote these stories exists now, a white friend to whom I related this incident said I should have taken down the officer's badge number.

The Los Angeles Times Book Review, June 30, 1991, p. 2.

Himes and Self-hatred

James Campbell

Chester Himes lived a life of almost constant agitation—Harlem, Paris, Spain—settling only once: to serve seven years of a twenty to twenty-five-year sentence in the Ohio State Penitentiary, the outcome of an armed robbery staged single-handed in a prosperous white neighbourhood in Cleveland. Nineteen when he entered prison in 1929, Himes had already been a thief, a pimp, a bootlegger, and a student at the University of Ohio [sic]. In prison, he switched to writing fiction, publishing his first short stories in *Esquire* and the black journal, *Crisis*.

The beginning and end of Himes's fifty-year literary career (he gave up the other one) are marked out by these two books: *The Collected Stories* contains sixty stories, probably all the short pieces he ever wrote, including previously unpublished and undated material; while *Plan B* is the "unfinished masterpiece" he supposedly left behind after his death. Unfinished the novel certainly is— there could be no other explanation for its dire quality—but the publishers present it as more of an enigma than is actually the case: "After his death in 1984, a rumor persisted that [Himes] had left a final unfinished Harlem story.... *Plan B* is that novel." The very same *Plan B*, as it happens, which was published in Paris, in translation, a year before Himes died, an event described in the informative introduction by Michel Fabre and Robert Skinner. Too ill to complete the work, Himes apparently went ahead and sanctioned publication in the country where he enjoyed his greatest popularity.

Confusion over Himes's publishing history is excusable: He wrote about twenty books, including two volumes of autobiography, but his novels have come out at different times under different titles, and during the 1950s and 60s most of them were published first in France, where Himes wrote detective novels for Gallimard's list of thrillers, *Série Noire* (as in "film noir", of course—nothing to do with *les noirs*). In 1958, he became the first non-French author to be awarded the Grand Prix de la littérature policière (for a novel known variously as *For Love of Imabelle, A Rage in Harlem, The Five-Cornered Square* and, in French, *La Reine des Pommes*). Himes went on to write eight more thrillers, none of which enjoyed much success, at least until recently, in his own country. Although he lived in France for many years, arriving in 1953, Himes never used it as a backdrop for his longer fiction. There is a tantalizing sketch in the *Collected*, set in the Latin Quarter in Paris, but for full-length thrills Himes always moved his imagination back to Harlem.

Virtually all Himes's writing, especially the early and late work, is characterized by brutality, anger and self-hatred. But the honesty with which he confronts this personal turbulence makes him, at times, an engaging writer. It grew" out of what Himes called a "life of absurdity" (though it was not absurdity in the sense that Camus or Beckett would have recognized). "Given my disposition", he wrote in the second volume of his autobiography—which he actually called *My Life of Absurdity* (1976)—"my sensitivity toward race, along with my appetites and physical reactions and sex stimulations, my normal life was absurd." In describing his own reactions—typically to someone whom he suspects of having put him down for being black—Himes uses phrases such as "My head was throbbing like a mashed thumb ..."; or "I'd feel my brain lurch". When a friend wrote to him from home about "the most popular of the colored writers", Himes noted his response to this simple information as "What motherfucking color are writers supposed to be?" His two-volume autobiography (the first installment is *The Quality of Hurt*, 1972) is at times a catalogue of misogyny, grievance and self-aggrandizement

Her eyes filled with conflicting emotions as she watched me go. Black pimps had taken thousands of white girls like her from the coal-mine towns of West Virginia and the little steel-mill towns of Ohio and put them to work as prostitutes in the ghettos. They liked it; they made the best whores.

Plan B has many similar passages (the introduction calls them "titillating"). The novel describes a plot by one Tomsson Black to instigate racial turmoil in America by supplying arms to blacks. Characters pop up and then disappear; plot-lines are left undeveloped; historical sketches are interleaved with contemporary events to no great effect. Even the two detectives who served Himes faithfully throughout his *Série Noire* productions, Coffin Ed Johnson and Grave Digger Jones, are sacrificed by their creator: Coffin Ed is shot by his partner, who in turn is killed by Tomsson Black.

By contrast, the very first (though not quite the earliest) story in the *Collected Stories* shows what a subtle writer Himes could be. In "Headwaiter", written in prison in 1937, Dick Small performs his nightly duties in the dining-room of the Park Manor Hotel with relentless courtesy and unstoppable efficiency. With the skill of a safe-cracker, Himes unpicks the headwaiter's mask—applied through years of fixed smiles—to reveal not bitterness, just the desire not to emulate the cruelty of some of his customers, and the need to maintain a balancing act between genuine humanity and the humility expected

of him. More than a mask, humbleness has become the man. On hearing of
the death of an elderly regular,

Dick went rigid. The brown of his face tinged ashily. Then he noticed that Mrs.
Miller's eyes were red and swollen from crying and he upbraided himself for not
having noticed immediately.
    He could find no suitable words for the moment. He pitied her in a sincere,
personal way, for he knew that the countess was the one person in all the world
whom she considered as a friend. But he could not express his pity. He was only a
head waiter.

    There are many other good stories in this edition, which lacks only an editor
to provide something more than the rudimentary bibliographical information
given here, and to arrange the material in a way that would show the writer in
the act of discovering his voice and range of techniques. By 1970, Himes's
fiction-writing was tailing off, and *Plan B* seems to have been the outcome of a
burst of racial fury around that date; "the most violent story I have ever
attempted", he called it, suggesting that craft—together with the irony and wit
and tenderness which informs Himes's best work—was not enough to give
shaping sense to a life of absurdity.

Times Literary Supplement, December 24, 1993, p. 17.

ESSAYS

Domestic Harlem: The Detective Fiction of Chester Himes

Raymond Nelson

In 1967, four years after he had left the United States to settle in France, Chester Himes began writing a remarkable series of novels about the adventures of Coffin Ed Johnson and Grave Digger Jones, a pair of touch Harlem police detectives. With characteristic irony Himes called this loosely sequential string of bloody narratives his "Harlem Domestic" series. Himes's interest in crime and violence was not new when these detective stories were first brought out for French audiences; he had long been regarded as one of the angriest black writers of the "school" of Richard Wright, and he had behind him several excellent naturalistic novels which must be counted among the most ragingly violent American fictions of our century.

What was new about the Harlem Domestic series was its variety of character-types, its grotesque comedy of violence, and its sparse, descriptive style. Because of these characteristics, and because of Himes's unabashed use of popular-crime formulae, his detective novels were indiscriminately labeled "potboilers," and in an amusingly unconscious confession of their own provincialism several American reviewers speculated that Himes was pandering to some depraved French taste for violence and flocculent sex in a sublimative Afro-America. I hope these lively tales did set Himes's pot to boiling—it was certainly time he made money—but his stories of criminal Harlem are more than commercial ventures. In them Himes moves beyond his earlier naturalism and embraces the rich folk-traditions of Black American culture. Judging from the responses of younger black writers, this shift of emphasis makes the Harlem Domestic series a seminal contribution to contemporary literature.

In an interview conducted by John A. Williams for *Amistad* magazine, Himes cryptically associates the beginning of the detective series with a "change from pessimism to optimism." We will probably have to wait for his autobiography to have that remark explained, but some of the dynamics of their origin can certainly be seen in the detective fictions themselves. Like his friend Richard Wright, Himes had been strongly influenced by the naturalism of the 1930's and 1940's. His earlier work was concerned largely with analyzing social and natural forces which his characters could neither understand fully nor control, but which imprisoned them in their own poverty, futility, and smoldering rage. Himes, however, is just old enough to remember also the 1920's and to have shared in the twilight days of that reinterpretation of Black culture and flowering of Black art known as Harlem (or Negro) Renaissance. In the Amistad interview Himes discusses his experience in that exciting, exuberantly self-conscious Harlem—as much a "place" of the mind as a geographical entity. He knew, then or later, such fine writers of the period as Langston Hughes and Wallace Thurman; he was photographed and catalogued by the ubiquitous Carl Van Vechten. Harlem Renaissance artists refused to be embarrassed by the "Negro characteristics" at which white Americans laughed; they discovered the sources of cultural pride in the folklore and the unique mores of the traditional black community. It would be surprising if a sensitive young writer had not been deeply impressed by their delighted urbanization of Black folk-culture, their hedonistic celebrations of Negro life in the streets and cafés, their loving attention to the intimate details of day-to-day life among black people.

There was more to the Harlem Renaissance, of course, than its superficial primitivism, far more to it than the popular image of happy Negroes who endlessly drank, fought, and danced, but even his most talented apologists soon discovered a frivolity about the period that Himes must have sensed also. When the deadly serious Great Depression ushered in a new literary era, Himes (perhaps regretfully) left Renaissance themes unexplored and turned instead to the literature of protest. In the Harlem Domestic series, however, he recaptures the spirit (without succumbing to the naïveté) of the Harlem Renaissance, and manages to mold the substance of two literary eras into a single balanced response to experience. Without sacrificing his bitter moral outrage, without taking his eyes from the ugly wound at which he has relentlessly pointed for some thirty-five years, he brightens his sordid criminal Harlem with the wild comedy, eccentricity of character, and exotic low-life that he inherited from the celebratory black writers of the twenties. The characters who crowd the pages of the detective stories are shockingly appropriate composites of Bigger Thomas and the lovable picaroons who wander in and out of Langston Hughes's tales of Jesse B. Semple. They are at once depraved and funny, grotesque and amiable, absurd and pragmatic, agonized and witty.

The Harlem Domestic novels (with the exception of the last) were first published in French translation in Gallimard's "Série Noire." The first, "For Love of Imabelle," appeared in 1958 and was followed (in order of composition) by "The Real Cool Killers," "The Crazy Kill," "The Big Gold Dream," "All Shot Up," "The Heat's On," "Cotton Comes to Harlem," and "Blind Man with a Pistol" (1969). Read as a chronologically ordered unit, the series offers a brief, imaginative history of the changing social and psychological orientation of black Americans during two explosive decades. It also shows how Himes has developed, both as an artist and as a man. Such simple inconsistencies as those in the characters of Coffin Ed and Grave Digger, who in the first book "took their tribute, like all real cops, from the established underworld catering to the essential needs of the people," but in the last "hadn't taken a dime in bribes," point to the values by which Himes refocused his vision as his stories grew.

While the first of the Harlem Domestic novels does roar with the frighteningly comic violence, grotesque characterization, and breathtaking "chase" sequences that inform the others, it is a detective story not yet fully realized. Himes's imagination is clearly engaged by the brutal action on which the later tales will depend, but "For Love of Imabelle" still draws its authority primarily from a naturalistic analysis of the invisible pressures that drive and control innocent black lives. He permits himself such images as that which describes Harlem's "Valley":

... waves of gray rooftops distort the perspective like the surface of a sea. Below the surface, in the murky waters of fetid tenements, a city of black people who are convulsed in desperate living, like the voracious churning of millions of hungry cannibal fish. Blind mouths eating their own guts. Stick in a hand and draw back a nub.

The aggressive naturalism of the image, the association of social conditions with malevolent natural forces, would be digressive in the subsequent tales, which can spare no time for analysis.

But essentially "For Love of Imabelle" is not a true detective story because it does not center upon the detectives. Coffin Ed and Grave Digger are important, but tangential characters—decent cops who are forced to be supremely tough by the unspeakable social context in which they work. Rather than the heroic figures they will become, they are themselves victims of an oppressive environment, cynical men seeking a basis for logical action in a brutally irrational world. Their extreme limitations are illustrated by the important waterfront scene in which a combination of accidents, mistaken identities, explosive human emotions, and simple darkness permits a cheap hoodlum the opportunity to throw acid into Coffin Ed's eyes. Blinded, thrashing about in agony, Coffin Ed knocks Grave Digger out with his pistol, and their prisoners escape. "For Love of Imabelle" has its own power and excellence, but it is, finally, less a detective story than a naturalistic novel about criminal sporting-life in Harlem.

In the five succeeding novels, however, Himes develops fully the embryonic form that we recognize in "For Love of Imabelle." He tells *Amistad's* John A. Williams that these stories grow naturally out of the experience of being black in America, and he argues that the detective novel is a native American genre which, for black people, isolates the most pertinent depravity of American life. Claiming only to have borrowed an ultimately appropriate mode already defined by its culture, Himes says this about his detective fiction:

It's a form, you know, and it's a particularly American form. My French editor says, the Americans have a style of writing detective stories that no one has been able to imitate .... There's no reason why the black American, who is also an American, like all other

Americans, and brought up in this sphere of violence which is the main sphere of American detective stories, there's no reason why he shouldn't write them. It's just plain and simple violence in narrative form....

    ... no one understands violence or experiences violence like the American civilians do. The only other people in the white community who are violent enough for it are the armed forces ... But of course they don't write about it....

    American violence is public life, it's a public way of life, it became a form, a detective story form.... the detective story originally in the plain narrative form—straightforward violence—is an American product. So I haven't created anything whatsoever; I just made the faces black, that's all.

We may be politely skeptical about Himes's disclaimer of originality and still recognize in his statement a confirmation of Edward Margolies' shrewd observation "that the kind of detective fiction he chose to write—implying, as it does, the comic, the violent, and above all the absurd—exactly suited his vision. In a peculiar fashion, for Himes the genre *is* the message."

    What we have, then, is a literature of violence, growing naturally out of a particular place and time, and formed, not by self-conscious artistry, but by a more organic esthetic that permits the laws of a specific way of life to find their own expression. The value of this literature is not in the form itself, but in the unique experience that produced it, and it is important to insisted upon the specificity of Himes' method. Under his hand, "it could only happen in America" (in this case, only in Harlem) becomes more than a truism. It is a structural principle as well. Only LeRoi Jones, that I know of, has taken the detective fiction seriously enough to recognize the significance of Himes's peculiar brand of regionalism. In his contribution to Herbert Hill's "Anger and Beyond," Jones writes:

It's all there, even to the Raymond Chandler-Dashiell Hammett genre of the detective novel, in Chester Himes' *All Shot Up* or *The Crazy Kill* or *The Real Cool Killers*, which are much more interesting, not only in regard to plot but also in terms of "place," a place wherein such a plot can find a natural existence. So that the Negro writer finally doesn't have to think about his "roots" even literarily, as being subject to some kind of derogatory statement—one has only to read the literature.

    Whatever we are to say, however, about their origins or the responsibility of their creator for their form, the five novels Himes wrote between 1958 and 1961 are classic detective stories. Each poses a problem, or a series of problems, usually expressed in hideous physical violence, which extends its corruption into personal and communal life, and threatens the always precarious balance by which individuals survive in Harlem. Each network of dangerous mysteries is explained by a single discovery of guilt, which restores that balance and redefines the worth of those characters with whom we sympathize. The discovery, of course, is made by Grave Digger and Coffin Ed, the heroic figures who embody all the attributes of the traditional literary detective. Opposed by violence and unreason, they struggle courageously to uncover truth; trapped in a hopelessly venal institution, they remain incorruptibly honest; burdened with a body of law ludicrously inappropriate to the conditions of Harlem life, they are lonely dispensers of justice. They

implement most of their solutions outside the law; many of their methods defy
it. The responsibilities and dangers involved in the search for decency rest upon
them personally rather than upon the institutional apparatus which supposedly
protects them.

But Grave Digger and Coffin Ed are more than familiar literary heroes; their
cultural antecedents ultimately give them the moral authority they exercise.
Simply enough, they are the "bad niggers" of Black folklore. They are Nat
Turners or Stackalees brought up to date and moved to the city, contemporary
avatars of one of the stubbornly pervasive motifs in Black American culture.
Like their less sophisticated ancestors, they are aggressively courageous and
utterly indifferent to physical danger, willing to submit without complaint to the
risk of the same ruthless violence by which they express their own naked force
of will. The raw personal power with which the "bad nigger" defies his world
has traditionally been celebrated in hyperbole, and there is a (never completely
formalized) refrain running through the Harlem Domestic series that rings with
unmistakable cultural reference:

Coffin Ed had killed a man for breaking wind. Grave Digger had shot both eyes out of a
man who was holding a loaded automatic. They story was in Harlem that these two
black detectives would kill a dead man in his coffin if he so much as moved.

These awesome detectives do not always limit their violence to the guilty—
they are, in fact, distressingly quick to beat on almost any black head they
encounter—and like all "bad niggers" they may seem at first glance improbable
(or undesirable) models for humanity. But the "bad nigger" is an emotionally
projected rather than a socially functional figure; he is valuable as a symbol of
defiance, strength, and masculinity to a community that has been forced to
learn, or at least to sham, weakness and compliance. As "bad niggers" Coffin
Ed and Grave Digger are part of the continuing evolution of a black hero, and
are thus studies in cultural lore rather than examples of individual character. In
the Harlem series they lay all of their traditional qualifications on the line in a
desperate fight against the crimes that endanger the integrity, even the
collective sanity, of the black community.

And, for all the socially dubious behavior the detectives find necessary, the
sense of community is strong in these novels. Himes remembers that he began
them in a state of "pure homesickness" as expressions of an exiled memory of
America, and he has made them alive with warm evocations of life lived in
what is a surprisingly *domestic* Harlem after all. Each story, for example,
examines one or more of the peculiar "institutions" through which the criminal
activity of Harlem is carried on. At times these oblique social commentaries are
morbidly bitter; more often they are softened by at least a hint of fondness. In
"The Real Cool Killers" the "institution" is the street gang; in "The Crazy Kill"
it is professional gambling. "The Big Gold Dream" looks at both evangelistic
Christianity (which, for Himes, is always a racket) and the numbers. "All Shot
Up" moves back and forth between politics and Harlem's homosexual sub-
culture, and "The Heat's On," by far the harshest and most grotesque of the
series, deals with heroin trade. None of these "institutions" are used simply as
background; they are explained in minute detail, often through portraits of the

individual personalities they have helped to shape, and information about them is often offered as much for its own sake as to meet exigencies of plot.

Himes does not depict only the criminal life in his cumulative panorama of Harlem, however; he also presents the less sensational aspects of the place, details of its special patterns of day-to-day life, with an intimacy that can make them either attractive or disgusting. He never tires of elaborate topographical descriptions of particular Harlem streets, the contents of store windows, the larger geography of the area. Famous Harlem landmarks—the Apollo Theater, Small's Paradise, the National Memorial African Book Store—are repeatedly described, both as geographical references and as settings for the action. The graffiti and stenches of slum tenements, the sounds of bars and jazz joints, the oppressive atmosphere of the pool-room and the prison: all add texture and density to the massive violence that moves this extra-legal (or sub-legal) Harlem. Himes's creative memory seems especially excited by the tastes he has left behind in America; the soul-food restaurant and the rich peculiarities of Afro-American cooking recur in sensual images of excess. And finally, of course, there are the street-scenes, the unending parades of Harlem life:

It was eleven o'clock Sunday morning, and the good colored people of Harlem were on their way to church.

It was a gloomy, overcast day, miserable enough to make the most hardened sinner think twice about the hot, sunshiny streets of heaven before turning over and going back to sleep.

Grave Digger and Coffin Ed looked them over indifferently as they drove toward Harlem hospital. A typical Sunday morning sight, come sun or come rain.

Old white-haired sisters bundled up like bales of cotton against the bitter cold; their equally white-haired men, stumbling along in oversize galoshes like the last herd of Uncle Toms, toddling the last mile toward salvation on half-frozen feet.

Middle-aged couples and their broods, products of the postwar generation, the prosperous generation, looking sanctimonious in their good warm clothes, going to praise the Lord for the white folks' blessings.

Young men who hadn't yet made it, dressed in light-weight suits and topcoats sold by color instead of quality or weight in the credit stores, with enough brown wrapping paper underneath their pastel shirts to keep them warm, laughing at the strange words of God and making like Solomon at the pretty brownskin girls.

Young women who were sure as hell going to make it or drop dead in the attempt, ashy with cold, clad in the unbelievable colors of cheap American dyes, some at that very moment catching the pneumonia which would take them before that God they were on their way to worship.

Despite its irony and sadness, this processional image is offered with the almost tender affection characteristic of much of Himes's evocation of Harlem culture, and it points to one of the subordinate purposes of his series: to envision a particular place at a particular moment of history—its customs, speech, topography, occupations, even its food—and record it for posterity.

Himes never becomes sentimental about Harlem; he permits himself no unrelieved nostalgia. The most prominent characteristics of the community that he chronicles are fear and brutality. His Harlem is an isolated world motivated and ordered by violence. The novels themselves are in a sense his violent assaults upon his reader. Himes is a fighter, a sort of literary Muhammad Ali (or, perhaps more accurately, Jack Johnson), and he writes with the same intense ferocity with which he might knock a man down. As he told John A. Williams—and the remark can be applied to the method as well as the theme of his series—"After all, Americans live by violence, and violence achieves— regardless of what anyone says, regardless of the distaste of the white community—its own ends." This emphasis on violence as a means—a revolutionary tactic, a method of survival, a mode of communication—helps to explain the troubling brutality with which the profoundly decent Coffin Ed and Grave Digger conduct their investigations. It is the only means at their disposal. They work within a system as closed as those electrical circuits that operate from a power-source since removed from the circuit itself—the works are set going but the first mover is withdrawn. Each problem the detectives face has its origin in the forbidden white city that surrounds Harlem. When Coffin Ed and Grave Digger confront criminal disorder they are thus limited to symptoms; the actual malfunction is inaccessible. Harlem problems are violent; they can be fought locally, and the delicate balance of community life sustained, only by an even more uninhibited violence. It is one of the brilliant ironies of the Harlem Domestic stories that the detective-heroes can express their genuine love for their people, their altruistic hopes for communal peace and decency, only through the crude brutality that has become their bitter way of life.

Himes's descriptions of physical violence itself are exquisitely detailed and deliberately repulsive. He wants to shove his reader's nose into them, and he has something more than mere education or social protest in mind. The violent scenes in the detective novels develop their own systems of imagery and their own concrete "meaning." Ultimately, they are the experiential base on which the fiction rests. Neither Himes nor his characters interpret the action they create—the violence is itself the message—but it is unlikely that recurring similarities of literary terrorism, such as those that define two typically grim scenes from "All Shot Up," are entirely coincidental.

The first of these exemplary scenes describes the death of a tire thief whom Grave Digger and Coffin Ed are pursuing because he has witnessed a murder that is the key to a complicated network of criminal activity. Ignorant of their intentions, however, the thief clings desperately to his instinctive habit of avoiding the police at all costs. He is riding a motorcycle, and as he leads the detectives through the crowded Harlem streets, he plans to squeeze through a narrow break in the traffic with his smaller vehicle, and leave his pursuers behind a truck. But the delicate timing of his maneuver is upset when Coffin Ed shoots out one of the truck's tires:

He [the tire thief] was pulling up fast behind the car carrying sheet metal when the tire burst and the driver tamped his brakes. He wheeled sharply to the left, but not quickly enough.

The three thin sheets of stainless steel, six feet in width, with red flags flying from both corners, formed a blade less than a quarter of an inch thick. This blade caught the rider above his woolen-lined jacket, on the exposed part of his neck, which was stretched and taut from his physical exertion, as the motorcycle went underneath. He was hitting more than fifty-five miles an hour, and the blade severed his head form his body as though he had been guillotined.

His head rolled halfway up the sheets of metal while his body kept astride the seat and his hands gripped the handlebars. A stream of blood spurted from his severed jugular, but his body completed the maneuver which his head had ordered and went past the truck as planned.

The truck driver glanced from his window to watch the passing truck as he kept braking to a stop. But instead he saw a man without a head passing on a motorcycle with a sidecar and a stream of steaming blood flowing back in the wind.

Himes continues to describe the progress of his grotesque apparition along the streets and on the sidewalks until the corpse finally goes limp, and the motorcycle comes to rest against the grating of a credit jewelry store.

A similar macabre sequence occurs later in "All Shot Up" when Big Six and George Drake, two sympathetic racketeers, are assigned to protect Casper Holmes as he leaves Harlem Hospital. Holmes is a familiar type: a crooked, a homosexually inclined, but a powerful Harlem politician, who because of the intricate system of checks and balances that keeps Harlem from exploding altogether, is arrogantly beyond the law. After arranging to have his campaign funds stolen and double-crossing his fellow thieves, he is attempting to escape into a private stronghold. As part of his erstwhile accomplices' plan to kidnap Holmes and recover the money, Big Six is lured from his car by an apparently drunken white man who urinates on a fender and spits out a racial insult:

… Big Six reached out a hand to clutch the drunk by the shoulder.

The drunk swung a long arc with his right hand, which he had held out of sight, and plunged the blade of a hunting knife through Big Six's head. It went in above the left temple, and two inches of the point came out on a direct line above the right temple. Big Six went deaf, dumb, and blind, but not unconscious. He teetered slightly and groped about aimlessly like an old blind man.

The narrative turns for a moment to the murder of George Drake, then returns to Big Six as he stumbles through the streets:

Big Six kept on slowly, lost to the world. "George!" he was calling silently in the rational part of his mind. "George. The mother-raper stuck me."

He started across Seventh Avenue. Snow was banked against the curb, and his foot plowed into the snow bank. He slipped but somehow managed not to fall. He got into the traffic lane. He stepped in front of a fast-moving car. Brakes shrieked.

"Drunken idiot!" the driver cried. Then he saw the knife sticking from Big Six's head.

He jumped from his car, ran forward and took Big Six gently by the arm.

"My God in heaven," he said.

He was a young colored doctor doing his internship in Brooklyn Hospital. They had had a case similar to that a year ago; the other victim had been a colored man, also. The only way to save him was to leave the knife in the wound.

Both of these episodes, however sensationalistic they may be, achieve their horrible intensity by concentrating on the continued function of bodies that have lost their essential consciousness, their essential humanity. They are grim parodies of the "mindless" life. The metaphorical quality of violence, the statement about a generalized cultural lobotomy, that such a paraphrase suggests, however, is only implicit; Himes never offers it as an intellectualized "meaning." We can push Himes's suggestion further by noticing similar patterns in the knifings of Big Six and of Leila, Holmes's wife, who later in "All Shot Up" is stabbed by the same white thug. Coffin Ed and Grave Digger discover her moaning softly, clutching the handle of the knife that has been plunged into her stomach, and "Grave Digger knelt down, pulled her hands away gently and handcuffed them behind her back. 'You can't pull it out,' he said. 'That would only kill you.'" It is as if Himes were saying that his characters, that black Americans in general, are forced to live with knives thrust into the sensitive areas of their bodies: if the blade is left in, it means blindness, impotence, helplessness, and above all pain; if the blade is removed, it is death. But Himes does not say this—at least not explicitly. Neither are these episodes expressions of a consistent thematic development that can be abstracted and analyzed. Rather, they are in effect visual analogues—small, carefully framed pictures which "mean" in and for themselves, but which also represent the "meaning" of "All Shot Up" as a whole.

Perhaps Himes's iconographic method can be seen more clearly in one of the spectacular scenes near the end of "Cotton Comes to Harlem." Grave Digger and Coffin Ed have unearthed two vicious mobsters hiding in a church, and engage them in a gun duel. Because they anticipated fighting in darkness, the detectives had loaded their pistols with tracer bullets, and everything they hit bursts into flame. Himes takes full advantage of his juxtaposition between the sacred objects in the church and the burning criminals, and the passage ends thus:

Upstairs in the church, light from the burning gunman on the floor lit up the figure of the gunman with his head on fire crouched behind the end of a bench ahead.

On the other side of the church Coffin Ed was standing with his pistol leveled, shouting, "Come out, other-raper, and die like a man."

Grave Digger took careful aim between the legs of the benches at the only part of the gunman that was visible and shot him through the stomach. The gunman emitted an eerie howl of pain, like a mortally wounded beast, and stood up with his .45 spewing slugs in a blind stream. The screaming had risen to an unearthly pitch, filling the mouths of the detectives with the taste of bile. Coffin Ed shot him in the vicinity of the heart and his clothes caught fire. The screaming ceased abruptly as the gunman slumped across the bench in a kneeling posture, as though praying in fire.

The scene offers an excellent capsulization of Himes's technique. Out of clichéd man's-magazine material, without diluting the fast narrative violence that is his "form," Himes has created a picture that Bosch might have painted of a ragingly moral world.

Despite such compressed flashes of imagistic brilliance, however, "Cotton Comes to Harlem" does not employ the techniques I have been describing with the consistency of the earlier stories. It and "Blind Man with a Pistol," the most recent Harlem Domestic novels, seem to be experiments, and may indicate that Himes is growing restless under the strict limitations of the detective format. In any case, he apparently is attempting to adapt his narratives to an increasingly ambitious symbolic and analytic purpose. His success is at best relative. As Himes himself has said, violence *is* its own form, and the detective story is formulaic and fixed; it brooks no tempering. Once the crisp, efficient rationale, the uninterrupted attention to plot demanded by a search for a single truth is violated, the form collapses into its component clichés and the unity of the work is lost. The "larger" concerns of "Cotton Comes to Harlem" and "Blind Man with a Pistol" (which, significantly, extend criminal investigation into the amorphous gray area beyond Harlem) are admirable in themselves, but they simply blunt the sharp edge of Himes' technique and adulterate the "message" of his genre.

"Cotton Comes to Harlem" parallels the story of the chase after Deke O'Malley, the crooked organizer of a "Back-to-Africa" movement, with a symbolic confrontation of black (the Harlem community in general) and white (an Alabama Colonel with an ideological mission to return the "Nigra" to the cotton-fields). The symbolic apparatus is broadly comic and refreshingly unpretentious, but it defies the fragile system of probabilities on which "belief" in the detective story is based. There is too much explicit racial commentary, too much protest, too much satire to be absorbed by what is fundamental an intellectual genre. The narrative of Colonel Calhoun and his Back-to-the-Southland movement would itself be irrevocably damaging to the integrity of a detective novel. Not only is the colonel a preposterously "literary" anachronism in modern Harlem, he is also the victim of implausible plot devices. In one of the primary "mysteries" of the narrative, he brings a symbolic bale of cotton to New York in order to hide in it the money he steals from the Back-to-Africa organization. Himes's attempts to weld together two unlike materials are sometimes hilariously successful, but the seams show, and, finally, the fusion does not old.

"Blind Man with a Pistol," in some ways the most ambitious novel in the Harlem domestic series, displays a further disintegration of the detective form. In fact, parts of it read like self-parody. The deterioration of narrative logic is deliberate in this impressively experimental novel; here, the *failure* of the genre is the message. There are several "plots" in "Blind Man with a Pistol"—two dealing with wildly grotesque murder, one with an apparently coincidental series of riots—and they are confusingly juxtaposed, perhaps in order to disturb our complacent sense of chronology. None of the plots go anywhere. Because of institutional pressures the murders are left unsolved; Coffin Ed and Grave Digger are forbidden to follow a path of investigation which would inevitably lead to powerful whites. As the narratives of detective action run down unresolved, the frustrations of the novel explode in a frantically culminative riot, symbolizing the inflammatory emotion the two detectives had once been able to suppress, but which, now released, threatens to destroy forever the delicate balance of life they had painfully sustained. The novel ends with the parable of the blind man with a pistol who, firing aimlessly at a fancied racial slur, touches off what is probably the same climactic riot, seen in another context. Certainly the statement that emerges from this maniacal collision of themes and movements is legitimate, and certainly it demands expression. But, again, it contradicts the faith in the ability of men to discover truth that is a basic condition of the detective genre. The wide range of reference, the tortuous complexity of motivation inherent in Himes's attempt to bring racist white society explicitly into his novel simply cannot be contained within the limitations of his form.

So the Harlem Domestic series as it now exists ends on a note of decay and frustration. "Blind Man with a Pistol" might almost be considered a literary ruin. But the artist who broke his own detective form is still writing, and we may happily anticipate that he will turn his hand to some new form that will express his genius even more appropriately. One almost wishes that Himes would go backward—repeat himself, and turn out more of these profoundly exciting tales of crime and violence. Whether he does nor not, we may be grateful for the substantial achievement he has already wrung from an improbable genre, and salute both the integrity and the force of imagination that conceived it. If the vehicle itself is small, Himes's accomplishments within it are not, and the residual portrait left by these books—of Coffin Ed and Grave Digger outlined against the dull, lurid light of a criminal city—is one of the compelling images of our time.

Virginia Quarterly Review, 48 (Spring 1972), 260–276.

Violence Real and Imagined: The Novels of Chester Himes

A. Robert Lee

Despite his persisting and highly particular talents, Chester Himes continues to be footnoted a Wrightian exponent of Black American literary protest given to reworking an inherited vein of angry naturalism. This blunt evasion of his forty years of craft and resource speaks worlds of criticism's stubborn unseeing before Black imaginative achievement and of its insistence of notions of hierarchy and diagnosis largely inappropriate, dull and racist. Although his imagination is hardly without flaw or unsteadiness, Himes has written fiction of considerable claim which explores a vital nerve in American life and which records with extraordinary eloquence racism's waste and damage. Acerbic in tone, firmly angled for the most part, subvertingly funny and threat-laden of late, his novels are addressed to the unflagging play of violence in America, its encasing pressures for those obliged to live out an aggregate identity determined by the crude basis of skin rather than by individual presence and need. The reaches of Himes' abilities, diverse and frequently compelling, deserve far better attention than that long remarked by a small enthusiastic readership.

Now in his middle sixties, a veteran of two decades of expatriation (he has made Alicante rather than Paris his residence), Himes first came into print in the early 1930s with a burst of stories dealing with his prison and city experiences. He looks back on a subsequently crowded career which takes in his essays and filmscripts, over twenty pieces of short fiction, a sequence of prose poems for the *Cleveland Daily News* (1939) and his magazine correspondence and interviews as well as, to date, fifteen full-length novels.[1] Of two volumes of promised autobiography, the first, *The Quality of Hurt*, appeared in 1972. Fast becoming something of an expatriate institution for younger Black writers (he has a following in Africa),[2] Himes has recently awakened in America enthusiasm of a kind more usually granted to Richard Wright, Ralph Ellison, and James Baldwin of the immediate post-war American circuit and to John A. Williams, Imamu Baraka, and Nikki Giovanni of younger Black moderns. In some degree this belated recognition for a talent reputed to be of minor key has been the by-product of Black cultural recovery during the 1960s, but more directly it has been caused by Himes' enormously popular, almost cultist, Coffin Ed/Gravedigger Jones novels, the Harlem detective saga which surfaced first as *romans policiers* in Gallimard's *Série Noire*.

Although Himes has acknowledged the hand of Dashiell Hammett in this later work (*La Reine des Pommes*, the first of the series, in 1958 won France's Prix du Roman Policier), the detective writing marks an achievement quite triumphantly his own with vital links back into the five novels he published in America between 1945 and 1955. The Harlem Himes puts on the page in the Coffin Ed/Gravedigger fables goes well beyond merely appropriate backcloth to a run of lively potboilers. It approaches inspired surrealism. Harlem comes through as an urban hothouse mean with exotic hustle and violence, a tangible asphalt jungle with its own abrasive laws of motion and boundaries and at the same time a mythical kingdom with properties of magic and violent farce. Though forever unlikely to earn comparison with, say Dickens' London or Joyce's Dublin (Chandler's Los Angeles, Claude McKay's Harlem, or Imamu Baraka's Newark might offer more precise frames of comparison), Himes' Black Upper Manhattan is charted with rich, if somewhat bizarre, authenticity.

With the exception of his *jeu d'esprit*, *Pinktoes*, published by Olympia Press in 1955, violence identifies all of Himes' fiction, violence both quietly corrosive and loudly expansive. The nine "Harlem domestic stories," as Himes terms the detective novels (only *Run Man Run* excludes Coffin Ed and Gravedigger), take up and magnify the violence of the earlier books. Himes has rendered the Harlem world they chart as one approaching an unprecedented total racial explosion. His Harlem explores an enclave of Black urban life constrained into exquisite heat and masquerade with the two Black detectives fighting a holding action against what, in the two most recent works, threatens as terminal violence, the holocaust of outright racial war. So unthinkable does Himes estimate this prospect that he has put aside a current novel in which Coffin Ed and Gravedigger are killed in the flames of massive Black insurrection. In recent interviews, and with bitter amusement born of long observation, Himes has warned that if America continues racist abuse at all levels, the prospect of a final chapter of civil war with armed Blacks forming a guerrilla underground could move over from fictional prophecy into live reality.

A prospectus on the historical magnetism of violence for *white* Americans was offered by Himes in an interview with a strong admirer of his talent, the novelist John A. Williams:

There is no way that one can evaluate the American scene and avoid violence, because any country that was born in violence and has lived in violence always knows about violence. Anything can be initiated, enforced, contained or destroyed in the American scene through violence; it comes straight from the days of slavery, through the Revolutionary War, the Civil War, the Indian Wars, the gunslingers killing one another over fences and sheep and one goddamned thing after another; they grew up in violence.... The only people that the American community has tried to teach that it is Christian to turn the other cheek and live peacefully are the black people.[3]

This pervasive legacy of violence presses close, mainly ruinously, upon the Black figures at the center of the novels prior to *Pinktoes* and provides the assumptions behind the detective writing. Read collectively, Himes' first five novels, not always without laboriousness, trace through an unfolding graph of injury and loss and of vital energies sapped and corroded. They chronicle fear, exhaustion, pursuit, individual need, and rebellion as decisive qualities in the lives of his major Black figures. With an unequivocal eye to the stab of controlling whiteness upon Black skins and psyches, Himes' fiction maps out interior landscapes of entropy, the process whereby unnourished selfhood runs down before its own impotence.

Himes' men and women in the early books, nearly all of articulate middle-class stock, find their very sharpness of consciousness punitive. By counterpointing the inner and outer textures of the violence that Willie E. Abrahams aptly calls "the language of white manliness."[4] Himes avoids formulaic angry novels (though there is anger in all he writes) and achieves a notable density and impetus to his writing. His detective novels are really logical points of arrival for an author to whom violence is both the essential condition, and the essential abuse, of the life before him. Himes should rank as a writer of serious, if uneven, accomplishment, a longstanding connoisseur of violence whose fiction achieves its own vital and challenging voice.

If He Hollers Let Him Go (1945) on first view might rank unambiguously as a race narrative, a fable of persecution written in brittle Hemingwayese. Its story is that of Bob Jones, an intelligent young UCLA graduate given token authority over an all-Black work crew in the World War II shipyards of Atlas, one of California's super-industries. Fighting to keep the affections of Alice, the daughter of Black professional parents, and hounded on all fronts by white authority, Bob gets trapped into a spurious rape charge by Madge, an abused but succulent Texan redneck. Beaten half to a pulp by Madge's avenging white menfolk (imported cheap Southern labor like herself, then pursued by police and put to trial, Bob is given the choice of Army or prison.

Reviewing *If He Hollers* for *PM* the year of its publication, Richard Wright perceptively noted the book's ordering paradoxes, the careful means by which Himes takes his first novel beyond casebook realism. Having described Bob as a man "reacting ... with nerves, blood and motor responses," Wright pointed "the transformations by which sex is expressed in equations of race pride, murder in the language of personal redemption and love in terms of hate." These transformations in fact contribute to the novel's thick tissue of existential metaphor, the dreams, images and fantasies which express the introverting consequences of racism. Bob, for instance, suffers the paradoxical ability of Atlas's white workers and the society of which they are a part, to transform him from a castrated Black fugitive into a sexually demoniac superman. And when he reflects grimly, "I had to get ready to die before I could leave the house," his comment is that of a worker whose working vitality is exhausted, a Black whose daytime life is the quarry for his night-time dreams of emasculation.

Instead of self-freeing relationships with women and the application of craft skills at Atlas, he feels only a cycle of control. Forced to hold two views of himself—on the one hand a conscious human being and on the other a mechanical functionary, a lover and yet a fiend of imposed sexual myth, a "man" who dreams endlessly of his own unmanning—Bob indeed personifies a living paradox, both in flight from and in combat against, his own finely tuned consciousness and the emasculating realities it reports.

Between anger and void, nightmare and consciousness, Bob thus lives a life which barely maintains the most delicate of balances. His body plays host to the motor responses underlined by Wright, the stings of pain and insult which assume almost psychosomatic character. When Madge, the degenerate but still proscribed belle, approaches him with fascinated curses and allure his body feels "electric shock." When he dreams of weight, nakedness, physical maiming—all indices of his manlessness—his body runs from hot to cold, feverish to dry. Bile gathers literally in his mouth in testimony to the outrage and need he is forbidden to speak. And when Madge's charge of "supermanliness," with promptness as arbitrary as is ironic, leads directly to the *formal* servitude of the Army, it makes the novel's ultimate paradoxical comment on a life so violently obliged to live out what does not want to be.

Further, Himes makes supporting metaphoric use of Atlas's world of heavy machines and industry. Bob describes himself explicitly as a "sort of machine." He works with his crew inside the skeleton of a ship under construction, amid entangling cables, girders, and workers infected by the rising fevers of war. The shipyard appears predatory, its heavy duty cranes "one-legged, one-armed spiders." Human and mechanical forces simmer in uneasy tandem very close to explosion. In Himes' paradox, white capitalist power, in the triad of government, Army and Business, mechanicalizes human vitality to build ships which ostensibly will destroy external fascism while allowing the brute processes of domestic racism which devour and cannibalize Bob Jones to pass unchecked, often willfully encouraged.

Like all of Himes' novels, *If He Hollers* opens up the sexual fibers of race, those flashes of taboo and myth which invest racial violence (and in this novel, most racial contact) with a sexual iconography. At a prime level, Bob's confrontation with Madge, Himes plays off against his encounters with Alice, his slightly androgynous, genteel girl. And as a man among men, Bob seeks endlessly standards of usable manhood. His search takes various forms—his bid for dignity before Atlas's white overseers, his adolescent machismo in driving to the shipyards with his Black workmates in a souped-up car. But fevered manlessness dogs his every turn. Not only does he endure dreams of being without work-tools, but his mind roams back to a Black audience he once saw applauding blind white acrobats performing at, of all places, the Lincoln Theatre. His desperation takes the form of hunting down a white "nigger-baiter," violence Himes depicts as possibly manning, up-grading. Finally, the pursuer turns pursued as the Los Angeles police narrow in on his lonely flight. These different tensions of flight and pursuit, role and rolelessness, amount to a sexual catalogue of violence, many of whose psychological implications Frantz Fanon explores in *Black Skins, White Masks.* Himes' irony has peculiar trenchancy, therefore, when he has Bob slotted into anonymous negro problem by Alice's white beau or when Herbie Frieberger of the Union plays down racism as a local variant of Marxist class war. The violence, real and imagined, in Bob's life, is too elusive, too compacted, for such facile categories.

The sharply unmanning directions of his life, with Alice as much as Madge, away from and inside Atlas, lead almost inexorably into the Court's reductive formula of the "rape and run" charge. Bob's emotions have been primitivized. His anger and despair turn self-destructively inwards. Throughout the novel Himes makes violence the reaction of both inner turbulence and the multiple external ways by which white society expresses its will over Blacks. Bob's relentless inner dream life and his own final act of external flight are made to match perfectly. For a first novel, *If He Hollers* offers a formidable log of violence's damage.

Heavy industry also forms the donnée of Himes' second and longest novel, *Lonely Crusade* (1947), a work which grants more comprehensive range to his diagrams of violence but which sags as an organic and formally arranged whole. The matrix out of which the novel grew is clearly discernible—Himes' direct involvement with the then newly minted C.I.O., his acid distrust of the Communist Party, and his close sense of Wright's *Native Son*. As an imaginative essay of unionism., West Coast politics, race and violence, it achieves far more than *If He Hollers*. The parts, however, lack the unified drive, the tautness, of the first novel.

Lonely Crusade recounts the troubled passage of Lee Gordon, a Black labor man hired to unionize the Black workers of Comstock Aircraft, like Atlas, a California war industry. Against the conspiring odds of historical communism, mainly personified by Luther McGregor, an opportunist Black brother and the Capitalist Right (Louis Foster, Comstock's boss), Gordon fights an uphill fight towards democratic unionism in company with a tough and by no means unracist assortment of union officials. Gordon's passage takes him through political chicanery on a number of fronts, through Hollywood parties and private sexual humiliations, a route of fear and emasculation which leads into a false murder charge. Finally, in a closing dramatic strike march outside Comstock, Lee seizes the union's banner from a fallen comrade and, with a policeman's gun leveled on his body, opts for the violent recovery of his right to a revolutionary destiny by rallying the strikers behind him.

Himes again links up the larger movements of violence at the surface of white-controlled society—murder, police brutality, bossism—to the inner trials of his main figure. Gordon's private struggle is to redeem his sexually injured manhood in the eyes of himself and his wife, Ruth, a woman who has long earned more money than he has and whose body he has come to regard as a source of pain rather than love. He abandons Ruth temporarily for Jackie, a young and attractive white Party agent eventually denounced by the Party to protect Luther's selling out the union to Comstock, an act which jeopardizes the loyalty of the Black workers. Himes thus keeps the narrative of Gordon's life alive at two primary levels, the first that of his struggle for attention and function in the world of Comstock, the second that of his inner life, the life of his battered psyche.

Despite the energy and intelligence of Himes' excursions into Marxism and race, especially his views of the Party's expedient uses of the American Black, and his scrutiny of labor and capital (scrutiny which extends to Jew and Black, color and sex), he doesn't altogether seat such concerns comfortably within the novel's imaginative structure. They tend to enter the narrative too stagily—in letters, newspaper clippings, heavy confessional scenes, party conversations in the Hollywood belt and in the long polemics of Rosie, a Jewish Party man closely derived from Max in Richard Wright's *Son*. The effect on the narrative is to retard the book's imaginative flow, veering it woodenly towards overt thesis fiction. But the novel does have filaments of great strength, amplifying Himes's inquiry into the racist technologies of white power, specifically in the violations of Lee Gordon's psyche and manhood.

Like Bob Jones, Gordon lives on the knife-edge of fear: "fear was the price he paid for living." When he first gets the union job, "he had once again crossed into the competitive white world where he would be subjected to every abuse concocted in the minds of white people to harass and intimidate Negroes." This fear empties his love for Ruth and keeps him a-dance before Joe Ptak, Marvin Todd, and Smitty of the union. Himes portrays fear resharpened at every turn, by Jackie's white body and her ambiguous attraction to Lee as a Black potency figure, by the newspaper account of a rape case she plants on him, by Luther's intimacy with white centers of power and money and his dissembling Sambo acts, and by Foster's veiled threats and the brute thrusts of enwalling police and corporate power. To one side of Lee's life resides the meticulous insanity of Lester McKinley, a Black worker plotting Foster's murder; to the other, the gregarious threat of Luther which finally breaks out in his blood-laden murder of a cop who has harassed him whilst Foster's bribes were being passed over and who has viciously beaten Lee. Each adds a sharp wrench to the twisting blade of Lee's fear.

As underpinning to Lee's insecurities, Himes points to the larger communal recollection of the Depression, the memory of massive collapse and the competing ideologies of the New Deal and the Party. Lee's commitment to industrial unionism, and to what in retrospect can be seen as nascent Black Power, represents a bid for stability and personal meaning within an unstabilizing and abusive tradition. The times, as Himes depicts them in *Lonely Crusade*, echo Bob's own sense of fraction and un-connection.

The sexual nervousness Bob feels with Jackie and his unease with the mixed marriages of Luther and McKinley Himes fits into the book's larger texture of eruptive and temporary liaisons—Blacks with whites, Party men with union workers, Hollywood liberals with the oppressed. Nervousness, flux, temporary alliances and accommodations of convenience Himes conveys with real sureness of insight as the keynotes of the times. He has Lee call the Los Angeles of 1943 the "bloated, mysterical, frantic, rushing city." Set to disentangle con-men and power-brokers, a Jewish dialectician and a coolly expedient Black Party leader (Bart), Lee stumbles more and more into himself, stung and whipped on by distorting graft and false accusations, his life violently and introvertingly determined by unscrupulous power-brokers. He cannot discover a place to stand still, to take stock, or to recover his severed manhood. Never sure that he can out-reach or repudiate an identity moulded to the typecasting and direction of others (Jackie, his wife, the union, Luther, Foster, etc.), he scuttles desperately through various sexual encounters, through

Luther's murder of the cop and the unadorned maneuverings of the Corporation and the police. Shrunken finally into "chaotic fear," he is forced to inhabit "deserted streets," a flayed survivor within his "dry and brittle shell."

Lee's violent apotheosis is to be beaten nearly to death in the police cells and put out on bail. The union gives him a last chance to bring out Comstock's Black workers. About him in the street scenes he sees a tapestry of violence and human wreckage which appears as one complement of his own condition. From amid the street's despoliation an instinct toward sympathy arises in him, a re-kindled instinct for the vital, the living, the revolutionary. His exultance suggests the low point of arrival for an isolate whose violation can go no deeper:

As he stood outside, ... images moved before his vision in startling clarity. Sounds came into his ears with clean fidelity. He saw the dirty facades of buildings and the filthy tatters of the bums, and heard the foul obscenities of decayed minds. He saw the ravages of dissipation in the faces of the winos and the reeking ruin of syphilis on the bodies of the shores. Yet everything he saw with compassion....

Liberated by the understanding of what have been made "black" recesses in his own life and the lives of others, his new compassion takes on strength. Despite some lingering self-doubts, his bondage becomes freeing. He opts for insurrectionary change, the manning repudiation of his life's straightjackets. History and confrontation make his choices clear (Sartre once remarked, "The French were never so free as during the German occupation"). Lee Gordon's redress of violence begins in the novel's closing moments as he watches Joe Ptak felled by the guards. His own willingness to take up the union banner and to face out the pointed gun of a white policeman expresses a crucial, though by no means final, stage in Himes' evolving embrace of Black Revolution. For Lee to confront the violence before him is for him to reach understanding of his psychological needs and to match, for the first time in the novel, the inner man in the outer identity. Lee's posture, no doubt heavy with romanticism, points uncertainly to an answer to racism through revolution and union solidarity.

Himes never explicitly acknowledges the hero of *Cast the First Stone* (1952), Jim Monroe, as Black, but his account of time-suspended claustrophobia in a Federal prison is loaded with analogies to the isolative and imprisoning sentences imposed by white society on Black. At the beginning of the novel the prison deprives Jim of name and history: "After ten days all information relative to my past and future, my body and soul, had been carefully recorded and filed. It had been done grimly and without sympathy." An ingénu, Jim gradually learns the ecology of prison routine, the high-temperature emotions of men placed under monitored physical constraint. He works first as a laborer in the prison's power-house (as a workhorse at the bottom of the machine, he is a part of a number of parallels to Black American history active throughout the novel). By a series of sexual and hustling moves he gains a position of handsome sufficiency, even triumph, among his fellow-prisoners. The universe into which he graduates smacks at time of Genet's in *Notre-Dame des Fleurs*, one of prison queens, alignments of guards and homosexual lifers and trusties, men hungry for touch and dominance. The fixed limits of Jimmy's universe Himes terms "stone and steel and concrete." A sensation of total control guides his sense of time: "Almost all the days belonged to the prison. They were steel-laced and unvarying, shaped and moulded for eternity. Another day. And then another...." Only the solace of Jimmy's lovers reaches certain wellsprings of emotion—Mal Steater especially, who becomes his "cousin," and Duke Dido, the artistic queen who finally hangs himself. Trying to write, wrestling down sexual self-contempt, and playing the card-school boss, Jimmy staggers through his sentence, a man without privateness or the fostered confidence of identity. Like the Biblical injunction from which the book takes its title, the prison envisions life as a storehouse of private miseries running down into spasms of hate and violence. The massive fire which kills a large number of prisoners acts as a powerful emetic to the congested cycle of abusive power in the prison, a further Himesian violent image of how repressive systems turn volcanic and eventually erupt. The analogies with racial repression, though implicit, are clear.

The outside world Himes only marginally keeps in view. Jimmy gets letters from his mother. Clothes, cigarettes and food are smuggled in on the prison underground. In the main, however, the prison is its own total world, inverting all normal canons of behavior. The prison hospital becomes a haven of sexual inversion rather than cure; prison reality to Jimmy is unreal; religious liberty is practiced in a guarded church. Love, need, human contact are made over into parasitic, threatening processes. In Jimmy's wait for outside life, "Thoughts of death touched me constantly...." And when Dido, the prison's most ravaged queen, writes a story, it depicts suicidal self-affright: "Shadows they are all about me. In the stench-laden corners of my dungeon they are black sentinels at the black gates of death, forbidding me sanctuary...." Like other fables of self-enclosure and escape, the novel is beautifully authenticated by Jimmy's reportorial "I." The recording consciousness as witness has a particular strength in Black American writing—stretching from oral slave narratives through the autobiographies of Booker Washington, Frederick Douglass, and James Weldon Johnson to the work of Malcolm X, Baldwin, Cleaver, Claude Brown, and yet more recently to the letters of George Jackson. So pervasive has this autobiographical mode been that it may well represent the most forceful province of Black letters. Survival in *Cast the First Stone* is elemental and deeply existential. In treading the paths of prison violence, Jimmy Monroe belongs patently enough with Bob Jones and Lee Gordon in Himes' special gathering of violated men.

The Third Generation (1954) acts as the diaristic record of a family's decline which works over a number of close autobiographical sources, now available in *The Quality of Hurt*. It lies near to Truman Capote's category of the non-fictional novel, personal history only lightly fictionalized. Crowded, at several points slack in laying out its heavy texture of detail—Himes was possibly too close to parts of the story—it maps out the dereliction of the Black bourgeois Taylor family, "Professor" Willie, his wife, and three sons. The Taylors take a downward journey from South to North involving dislocation which is a direct consequence of the mother's blighting pride in the lightness of her skin (she can pass) and the conviction that her white heritage confers a mark of racial specialness (it does, a victimizing mark), a reprimand to her husband's Black and artisan lowliness. The mother's implosions of anger and pain and their impact on her darker-skinned husband, a personable teacher of ironcraft, bequeaths to Charles, the youngest son, on whom the novel comes to focus—he is 18 in the late 1920s—a new set of embitterments. The family's sober picaresque travels from town to Southern town—Himes offers several excellent lyric vignettes of childhood—and their eventual migration into urban Cleveland give spatial definition to Charles' private awakenings and the parents' domestic storms. In the distant hinterland, touching the Taylor family only at margins, stands the Twenties' other face, the wealthier exuberance of Flapper and Jazz baby whose literary custodian was Scott Fitzgerald.

Of the Taylors as individuals, the father, deprived of his professor's status on the Black campuses of the South, dies in a knifing. Tom, the eldest boy, drifts into obscurity. Charles, self-accusing, lonely, an artist manqué, drops out from college into the petty crime which puts him in prison and into the charge of the courts. The mother, for whom the legacies of color have reserved their most ingenious devising, slows down finally, a female Sutpen alone in the city who broods over her dynastic embers and fades sadly into senescence. Only William Lee, Jr., the son blinded in a gunpowder accident, finds an accommodation with his life. Like Himes' own blind brother he moves into academia. The cruel freak of blindness removes from his sight, at least, the disabling spectacles of segregation, the thrash of Lilian Taylor to de-negrify her family.

The Third Generation, in fact, amounts to an anthology of experiences which pain and violate, though the book has sweeter rural moments—the slow drive into Delta Mississippi, for instance, or the hilarious hallelujah sermon "Dry Bones in the Valley." The mother's wedding night ("She was never able to separate the blackness of his skin from the brutality of his act") and the unrelieved fury she feels at the Black part of her racial heritage ("she wasn't white like other white people, because she lived with negroes") make up the central spine of this anthology of pain, though Himes draws supporting detail from the slangings of husband and wife (he "a shanty nigger," she "white men's leavings") from William's question to his mother, "Are we bad because we're colored?" and her answer, "You have white blood—fine white blood—in your veins," and from the array of incidents which educate the children into the different grammars of racism. Mrs. Taylor's angry impotence (at the white dentist's where she tries to pass, or on a train journey in which she refuses apartheid seating), and her swelling skirmishes with the system which places so ambiguous a gloss on her identity (her portrait is done with great sympathy) serve as a chorus on the family's coming rupture and ultimate decay. Her need to reverence the imagined aristocracy of her planter-forbears causes her to repress the historical rape which blended her color and brings down an inevitable curtain of violence on her family. The "old bitterness of color," in the book's phrase, asserts itself in the divided future the Taylors anticipate for their children: "She wanted to rear them in the belief that they were, in large part, white; that their best traits were from this white inheritance. He wanted to prepare them for being black...." "Preparing for being black" for Charles amounts largely to an unsuccessful course in self-survival. Like accusing shadows around him stand his father's capitulation, the draining anger of his mother, Tom's disappearance, and William's sightlessness. Himes gives his firmest attentions to Charles' adolescence (*The Third Generation* is something of a portrait of the artist as a Black disaffiliate) and to the Jim Crow equations which stiffen the boy's evolving consciousness. The sight in childhood of a cart puncturing the body of a woman haunts him like a spectre. Within him lurks a feeling for art and possible imagined worlds. The frustration of these creative drives blisters out into petty crime and his ventures on Cedar Avenue, the city's numbers and red-light district. The despair brought on first by the divorce, then by the death of his parents and his resorting to the bright-eyed rapacities of the block, a recess of hustlers, pimps and whores, brings on a final enervation. His obvious energies and creativity lie in abeyance, tired and unrealized. In any event Charles/Himes, we now know, loosened the blockage with a cascade of short stories in the Thirties. The novel ends on a temporary and foreboding note of quietness.

The Primitive (1955) is Himes' best novel. It's an interior life which outstrips anything in the previous work. The circuits of failure and exhaustion which connect Jesse Robinson and Kriss Cummings, veteran isolates, even by Himes' standards, are laid out through careful shifts of viewpoint and interior flashback. Robinson, who might well be a grown Charles Taylor, and his equally ravaged, self-avenging white woman, fight literally to the death a sexual battle whose weaponry is racial taunt and the broker's relationships which scar them and their frenzied inter-racial circle. The booze-laden weekend they spend together at Kriss's New York apartment, intensified by visits from other friends and lovers and by fresh deliveries of drink, Himes works as a memory theatre for their two lives. His knit of recollection dream, and live battle is set to a fluent and accelerating rhythm. The net of mutual revelation spreads painfully wide, into a hate which was once love for each other and into an accusing past of bad marriages, Kriss's conquests at parties and in bed, and Jesse's struggles to get published. Himes pulls together the whole with considerable narrative astringency.

From the parallel first two chapters which diagnose the linked insecurities of Kriss and Jesse, Himes matches the line of their sexual and racial experience to an interior psychology of ravage. Their weekend's descent into hell is measured through window and mirror gazing, through the inner imaginings of nightmare and abuse and subliminal television newscasts which garble snatches of contemporary history and include, as part of the general context of dislocation, an interview with a prophetic chimpanzee emblematizing a Darwinian reversal whereby Jesse exists only at a prehuman level. If consciousness is having others see us, *The Primitive* draws on a texture of watchings, gazings, alcoholic dream, and memory. Jesse especially is the victim of his dream-life. The book first mentions him in his dream of drowning in icy water. And Kriss, from waking out of fear and aloneness, tries to suppress the threat of her inner mind. She depends upon pills, drinks, and a compensating run of lovers and squires to bolster a psyche which, left to itself, might collapse into chaos. Himes offers the rituals of titillation and sexual challenge as husks of ferment within.

Jesse's imagination constantly dreams up possible books, literary steadying to his fertile, but paradoxically un-manning, bank of experience. He casts about for shape and meaning to his broken marriage with Becky, to the rejections of white publishers, and to his false arrest in a car accident. The homosexuals he boards with in a run-down Harlem tenant house give further index to this inner dislocation and self-loss. Similarly, Kriss though outwardly more assured in her role of executive in a Madison Avenue foundation bringing already rich students to America from India, looks back in her early-morning reveries to a private trail of pain—to a girlhood abortion, her lost homosexual Mississippian husband, her demeaning availability to his many successors. These two troubled isolates move together inexorably. Their intricate afflictions of race and sex finally break out into a savage, sometimes comic, sexual dance, ritualistic violence which anticipates the acerbities of Edward Albee's *Who's Afraid of Virginia Woolf?* Taunted, provoked, and denied by Kriss's white body, Jesse drinks more and more, seeing in her the bitter manipulation of his manhood. His inner drives to revenge drunkenly take over. He stabs Kriss in a miasmic trance. His act registers Himes' most complex instance of risen violence, identity seized confusedly at an almost inevitable price of murder.

Himes beautifully concentrates the absurdist thrusts of Jesse's dream life, often redolent of Poe or De Quincey, in one of his most powerful visions of paradox and the hunt for sustaining identity:

He dreamed he was in a house with a thousand rooms of different sizes made entirely of distorted mirrors. There were others besides himself but he could not tell how many because their reflections went on into an infinity in the distorted mirrors. Nor could he see their true shape because in one mirror they all appeared to be obese dwarfs and in another tall, then, cadaverous skeletons. He ran panic-stricken from room to room trying to find a familiar human shape, but he saw only the grotesque reflections, the brutal faces that leered from some distortions, the sweet smiles from others, the sad eyes, the gentle mouths, the sinister stares, the treacherous grins, the threatening scowls, hating and bestial, suffering and saintly, gracious and kind, and he knew that none of them was the true face and he continued to run in frantic terror until he found a door and escaped....

Hurrying from an outer world of normal existence itself racked by emotional idiocy, Jesse has to live with the hallucinatory play of his own imagination running amuck. He lives in a cruel house of mirrors which denies him an even and useable image of himself. The distorting white envelope of flesh into which his life has been thrust and Kriss's vamping before him and her other Black lovers fuse dizzily into a single locus of pain. Killing her certifies his membership in the human race; he believes himself to have joined the mainstream American norms of violence. Jesse muses, "You finally did it.... End product of Americanism on one Jesse Robinson—black man. Your answer, son. You've been searching for it. *Black man kills white woman....* Human beings only species of animal life where males are known to kill their females. Proof beyond all doubt. Jesse Robinson joins the human race." A considerable distance from Bob Jones' dream of impotence, Himes thus completes the graph of violence in his first novels with an appropriate diagram of what has brought murder into Jesse's soul. Himes' skills with tone and with declarative prose that traps the stinging edge of sensation gives concentration, and just the right engraving, to *The Primitive's* envisionings of violence. When Jesse phones the local police precinct with news of what he has done, the cryptic idiom he drops into could well come from a voice out of Gravedigger's Harlem: "'I'm a nigger and I've just killed a white women,' Jesse said, giving the address and hung up. 'That'll get the lead out of his seat,' he thought half-amused." The detective work lies close ahead.

Some of the groundwork for Coffin Ed/Gravedigger fiction was prepared in *Pinktoes*, Himes' light-hearted mixture of Harlem anecdotery and erotica. An odyssey of double-entendres, sexual puns and scandal, it makes of inter-racial liberalism, the parties and good-mixing especially, a bed-hopping comedy to be ranked, perhaps, with Terry Southern's *Candy* or with the lighter sexual badinage of Henry Miller or William Melvin Kelley. Mamie Mason, "the hostess with the mostess," the presiding, and overweight, genius of "la Société des Mondaines du Monde de Harlèm," gathers about her a motley of publishers, artists, college, and foundation presidents, actors and clerics in hues from the pinkest of pinks to the jettest of blacks. Together with their various paramours and wives she conducts, with appropriate Rabelaisian bravura, a sexual barn dance whose antics beautifully undercut the usual solemn masquerades of concern with "the problem." *Pinktoes* performs an attractive exercise in scatology, a bawdy tilt at middle-class American urban liberalism. It romps through the sexual and emotional manners of racial good-feeling, an extravaganza with the usually unmentionable premise that sexual fascination is the prime mover for most bourgeois racial contact.

Read in sequence, Himes' detective novels unveil a far meaner underside of Harlem. Coffin Ed Johnson and Gravedigger Jones, his two rough-hewn lawmarshals with their own approximate standards of justice, patrol an overcrowded kingdom of Black life, a gallery of the living violent and bizarre. With the Harlem he has called "the Mecca of the black," Himes has taken enormous care. He displays a geographer's scruple for accuracy and detail even to the point of having made regular trips from Europe to New York in a bid to keep his knowledge of the changes in Harlem's landscape up to date.

A laconic archivist he successfully puts on view the feeling of Harlem's pulse and argot, its music, dishes and flavors, the sweltering summer landscapes of brownstone and tenement, the motley of bars, whorehouses, churches and pawnshops. Himes abundantly knows his Jazz and blues, his soul-food and pig-knuckles. Book after book offers a milling population of preachers and politicians, sober matriarchs and mock religious prophets, pimps, and their chippies, drug-pushers and wheel-thieves, transvestites and conmen, shysters of every kind and sex. Gravedigger and Coffin Ed are adepts in reading the deceits and false fronts of Harlem's netherworld, a territory prone to the wildest species of violence (knifings, acid-throwing, torture to the point of overspill, street-shootings, and throat-cuttings figure most prominently). From this carefully observed domain Himes authenticates the complex—sometimes hilarious, at other times scarcely credible—spirals of violence and crime unraveled by his two Black cops.

Each of Himes' (to date) eight Coffin Ed/Gravedigger Jones novels[5] is, he has rightly insisted, a barely fictive essay in violence, a witty, complicated, often anarchically grotesque and funny tale of detection bulging with mayhem, predatory hustle, and murder. Each individual narrative he writes to an involuted but rigorous logic. "Those two Harlem Sheriffs," as he calls his detectives in *The Crazy Kill* (does Loop Garoo in Ishmael Reed's mock frontier novel *Yellow-Back Radio Broke-Down* owe anything to Himes' uniquely conceived pair?), have the unenviable task of bringing to some level of tolerable order the eruptive undergrowth of crime and communal self-violence which result from straight-jacketing half a million people into a suffocating urban enclave. Of his novels and their violence Himes has remarked, "They're based on one thing; black people want money through crime. They don't have any choice."[6] Himes' eight novels (and *Run Man Run*[7] is no different in this respect) propose ingenious map-readings in violence, deciphering of a mask-ridden world whose sober baselines he nevertheless insists upon, as in this description of a Harlem street in *The Crazy Kill*:

Unwed young mothers, suckling their infants, living on a prayer; fat black racketeers coasting past in big bright-colored convertibles with their solid gold babes carrying huge sums of money on their person; hard-working men, holding up buildings with their shoulders, talking in loud voices up there in Harlem where the white bosses couldn't hear them; teenage gangsters grouping for a gang-fight, smoking marijuana weed to get up their courage; everybody escaping the hot-box rooms they lived in, seeking respite in a street made hotter by the automobile exhaust and heat released by the concrete walls and walks.

He almost invariably makes the foreground of the novels an act of macabre violence, an event outrageous to at least one of the five senses. Philip Oakes, in a profile of Himes, after observing that in the novels, "Death is not only seen as grotesque, but grotesquely funny," offers this sample list of their violent wares:

A hit-and-run victim, jammed against a wall, and frozen stiff on a sub-zero night, is stripped of her finery and revealed as a transvestite. Dr. Nubutu, inventor of an elixir distilled from the mating organs of baboons, rabbits, eagles and shellfish, is butchered while arguing the true cost of rejuvenation. A white homosexual, whose jugular has been severed, expires on the sidewalk, remarkable only because he's not wearing trousers.[8]

To these choice items, which describe in turn *All Shot Up* and *Blind Man With a Pistol*, might be added a transvestite nun with "his" throat cut open in a chase after fool's gold (*A Rage in Harlem*); a white King Cola salesman, the flagellant of teenage black girls, shot by the marijuana-high leader of a teenage gang of Moslems (*The Real Cool Killers*; the death by religious ecstasy of Alberta Wright, a follower of one Sweet Prophet Brown, which puts in train the murderous search for a Numbers Fortune hidden in an armchair (*The Big Gold Dream*); and the corpse of a headless tire-thief riding the Harlem streets on a motorcycle and crashing into a store with the shopfront motto "We Will Give Credit to the Dead" (*All Shot Up*). This cryptic resource of Himes' imagination comes over time and again in like situations. Such unlikely donneés usually constitute the starting point for his two detectives whose own arrival at the scene of any crime is itself a mixture of comic high *kitsch* and genuine threat. Take this moment from *The Crazy Kill*:

An inconspicuous black sedan pulled out from the kerb and parked at the end of the block unnoticed, and the two tall, lanky colored men dressed in black mohair suits that looked as though they'd been slept in got out and walked towards the scene. Their wrinkled coats bulged beneath their left shoulders. The shiny straps of shoulder holsters showed across the fronts of their blue cotton shirts. The one with the burnt face went to the far side of the crowd; the other remained on the near side. Suddenly a loud voice shouted, "Straighten up!" An equally loud voice echoes, "Count off!"

"The one with the burnt face" is Coffin Ed, the victim of an acid-throwing attack which has left him twitchy and psychopathic (the details are in *A Rage in Harlem*, Chapter 12) and whose subsequent skin-grafts make fearsome basilisks to wrong-doers.

Between them Coffin Ed and Gravedigger Jones run a curious show. Although they live outside Harlem they have it cross-webbed with stool-pigeons and informants and know its every crevice. Their inwardness with Harlem represents an endless bafflement to their white precinct officer, Lieutenant Anderson, who suffers the kind of inadequate racial vision which underpins Ralph Ellison's *Invisible Man* and which William Melvin Kelley develops into surreal comic nightmare in *dem* (1967). They keep to certain guidelines, laying off brothels, numbers, houses and bars intrinsic to Harlem life, but pistol-whipping their way over anybody bringing violence upon an already violated community. Their code Himes explains in *A Rage in Harlem*:

Gravedigger and Coffin Ed weren't crooked detectives, but they were tough. They had to be tough to work in Harlem. Colored folks didn't respect colored cops. But they respected big shiny pistols and sudden death. It was said in Harlem that Coffin Ed's pistol would kill a rock and that Gravedigger's would bury it. They took their tribute, like all real cops, from the established underworld catering for the essential needs of the people—gamekeepers, madams, streetwalkers, numbers writers, numbers bankers. But they were rough on purse snatchers, muggers, burglars, con-men, and all strangers working any racket. And they didn't like rough stuff from anybody but themselves. "Keep it cool," they warned, "Don't make graves."

Himes' two latest contributions to the sequence, *Cotton Comes to Harlem* (1963) and *Blind Man with a Pistol* (1969), strike me as noticeably widening both the range and violence as a theme in his work and the straight, however distinctive, thriller-detective format which identifies the run from *A Rage in Harlem* (1957) to *The Heat's On* (1961).

Cotton Comes to Harlem, the first of what is becoming a film series directed by Ossie Davis with Raymond St. Jacques and Godfrey Cambridge in the detective roles, spans out from a death-strewn Back-to-Africa caper into more inclusive considerations of race-war in Harlem and America at large. Underpinning Himes' customary recipes of death and violent mayhem lies a pressing regard in this novel for Black American history which he brings to focus by making his central and reverberative point of reference a bale of white Alabama cotton. Himes frames his gunbattles and violent inflections of the comic-grotesque (the "Holy Dream" pitch deserves a special mention—a thief cuts the skirt from a Church-sister's backside in a bid to get her hidden purse while his accomplice enthralls the good woman with details of a conversation he has held with Jesus in a dream), within a subtle historical parallel. He offsets a latter-day Garveyist extravaganza against a "Back to the Happy Southlands" scheme run by a crooked neo-Confederate colonel who suggests throughout Harlem that the Back-to-Africa movements, and the racial awareness they provoke, are un-American. Himes thus dovetails the cult of Mother Africa into the communal memory of cotton slavery and subsequent Black fortunes in America. Harlem is made a point of intersection, deeply explosive, between a chattel slave past, a future bound up with the politics of negritude, and a highly dangerous urban present. The task of Gravedigger and Coffin Ed, apart from sorting out the gory complexities of the Reverend Deke O'Malley and Colonel Robert L. Calhoun and their respective gangs, is to keep a harder-than-usual rein on a situation which brings into visible clash white retrenchment and the political arms of Black Power (the Black Muslims, significantly, appear for the first time in his work). In other words, *Cotton Comes to Harlem* takes the subject of violence beyond the immediate demands of the detective yarns into the wider reach of the political, or perhaps racial-political, parable.

This widening of theme and narrative kind applies even more to *Blind Man with a Pistol*, a title Himes deliberately chose to emblematize the unseeing thrust of "all unorganized violence."[9] Retitled *Hot Day Hot Night* in the American re-issue, this latest novel, probably the richest imaginatively in the detective series, binds together a number of seemingly disparate themes: an inter-racial sex scandal which brings into play Himes' unflagging genius for the grotesque and comic; a rejuvenation caper with a Black Mormon and his wives with leads into Syndicate crime; and a spate of Black protest marches, political and religious, which put Harlem on a nervous, insurrectionary edge. For the first time in the series, Gravedigger and Coffin Ed are barely able to contain the flare-ups; and their ambiguous status as Black cops is challenged by new-wave militants. Tired, obviously aging, the pair learn more clearly than ever that Black ghetto crime derives, in large part, from the wider national equations of racism and power. The "Afro" explosion, the Sixties moves to alter and revolutionize Black Consciousness, lie pressingly to hand. *Blind Man with a Pistol* makes copious reference to Black Power, to the heirs of Malcolm X, and to the rising energies of confrontation and shoot-outs. Gravedigger and Coffin Ed inject a more explicit political character to their musings when they talk of Malcolm:

"You know one thing, Digger. He was safe as long as he kept hating white folks—they wouldn't have hurt him, probably made him rich; it wasn't until he began including them in the human race they killed him. That ought to tell you something."
 "It does. It tells me that white people don't want to be included in a human race with black people."

The violent train of events which Himes weaves and counterpoints throughout the novel comes to a turbulent close with a berserk pistol-firing of a blind man. As he flails about at the end of a bizarre chain of events, his contortions articulate the absurd, apocalyptic threat Himes reads in his times. His gun blasts off indiscriminately, and "Everyone thought the world was coming to an end; others that the Venusians were coming. A number of white passengers thought the niggers were taking over; the majority of the soul people thought their time was up." The blind man suggests confusion and sightless riot. Himes uses him as a living token of what can ensue from white supremacist dreams. The detective novels have almost ceded their place to a prophecy of anarchic racial apocalypse in which not even Coffin Ed and Gravedigger can exert a restraining hand.

Two recent observations by Himes offer useful angles on his writing. On the origins of violence as a root and branch theme in his books he comments: "If I had wanted to express my revulsion for violence then I would have made the violence even more repellent, really repellent. I am simply creating stories that have a setting I know very well...."[10] In drawing from "a setting I know very well" Himes, obviously enough, is transcribing violence personally witnessed which he takes to characterize the pervasive racist grain of Black American experience. The life which gives shape to his writing undoubtedly is violent enough—at an inner level in terms of racist damage to personality and at an outer level in the matching landscapes of ghetto, color-line, and sheer human blight. We might be grateful for being spared "really repellent" violence. Among other things, Himes undoubtedly has in mind, as always, the terminal violence of unconstrained racial warfare.

Himes' other comment links violence to the narrative disposition of his detective works:

My French editor says, the Americans have a style of writing detective stories that no one has been able to imitate.... There's no reason why the black American, like all other Americans, and brought up in this sphere of violence which is the main sphere of American detective stories, there's no reason why he shouldn't write them. It's just plain and simple violence in narrative form.... American violence is public life, it's a public way of life; it became a form, a detective story form.[11]

"Violence become a form" might stand more widely for nearly all of Himes' novels. In opening up his vistas on violence with so careful a controlling lens, Himes has mounted a record, both in terms of a major theme and in the resources of his narrative form, not to be put aside with complacency. His novels, lexicons of the workings of racist violence, can lay persuasive claim to our attention.

NOTES

1. Himes has published a selection of his stories, essays and the film scenario "Baby Sister" as *Black on Black* (New York: Doubleday, 1973).

2. Cf. Le Roi Jones, *Home: Social Essays* (New York: Apollo, 1967), p. 123: "And one can find more moving writing in any of Chester Himes' bizarre detective novels than in most serious efforts by Negroes, just because Himes' main interest must be in saying the thing like it is."

3. "My Man Himes," Interview with John A. Williams, in *Amistad: Writings on Black History and Culture*, eds. John A. Williams and Charles F. Harris (New York: Vintage Books, 1970), pp. 66–67.

4. William Melvin Kelley, *dem* (New York: Collier, 1969), intro., p. VIII.

5. In order of publication the novels are *A Rage in Harlem* (1957), *The Real Cool Killers* (1958), *The Crazy Kill* (1958), *The Big Gold Dream* (1959), *All Shot Up* (1960), *The Heat's On* (1961), *Cotton Comes to Harlem* (1963), *Blind Man with a Pistol* (1969).

Run Man Run was published in 1959. A bibliography for Himes is appended to John A. Williams' interview (*Amistad*, op. cit.) and can be supplemented from Darwin T. Turner, *Afro-American Writers* (New York: Appleton-Century-Crofts, 1970) and Arthur P. Davis, *From The Dark Tower: Afro-American Writers 1900 to 1960* (Washington: Howard University Press, 1974).

6. (London) *Sunday Observer*, June 29, 1969.

7. *Run Man Run* is perhaps the nearest of Himes' later works to the straight detective story. At its center is the story of a white psychopathic cop taking out on blacks and women the violence he can no longer distance himself from.

8. (London) *Sunday Times Magazine*, November 9, 1969, p. 69.

9. Himes offers the full origin of the title in a preface to the novel: "A friend of mine, Phil Lomax, told me this story about a blind man with a pistol shooting at a man who had slapped him on a subway train and killing an innocent bystander peacefully reading his newspaper across the aisle and I thought, damn right, sounds just like today's news, riots in ghettos, war in Vietnam, masochistic doing in the Middle East. And then I thought of some of our loudmouthed leaders urging our vulnerable soul brothers on to getting themselves killed, and thought further that all unorganized violence is like a blind man with a pistol."

10. *Nova*, January 1971, p. 52. In this same article Himes is quoted as holding the following political view on violence: "All of the so-called leaders of the Black people in the United States are effectively neutralized by publicity. I have never fully endorsed the black movements although I have supported both the Black Muslims—I was a friend of Malcolm X—and the Panthers. I don't think they will succeed because they are too used to publicity, and a successful revolution must be planned with secrecy, security. Yet there is no reason why 100,000 Blacks armed with automatic rifles couldn't literally go underground, into the subways and basements of Manhattan—and take over. The basements of those skyscrapers are the strongest part of the building.... This was the novel I was writing, and I don't know if I have the energy or determination to finish it.... The whites are going to have to back down, and I don't know if they can bear to do that. I believe in organized revolution with violence as the only way for the Blacks to instill enough fear into the whites to make them back down."

11. *Amistad*, Interview with John A. Williams, pp. 48-49.

"Violence Real and Imagined: The World of Chester Himes' Novels" *Negro American Literature Forum*, 10 (Spring 1976), 13–26.

Chester Himes: "A Nigger"
Maureen Liston

Chester Himes is perhaps best known as the creator of Grave Digger and Coffin Ed. That he has also written and published short stories, a play, essays, novels other than detective, and a two-volume autobiography is little known, save to Black writers and Black literature scholars. During his writing career—which spans some forty-plus years—Himes has published "six major novels";[1] some twenty-two short stories in periodicals; a series of detective novels; essays on a variety of subjects; and a collection including a film scenario as well as short stories and essays, some of which had been printed earlier in *Esquire*, *Coronet*, *Crisis*, *Opportunity* and *Negro Study*.

Born 29 July 1909 in Jefferson City, Missouri, Chester Himes was the youngest of three sons. His mother was an octoroon; his father, Professor Joseph Sandy Himes—a teacher at the Lincoln Institute, a Negro college—was "a short black man with bowed legs, a perfect ellipsoidal skull, and an Arabic face with a big hooked nose."[2] Several years after Chester's birth, the family moved to Mississippi, where Professor Himes became head of Alcorn A & M's Mechanical Department. Around 1917 Chester Himes also spent a year in Augusta, Georgia, when his mother taught at the Haines Institute.

Chester and his brother Joe were educated at home until 1917; both children were better educated than most blacks of the same age. In 1921, when Prof. Himes went to Branch Normal College, Pine Bluff, Arkansas, Joe and Chester enrolled in the college, later to be known as Arkansas A & M. About a year later, Joe was blinded by a chemistry explosion in a school demonstration; the family returned to St. Louis in order to get better treatment for him. This episode played an important role in Chester's development and he devoted several long sections in the first volume of his autobiography to his closest brother's accident, subsequent reeducation and success. In 1923 or 1924, motivated by unemployment, racial inequality, and the inability of the Barnes Hospital to further help Joe, Prof. Himes moved his family to Cleveland, Ohio, where he had relatives.

In January of 1926, due to a clerical error, Chester Himes was awarded his high school diploma. In order to earn money for college, he took a job as busboy at Wade Park Manor, where malfunctioning elevator doors caused him to fall about forty feet down an empty elevator shaft; the result was three broken vertebrae, a broken jaw, shattered teeth, a broken left arm and a ruptured urethral canal. Hospital expenses were paid by the Ohio State Industrial Commission, as well as a pension.

In September 1926 Himes entered Ohio State University in Columbus. He quickly tired of university, and by the end of the second quarter was allowed "to withdraw for reasons of 'ill health'" (Himes, p. 31). On his return to Cleveland, he was introduced to gambling and, in 1928, participated in his first burglary. Himes' family was breaking up—his parents' quarrels, which had been going on for years, were becoming more violent—and he seemed to seek security and relief from emotional pressures in the gambling halls, with prostitutes, and in burglary. "I discovered that I had become very violent," writes Himes in his *Autobiography* (p. 47); by the end of 1928 he had been arrested in Chicago for first-degree armed robbery. Sentenced to twenty-to-twenty-five years of hard labor, Himes served only seven-and-a-half years of his sentence, in the Ohio State Penitentiary; here he began to write.

In 1936 Himes married his first wife, Jean, in Cleveland. He wrote a few short stories, and wrote for the WPA and the Ohio Writers' Project. Sometime after the beginning of the Second World War, perhaps in 1940, Himes and his wife travelled by Greyhound to Los Angeles. (*If He Hollers Let Him Go* concerns this period in his life.) Four years later he travelled east to New York City.

The next two years were spent in California and on the East Coast, Himes going from job to job, supported mostly by his wife. *Lonely Crusade* was published in 1947 and, with the total rejection of the book, a five-year-long writer's block set in. By 1952 Himes' marriage to Jean had broken up, and in 1953 he finally left America for France. The last twenty years have been spent mostly in Europe—with infrequent trips to the United States—mainly in France and in Spain; Himes and his second wife, Lesley, travel a lot, frequently to escape other "expatriate" black writers, and have recently completed a villa in Alicante, Spain.

These biographical facts are of importance for a writer such as Chester Himes, especially since Robert Bone assigns him to the "Wright School,"[3] a 1940's "urban realism" movement.[4] The following quote explains the need for autobiographical content in Himes' writings and the role of the Wright School.

For the Wright School, literature is an emotional catharsis—a means of dispelling the inner tensions of race. Their novels often amount to a prolonged cry of anguish and despair. Too close to their material, feeling it too intensely, these novelists lack a sense of form and of thematic line. With rare exceptions, their style consists of a brutal realism, devoid of any love, or even respect, for words. Their characterization is essentially sociological, but it may contain a greater attempt at psychological depth than is usually associated with the naturalistic novel. Their principal theme, reminiscent of Sherwood Anderson, is how the American caste system breeds "grotesques." The white audience, on perceiving its responsibility for the plight of the protagonist, is expected to alter its attitude toward race.[5]

Bone also comments that "many of these authors served their literary apprenticeship as newspaper writers."[6]

Wright was the first black to approach the situation of the urban Black naturalistically.[7] The Wright School movement followed a decade after the social protest expressed most frequently in the American novel in the Depression years. Not only a journalist, "Himes, like Wright, is a product of the Great Depression, of association with the labor movement, the Federal Writers' Project, and the Communist Party."[8] Whitlow comments that "Most of the writers of the movement are mediocre."[9] John A. Williams, however, states that "Himes is perhaps the single greatest naturalistic American writer living today."[10]

Himes' "six major novels" are as follows: *If He Hollers Let Him Go* (1945); *Lonely Crusade* (1947); *The Third Generation* (1954); *The Primitive* (1955); *Cast the First Stone* (1952), and *Pinktoes* (1961/62 and 1965).[11] In 1966 Himes wrote that "the Negro novelist, more than any other, is faced with this necessity [to find justification for existence]. He must discover from his experiences the truth of his oppressed existence in terms that will provide some meaning to his life. Why he is here; why he continues to live. In fact, this writer's subject matter is in reality a Negro's search for truth."[12] The first two novels—both highly autobiographical—deal with race, sex, and the labor movement of the 1940's. (In Volume 1, Book 1, Section 2 of *The Quality of Hurt*, he writes about the composition and background of these two books.) The next three novels advance along the same lines: autobiographical, racial, sexual. Himes writes not only of the place of the Black in American (western) society, but of humanity in a diseased world. Of the six, only *Pinktoes* has had any real commercial success.

Pinktoes, which was first published in Paris as *Mamie Mason*, is a sometimes successful satire on race. Compared to the other "serious" novels, it is the least well-written but also the least violent. It is at times funny, this story of an up-and-coming lack Harlem hostess, whose sexual adventures are probably the selling point of the book. (Himes seems to have added sexual scenes for the American edition of the book; he claims the publishers asked for more explicitness.)[13]

Against these novels can be set the nine more successful—and much more readable—"detective" novels. Strangely enough, all but one of the nine were first published in France, in French: the first, *La Reine des Pommes* (Série Noire-Gallimard, 1957), won the *Prix du Roman Policier* in 1958 and appeared in the United States as *For Love of Immabelle* in 1959; the latest *Blind Man With a Pistol*, was published in 1969.

Coffin Ed Smith and Gravedigger Jones, the "heroes" of the novels, are two black cops in Harlem. They are tough, violent, hated, feared, and beaten-up by the blacks among whom they work. They twist the law to keep the law, sometimes even committing crimes to catch the bad guy. The novels are all set in Harlem, and, with the possible exception of *Blind Man With a Pistol*, are relatively easy to read. Himes captures in his prose the spirit of Harlem—the violence, the brutality, the simple joys, the sexuality.... It is in these books, not in his more serious attempts as a writer, that his talent is revealed.[14] Descriptions of street-corner preachers, lesbian strippers, transvestite "sisters," sleazy prostitutes—descriptions of the street, with its thousands of different characters and the ever-present possibility for violence—jerk and jive into real life. The dialogue is a mixture of Black English, underground slang, dope colloquialisms, black dialects, and patois. Even the smallest details are not too small for Himes: pages are devoted, for example, to the different eating places and to the different kinds of food in Harlem. It is a terrible world Himes is presenting, filled with sex and violence, and the energy of Harlem life is caught on every page. This crazy life which is often out of control is controlled by Himes: the plots work; each made incident somehow fits into the story being unfolded, each mystery is somehow solved, each bad guy is caught, or killed, or maimed, or punished. The violence which is always there suddenly erupts into blood, and the blood flows until somehow the book—this one incident being related, not the violence and not Harlem—comes to an end. As Himes would say, the books are "titillating."[15]

It is in this setting that one can approach the short stories. In Himes' "forword" to *Black on Black* he writes the following:

These writings are admittedly chauvinistic. You will conclude if you read them that BLACK PROTEST and BLACK HETEROSEXUALITY are my two chief obsessions.

And you will be right. I am a sensualist, I love beautiful people, I have SOUL. At the same time I am extremely sensitive to all the humiliations and preconceptions Black Americans are heir to. But I think my talent is sufficient to render these chauvinistic writings interesting, or at least provoking....
. . . .
With the exception of "Tang," which I wrote in Alicante in 1967 when my thoughts had concentrated on a BLACK REVOLUTION, I wrote the first nine short stories during the Depression of the nineteen thirties and the first years of the Second World War.
. . . .
I wrote the last short story, "Prediction," in Alicante in 1969 after I had become firmly convinced that the only chance Black Americans had of attaining justice and equality in the United States of America was by violence.[16]

Many of the stories appear in varied forms in the detective novels, as do many of Himes' early characters.[17] The preacher in "Pork Chop Paradise" (1938) appears in some form in every Harlem novel; in the short story the preacher is recognized as God because he feeds his people with pork chops. In the novels he uses other ploys to make money or to become God, but he is still the preacher who "carried his pulpit about in his hand and set it upon street corners and wrestled with the sin of the world as ardently as if he, himself, had been forever sinless" (p. 165).

He rocked his congregations, he scared them, he startled them if by nothing else except his colossal ignorance, he browbeat them, he lulled them, he caressed them. He made hardened convicts want to shout, he made gambling addicts repent and give away their ill-gotten gains and stay away from the games for two or three whole days. He played upon people's emotions. His voice was like a throbbing tom-tom, creeping into a person's mind like an insidious drug, blasting the wits out of the witty and filling the hearts of the witless with visions of everlasting bounty.

It had an indescribable range, sliding through octaves with the ease of a master organ. It was like a journey on a scenic railway, dropping from notes as clear and high as Satchmo ever hit on his golden trumpet, like the sudden, startling dive of a pursuit plane, to the reverberating roar of heavy artillery. You could see hell, in all its lurid fury, following in its wake, and then with as abrupt a change the voice took you to green pastures lush with manna. (p. 164)

In "Pork Chop Paradise" Himes explores the personality of "an illiterate black man" (p. 161); in "Headwaiter" (1938; pp. 144–60) that of a black headwaiter willing to do anything to please the white customers; in "Da-Da-Dee" (1948, pp. 167–74) a drunken writer. "To the Negro writer who would plumb the depth of the Negro personality, there is no question of whether Negroes hate white people—but how does this hatred affect the Negro's personality? How much of himself is destroyed by this necessity to hate those who oppress him? Certainly hate is a destructive emotion. In the case of the Negro, hate is doubly destructive. The American Negro experiences two forms of hate. He hates first his oppressor, and then because he lives in constant fear of this hatred being discovered, he hates himself—because of this fear."[18] These sentences, written in 1966, could be a description of Himes' "A Nigger," written in 1937.

There are autobiographical elements in "Nigger": the setting, for example, is Cleveland, Ohio, probably sometime between 1935 and 1937. Joe Wolf, a writer between 24 and 26 years old, goes to visit his mistress Fay after her common-law husband leaves for the afternoon. Mr. Shelton, Fay's white John, appears on the scene, and Joe is forced to hide in the closes closet. As Mr. Shelton leaves, he opens the closet door by mistake; Joe thinks he has been seen and, when Fay returns to the room, erupts into violence. After he escapes to his room, eight blocks away, Joe realizes he is an Uncle Tom.

The most interesting elements of "A Nigger" are neither the simple plot line nor the narrative techniques employed but the main character's reactions to the situation. Fay is "kept by a rich white John out of Shaker Heights, and living with a fine-looking, hard-working, tall yellow boy on the side who dumped his paycheck to her as regular as it came, then cheating on them both with this broke, ragged lunger who claimed he was some kind of writer or poet or something" (p. 125). Himes' ironic view of what is possibly a recreation of himself continues throughout the piece, communicated not only through the narrator's retelling of the events but also through Joe's interpretation of what occurs. Joe's first reaction, in "the cluttered closet" (p. 126), is "laughingly, *what a bitch!*" (p. 126). Mr. Shelton's voice is "smug and condescendingly possessive," and Joe thinks "*why, you old bastard*" (p. 126). Mr. Shelton is going East, and wants to leave enough money for Fay, who secretly uses it to support Joe, thus making him indirectly dependent on Mr. Shelton.

Joe begins to get angry when he hears Mr. Shelton insisting on the same respect for Mrs. Shelton that Fay demands from Joe for Mr. Shelton. The dialogue between the John and Fay is a sugary parody of a lovers' dialogue. While Mr. Shelton complains about Roosevelt, Joe is distracted by his thoughts on "*old sons of a bitches like this....* (p. 127). When he again listens, Fay is obviously trying to get Mr. Shelton to make love to her:

What in the hell is she trying to do? But Joe was too proud to bend down the keyhole to see for himself. He stood sweating in the center of the closet between the two racks of close-packed garments bought for her by *Mr. Shelton*—he thought of him as *Mr. Shelton* without being aware of it—his stockinged feet cramped and uncomfortable among the scatter of shoes, suddenly overcome with the sense of having sold his pride, his whole manhood, for a whore's handout, no better than the pimps down on Central Avenue, only cheaper—so damn much cheaper. One flicker of light came through the keyhold to which he was too proud, even to bend down and look at the man who had controlled his eating of the past five weeks, and now at this moment was controlling his movement and emotions and even his soul. Too proud to look even while accepting the position, as if not looking would lessen the actuality; would make it more possible to believe he hadn't accepted it. Sweat trickled down his face and neck and legs and body like crawling lice, and the mixture of the scent of the twelve bottles of perfume she kept on her dresser like a stack of thousand-dollar bills, along with the sharp musk scent of her body, stale shoe smell and underarm odor, in the dense sticky closeness, brought a sickish taste to his mouth.... (p. 128).

At the same time, Joe tries to maintain an artistic distance from the situation: "*If I can only get it funny*, he thought."

He tried to get far enough away from it to see it like it was. The guy was just another square. Just like all the other white squares he'd seen being debased by Negro women after their sex had gone from their bodies into their minds, no longer even able to give or receive any vestige of satisfaction from younger women of their own race, their wives long past giving or requiring. Turning to Negro women because in them they saw only the black image of flesh, the organ itself, like beautiful bronze statues endowed with motion, flesh and blood, instinct and passion, but possessing no mind to condemn, no soul to be outraged, most of all no power to judge or accuse, before whom the spirit of exhausted sex could creep and crawl and expose its ugly nakedness without embarrassment or restraint (p. 129).

Joe remembers an incident which occurred in 1928, an incident which was at the time funny. He had been a voyeur when a black prostitute had been paid to debase a white man. "But it wasn't funny now. He couldn't get it funny. The fact was, he, Joe Wolf, had been maneuvered by a whore into a spot too low for a dog" (p. 130). As Himes became aware in the 1920's of his growing violence, Joe becomes aware of his, and forms a garrote out of a hanger. "His breath oozed out and with it his determination—*God knows, I don't want to kill them. But he knew that he would; he always did every crazy thing he knew he shouldn't do*" (p. 130).

The closet door opens and "Joe blinked into the light, and for one breathless instant he stared straight into the small blue sardonic eyes of a stout bald-headed white man with a fringe of gray hair and a putty vein-laced face" (p. 130). After Mr. Shelton leaves, Joe realizes: "All of a sudden it hit him that *Mr. Shelton* had opened the door deliberately, knowing he was there, and after having satisfied himself that he was right, had refused to acknowledge Joe's existence" (p. 131). "*Why he had not only refused to recognize him as a rival, not even as an intruder; why, the son of a bitch looked at him as if he was another garment he had bought for her.* It was the first time he had ever felt the absolute refusal of recognition" (p. 131). Fay's "Suppose he did see you—so what? He didn't let it make any difference" (p. 131) drives Joe to violence; he lashes out at her with the wire. "*Trying to make him accept it! The man refused*

to even acknowledge his existence. And she wanted him to accept it!" (p. 131).
His rage disappears when the landlady shoots at him with a .38, and he flees to
his boarding house.

... deeper than his resentment was his shame. The fact was he had kept standing there,
taking it, even after he could no longer tell himself that it was a joke, a trim on a sucker,
just so he could keep on eating off the bitch and people wouldn't know just how hard up
he really was. Just to keep on putting up a cheap front among the riffraff on Cedar
Street, just to keep from having to go back to his aunt's and eat crow, had become more
important to him than his innate pride, his manhood, his honor. Uncle Tomism,
acceptance, toadying—all there in its most rugged form. One way to be a nigger. Other
Negroes did it other ways—he did it the hard way. The same result—*a nigger* (p. 132).

It is never ascertained whether or not Mr. Shelton saw Joe. In any case, it is
this probability that drives Joe to action. "He stood there, unable to breathe,
feeling as foolish and idiotic as a hungry man leaving a cathouse where he'd
spent his last two bucks. Then rage scalded him from tip to tow. He flung open
the door to spring into the room, slipped on a shoe and went sprawling, the wire
garrote cutting a blister across the back of the fingers of his left hand" (p. 130).
As Joe Wolf has tried to "get it funny," Himes presents a potentially slapstick
scene less the irony of which is lost in the pathos. Joe's leap from the closet in
which he has been imprisoned leads not into freedom but into a more existential
confinement where he is both prisoner and jailer. The realization that he too is a
"nigger" shames him; he wants "to just crawl away somewhere and die" (p.
132). His inability to act against oppression places him the same position as the
other blacks he knows. Keith Richards, the protagonist of "All God's Chillun
Got Pride" (1944; pp. 239–46), becomes proud enough to react against being a
nigger and ends up in a guardhouse. Joe Wolf is incapable of overcoming his
oppression and his fear.

Joe's interior monologues followed by a short but intense bursts of violence
make the ending somewhat anticlimactic. The sudden activity juxtaposed with
Joe's final discovery deprive the truth of having the impact it deserves. The
ineffectuality stems not from Himes' philosophy—he had already discovered
his potential for violence—but from the way in which he tries to handle the
theme. Joe's discovery of his imprisonment would have been much more
powerful if he had not burst from the closet, taken a pratfall, and attacked Fay
and Miss Lou.

"A Nigger" is perhaps most interesting as a psychological study and as an
introduction to many of Himes' major themes: Uncle Tomism, violence, race,
manhood. The elements of social protest, emotionalism, sociological and
psychological characterization, and intensity are shared by the other members
of the Wright School. And the reader, "on perceiving its responsibility for the
plight of the protagonist, is expected to alter its attitude toward race."

The idea of "nigger" is developed well through the ruminations of Joe Wolf.
But as a short story, just like all of Himes' short stories, "A Nigger" is a
lightweight. Himes' ideas towards violence seem to constantly lead him towards
some kind of writer's block; since 1969 he has published the collection *Black*

on Black and his two-volume autobiography, but no fiction. As Margolies notes:

There can be little question that the tone of Himes's work has changed since his departure for Europe. As he himself noted he can no longer bring himself to write protest novels. Which is not to say that any of Himes's intensely bitter racial feelings have waned. Perhaps the opposite is true. His years abroad have lent him time to brood about the injustices, the tragedy of it all.... And if we read these expatriate works correctly we see that, if anything, Himes's European perspective has left him even more pessimistic....[19]

The violence which runs throughout *Blind Man With a Pistol*, his last published novel, and "Prediction" (1969; pp. 281–87), his last published short story, has been wholesale, random, futile; Himes now believes "that only organized violence on the order of Viet Cong violence can effect social change."[20] His pessimism and brooding—what is perhaps still hate—are not creative but, as Himes himself realized a decade ago, "destructive" emotions.

Himes will be 68 this year. It can only be assumed that the life he has led— or has been forced to lead—has finally destroyed whatever fictive powers he ever possessed. Perhaps Chester Himes has been exploited; the ideology he has adopted to combat this exploitation has led to an impasse in his creative powers. Most likely the evaluation of his writing will agree with Bone's criticism of *If He Hollers Let Him Go* as "an impressive failure" and with Margolies' limited view that the detective novels are "some of his best prose."[21]

NOTES

1. Edward Margolies, *Native Sons: A Critical Study of Twentieth-Century Black American Authors* (New York, 1968), p. 87.
2. Chester Himes, *The Quality of Hurt: The Autobiography of Chester Himes* (London, 1972), p. 5.
3. Robert Bone, *The Negro Novel in America* (New Haven, 1965), p. 157.
4. Roger Whitlow, *Black American Literature: A Critical History* (Chicago, 1973), p. 115.
5. Bone, p. 158.
6. *Ibid.*, p. 157.
7. *Ibid.*
8. Bone, p. 173.
9. Whitlow, p. 117.
10. John A. Williams, "My Man Himes," in *Amistad 1* (New York, 1970), p. 27.
11. *A Case of Rape*, published only in French, is a novel virtually unknown to the American reading public.
12. Chester Himes, "Dilemma of the Negro Novelist in the United States," in John A. Williams, ed., *Beyond the Angry Black* (New York, 1966), pp. 74–75.
13. Edward Margolies, "Experiences of the Black Expatriate Writer: Chester Himes," *College Language Association Journal*, 15 (1972), 426.
14. "In certain respects I think Himes's works about a couple of hardboiled detectives represents some of his best prose. Possibly because he thought he was writing potboilers, possibly because he could relax more within the framework of the detective

genre, writing for a French audience about the kind of life he knew very well."
Margolies, p. 426. Himes claims he started writing detective fiction because he needed
the money. See Williams, p. 32.

15. Titillating, "one of Himes' favorite words in describing the effect black people
have on white people." Williams, p. 28.

16. Chester Himes, "Foreword," *Black on Black: Baby Baby Sister and Selected
Writings* (New York, 1973), pp. 7–8. Further references to this volume will appear in the
text.

17. In response to Williams' question concerning Himes' memory of detail:

Well, some of it comes from memory; and then I began writing these series [Série
Noire] because I realized that I was a black American, and there's no way of escaping
forty some odd years of experience, so I would put it to use in writing, which I had been
doing anyway.... Well, then I went back—as a matter of fact, it's like a sort of pure
homesickness—I went back, I was very happy, I was living there, and it's true. I began
creating also all the black scenes of my memory and my actual knowledge. I was very
happy writing these detective stories, especially the first one, when I began it. I wrote
those stories with more pleasure than I wrote any of the other stories. And then when I
got to the end and started my detective shooting at some white people, I was the
happiest. Williams, pp. 49–50.

18. Himes, "Dilemma of the Negro Novelist," pp. 78–79.

19. Margolies, pp. 426–27.

20. *Ibid.* Margolies also refers to an interview with Himes "granted to Michel Fabre
on June 12, 1970 and then edited and translated into French for *Le Monde*." p. 426,
footnote 6.

21. Bone, p. 173; Margolies, p. 426.

PRIMARY SOURCES

See Michel Fabre's "Chester Himes' published Works: A Tentative Check List" in *Black
    World*, 21 (March 1972), 76–78, for a complete listing.
Fuller, Hoyt W. "Traveler on the Long, Rough, Lonely Old Road: An Interview with
    Chester Himes." *Black World*, 21 (March 1972), 4–22, 87–98.
Himes, Chester. *Black on Black: Baby Baby Sister and Selected Writings*. New York, 1973.
———. "Dilemma of the Negro Novelist in the United States," *Beyond the Angry Black*.
    Ed. John A. Williams. New York, 1966.
———. *My Life of Absurdity: The Autobiography of Chester Himes*. Volume 2. New
    York, 1977.
———. *The Quality of Hurt: The Autobiography of Chester Himes*. Volume 1. London,
    1973.
Williams, John A. "My Man Himes: An Interview with Chester Himes," *Amistad 1*. Ed.
    John A. Williams and Charles F. Harris. New York, 1970, pp. 25–93.

SECONDARY SOURCES

Becker, Jens-Peter. "'To Tell It Like It Is': Chester Himes." In Sherlock Holmes and Co.:
    Essays zur englischen und amerikanischen Detektiv-literatur. München, 1975.
Bone, Robert. Negro Novel in America. New Haven, 1965.
Fabre, Michel. "A Case of Rape." Black World, 21 (March 1972), 39–48.
Lundquist, James. Chester Himes. New York, 1976.

Margolies, Edward. "Experiences of the Black Expatriate Writer: Chester Himes."
      College Language Association Journal, 15 (1972).
_____. "Race and Sex: The Novels of Chester Himes." In Native Sons: A Critical
      Study of Twentieth-Century Black American Authors. Philadelphia, 1968.
Milliken, Stephen F. Chester Himes: A Critical Appraisal. Columbia, 1977.
Reed, Ishmael. "Chester Himes: Writer." Black World, 21 (March 1972), 24–38, 83–86.
Whitlow, Roger. Black American Literature: A Critical History. Chicago, 1973.

The Black American Short Story in the 20th Century: A Collection of Critical Essays
(Amsterdam: B. R. Grüner, 1977). Pp. 85–97.

The Use of the Doppelganger or Double in Chester Himes' *Lonely Crusade*

Ralph Reckley

Chester Himes' second novel *Lonely Crusade* has not received the critical attention it merits. Critics have praised it for its protest and its naturalistic tendencies, or damned it for its Communistic implications, but so far no one has bothered to study the novel to ascertain how skillfully Himes uses doubles throughout the novel to propound his philosophy of the emasculation of the Black male. This paper, therefore, will be concerned with analyzing three of Himes' Black male characters: Lee Gordon, Lester McKinley and Luther McGregor, so that we can better understand Himes' use of doubles.

Set in Los Angeles during the war year of 1943, *Lonely Crusade* is concerned with the efforts of Lee Gordon, a college educated Black, to recruit the Black laborers of Comstock Aircraft Corporation and organize them to form a local union. His success as an organizer is impeded on the one hand by Comstock Corporation and its major shareholder-manager, Lewis Foster, who is symbolic of the socio-economic complex which discriminates against Blacks and blocks their social mobility, and on the other by the Communist and communistic forces that would infiltrate the union for its own purposes.

In addition to Lee there are two other characters, Lester McKinley and Luther McGregor, who, in mental attitudes and social traits, act as doppelgangers or doubles to Lee. Robert Rogers, in his work, *A Psychoanalytic Study of the Double in Literature*, maintains that doubles and/or multiple characters might exist independently in a work but they are generally "fragments of some other characterological whole." Further, Rogers explains that there is doubling by division which involves "the splitting up of a recognizable, unified psychological entity into separate complementary distinguishable parts represented by seemingly autonomous characters."[1]

Using the terms decomposition, doubling and fragmentation as synonyms (terms which will also be used in this paper as synonyms), Rogers maintains that a doppelganger might be a secret sharer or an opposing self. The secret sharer is a latent decomposition that has been "compounded and fused within the crucible of art by the catalytic heat of creative fire."[2] According to Rogers such a double is difficult to define, not because he may exist as an independent entity, but rather because he is so deeply woven into the structure of the work that he becomes difficult to identify as a double.

The opposing self is the opposite of its double: for example, the bad self and the guardian angel, the normal self and the diabolical self. The opposing self might also symbolize possible alliances and divisions among the Id, Ego, and Super Ego.[3]

Lester McKinley and Luther McGregor embrace Robert Rogers' definitions of doubles because they seem to exist independently of the protagonist. They are fully aware of their environment, and psychologically they function autonomously. However, the doubling motif which girds the novel, the coupling of incidences, both internal and external, the relationship between Lee and the decompositions—their affinities and their antagonism, and the similarities of their names—all suggest that Lee Gordon is a composite character and that Lester McKinley and Luther McGregor are the components that formalize the composition of the protagonist, Lee.

While Lester and Luther are not mirror images of Lee, there is ample evidence in the novel which indicates that these three characters are bound together in more than a haphazard relationship. For example, all three are involved with Foster and Comstock Aircraft Corporation. All three are fighting the socio-economic-industrial complex. All three are boxed in by discrimination.

However, the most obvious doubling technique in the novel, one which indicates that Himes' use of doubles could have been a conscious effort, is the naming of the characters: Lee Gordon, Lester McKinley, and Luther McGregor. At once the similarity strikes the reader as more than coincidental. It becomes obvious that phonetically the names are similar, especially in the persistent use of liquids in the first names—Lee, Lester, Luther. Linguistically, it appears as though the novelist wants us to see these three figures as one composite character. The mystery surrounding McKinley's name also encourages speculation of the doubling motif in the novel. The character changes his name to Lester McKinley after he becomes an adult, an act which might imply that during his formative years he conceived of himself as Lee, for as this essay will indicate, they do have similar experiences.

One finds too, on perusing the novel, that the similitude of names blurs the characters in the reader's mind; as a result, a reader could easily mistake Lester for Luther, or Luther for Lee. This identity crisis is especially true in the case of James Lundquist, who has published recently a critical study of Himes. In his work, *Chester Himes*, Lundquist makes several references to Lester McKinley, but he accidentally refers to Lester McKinley as Luther McKinley.[4] While Lundquist does not discuss the doubling technique in the novel, subconsciously he sees Luther and Lester as one. The fact that a critic confuses these characters suggests that there is a need to study Himes' use of the double in *Lonely Crusade*.

It was stated earlier that the minor characters are not mirror images of the protagonist but rather extensions of him. A close analysis of the experiences of the characters, Lester and Luther, in comparison with the experiences of the composite, Lee, will demonstrate their similarities (and apparent differences) by establishing how they help to complete the character of Lee.

As a youngster, Lee was informed by one of his teachers that Blacks were heathens and that many of them were cannibals. Attending a predominantly white school, Lee observed the white males to see if there were any differences between whites and blacks that would make whites superior. Finding no differences between them and him, he hid in the girls' locker room to see if they were different. The Gordons were harried out of town for their son's act.

The family moved from Pasadena to Los Angeles, but one night while Lee's father was coming home from his janitorial job, he was accidentally shot and killed by a police officer who thought that he was a burglar. The city dismissed the killing as a natural mistake, implying that all Blacks were burglars. The traumatic experiences of Lee's youth terrified him. Because of the incidents, Lee suffered from "pure and simple fear of white folks"; further, he came to the conclusion that his destiny would be governed by the whims of whites.

As a college educated adult, Lee could not find employment for which he had been trained. The constant discriminatory practices of prospective employees, despite President Roosevelt's Executive Order 8802, turned Lee Gordon into a neurotic. The protagonist describes his emotional state in this way:

If you have never lain sleepless for seven straight nights, your navel drawing into your spine at the slightest sound, your throat muscles contracting into painful strictures, terrified by the thought of people whom you have never seen and might never see, then you would not understand. Living in the world outnumbered and outpowered by a race whom you think wants to hurt you at every opportunity.[5]

The image presented here is one of a broken man. The sleeplessness, the constricting of the abdominal muscles, the tightness of the throat, and above all, the unknown fear of unknown people—all indicate that Lee is at the breaking point. Where Lee has reached that point Lester, his double, has passed it.

Lester McKinley's experiences parallel those of Lee's. If anything, they are more dramatic. Growing up in Georgia, Lester suffered from the same kind of racial pressures his other self, Lee, experienced. At the age of twelve he witnessed the lynching of a Black man, and from that day he had an overwhelming compulsion to kill whites. Lester attended Atlanta University and became a brilliant scholar in Latin, but his homicidal tendencies overpowered him. As a result, he left the South and moved to Albany, New York, hoping that his psychopathic inclinations would abate. Finding no respite in the North, he visited a psychiatrist who suggested that he marry a white woman and that such a union would lessen his compulsion to kill white men. Lester married a white woman and settled in California, but Lester, like Lee, could not find employment for which he had been trained. Prejudice and discrimination, combined with his compulsion to kill whites, had warped Lester's personality and rendered him insane. He had reached the stage where he was now.

Sitting in his living room, plotting the murder of Lewis Foster, McKinley knew that he was insane, but the knowledge did not terrify him because he was through fighting it. He would kill this white man he resolved, and if that didn't do any good he would kill himself.[6]

Lee's and Lester's experiences are the same, for Lee also believed that he had been "oppressed by white people to the point of criminal compulsion." But where Lee becomes passive and internalizes his fear, Lester becomes aggressive and seeks release in the external world. (It should be noted, however, that while Lester plans murder, he never commits murder.) Lester is Lee driven to extremes by a society which humiliates and degrades him. Lundquist maintains that Lee and Lester share many impulses, but that Lee lacks Lester's craze "only because his [Lee's] despair has not yet become so deep."[7] I contend that Lester's desperation is no greater than Lee's. Lester is Lee, a psychotic Lee who objectifies his psychopathic tendencies.

In addition to Lester's and Lee's traumatic experiences there is other evidence of doubling in their moral traits and in their social stance which yokes the two characters together. For example, both Lester and Lee are college educated, and because of their education, both have a tendency to be contemptuous of Blacks who are not educated. Both are under-employed, both are propositioned by Lewis Foster to betray the union; both refused. Both are embroiled in domestic problems because they cannot meet their obligations. And finally, both are destroyed because they refuse to be less than men in the white man's world. These parallels are not accidental. They are indicative of the doubling technique found throughout the novel.

That Lester is Lee's alter ego is exemplified in yet another manner. Lee sees himself as an honest individual surrounded by unprincipled Communists and industrialists. Lee projects this attribute of honesty to Lester. He conceives of Lester as the only source of truth in a jungle of conspirators. When attacks and counter-attacks are made by both Communists and industrialists and Lee loses his perspective, he turns to Lester. On several occasions he tries to reach McKinley because he believes that McKinley would be sympathetic and honest. He "was positive that Lester knew the truth" and would help him to gain a new perspective of his dilemma. Lee's projecting one of his own character traits on to Lester and his expecting sympathy from Lester suggest that there is a common bond between the two characters.

Luther McGregor is the other component of the character, Lee. Where Lester is an extension of Lee, Luther becomes the opposing self. Where Lee has an affinity for Lester he despises Luther. But Luther has the intestinal fortitude to act—a quality which is lacking in Lee and to some extent in Lester.

Little is known of Luther McGregor except that he is from Mississippi where he has spent time on a chain gang. A former WPA worker, he was sunning himself on a Los Angeles beach when a rich white woman picked him up and took him home as her paramour. Another white woman, Mollie, stole him from his first lover.

McGregor is not only a gigolo, he is a card-carrying Communist and a part-time union organizer. He is neither handsome nor intelligent. Mollie refers to him as her Caliban with a pygmy brain. He is further described by the omnipotent narrator in this manner:

Fully as tall as Lee, his six-foot height was lost in the thickness of his torso and the width of his muscular shoulders that sloped like an ape's from which hung arms a good foot longer than the average man's. His weird, long-fingered hands of enormous size and grotesque shape ... hung placidly at his side, and his flat splayed feet seemed planted firmly in the mud. He wore a belted light-tan camel's hair overcoat over a white turtle-neck sweater above which his flat-featured African face seemed blacker than the usual connotation of the word.[8]

Lee and Luther also differ in their racial assumptions. Lee believes his color is a handicap, and as a result, he rejects his Blackness. Luther, on the other hand, accepts himself for what he is. He takes advantage of his racial features. Arriving at the conclusion that all the white world saw in him was a "nigger," Luther becomes a professional Black who insists that whites will have to pay to exploit his Blackness. He informs Lee:

Look, man, as long as I is black and ugly white folks gonna hate my guts. They gonna look at me and see a nigger. All of 'em Foster, and the white folks in the party and the white woman in the bed, but I is always gonna make it pay off, man.... 'Cause I is gonna be they nigger and they proof and make 'em pay for it.[9]

Luther is also different from Lee in his attitude toward white women. Lee deserted his Black wife, Ruth, for Jackie Folks, a white friend who was really a Communist agent sent to gain his confidence and to sabotage his plans for the union. To Lee, Jackie was a lady, his "immortal woman." Luther, on the other hand, saw no saving grace in the white female. Molly, his paramour, wanted him for one reason and he realized that fact. He was her "air hammer," her "fire and bone" and steel-driving man.

On the narrative level Luther demonstrates all of the character traits Lee detests. Luther is unscrupulous. He is cunning. He is anti-social. He hates society and he doesn't hide his hate. Industry attempts to manipulate him, but he outmaneuvers industry instead. He would brutalize and/or kill anyone who threatens his well-being, and his cynical attitude towards his women borders on hate. On the psychological level, however, all of the traits that Luther exhibits are present in Lee. Although Lee does not verbalize his thoughts, his animosities towards Foster and the industrial complex are just as strong as Luther's. And like Luther, he is always thinking how he could manipulate them to his advantage. While he does not release his aggression on those whites who affront or humiliate him, he releases his hostilities on his wife by beating and raping her. He does not want to admit it, but he realizes, as Luther said, that he is just a stud and a pimp to his white lover. For even Jackie admits to Lee: "I'd be your white whore and make you a hundred thousand dollars and the proudest black man who ever lived."[10] Physically, and on the narrative level, then, Lee and Luther appear to be different, but the psychic similarities suggest that they share, conjointly, the same thoughts, the same emotions. And it is these thoughts and emotions which suggest that Luther is a decomposition. He is Lee's opposing self.

Another suggestion of doubling is found in Luther's behavior towards Lee. Luther's familiarity with the protagonist intimates a foreknowledge of Lee. On their initial meeting Luther presents himself as though the introduction should remind Lee of past experiences. Lee's hesitation causes Luther to insist: "You know me! I'm Luther, man, I'm Luther"[11] Luther further implies that he had known Lee for a long time. He explained that it was he who caused the union to hire Lee. When Luther drives Lee home he continues this behavior. He stalks into Lee's house and pokes around as though he lived there, as though he were Lee. Luther's acts might be attributed to his uncouthness. I suggest, however, that Luther's prescience is an indication of Himes' double motif.

Still another example of doubling is evidenced in Luther's killing of Paul Dixon. Paul and several other deputies, under the aegis of Foster, had brutally beaten Lee when he refused to accept money to betray the union. As a result of this encounter Lee wanted to kill Paul. (Lee's thoughts are conveyed to us through Ruth, his wife.) However, it is Luther who, in their second encounter with Paul, stabbed him to death when he, Luther, suspected Paul of duping them out of their fair share of the loot. In killing Paul, Luther becomes Lee's defense against external aggression in that he acts as a surrogate for Lee.

So far, we have limited our discussion to Lee and his doubles. However, in looking at the protagonist and his components, it becomes obvious that certain parallels exist between them and their creator which suggest that doubling exists between the component character and the novelist, Chester Himes.

For example, all three of the characters are emasculated and eventually destroyed either physically or psychologically. Luther McGregor is shot to death by the police, and when the novel ends policemen are about to shoot Lee Gordon. Lester McKinley, who has reached that state of complete social alienation and mental and emotional instability, literally runs from Los Angeles. Himes had the same experiences in California as his characters did. He maintains that when he went to California he was full of hopes. He had great aspirations, but race prejudice in Los Angeles prevented him from realizing his potential, and not being able to realize his goals he became bitter and frustrated. When he went to California he was emotionally stable. He states, however, that when he left he was shattered.

All three of the characters either conceived of murder or committed murder because of racial oppression. And Himes, like his creations, affirms that he not only believed himself to be capable of murder but that he might be forced to commit murder in order to defend his honor or his life.[12] All three of the characters had stormy affairs with white women. Himes' first autobiography, *The Quality of Hurt*, seems to be concerned, for the most part, with his disastrous affairs with white women.

In addition to the similarities Himes shares with the characters in general, there are psychic features and/or social experiences that Himes shares with each of the fragmented characters. Luther, for example, is given to bursts of violent temper, a trait demonstrated in his attitude toward his paramour, Mollie, and his killing of Paul Dixon. And Himes said that while he was living in Spain, he suffered from "blind fits of rage in which it seems my brain [had] been demented." Luther spent time on a Mississippi chain gang and Himes spent time in the Ohio State Penitentiary. Like Lester, Himes had attended college, and like his intellectual double, he could not find a job for which he had been trained. (During a period of three years in California Himes says he had twenty-four jobs. Twenty-two of these assignments were as a common labourer or a domestic, and two were semi-professional.) Also like Lester, Himes suffered emotionally because of his inability to find suitable employment.

Himes states that he suffered from periods of blankness, periods during which he could not account for his actions. Lee, the protagonist of *Lonely Crusade*, suffers from like attacks. Himes was jealous of his wife's success. He says:

It hurt me for my wife to have a better job than I did and be respected and included by her white co-workers, besides rubbing elbows with many well-to-do blacks of the Los Angeles middle-class who would not touch me with a ten-foot pole. That was the beginning of the dissolution of our marriage.[13]

In the novel, Lee, the protagonist, and Ruth, his wife, have the self-same problem. Lee cannot find employment while his wife has a white-collar post. Because of her working with whites, Lee accuses her of conspiring with them to emasculate him. In short, Lee's marriage, like Himes', disintegrates because his spouse has a better job.

All three of the characters, individually and collectively, have experiences that parallel Himes' own experiences. Further, all three display character traits common to their creator. It is fair to conjecture, then, that the characters, individually and as a composite represent aspects of Chester Himes and that they function as surrogates for Himes. Like Richard Wright, Himes felt the need to release his aggression, but not wanting to vent his hostilities on society, he created combative characters and lived vicariously through them.

By using characters as surrogates for himself, Himes probably purged himself of those emotional tensions that plagued him. Within the novel, however, the doubling technique has other values. By creating the composite character, Himes gives us a triple view of the effects of discrimination on the black male. Robert Rogers stated that one aspect of doubling deals with the alliances and the divisions among the Id, the Ego and the Super Ego. If we conceive of Lee as representing the Ego, the balance between the two extremes, and Luther as the Id, and Lester as the Super Ego, we might conclude that when racial pressures affect us at the primal level we could react violently as Luther McKinley did. When they affect us at the level of the higher self we could attempt to control our aggression, but in so doing, we could become psychotic as Lester McKinley did. When they affect us on the level of the ego, we could become like Lee, spiritually and physically emasculated.

Finally, the doubling technique preserves the integrity of the protagonist, Lee Gordon. Our moral sensibilities would be stunned if Lee behaved as Luther did. On the other hand, Lee would become the object of pity if he behaved as McKinley did. However, through the technique of doubling, the integrity of the protagonist is preserved and Himes still has the opportunity to bring before the reader aspects of Lee's thoughts and actions. The doubling technique results in complexity of structure in the novel. Further, it intensifies Himes' protest theme by giving us not one but three examples of the effects of racism on the black male.

NOTES

1. Robert Roger, *The Double in Literature* (Detroit: Wayne State University Press, 1970), p. 6.

2. Rogers, p. 40.

3. Rogers, p. 62.

4. James Lundquist, *Chester Himes* (New York: Frederick Ungar Publishing Company, 1976), p. 58.

5. Chester Himes, *Lonely Crusade* (New York: Alfred A. Knopf, Inc., 1947), p. 126.

6. *Lonely Crusade*, p. 71.

7. Lundquist, p. 58.

8. *Lonely Crusade*, p. 28.

9. *Lonely Crusade*, p. 329.

10. *Lonely Crusade*, p. 286.

11. *Lonely Crusade*, p. 29.

12. Chester Himes, *The Quality of Hurt* (New York: Doubleday and Company, Inc., 1972), p. 76.

13. *The Quality of Hurt*, p. 75.

CLA Journal, 20:4 (June 1977), 448–458.

Chester Himes
and the Art of Fiction
Angus Calder

Part I

i

Literature is too serious a matter to be taken altogether seriously. The books which people read in moments of relaxation, however casually they are picked up, no matter how escapist the pleasure taken in them, influence them more than superficially. They present myths, they provide worldscapes, they insinuate values. It is time that intellectuals in East Africa should divert some of the energy which they now devote to telling people what they *should* read to examining what people actually *do* read; it is time for a descent into the hectically coloured world of the imported imagination.

The most popular writers in Kenya, from my own observation, are not James Ngugi and Grace Ogot; they are Peter Cheyney, James Hadley Chase, Ian Fleming and Harold Robbins, the masters of the quick-talking, quick-shooting, quick-sex, cynical best-seller. While literati through the newspapers extol the nation-building merits of African novels and poems, the cultural battle is being lost on the streets of Nairobi and the beaches of Mombasa, where the myths accepted are those of Hollywood and the Cold War, where the worldscape viewed through books is that of a cosmopolitan, Americanised elite, and where the values imbibed are those which condone easy money, easy violence and easy lays.

It is time that East African critics began to analyse and take apart, as publicly as possible, the pseudo-aristocratic but in fact super-bourgeois Bond myth, for instance; as George Orwell many years ago exposed the sheer nastiness of James Hadley Chase.[1] But such analysis will show how very important it is that the new Africa should develop its own brands of popular fiction. A best-seller need not be a bad book. The thriller may be a work of art. A novel concerned with sex is not necessarily immoral. In fact, most of the major works in most literatures have been written in 'popular' forms. It is the strength of a Sophocles, a Po Chu-yi, a Seami, a Shakespeare, a Dickens, a Tolstoy or a Brecht that he writes in forms acceptable to a wide public and draws sustenance from the popular culture of his day. The humour of the streets overflows in the plays of Aristophanes; folklore and popular culture pervade the novels of Scott and Dickens.

The novel in Africa, written by Africans, is in some danger of perishing from its own high seriousness. So many painstaking, painful, descriptions of village life viewed with the self-conscious eyes of the exile and stultified by the attempt to prove to the world that rural Africans are not people but lay saints. So many stereotyped cameos of corruption in high places. More dangerously still, perhaps, in novels like *The Interpreters, The Beautyful Ones Are Not Yet Born* and Kibera's *Voices in the Dark,* so much intellectualism. Can *anyone* without Kibera's education get much from his novel? Where has the writer gone who, in *Potent Ash,* showed promise of developing a lively mode of dealing with the village and the servants' quarters?

Against the bores and the brilliant hermits we can set Ngugi, Achebe, Oyono, Ousmane—writers with the classic virtues of clarity and proportion whose books should deservedly form part of the common property of a continent. They are writers whose novels are about, and for, common men. But they are too few, and their books are not built for weary minds seeking relaxation after a day's work.

What about Ekwensi, too glibly dismissed very often as a mere 'entertainer', but in fact a writer with 'serious' preoccupations? Even at his worst he is most readable. The trouble with Ekwensi, except in that underrated novel *Jagugi Nana,* is that his moralising is inept and his values are inadequate. He flounders into sentimentality when he attempts to set against the confused and debased values of his city people—whores, hustlers, bandleaders, political bosses—a romantic idealisation of rustic values on the one hand or bourgeois values of the shallowest species on the other. Thus, Sango in *People of the City* and Iyari in *Beautiful Feathers* settle for bourgeois 'success' and bourgeois domesticity as a valid release from their confusion.

Recently, two East African writers have published novels in a 'popular' style. Eneriko Seruma's attempt, in *The Experience,* to marry dash and punch to the theme of race relations shows more promise than achievement; the effect is one of vigorous caricature. Charles Mangua's *Son of Woman,* in spite of its treacherously bourgeois conclusion, looks already like a solid beginning for an authentically popular application of the novel form in East Africa. The over-hanging 'serious' themes are all there—colonialism, crime and corruption, city *versus* country—but they are explored without self-defeating portentousness. The people are solid, like Breughel's—far from any ideal, but full of life. The pace is fast and the book is funny, not in the 'dry titter' category where *Voices in the Dark* falls, but in the 'belly-laugh' club.

But Mangua's success is achieved at the expense of over-obvious imitation of Peter Cheyney. One can believe that there are people in Nairobi who talk like his hero Dodge, because one has met them; they, too, have read Cheyney. But when *all* the characters talk in a racy mid-Atlantic idiom, the effect cannot be convincing. And there are much better models than Cheyney.

There is Georges Simenon. There is Raymond Chandler. And there is Chester Himes, the author of the popular Harlem crime thrillers. My purpose in this essay is to establish, through a consideration of Himes, that a 'popular' novelist may be a more effective 'serious' novelist than most of his 'serious' contemporaries. The case shouldn't need proving—Dickens has been there for a hundred years as blatant evidence in its favour. But it does, because 'serious' critics are infested with all kinds of irrelevant notions about what 'serious' achievement in fiction consists of; and for ninety of those hundred years, until his very recent comeback, Dickens has been snubbed by 'serious' critics. Graham Greene, a major writer with intense moral and political commitments, has been curiously underrated, perhaps because he has written thrillers and 'entertainments' for the mass market. Chandler, one of the finest prose stylists of our time and a piercing critic of the moral inanity of Southern California, is relegated to minor status. One could go on with books, but examples from other art forms make the same point. In spite of the revolutionary skill of its best exponents, and its world-wide impact, jazz is still automatically discounted as non-art by most 'serious-minded' people (including African intellectuals who consistently fail to recognise it as the most developed and influential artistic expression, in modern times, of black genius.) Such serious-minded people, rendered blind and spastic by their rigorous solemnity, will accept a scrappy, pretentious film by Jean-Luc Godard as 'art', but will ignore the magnificent craftsmanship of Anthony Mann, who chose to reveal his artistry and his seriousness in Westerns and film 'epics'.

The excursion into jazz and cinema is most pertinent to an essay on Himes. He is a writer drawing his material from the black American culture which produced jazz. And like Greene and Ousmane he is a brilliant technician in narrative who has absorbed certain advances in story-telling which the cinema has promoted, with his hard bright images and his deft cuts. But it is necessary, first of all, to consider him in relation to the history of the novel.

ii

The publisher's blurb inside the front cover of Himes's *Crazy Kill,* in the Panther paperback, cites a gentleman otherwise unknown to me called Anthony Boucher on Himes's 'Perverse blend of sordid realism and macabre fantasy humour'. What interests me here is the suggestion that 'macabre fantasy' is necessarily different from 'realism'. Alas, I fear it isn't. I would refer, if there were space, to first-hand accounts of tortures enacted upon slaves before 'emancipation', of the conduct of staff in German concentration camps, and of the bombing of Dresden, Nagasaki and Hiroshima.

I suspect many readers will react to Himes as critics for so long reacted to Dickens; they will enjoy him, but will find him an author who departs too far from 'realism' to be taken 'seriously'. There is a tendency abroad which confuses 'realism' with what I will call 'normalism', because, bless its noble heart, it confuses 'reality' with 'normality'.

A list of major novelists who present us in their works with 'normal' people would include most of the writers used as an explicit or concealed standard by contemporary British and American critics. It would almost complete the currently accepted 'tradition' of the 'classic' novel; from Fielding to Scott and Jane Austen, to George Eliot, Turgenev, Tolstoy (in *War and Peace* and *Anna Karenina),* Henry James, Chekhov, Hardy and Forster.

These writers, to be crudely brief and briefly crude, stress in their presentation of human nature those qualities which, binding men together in social fellowship, make 'normality' possible. To co-exist in a reasonably orderly fashion men must be, in general, sociable, loving, pious and good-humoured, and this is how the 'normalist' novelist, in general, sees them. He works backward from the fact that the society he describes, or writes for, is stable, towards a definition of man as 'normal'. Against the standard provided by this definition, the anti-social, the cruel, the perverted and the pompous may be judged and condemned—not without compassion, but stringently. Affection for the scapegrace and the rebel is in order. Indeed, the rebel may sometimes suffer for embodying the 'normal' virtues more purely and strongly than the people around him, as Jane Austen's Fanny does in *Mansfield Park* and Tolstoy's Pierre in *War and Peace.* But the tragic Anna Karenina must be judged, ultimately, by the standards of the home-making, loyal, long-suffering Dolly. The continuities in *Howard's End* ultimately weigh more than the acts of rebellion. For a normalist writer the social system, even if it is not perfect, is perfectible without violent change. Drastic social upheavals would involve widespread violations of the 'normal' code. You can't make a revolution without breaking norms.

In the American novel, which reflects a society based on change and unsettlement, the norm works rather differently. What one finds in a Twain, or a Hemingway, or a Bellow is the notion that man, while essentially not sociable, is nevertheless basically pious, loving etcetera. It is the glory of the individual that he is good, as Huck Finn is good. Positive goodness is vividly present in the riff-raff of the countryside and the sweepings of the slums of Europe. This after all is what the American Dream is based on, and for the novelist who accepts the Dream it provides a climate of facile Pelagianism.

But now let us consider a list running parallel to the first. Sterne, to begin with. Balzac, Emily Bronte, Dickens, Gogol, Tolstoy (in *Resurrection),* Dostoevsky, Melville, and in our own time Faulkner, Greene and V. S. Naipaul. It is a roster as formidable as the first one, including as many writers of steady appeal, and perhaps more of widespread and enduring influence. But Sterne, for all his more immense and decisive contributions, gets less space in Eng Lit books than Fielding. And this list is much less 'respectable'. These men are acclaimed, or mistrusted, as brilliant oddballs, not stalwart 'classics'. They are laws, we are given to understand, unto their grotesque and misshapen selves; great writers, perhaps, but impossible to hold up as standards.

And if we believed a quarter of what they tell us about human nature, we would either go mad or resolve to change the world which permits such distortions. These writers may be described as 'abnormalists'. It is not that they are 'anti-normal', not that they are insensible of the virtues extolled in Mosaic Law and in the sayings of Confucius. They are, on the contrary, passionate moralists. But their work shows how far human nature, almost always, falls short of a working application of the ideal. Goodness itself in their worlds is so abnormal that demented Uncle Toby, illiterate Joe Gargery and epileptic Myshkin are its appropriate embodiments. After Father Zossima makes his immense speech in favour of virtue, Dostoevsky, wickedly, lets him die, rot and stink. As these writers portray it, the nature of man is dubious; his societies are radically unsettled, his future is insecure. He is lonely rather than sociable (but he is not necessarily individualistic). He is obsessive rather than sensible. He is capable of fierce irrational loves and hatreds, monstrous impieties, and terrible breaches of faith and order. He is Vautrin, he is Heathcliff, he is Chichikov. Just as perversely, he is Micawber and Biswas. He is St. Francis and he is Hitler, and he is also Charlie Chaplin.

But 'comedy' in the Aristotelian sense doesn't apply very well to the abnormalists, although they certainly include the funniest writers in their number. Naipaul, in his description of the rootless, racially divided Trinidad society, concluded that by a definition which sees 'comedy' as depending on 'a strong work of social convention', the West Indian writer 'is incapable of comedy.' As he defines it, the situation is, in my sense, inherently 'abnormal':

There is no set way in Trinidad of doing anything. Every house can be a folly. There is no set way of dressing or cooking or entertaining. Everyone can live with whoever he can get wherever he can afford. Ostracism is meaningless; the sanctions of any clique can be ignored. It is in this way, and not in the way of the travel brochure, that the Trinidadian is cosmopolitan. He is adaptable; he is cynical; having no rigid social conventions of his own, he is amused by the conventions of others. He is a natural anarchist, who has never been able to take the eminent at their own valuation. He is a natural eccentric, if by eccentricity is meant the expression of one's own personality, unhampered by fear of ridicule or the discipline of class.... The Trinidadian has no standards of morality.[2]

This moral anarchy expresses itself in his novels both as 'humour' (in the sense which applies also to Dickens) and as pathos; the pathos inherent in limitation and waste, where the noble word 'love' has no direct application and yet something like love is latent, exists and is thwarted. Because such excludes dignity, it excludes 'comedy'; it proliferates in absurdity. The great 'comic' writer Dickens and his great 'serious' disciple, Dostoevsky, operate alike on the basis of a world view where if God exists he is most loth to reveal His existence, and the powers effectively in control are named Accident, Despair and Laughter.

So also tragedy, where it conforms to the Aristotelian formula, is normalist. It involves an assault upon the dignity of man, heroically embodied by remarkable individuals, made by a Fate which has justice on its side. The assault may, as in *Antigone,* expose the internal contradictions of the norm; but Sophocles is the supreme normalist. We find abnormalism tampering already with tragic spirit in the works of his younger contemporary Euripides, in *The Bacchae* and *Women of Troy* teeter constantly on the brink of the Absurd. The Absurd is defined by the absence of either dignity or justice. The great abnormalist writers can display human nature neither as high', in Aristotle's sense, nor as 'low', because 'low' can only be defined by contrast with 'high'. For them, human nature is malleable, vulnerable, and amorphous; so fickle that even in the midst of chaos we may have Dickens's happy endings, or Dostoevsky's Alyosha existing as support for the proposition that *even* happiness and goodness may be possible.

I am not going to argue that 'abnormalist' writers are necessarily better than 'normalist' ones; my own favourites, as it happens, are found in each camp. My point is that critics conventionally talk as if sober truth lay with the normalists and inspired fantasy with the brilliant deviants. In fact, both kinds of viewpoint are equally selective, both kinds of viewpoint are equally 'true'. Societies do in fact cohere over long periods of time (two thousand five hundred years in the case of China) and large areas of space (as large as China.) Mysteriously, people are not always cutting each other up or torturing those they love. Dignity, that prodigy, manifests itself. Those novelists, the normalists, who select from reality tokens of coherence, stability and progress present not only ideals, but facts. The abnormalists tend to ignore those facts. But Auschwitz was a fact. The man who raped a little baby and gave it syphilis is a recent, local fact. Nairobi is a fact.

In practice my divisions have been both over-neat and unhistorical. (Such divisions invariably are, which is why we must use them with nervous caution.) The greatest normalist writers pay their tribute to the most unpleasant facts. The vision of Jane Austen may exclude violence, but Chekhov's certainly doesn't. Conrad seems to me to be a normalist exploring the no-man's-land where norms break down. Lawrence, who thought Dostoevsky's people were sick, can hardly be accused of ignoring the forces of lust, obsession and violence, though he struggles, I think, for a norm. Most contemporary novelists reflect the influence of both normalist and abnormalist predecessors.

But then, in the twentieth century the world has looked less and less like a place where people can live even moderately happily ever after, or where delicate moral discriminations are the most vital of our concerns. In the theatre the Absurd and the Epic have advanced to the point where comedy and tragedy no longer have important existence. In poetry, rhetoric collapses and the accidental plays a larger role. Capitalism, colonialism and science between them have reduced 'normality' to threatened pockets over the entire world. If British critics in particular confuse 'normality' with 'reality', this clearly reflects the fact that they mostly live in such pockets, dwelling in quiet streets, teaching in unriotous universities. If you yourself happen to be doing all right, it is pleasant, indeed necessary, to believe that there is nothing much wrong with the world which cannot be ousted *à la* Forster, by a little more kindness here, a few more moral scruples there. Elsewhere, the cultural conflicts created by colonialism, the brute facts of capitalist exploitation and the explosion of perspectives by scientific discovery and technological change are much more obvious. Normalism will have to run very fast if it is to catch up with heart transplants. And how do you write a normalist novel about Mathare Valley?

In fact, normalism has always been at a disadvantage in the metropolis. The chaos of values in Dickens's London or Dostoevsky's Petersburg, with their hordes of social isolates of indeterminate class and marginal occupation, those freaks who do not meet but collide, who talk at each other rather than with each other, was surely not invention; in Nairobi we have the evidence before our eyes. Rather like Naipaul's Trinidad, Nairobi is characterised by the absence of settled standards, where God, Ngai, Jok, Allah, Krishna, Kenyatta and Mammon are variously respected, in various permutations. and where the legless beggar beneath the Hilton is a symbol already reduced to cliché of the lack of any coherent system of social values. The modern city is at best a chaotic system of smaller communities, each separated from the others by race, class or religion, or by a combination of all three. At worst, it is a complex of isolation wards with no doctor in attendance.

Achebe in *Arrow of God* is a very convincing normalist tragedian; indeed, his most important success lies in persuading us that traditional Ibo society was sanely, validly 'normal'. (By contrast, Oyono in *The Old Man and The Medal* presents an African community where 'things have fallen apart' to the point where an 'abnormalist' style of characterisation is appropriate.) But Achebe's tragic normalism is sustained in *No Longer at Ease* only at the expense of drastic selectivity. The reeking streets of Lagos as Ekwensi at his best presents them would make nonsense, if much about them were included, of Achebe's liberal-humanist norms. If Armah in *The Beautyful Ones* excludes almost everything *but* rot and corruption, Achebe is open to the equal and opposite charge that he makes his Obi shadowy and even incomprehensible by excluding the ripe and reeking urban ambience which makes his lapse both partly excusable and almost wholly inevitable. It is significant that in *Man of the People,* a far more powerful book, Achebe takes several strides towards abnormalism. The major characters, when they switch at will from English to Pidgin to mother-tongue, exemplify thus the absence of 'normality' in urban Africa, of which the celebrated 'clash of cultures' is both a cause and a symptom. The case against Ekwensi's worst writing, for that matter, is that he strives to make us judge his characters by 'normal' standards in a situation which, as he describes it, is wholly abnormal.

Nowhere more than in urban Africa do Marxist theories of alienation make obvious sense. When capitalism is dominant, as in our place and time, it is a further asset of the abnormalist writer that his methods can convey alienation directly, through 'grotesque' detail and 'imaginative' texture. The suppression by man of his own nature and his reduction of himself to the level of commodity, machine, tool and environment can be presented by the normalist on a theoretical level, as Conrad shows so memorably in *Nostromo,* but cannot be embodied (as it were) in description and characterisation, because alienation deprives man of the dignity which is indispensable to the normalist view of his nature. Gould and Nostromo continue to look and sound 'normal' while they are destroying themselves with the silver of the mine. But Gogol's Plyushkin or Dickens's Merdle represents, in his grotesque insentience, his horrifying lack of human substance, the social-psychological phenomenon on the material plane.

Obi acts out a moral drama typical of Lagos, but not rooted in Lagos; the normalist emphasises the separateness of man from his environment, his reputed ability to make significant moral choice. Whereas Armah's Man, the only remotely 'normal' human in a dehumanised world, moves through a dense current of urban particularities which locate the concept of corruption very aptly in the sewage system. For the abnormalist, men have capitulated to their environment; this is the point in common between Gogol's Sobakevich, looming bear-like among his bear-like furniture, Dostoevsky's Raskolnikov narrowed humanly by his narrow little room and Naipaul's Biswas whose soul is usurped by the image of a house.

Finally, the thriller form is especially useful both for a writer with an abnormalist imagination and one who wishes to cope somehow with the modern city. Along with alienation in capitalist society, and very much a part of it, come the division of labour and the isolation of man from man so perversely characteristic of the metropolis. Scott was probably the last novelist in a position to study and describe without effort the whole range of human working activities in coherent relationship to each other both in town and country; even so his Edinburgh viewpoint excluded the industrialism of Glasgow. With the growth of enormous cities, the ramification of specialised industries and the proliferation of intricate specialisations even in the service trades, and with mass-production, the occupations to which most men devote the greater part of their waking lives present an impossible subject for study, let alone for absorption into the literary imagination. It is the difference between the family grocer and the chain store, the blacksmith and the skilled aero-engineer, the apothecary and the brain surgeon, which I draw to your attention here.

Scott was the founder of the 'social novel'. Perhaps I should say 'societal novel', for by this term I refer to the work of fiction which aimed to present a study and a critique of a whole society, not just a study of individuals, groups or classes. (Jane Austen is not, in my sense, a 'societal' novelist.) But Scott wrote at precisely the moment when industrialisation and urbanisation were rapidly rendering his range inaccessible. Subsequent societal novelists might leave the city out, as George Eliot did in *Middlemarch* and as Hardy and Faulkner did in their respective creations of Wessex and of Yoknapatawpha County, but only at the expense of limiting their societal comment to untypical, because old-fashioned, situations. As fine a novelist as Joyce, tackling the city of Dublin in the most intensive fashion possible, was limited to the presentation of leisure activities, of men as consumers rather than producers, and even then to a petty-bourgeois segment of them.

But the eye of the journalist could still assemble, out of chance impressions, insightful deductions and systematic investigations, a much wider picture. The world of work, as Scott had referred to it, was lost and could never be wholly recaptured. But the homes, the streets, the physical types, of various kinds of workers need not be lost. The amazing novels of Dickens's middle age— *Dombey and Son, Bleak House, Little Dorrit* and *Great Expectations*— accomplished the feat of suggesting a whole society, railway workers as well as seamen, aristocrats as well as crossing sweepers, dancing masters as well as lawyers. It is an anti-social society, of freakish isolates; but the novel, as distinct from the society, is held together by the symbolism of a prose poet, and by a plot hingeing on crime, mystery and detection.

Crime slashes across the classes. Slum boys cosh rich ladies, swindles entangle rich and poor together. A single crime may involve all levels of society, as in *Bleak House,* where Dickens introduces Inspector Bucket, the first important detective in fiction. The criminal investigator, knocking on the doors of mansions and hovels alike, can traverse society in step with the inquisitive eye of the novelist-journalist.

Besides this, crime is not only a prevalent feature of cities which cannot be ignored, it raises, along with the question of justice for the individual, that of social justice, which in an abnormal situation by definition cannot exist. Dostoevsky's four great novels involve violent crime in the absence of evident justice. When Tolstoy finally confronted the city and the Russian proletariat, in *Resurrection,* his plot involved a fruitless quest for justice following a legal miscarriage of it. Richard Wright's *Native Son* is a classically simple and direct modern reworking of *Crime and Punishment.* The crime novel has hardly maintained its early promise. But Chandler follows Dickens, Dostoevsky and Tolstoy in his presentation of the relativity of justice in a class society; one law for the rich, as we all know perfectly well, and a much harsher one for the poor. Napoleon, as Raskolnikov points out, gets away with mass murders; why not me? Bigger Thomas, as Wright so memorably stresses, would be judged guilty of the crime which he never morally committed even if he hadn't physically committed it.

The case I wish to make for Chester Himes should by now be more or less clear. He is an author of best-selling detective stories, but this does not mean he need be taken lightly. He is an 'abnormalist', but this does not prevent him from being, in the best sense, a realist. His presentation of Harlem is densely detailed, to the point of apparent redundancy, but this richness of 'background' is associated, as in Dickens, with a view of character in which character and environment are morally indistinguishable. He is a 'societal' novelist, employing the useful convention of the crime thriller in order to ransack Harlem (conceived by him as a distinctive community) from east to west and from top to bottom. And he is a 'committed' novelist whose thrillers embody a splendidly intransigent refusal to come to terms with contemporary American values, to accept even one lie or subscribe to even one illusion. His crime stories are powerful fables: presenting the dehumanisation extant in any capitalist-racist situation.

He is a major novelist, as good as Wright, I think, and very much better than Baldwin or Ellison, to name the most fashionable Black American writers in White American circles. But even this comparison does him the obvious injustice which is bound to occur when a Black writer is compared only with other Blacks. I think he is a more profound writer than Chandler, and I think Chandler is a more profound writer than either Hemingway or Scott Fitzgerald.

It is time Himes is set in his proper place. One critic who made a start towards putting him there was Leroi Jones, a few years ago, when he wrote, 'One can find more moving writing in any of Chester Himes's bizarre detective novels than in most more "serious" efforts by Negroes, just because Himes's main interest must be in saying the thing like it is'[3] For those who think thrillers 'unrealistic' by definition, this verdict will seem self-contradictory. But it gathers weight from Himes's own remarks on the thriller form in a recent interview:

... No one, *no one,* writes about violence the way that Americans do. As a matter of fact, for the simple reason that no one understands violence or experiences violence like the American civilians do.... American violence is public life, it's a public way of life, it became a form, a detective story form. So I would think that any number of black writers should go into the detective story form.[4]

So in his own view, the thriller offers Himes not merely a suitable vehicle, but perhaps *the* most suitable vehicle for exposing and discussing the violence which he holds, with evident plausibility, to be the dominating and distinctive feature of American society. (One can argue about this viewpoint, but there are statistics which support it strongly.) I will add at this point only that I think that *Run Man Run,* by Himes, is perhaps the most fully convincing fictional treatment of violence which I have ever read.

iii

Himes has finished a volume of autobiography which is not yet to hand. It seems that he began to write novels after a wide experience of life on the lower reaches of American society, including a long spell in prison. He was in his late thirties when his first novel, *If He Hollers Let Him Go*[5] was published, in 1945. According to Himes, it was shaping up as a best-seller but the publishers wouldn't meet the demand by reprinting. In view of the book's dominantly proletarian character and its bracing refusal to be optimistic about the race situation, this is not surprising. However, Frantz Fanon was able to secure it, and was greatly impressed with Himes's psychological insight, though he distorts the plot considerably when he refers to it in *Black Skin White Masks.*[6]

In the following ten years, Himes published four more 'serious' novels: *Lonely Crusade* (1947); *Cast The First Stone (1952); The Third Generation* (1954) and *The Primitive* (1955). (These have been intermittently in print over the past few years, but I haven't managed to see them.) Meanwhile, Himes had migrated to France, where he became Richard Wright's close friend in the pioneer Black novelist's voluntary exile. In Baldwin's memoirs of the Paris scene, the figure of the 'tough and loyal Chester Himes' is made to shine out amongst the crowd of Wright's hangers-on; the adjectives define qualities which Himes, on the strength of his writings, values very highly.

Himes still lives in Europe.

It was for money that he began to write his Harlem detective stories, for a French publisher; all but the last of the series appeared initially in French. So did *Pinktoes* (1961), a 'pornographic' burlesque, on the theme of miscegenation (with variations), which finally established Himes as a best-seller in the USA. *Pinktoes,* like all Himes's writing, radiates magnificent intelligence, and from the sexual romping 'serious' satirical points emerge. But it must be regarded as thoroughly good fun rather than major fiction.

However, there is no necessary contradiction between writing for money and writing as an artist. As Himes himself reminds us, Dostoevsky produced major novels under extreme financial pressure: 'There was a man who wrote very rapidly and very brilliantly all the time, and the reason that he did so was that he needed money all the time.[7] So Edward Margolies seems to me to be begging questions when, in his survey of Black American writing, *Native Sons,* he dismisses the Harlem thrillers as 'lively pot-boilers'.[8]

Which brings us to Himes's critical status, as reflected in current works of reference by (white) academics. Robert A. Bone (in *The Negro Novel in America)* and David Littlejohn (in *Black on White)* concentrate on *If He Hollers Let Him Go* and establish something like a consensus with Margolies over that novel. It is seen as belonging to the 'school of Wright', as a 'protest' novel and as a 'race-war' novel. It is critically identified by Bone as 'an impressive failure with accent on the adjective'[9] and dismissed more lightly by the ineffable Littlejohn, who describes the hero as 'race-mad almost to the point of hysteria'.[10]

Several kinds of unhelpful preconception are involved in these verdicts. One involves the white predilection for casting black novelists as 'race' writers and then turning round to complain that they're nothing more. 'Himes has considerable narrative power,' says Margolies, 'and startlingly clear psychological insights. Perhaps what his novels now require is a European setting'.[11] ('Mr Joyce is a most interesting writer,' one might paraphrase: 'Perhaps what his fiction now requires is a Swiss setting'). There is a refusal to accept that the fact of race prejudice in the USA is no more intrinsically a 'narrow' theme than the factual relationship between marriage, money and class in early nineteenth century England which provided Jane Austen with virtually her whole subject matter. The typecasting of Himes as 'school of Wright' suggests, quite falsely, that he is imitative. In fact he is a very different novelist. He has what Wright lacks most of all, a gift for humour and satire, and the density of social detail which he offers contrasts sharply with the spareness of *Native Son.*

There are also the false assumptions which make many critics separate 'form' from 'content' before judging a novel in terms of its 'form'. Margolies makes the point that *If He Hollers* begins with such intensity that the build-up of tension desired in a novel cannot take place; so much, one might say, for *Crime and Punishment.* If the situation is diagnosed by Himes as one which produces constant tension, how can he honestly present it otherwise? Bone's conclusion is worth quoting:

> At bottom the problem is ideological: neither revenge nor accommodation is acceptable to Himes, and as a result, the novel flounders to an inconclusive finish.... The novel suffers ultimately from a one-to-one correlation between form and content: in portraying a divided personality, Himes has written a divided novel. But formless and chaotic is precisely what art cannot afford to be.[12]

But what if life is 'formless and chaotic'? And what about those notoriously 'formless and chaotic' writers, Dickens and Dostoevsky? Why *can't* form correspond to content? If Himes can see no immediate resolution of the problem he presents in the novel, must he lie, in effect, in order to satisfy the demands of academic aesthetics? Bone should be clear (but isn't) that when he objects to Himes's anti-climactic ending his objection is to the *content* of Himes's book. In my own opinion this ending is much more convincing than Ralph Ellison's consolatory word-play at the end of *Invisible Man,* which Bone considers 'quite possibly the best American novel since World War II'.[13]

The key word perhaps, is 'American.' The most obvious reason why white academic critics are not prepared to give Himes more than the devil's due is that he refuses to imply the soothing things which Ellison implies about race relations, to kowtow to the Frontier Spirit and the American Dream as Ellison does. Margolies remarks ominously that 'Himes, one suspects, regards the American scene as beyond redemption.'[14] So he clearly can't be a major American novelist, can he? What both critics want is a 'normalist' writer who will offer a suitably optimistic 'American' message.

It is worth looking at *If He Hollers* now, in order to defend Himes against such irrelevant criticism, and to present the positive virtues of his style, which are virtues still present in the Harlem thrillers.

The novel deals with Robert Jones, a well-educated black who is the first of his race to be employed as a 'leaderman' in a certain West Coast shipyard during the Second World War. Though in theory he has the same authority as a White leaderman, in practice he does not, and he is bitterly aware of the fact, which is proven when he is demoted for swearing back ('cracker bitch') at a white woman employee who calls him a nigger. He has a near-white, bourgeois girl friend, Alice, who urges him to accept the limitations imposed on coloured people by white racism and to become a successful black lawyer. 'You need some definite aim', she tells him, in her social-worker's idiom, 'a goal that you can attain within the segregated pattern in which we live.... There is no reason a Negro cannot control his destiny/within this pattern.' Bob, in a calm moment, replies, '... I've already made up my mind to conform ... But please don't tell me I can control my destiny, because I know I can't. In any incident that might come up a white person can use his colour on me and turn it into a catastrophe and I won't have any protection....'[15] What follows proves his point, and makes it simply impossible for him to conform. The white girl employee, Madge, frames him, putting him in a position where he seems to be raping her. The white workers beat him up. He runs from the police. Alice refuses to help him escape. The authorities, realising that the false charges against him won't stick, but not prepared to let him off, 'release' him on condition that he joins the army. The book ends with him marching off to join the army. Though the rape motif of *Native Son* is repeated in this book, Bob is nothing like Bigger Thomas. He is a tough and intelligent man who should clearly be accepted as free and equal in any society, not, like Bigger, a pitiful creature depraved by the slums. He is torn between conforming, accepting inferior status, and the futile revolt which his rage and frustration urge him to. At one moment he resolves to kill a white who has hit him and go, like Bigger, a proud man to the electric chair. He plots to seduce the white woman who insulted him, but in the end humiliates her by *not* taking her.

Meanwhile, Himes's subtle and moving presentation of Alice makes his point that compromise doesn't really solve anything very clear. Her brittle socialite poses mask a strain as constant as Bob's, and her Lesbian proclivities reflect the distortion wrought by this strain upon her personality. Himes views racism and its effects clinically, but with surprising compassion. He diagnoses its many varieties, from the Southern white 'cracker bitch', through the Fascist leader-man who takes Bob's job, to the pseudo-liberal employer and the well-meaning but uneasy Communist. It is a deforming disease, and the diagnosis seems to be that only the knife, only violence, can cure it.

This sober and powerful book already displays the essentials of Himes's style and vision. There is the 'brutal' realism beloved of Paperback blurb-writers, though I would prefer to call it 'clinical'. There are also vast resources of psychological subtlety, and of humour, which Himes deploys so easily that one takes them for granted. His very fine ear for dialogue is shown in the inconsequential exchanges between Bob's fellow black shipyard workers. They yield a strong flavour of the particularity of black culture, which is something Himes emphasises strongly; but they are also there to assist the making of another stern Himes point. Early in the novel, Bob thinks, 'We're a wonderful, goddamned race ... Simple-minded, generous, sympathetic sons of bitches. We're sorry for everybody but ourselves; the worse the white folks treat us the more we love 'em.'[16] Sure enough, Bob's black co-workers do nothing to support him when he is demoted, and work gratefully for the racist white replacement who is able, because he is white, to get them a cosier job in the yard. Himes diagnoses another disease; the black disease of feckless, happy-go-lucky indifference to the true interests of black people. The Harlem thrillers are concerned throughout with this disease.

My contention is that when the thrillers are set beside *If He Hollers* it is plain that Himes, in adjusting his methods to the pace obligatory in the thriller genre, does not violate the essentials of his serious style. The realism is as clinical, the dialogue is as vivid, and the view of character is essentially the same.

Himes has the gift of bringing a character to life in a few strokes. Here are two examples from *If He Hollers:*

> She was a small, compact, black-haired woman with sharp brown eyes and skin that was constantly greasy. She looked thirty and she was hard as nails. (The Boss's secretary)
> Dr. Harrison answered my ring. He was dressed in a brown flannel smoking jacket with a black velvet collar. He waved a soggy cigar butt in his left hand, stuck out his right. (Alice's father)[17]

The knack, as with any good novelist, is to give just enough detail to make the character vivid and distinctive, without slowing the story to a halt, and to make this detail significant. But I want to examine the direction established by Himes's characteristic choice of detail.

The woman described above is a kind of white person Himes likes; hard, no nonsense, unhypocritical. But he does not direct our sympathy towards her by emphasising anything obviously attractive about her. The selection of her 'greasy skin' for comment does give her fullness of bodily function, fullness of life, but it is at first sight disagreeable. The detail emphasises her *physical* life, and the phrase 'hard as nails' refers to a quality she has in common with inanimate objects; that the phrase is a cliché doesn't alter this point.

Harrison, whom Himes doesn't like at all, is first presented entirely in terms of his clothes and his cigar butt. The lush dress pins him down as a ostentatious black bourgeois. The soggy cigar butt deprives him of dignity, directs us to bodily function, and implies the sogginess of his compromised character. Both descriptions direct us towards a definition of man as animal, and as creature of his environment, rather than man as a spiritual entity capable of free motion.

In the Harlem thrillers, Himes presses on in this direction to the point where the possibility of free spiritual life is almost completely ruled out in our first meetings with his characters:

Imabelle was Jackson's woman. She was a cushioned-lipped, hot-bodied banana-skin chick with the speckled-brown eyes of a teaser and the high-arched, ball-bearing hips of a natural-born *amante*. (*A Rage in Harlem*, 7–8)[18]
He was a small, elderly man with skin like parchment, faded brown eyes, and long gray bushy hair. His standard dress was a tail coat, double-breasted dove-grey vest, striped trousers, wing collar, black ascot tie adorned with a gray pearl stickpin, and rimless nose-glasses attached to a long black ribbon pinned to his vest. (*A Rage in Harlem*, 13)

In the first description, of the fickle sex-pot who is probably the chief character in the novel, exact definition of the body, and appraisal of it in purely sexual terms, leaves no room for moral comment. H. Exodus Clay, the undertaker, *is*, essentially, his clothes, which define his function and his place in society. To repeat my earlier point; character and environment are morally indistinguishable.

The quick-fire style of the Harlem novels, where Himes is handling a vast number of characters in a small number of pages, certainly depends on something close to 'caricature'. But the underlying viewpoint is the same as in the remarkable second chapter of *If He Hollers*, perhaps the most original in the novel.

It is just Bob driving to work, picking up his workmates on the way, listening while they chaff each other. He is tense; his exposed position in the shipyard is giving him bad dreams. The manner of his driving illustrate his tenseness, but also his power, his capacity:

... I was coming up fast in the middle lane and some white guy in a Nash coupe cut out in front of me without signalling. I had to burn rubber to keep from taking off his fender; and the car behind me tapped my bumper. I didn't know whether he had looked in the rear-view mirror before he pulled out or not, but I knew if he had he could have seen we were a carful of coloured—and that's the way I took it. I kept on his tail until I could pull up beside him, then I leaned out of the window and shouted, "This ain't Alabama, you peckerwood son of a bitch. When you want to pull out of line, stick out your hand."[19]

It takes an abnormalist to recognise how car driving exposes the sharp edges of character; simply as a 'realistic' description of traffic behaviour, the passage is very good. But it also establishes the character of Bob, who unlike Clay or Imabelle is subjected to depth study, in relation to his environment, which is seen to surround him and also to trigger him. An image of California is established; a place where everyone wants to get ahead fast, like Bob, and where friction and collision are inevitable. The physical ambience and the moral ambience are identical; they dominate Bob and determine his behaviour. California is a trap. Only if he escapes and redefines himself in a different environment can he begin to exercise the control over his destiny which he craves. Hence our relief (I think) when Bob marches off to join the army. Perhaps we have here the motive underlying Himes's own self-exile. In America he was doomed to be another 'Black Protest' novelist; in France, Jean Cocteau and Jean Giono might (and did) acclaim him as a remarkable novelist in his own right. The insider desperately looking out, in *If He Hollers,* with its many pages of agonised 'visceral' description of Bob's emotions, becomes the much more mature Himes of *Run Man Run,* an outsider calmly looking in, 'saying the thing like it is,' more clinically than ever examining the fears and confusions of an educated young black, much like Bob in some respects, trapped in a similar claustrophobic ambience of race prejudice, and rescued by his own resourcefulness and by a slow, almost grudging application of elementary justice on the part of a hard, but decent, white cop.

NOTES

1. *George* Orwell, 'Raffles and Miss Blandish', in *The Collected Essays, Journalism and Letters of George Orwell,* Vol. 3, London (Secker and Warburg) 1968, pp. 212–224. My colleague Mr. Tom Gorman, who has studied the reading habits of Kenyan school-students, confirms my suspicion that Chase, Robbins and the others I mention are, amongst men, the most popular reading. Girls, it seems, go for Denise Robins.

2. V.S. Naipaul, *The Middle Passage,* London (Penguin) 1969, p. 75

3. Leroi Jones, *Home: Social Essays,* New York (Morrow) 1966, p. 123.

4. John Williams, 'My Man Himes: An Interview with Chester Himes', in *Amistad I,* ed. J. Williams and C. Harris, New York (Vintage) 1970 p. 49.

5. I refer to the 1967 paperback reprint of *If He Hollers Let Him Go,* by Sphere Books (London).

6. Frantz Fanon, *Black Skin White Masks,* London (Paladin) 1970, pp. 99, 110, 125.

7. 'My Man Himes', *Amistad* I. p. 77.

8. Edward Margolies, *Native Sons,* New York (Lippincott) 1968, p. 87.

9. Robert A. Bone, *The Negro Novel in America,* revised edition, Yale UP 1965, p. 173.

10. David Littlejohn, *Black on White: A Critical Survey of Writing by American Negroes,* New York, (Grossman) 1966, p. 142.

11. Margolies, op. cit., p. 101.

12. Bone, op. cit., p. 176.

13. *Ibid.,* p. 212.

14. Margolies, op. cit., p. 89.

15. Himes, *If He Hollers ...,* pp. 155–6.

16. *Ibid.,* p. 11.

17. *Ibid.,* p. 31, p. 77.

18. The page references given after my quotations here and later from the Harlem thrillers are for the following British editions: by Panther Books, London (paperback)—*A Rage in Harlem* (1969); *The Real Cool Killers* (1969); *The Crazy Kill* (1968); *Run Man Run* (1969); *The Big Gold Dream* (1968); *All Shot Up* (1969);

The Heat's On (1968) and *Cotton Comes to Harlem* (1967): by Hodder and Stoughton, London (hardback)—Blind *Man With a Pistol* (1969). *Pinktoes* was published in British paperback by Corgi Books (1967).

    19. *If He Hollers*, pp. 17–18.

Journal of Eastern African Research and Development, 1:1 (1981), 3–18.

Chester Himes and the Hard-Boiled Tradition

Jay R. Berry, Jr.

The hard-boiled, or tough-guy, novel is a uniquely American creation. It represents a reaction against the classical school of mystery writing, which is generally characterized as being comprised of novels of manners. The style and dialog of the latter are slick and polished, character motivation is often weak, and the genre's central concern is the solution of a complex puzzle. The society and world at large are seen to be orderly and rational in their operation, and crime is seen merely as an aberration. Once the crime is solved and the aberration eliminated, the world can resume its orderly function.

The hard-boiled genre, on the other hand, presupposes an entirely different view of the world, one shaped by the general disillusionment and cynicism following World War I, Prohibition, and the Depression. The moral climate of these novels, as Herbert Ruhm points out, "was one of chaos; individual conscience, wit, or cunning triumphed rather than any social order. The world depicted in the tough guy novels was irrational and disorderly. Violence was the means to all ends."[1]

Tough guy novels are written in the American grain, using colloquial vernacular, emphasizing characterization and motivation, action, and often a moral and ethical code that governs the behavior of the private eye. These novels are set in urban America, for it is in the streets of the city that society's chaotic and disordered moral climate is reflected most effectively. "Events were depicted in the language of these streets; mean, slangy, prejudiced, sometimes witty and always tough. It was a language that could be made to say almost anything."[2] The solution of the puzzle is not nearly as important as the implicit and explicit social criticism that one generally finds in these novels, as well as the interaction between characters.[3] These general characteristics represent a definite break with the classical tradition of mystery writing.

The first writer to substantially develop the tough guy genre was Dashiell Hammett, who, with the creation of the Continental Op and, later, Sam Spade, first articulated the essential ethical and moral code of the private eye—honesty, dedication to the profession, loyalty to one's partner and one's client's interests.[4] He was also the first hard-boiled writer to fully develop a lean, detached and objective narrative style which fell within the Naturalistic tradition (characterized by a profound sense of pessimism, determinism, and randomness in an irrational world) of American literature. In the ensuing decades, Raymond Chandler and Ross Macdonald expanded the scope of the genre by creating more complex and human protagonists (with varying degrees of sentimentality and compassion), by evoking a definite sense of place through the use of descriptive passages integrated into the story, and in the case of Chandler, by injecting humor effectively into the novels.

The tough guy novels of Chester Himes are an important part of the Hammett/Chandler tradition of detective fiction, working both within the scope of the genre as well as going beyond the strict limits of the form in the last few novels (especially *Cotton Comes to Harlem*), where Afro-American history becomes an integral part of the novel.[5] This paper will examine Himes's detective fiction in a general way, noting his place in the tough guy genre through his use of common themes and motifs that persist throughout the series, and commenting upon his innovations in the genre.

Four years after leaving the United States to reside permanently in Europe, Chester Himes turned away from the protest writing that had characterized his career, and turned to writing detective fiction. It took Himes many years to discover that the demand for protest novels was small, and in the late 1950s he found that he could earn a decent living by writing detective fiction for Marcel Duhamel's "Serie Noire."[6]

The decision to make a total commitment to the detective novel was not an easy one for Himes. As Stephen Milliken points out:

The decision meant turning aside from the high ambitions, the lofty dedication, that had kept him going for so long, but his head had been pretty thoroughly battered and he was ready for a rest. The most important aspect of the decision, however, was the fact that it meant that he would have to concentrate exclusively on the most violent and sordid aspects of black life in America.[7]

Indeed, Himes's world in his Harlem detective novels is sordid, chaotic, and violent. Although the tough guy novel has always been violent, in post World War II America the level of violence increased tremendously in many of these novels. One has only to examine, however briefly, the novels of Mickey Spillane—*I, the Jury, Kiss Me Deadly* etc.—to understand this point. Some critics have argued that the acceptability of increased violence was due, in part, to a shift in American culture and values in the postwar years towards an acceptance of a kind of G.I. mentality.

Many of the more recent fictional tough guys were veterans of World War II and the Korean War who came home to find the country radically changed and corrupted (at least they perceived it this way) by organized crime syndicates. In the novels they assume the moral burden of eradicating the widespread corruption. Given their war experience, violence is seen as the only feasible recourse. This phenomenon in the tough guy genre is called the "vengeance variation,"[8] and to some extent Himes's protagonists, Grave Digger Jones and Coffin Ed Johnson, subscribe to this type of violence.

At times they kill for revenge (e.g., *For Love of Imabelle,* where Digger shoots out the eyes of the man who threw acid in Ed's face), and they often fly into violent rages during the course of each novel. They are intimidating and often cruel in their treatment of suspects (e.g., *The Crazy Kill,* where Digger and Ed handcuff a suspect's ankles together, suspend him upside down from the top of a door, and slowly push down on his armpits with their feet in order to get information). Finally, they have been known to perform illegal acts in order to wage their battles against the Harlem underworld.

The description of violence in Himes's novels, not surprisingly, is very detailed, deliberate, and gruesome, perhaps because the core of reality in Himes's Harlem is the presence of violence. Therefore, in *All Shot Up* (1960), a motorcycle rider is decapitated, and the scene is depicted quite vividly, even though no such detail is important to the actual story line itself:

The motorcycle rider was pulling up fast behind the car carrying sheet metal when the tire burst and the driver tamped his brakes. He wheeled sharply to the left, but not quickly enough.

The three thin sheets of stainless steel, six feet in width, with red flags flying from both corners, formed a blade less than a quarter of an inch thick. This blade caught the rider above his woolen-lined jacket, on the exposed part of his neck, which was stretched and taught from his physical exertion, as the motorcycle went underneath. He was hitting more than fifty-five miles an hour, and the blade severed his head from his body as though he had been guillotined.

His head rolled halfway up the sheets of metal while his body kept astride the seat and his hands gripped the handle-bars. A stream of blood spurted from his severed jugular, but his body completed the maneuver which his head had ordered and went past the truck as planned (*All Shot Up,* p. 83—hereafter referred to as *Shot*).

Later in the novel a man is knifed in the head; and, as he staggers around like a blind person, passersby ignore him as they would one of the neighborhood drunks. Himes again takes great pains to be as detailed as possible in the description of this almost incredible act of violence in an effort to drive home the point that reality in Harlem, as he sees it, is violence or the threat of violence.

In the midst of this chaos and senseless violence, Harlem police detectives Grave Digger Jones and Coffin Ed Johnson try desperately to bring peace and order to an irrational world. "'This mother-raping senseless violence!' Grave Digger exclaimed upon seeing someone with his throat cut. 'Yeah, but what you gonna do?' Coffin Ed said, thinking about themselves. 'Hell, meet it is all'" (*The Heat's On,* p. 94—hereafter referred to as *Heat*).

One look at the two black detectives—who were modeled on two black police officers in Watts, California, one of whom shot the other for seducing his wife[9]—tells the reader that one is dealing with a couple of very rough characters:

Their faces bore marks and scars similar to any other colored street fighter. Grave Digger's was full of lumps where felons had hit him from time to time with various weapons; while Coffin Ed's was a patch-work of scars where skin had been grafted over the burns left by acid thrown in his face (*Heat,* p. 32).

Despite their rough edges, Grave Digger and Coffin Ed are familiar literary heroes. Their cultural antecedents give them the moral authority that they exercise—from folk culture they are the "bad niggers" in the tradition of Stackalee. "Like their less sophisticated ancestors, they are aggressively courageous and utterly indifferent to physical danger, willing to submit without complaint to the risk of the same ruthless violence by which they express their own naked force of will."[10]

It is ironic, then, that the detective heroes "can express their genuine love for their people, their altruistic hopes for communal peace and decency, only through the crude brutality that has become their bitter way of life."[11] Despite this paradoxical situation, Coffin Ed and Grave Digger do possess an ethical code of behavior that has its roots in the Hammett hero:

Hammett's Continental Op is on the side of right, but he is in many ways as cruel and unscrupulous in pursuing his cause as his opponents are in pursuing theirs. He is a deadly shot with a pistol, able to give and take vicious beatings with his fists, and he foreshadows Coffin Ed and Grave Digger in these respects.[12]

Ed and Digger also possess the other important traits of the hard-boiled detective: honesty, loyalty to one's partner, a dedication to one's profession of helping to form a better community, and, if necessary, a willingness to take the law into one's own hands to ensure that justice prevails. With the progression of the series, one can see Ed's and Digger's ethical code becoming more clearly delineated and complex.

In *For Love of Imabelle* (1957), for example,

Grave Digger and Coffin Ed weren't crooked detectives, but they were tough.... *They took their tribute, like all real cops, from the established underworld catering to the essential needs of the people....* But they were rough on purse-snatchers, muggers, burglars, con men, and all strangers working any racket (*Imabelle,* p. 59, emphasis mine).

It is hinted, though, that they do accept some sort of compensation from the underworld for ignoring activities relating to essential needs of the people of Harlem (e.g., prostitution, gambling, etc.), carrying on a symbiotic relationship with it.

In subsequent novels, however, the detectives' honesty and integrity are never questioned. When the proprietor of a Harlem restaurant refuses to let Ed and Digger pay for their dinners in *The Heat's On* (1964), ostensibly to accrue some favors to be used at a later date, Digger replies harshly, "'Just don't think it buys you anything,'" (*Heat,* p. 38). Later in the novel when a bribe is offered to Ed in order to persuade him to abandon his search for the gunmen who wounded Digger, he says, "'Is everybody crooked on this mother-raping earth?... You think because I'm a cop I've got a price. But you're making a mistake. You've got only one thing I want. The truth'" (*Heat*, p. 185).

In *The Maltese Falcon* one of Sam Spade's motives in solving the case is to have his partner's murderer arrested, and in Himes's novels partner loyalty is also extremely strong. When a felon throws a glass of acid in Coffin Ed's face in the first novel, his first thought is of his partner: "'Where are you, Digger? Speak up, man.' Despite the unendurable pain, his first duty was to his partner" (*Imabelle*, p. 84). Loyalty to Ed motivates Digger to avenge his partner's injury by shooting the acid thrower through both eyes. After Grave Digger is critically injured by two gunmen searching for a lost heroin shipment in *The Heat's On*, Coffin Ed tracks down the gunmen even though he and Digger were suspended from the police force earlier in the novel for unnecessary brutality.

Like Raymond Chandler's Philip Marlow, Grave Digger and Coffin Ed possess a moral conscience concerning the formation of a better Harlem community. Although it is not as complex or clearly stated in the first five novels, one can still catch glimpses of this conscience cloaked in cynicism. In *The Crazy Kill* (1959), Digger and Ed are trying to find out who stabbed the brother-in-law of a powerful gambling figure. While interrogating one of the suspects Ed says, "'Me and Digger are two country Harlem dicks who live in this village and don't like to see anybody get killed. It might be a friend of ours. So we're trying to head off another killing'" (*The Crazy Kill*, p. 124).

Later novels, such as *The Heat's On* and *Cotton Comes to Harlem*, are more explicit in their treatment of the detectives' moral conscience. As Ed says, "'Folks just don't want to believe that what we're trying to do is make a decent peaceful city for people to live in, and we're going about it the best way we know how'" (*Heat*, p. 220).

In *Cotton Comes to Harlem* (1965), one sees Digger and Ed most clearly possessing a moral conscience. When 87 black families lose $87,000 in a religious Back-to-Africa swindle, they try desperately to recover the money:

Grave Digger and Coffin Ed knew that these families had come by their money the hard way. To many it represented the savings of a lifetime. To most it represented long hours of hard work at menial jobs. None could afford to lose it. They didn't consider the victims squares or suckers. They understood them. These people were seeking a home—just the same as the Pilgrim Fathers. Harlem is a city of the homeless.... Everyone has to believe in something; and the white people in America had left them nothing to believe in. But that didn't make a black man any less criminal than a white; and they had to find the criminals who hijacked the money, black or white (*Cotton Comes to Harlem*, pp. 34–36—hereafter referred to as *Cotton*).

The detectives' code of behavior is not the only element of Himes's novels that is part of the hard-boiled tradition. Narrative point of view and plot structures are also very much a part of that tradition.

Himes's use of the omniscient third person point of view in his novels is a somewhat unusual, but not unique, practice in the genre. Most writers, including Ross Macdonald, Raymond Chandler, and Dashiell Hammett (in three of his five novels) employ the first person point of view.[13] Given the chaotic world-view that most tough guy writers adhere to, it is logical to have the individual perceptions of the protagonist serve as the narrative mode rather than those of an omniscient narrator. Omniscience suggests a sense of order and external control that is not seen much in the world of the hard-boiled writers.

The third person point of view is strategically used in Himes's novels for several reasons. One reason is to prevent the detectives from dominating all aspects of the novels. By using the third person, Himes is not forced to have Ed and Digger in every scene. In fact, the first few novels feature the two detectives in supporting roles. Since one of Himes's strongest attributes is the ability to create a host of memorable minor characters, it is important that Ed and Digger do not overshadow them.

Another reason for Himes's use of the third person is that it enables him to jump back and forth in time and space between chapters (sometimes annoyingly so), to narrate the story from a variety of perspectives. In *All Shot Up,* for example, the action of the first chapter is seen through the eyes of a petty thief who happened to see a hit and run accident. The second chapter retells the action of the first, but from the perspective of another character—the driver of the hit and run vehicle. Ideally, this device gives the author a freedom of movement in telling the story; sometimes, as in the case of some of Himes's work, it gives the novels a sense of disjointedness and choppiness, eliminating the fluidity of the story line.

A third, and perhaps the most obvious, reason for using the omniscient narrator is that it enables the author to withhold information from the reader for revelation at a later and more dramatic time without being accused of cheating. A true first-person narrative requires that the narrator articulate to the reader all important assumptions, observations, and deductions made during the course of the novel.

One of Himes's favorite structural motifs—a variation on *The Maltese Falcon* plot[14]—also lies within the tough guy tradition. In novels using this motif, all of the major characters are trying to acquire some object(s) that they believe to be extremely valuable, and the plot is structured around the frantic search for the object. Himes, like Hammett, often uses this device in an ironic manner by revealing the object of desire to be worthless or non-existent, and this twist is especially effective as a mode for social criticism.

The object in *For Love of Imabelle* is a trunk of fool's gold, mistakenly thought to be gold ore. This ore is the cause of much of the trouble surrounding the innocent victims Jackson and Imabelle when three southern con artists attempt to establish a phony gold mine racket with Imabelle's "gold," leaving several corpses in their wake.

The objects of desire in *The Heat's On* are five eels stuffed with heroin that has been shipped in from France, but the reader discovers at the end of the novel that the eels were inadvertently destroyed before the actual story opened. Thus all of the killing and scheming is pointless, and the novel assumes a grotesquely comic and ironic position, echoing Raymond Chandler's statement: "It is not funny that a man should be killed, but it is sometimes funny that he should be killed for so little, and that his death should be the coin of what we call civilization."[15]

In *Cotton Comes to Harlem* the object is real enough—$87,000 stolen by a neo-Confederate colonel at a Harlem Back-to-Africa rally. The money is hidden in a bale of cotton, the symbol of his Back-to-the-Southland movement, which is lost during a chase scene. The bale is found by an old junk collector who eventually discovers the hidden money and uses it to go to Ghana—another ironic twist. Again there is senseless violence amidst a chaos of events, and the original $87,000, having disappeared earlier in the novel, is never recovered by those who were involved in a frantic search for it.

Through the use of this plot device, Himes is able to work within the conventional limits of the hard-boiled detective novel. But Himes also surpassed the limits of the genre in two important respects—through his innovative use of Afro-American history as an integral part of his later novels and his evocation of a sense of place, grounded in the Harlem area, which rivals Chandler's Los Angeles.

Cotton Comes to Harlem is Himes's penultimate Coffin Ed Johnson/Grave Digger Jones novel to date. Central to the story are a bale of cotton, a southern colonel who heads a Back-to-the-Southland movement, a Back-to-Africa movement, and the appearance of black militancy—all very important elements in Afro-American history. These elements, when placed in their historical context, help enrich the reader's understanding of what Himes is trying to accomplish in the novel.

The novel opens with a Back-to-Africa rally being held in a vacant Harlem lot by a con artist (Deke O'Hara) posing as a minister. He has managed to con 87 families out of $87,000 by promising them passage to Africa. Before he is able to slip away with the money, however, three masked gunmen in a meat truck escape with the money. O'Hara and a few of his security guards pursue the robbers in an armored truck. In the middle of the chase, a bale of cotton falls from the rear of the meat truck, and is picked up by an old junk collector. The robbers escape; and O'Hara, going into hiding, contemplates how he will try to recover the money.

Grave Digger and Coffin Ed are unable to find either O'Hara or the robbers, and the next day a Back-to-the Southland movement is established in Harlem by Colonel Calhoun and his nephew from Alabama. The movement is used as a front for the gang of thieves as they endeavor to recover the lost cotton (containing the $87,000).

Five corpses later, Grave Digger and Coffin Ed discover the significance of the cotton and the role of Colonel Calhoun and Deke O'Hara in the drama. They stake out the colonel's office, apprehending him and the nephew as they bring the recently discovered cotton into the office. When they discover that the money is gone, Digger and Ed make a deal with the colonel—if he reimburses the Harlem families for the $87,000 that was stolen, he and his nephew will be allowed a twenty-four hour head start in their escape.

The novel closes with the Harlem families having their money returned, the old junk collector going to Ghana with the original $87,000, and the state of Alabama refusing to extradite Colonel Calhoun and his nephew for a murder they committed while trying to get the bale of cotton.

Himes's use of the bale of cotton obviously suggests historical images of torture, cruelty, and hardship that Afro-American slaves were subjected to; and in this novel those conditions, metaphorically speaking, are seen in the North as Digger suggests: "'This mother-raping cotton punished the black man down south and now it's killing them up north'" (*Cotton*, p. 153). It is also ironic that Uncle Bud, the junk collector, should find his passage to Africa—and hopefully to happiness—in that bale of cotton, thus terminating an historical cycle.

Colonel Calhoun (even the name's significance is painfully obvious) is dedicated to keeping the black race subservient to the white. He refers to all those "nigras" involved in the Back-to-Africa movement as anti-Americans, and tries to entice blacks back to the South to work at menial jobs by offering $1,000 bonuses to the first families to sign up. The colonel's white supremacist movement is a tongue-in-cheek parody of Marcus Garvey's Black Nationalist movement during the 1920s. The African movement represented by O'Hara is also an ironic twisting of Garvey's philosophies since it is being headed by a con man using the cloak of religiosity.

Black militant insurgence, reaching fruition in the 1960s, emerges twice in the novel. The first occurs when the B.T.S. office opens in Harlem—there is a move to protest its opening that becomes increasingly militant until the police break it up—and later an angry mass of black Protesters converge on the B.T.S. headquarters, threatening to erupt as a riot, until Grave Digger and Coffin Ed break up the march. Himes is not, I think, trying to say that black protest is ineffectual, for his latest novel, *Blind Man With a Pistol* (1969), ends amidst a racial riot. Himes is arguing that unorganized violence is like a blind man with a pistol, and that organized violence is the correct route to pursue.

Himes's other important contribution to the tough guy novel lies in his evocation of a sense of place. Using the black community of Harlem as the setting for his novels, he has created a society that has a life of its own. Although his physical description of Harlem is rarely pretty, one cannot help being impressed by the power of his images.

Black-eyed whores stood on the street corners swapping obscenities with twitching junkies. Muggers and thieves slouched in the dark doorways waiting for someone to rob; but there wasn't anyone but each other. Children ran down the street, the dirty street littered with rotting vegetables, uncollected garbage, battered garbage cans, broken glass, dog offal—always running, ducking, and dodging. Listless mothers stood in the dark entrances of tenements and swapped talk about their men, their jobs, their poverty, their hunger, their debts, their Gods, their religions, their preachers, their children, their aches and pains, their bad luck with numbers and the evilness of white people (*Cotton,* p. 47).

The description of the physical surroundings that one finds in the vast majority of tough guy novels is of minor significance, but for Himes the very action and violence that dominates his writing calls for a very special sense of place, and calls for detailed descriptions of the physical surroundings that one finds in his work. It is as if Himes is compiling a naturalistic case-study of various aspects of Harlem life in each of his novels through the use of stark details.

Himes's description of such facets of Harlem life as restaurants and foods, music, and entertainment also help to create a sense of place in his works. The minor characters who reappear throughout the series—Jackson and Imabelle; H. Exodus Clay, the mortician; Fats and Mammie Louise, owners of popular Harlem restaurants; and Uncle Bud, the old junk collector—give the series a sense of continuity and community.

Like all writers in the genre, Chester Himes imitated existing literary conventions, but he always added an interesting twist (e.g., his plot structures, similar to that of *The Maltese Falcon,* are carried to their logical extremes in the novels). His innovations in the realm of Afro-American history, in the evocation of a sense of place, and in the creation of Afro-American detective heroes are of great importance in expanding the genre's scope. Himes should be recognized as a capable, and at times outstanding, practitioner of the art of detective story writing.

NOTES

1. Herbert Ruhm, Introduction to *The Hard-Boiled Detective* (New York: Vintage, 1977), p. viii.

2. *Ibid.*

3. E.g., Dashiell Hammett's *Red Harvest* and Raymond Chandler's *Farewell, My Lovely* are sharp, biting criticisms of corrupt small-city politics, and Hammett's *The Thin Man* attacks what he felt to be a savage and cruel society on an individualistic level.

4. Hammett's detective, however, was not the first tough private eye. Carroll John Daly's Race Williams is credited with being the prototype of the tough guy. He first appeared in *Black Mask* in 1923, and many times thereafter. Williams was very crudely drawn and Daly's style was never very good—it was trite, riddled with clichés and stock situations—so Hammett's Continental Op is really the first substantive private-eye character.

5. Himes has written eight detective novels in all, and in order of composition they are: *For Love of Imabelle, The Real Cool Killers, The Crazy Kill, The Big Gold Dream, All Shot Up, The Heat's On, Cotton Comes to Harlem,* and *Blind Man With a Pistol.*

6. Stephen F. Milliken, *Chester Himes, A Critical Appraisal* (Columbia: University of Missouri Press, 1976), p. 208.

7. *Ibid.,* p. 211.

8. William Kittredge and Steven M. Krauzer, Introduction to *The Great American Detective* (New York: New American Library, 1978), p. xxiv.

9. Edward Margolies, "The Thrillers of Chester Himes," *Studies in Black Literature,* 1 (1970), 2.

10. Raymond Nelson, "Domestic Harlem: The Detective Fiction of Chester Himes," *Virginia Quarterly Review,* 48 (1972), 266.

11. *Ibid.,* 270.

12. James Lundquist, *Chester Himes* (New York: Ungar, 1976), p. 108.

13. Several of the best hard-boiled novels, however, employ the third-person point of view, notably Hammett's *The Maltese Falcon* and *The Glass Key,* as well as the Perry Mason novels of Erle Stanley Gardner.

14. Milliken, pp. 217–18. Himes uses this plot device in six of his eight Harlem series novels—*For Love of Imabelle, The Big Gold Dream, All Shot Up, The Heat's On, Cotton Comes to Harlem,* and *Blind Man With a Pistol.*

15. Raymond Chandler, "The Simple Art of Murder," in his *The Simple Art of Murder* (1950; rpt. New York: Ballantine, 1977), p. 20.

The Armchair Detective, 15:1 (1982), 38–43.

In America's Black Heartland: The Achievement of Chester Himes

James Sallis

In one early short story Chester Himes writes of a black man who, because he will not step off the sidewalk to let a white couple pass, has his feet doused with gasoline and set on fire, consequently losing them. At the end of the story another white man becomes enraged when at a movie theater he fails to stand for the playing of the national anthem, even though it is pointed out he has no feet.

A more recent story, "Prediction," opens with the black janitor of the city's Catholic cathedral sitting astride the public poor box with a heavy-caliber automatic rifle, waiting at the end of "four hundred years" while six thousand white policemen parade in the streets below. The ensuing massacre is described with characteristic intensity and shocking detail: rank after rank of policemen are mowed down; shards of bone, lariats of gut and pieces of brain spin through the air. A riot tank is dispatched and, unable to find a target, turns its guns on black plaster-of-Paris mannequins in a nearby store window, then on the policemen themselves, killing 29 and wounding another 117. Finally the black janitor's location is discovered. The tank turns to the stone face and stares a moment "as if in deep thought," then levels the cathedral. But his symbolic action strikes a resounding blow: "In the wake of the bloody massacre the stock market crashed. The dollar fell on the world market. The very structure of capitalism began to crumble."

These two visions, the naturalist-didactic and the apocalyptic, largely define Chester Himes' career and work. The first of the stories, in its limning of the way in which white society makes demands on the black which that same society has assured he cannot fulfill, shares with the second a parabolic intensity common to Himes; each suggests, as do his later Harlem detective novels, that the forces of law and order only serve to amplify the disorder and chaos of American urban life. For Himes, the roots of our society are so thoroughly corrupt as to forbid anything approaching normal growth. Though he often has been labeled such, he is not a protest writer, for that term carries an implicit sense of meliorism, of redemptive change, a sense rarely manifest in Himes' work. The sense one *does* receive is that of a vast pall of futility, a huge sea of inaction and impotence relieved by sudden islands of violent, random motion: the crushing weight of centuries. And his interest from the first has been the individual human consequences of so distorted a society. Of his early naturalism he retains always determinism: if his people are monsters, misshapen, grotesque things, it is because the egg they formed in forced them to that shape.

In other respects Himes' naturalism has undergone a progression unique to American letters. Reminiscent of Richard Wright and proletarian work of the Forties, the early naturalist novels yielded, with their author's expatriation, to the serial exploits of a team of black Harlem detectives, Grave Digger Jones and Coffin Ed Johnson. These have proved quite successful in France and other European countries, in fact winning Himes the Grand Prix Policier, but American publication has been perfunctory. Brought out indifferently by various publishers, most if not all these books are now out of print. Critics typically considered the Harlem books potboilers, pandering to excessive violence and grotesque characterizations, and not a few bemoaned the loss of a talented serious writer. Himes was caught in a curious middle ground: habitual readers of detective stories demanded clear plot and resolution, which he did not provide, and more literate readers (at least in America) believed this sort of ephemera undeserving of their attention. The dilemma was not new to Himes. His second and third "serious" novels had been attacked diversely by white racists, black racists, fascists and the Communist Party. Himes' books were never comfortable spots for the ideologue.

Himes did achieve brief celebrity in 1965 with *Pinktoes,* his satire of black-white (mostly sexual) relations, and in 1970 a popular movie was made from one of the Grave Digger/Coffin Ed books, *Cotton Comes to Harlem.* He then seemed to enter yet another phase, with a two-volume autobiography (The *Quality of Hurt* in 1972, My *Life of Absurdity* in 1976) and a retrospective of shorter work (*Black on Black,* 1973). There has been no new fiction, and despite the fact that Chester Himes is arguably among America's most powerful and original novelists, despite, too, a gathering critical acclaim, he remains largely unknown. His expatriate status and the biform nature of his work certainly contribute to this, but that work deserves and demands wider recognition. Perhaps no other novelist has so succeeded in capturing the heavy beat of blood, the heaving desperate breaths of the American city and its inhabitants.

I first came to Chester Himes in the wake of his success with *Pinktoes.* I saw *Cotton Comes to Harlem* in an uptown New York theater shortly thereafter. Reading those books; stepping over bag ladies and drunks asleep in my apartment vestibule or various odd corners of the street; watching the parade of hustlers, wounded and great American glitter as the city always just managed to heave itself up for another day out of that black night, like a wounded whale on to the beach—somehow all this became of a piece, and after leaving New York I read nothing more of Himes for many years. But whenever I returned on visits, or thought of the city, I remembered those novels.

I admired their singular voice, the precise economy of Himes' imagery amid description, the outlandish rightness of his characterizations and the velocity he generated in his narratives, their sheer force of imagination. Even more, I admired his creation in these novels of a world unto itself—not Harlem, certainly, but a *response* to Harlem. "I got the story out of the American black's secret mind itself," Himes has said.

Always together, Grave Digger and Coffin Ed prowl the streets in their beat-up, souped-up Plymouth, looking like "two hog farmers on a weekend in the Big Town," connecting with a broad network of junkies, stool pigeons, whores and pimps and maintaining law and order primarily by bashing heads and making deals, in the interim shooting off their mouths and identical long-barreled, nickel-plated .38 revolvers on .44 frames (they have a particular affinity for tracer bullets). Grave Digger, the more articulate of the two, has smoldering reddish brown eyes, a "lumpy" face and oversize frame, and always wears a black alpaca suit with an old felt hat perched on the back of his head. Coffin Ed's face, disfigured by thrown acid in the first of the novels, has earned him a second nickname, Frankenstein, and he often must be restrained from impulsive violence by Grave Digger. The two live near one another, with their families, on Long Island. They share a considerable courage, a sure knowledge of street ways, studied flamboyance—and an abiding pragmatism. They know that nothing they can do is likely to have much real effect, and maintain what order there is chiefly by improvisation, threat and brutality, generally adding appreciably to the toll of bodies and confusion. Here is their first appearance, from *For Love of Imabelle* (also issued as *A Rage in Harlem*):

They were having a big ball in the Savoy and people were lined up for a block down Lenox Avenue, waiting to buy tickets. The famous Harlem detective-team of Coffin Ed Johnson and Grave Digger Jones had been assigned to keep order.

Both were tall, loose-jointed, sloppily dressed, ordinary-looking dark-brown colored men. But there was nothing ordinary about their pistols. They carried specially made long-barreled nickel-plated .38-calibre revolvers, and at the moment they had them in their hands.

Grave Digger stood on the right side of the front end of the line, at the entrance to the Savoy. Coffin Ed stood on the left side of the line, at the rear end. Grave Digger had his pistol aimed south, in a straight line down the sidewalk. On the other side, Coffin Ed had his pistol aimed north, in a straight line. There was space enough between the two imaginary lines for two persons to stand side by side. Whenever anyone moved out of line, Grave Digger would shout, "Straighten up!" and Coffin Ed would echo, "Count off!" If the offender didn't straighten up the line immediately, one of the detectives would shoot into the air. The couples in the queue would close together as though pressed between two concrete walls. Folks in Harlem believed that Grave Digger Jones and Coffin Ed Johnson would shoot a man stone dead for not standing straight in a line.

In a later novel, urged by their Lieutenant to "play it safe" and avoid unnecessary violence, Grave Digger responds: "We've got the highest crime rate on earth among the colored people in Harlem. And there ain't but three things to do about it: Make the criminals pay for it—you don't want to do that; pay the people enough to live decently—you ain't going to do that; so all that's left is let 'em eat one another up."

As H. Bruce Franklin points out in an excellent piece on Himes in *The Victim as Criminal and Artist*, the varieties of violence inflicted on blacks by blacks, finally represented by the two detectives as much as by the criminals they chase, become the persistent theme of the Harlem novels. But, he adds, these two black cops know who the real enemy is. In *The Real Cool Killers*, after a rare exercise of traditional detective methods to discover the killer, Grave Digger conceals her identity, chiefly because she is one of the rare Harlem inhabitants who has struck out—in this case against a wealthy white sadist who comes uptown to beat young girls.

Though the Harlem novels develop in a fairly clear line from the modern detective novel as established by Hammett (particularly *Red Harvest)* and Chandler, they were never true genre pieces, fulfilling few traditional expectations, and as they continued, they in fact withdrew further from preconceived notions of the detective story. Specific crimes are solved in the early books (albeit rather incidentally), but there is a progressive movement towards concentration on the scene itself, on Harlem as symbol, using the detective story framework as vehicle for character amid social portraiture. And as this shift occurs, absurdities, incomprehensible events and grotesqueries proliferate. The books close on greater disorder and confusion than they began with, as James Lundquist observes in his book-length study of Himes: "Order and reason are left farther and farther behind as the crimes Grave Digger and Coffin Ed must solve and the means of solution become ever more outrageous." This is of course nihilism—and a near perfect reversal of Gide's description of the detective story as a form in which "every character is trying to deceive all the others and in which the truth slowly becomes visible through the haze of deception."

Himes did not plan this evolution; it grew quite spontaneously out of the material he was working with in the Harlem novels, and what he himself was. In *My Life of Absurdity* he describes writing these novels:

I would sit in my room and become hysterical thinking about the wild, incredible story I was writing. But it was only for the French, I thought, and they would believe anything about Americans, black or white, if it was bad enough. And I thought I was writing realism. It never occurred to me that I was writing absurdity. Realism and absurdity are so similar in the lives of American blacks one can not tell the difference.

These trends culminate in *Blind Man With a Pistol.* Assigned to find the killer of a cruising white homosexual, Grave Digger and Coffin Ed roar through a landscape of crazy preachers, children eating from troughs, the cant of black revolutionaries, and a gigantic black plaster-of-Paris Jesus hanging from the ceiling with a sign reading *They lynched me.* (Lundquist has called the first chapter of this book "one of the strangest in American literature.") Neither the original nor subsequent murders are solved; the sole connecting link is an enigmatic man *(or men)* wearing a red fez. The two detectives are confounded and frustrated at every turn: politically protected suspects, payoffs and neatly contrived "solutions," diversionary cleanup campaigns and bureaucracy. Halfway through the novel they are taken off the case, in fact, and assigned to investigate Harlem's swelling black riots. "You mean you want us to lay off before we discover something you don't want discovered?" Grave Digger asks point blank. But he already knows; they all do, and the rest is little more than ritual dance. This is where Himes' work breaks off most surely from its forebears. With Hammett, Chandler or Ross Macdonald, the corruption, however profound, would at last be penetrated; with Himes, it is so pervasive, its signature so universal, that it cannot be.

Towards the novel's end, in a scene paralleling that of their debut in *For Love of Imabelle,* Grave Digger and Coffin Ed are standing on the corner of Lenox and 125th shooting rats as they run from buildings being demolished. Their function, and efficacy, have been so abridged.

Meanwhile a belligerent black man who wants no one to know he is blind, walking streets and riding subways by memory, has become involved in an argument with a gardener (for whites, of course) who thinks the blind man is staring at him. Soon involved as well are a white truck driver and a black clergyman who intervenes to preach against violence. Attacked by the truck driver, the blind man draws a pistol and fires, killing the preacher. He continues to fire as the subway pulls into the 125th Street station, then staggers up onto the street close behind the gardener and truck driver, where he is shot to death by white police watching Grave Digger's and Coffin Ed's display of marksmanship. Immediately the cry goes out that "Whitey has murdered a soul brother!"

> An hour later Lieutenant Anderson had Grave Digger on the radio-phone. "Can't you men stop that riot?" he demanded.
> "It's out of hand, boss," Grave Digger said.
> "All right, I'll call for reinforcements. What started it?"
> "A blind man with a pistol."
> "What's that?"
> "You heard me, boss."
> "That don't make any sense."
> "Sure don't."

Thus the book ends on a familiar theme: having abrogated their authority, the Lieutenant absurdly expects his detectives still to function. And just as Himes had discovered in his mythical Harlem a correlative for the absurdity of the urban black's life, so lie found a final metaphor for the mindless ubiquity of violence against and within those same people.

Returning to Chester Himes' work after several years, and following that to the man (for his work, I found, passed from autobiographical novels through the Harlem fables I already knew to direct autobiography), I discovered an individual quite as unconforming and cryptic as those in the Harlem novels.

Repeatedly, unaccountably, he has let himself drift or be pulled, knowing fully the consequences, into impossible situations, as when he accompanies a singularly callow and unattractive girlfriend to her home in Germany. There is about him always a baffling passivity, a disengagement, which reminds us that he spent formative adult years (from age nineteen to twenty-six) in prison. And yet, living in France for many years, he refused to learn the language: clearly a willful defiance. Similar contradictions appear in his thought. He seems astounded that his actions often have (quite predictably) led to disaster; he remarks that "Nothing happened in prison that I had not already encountered in outside life," yet begins his autobiography by intimating that prison left scars too deep for probing; hating whites, he chooses to live exclusively with white women.

Himes is not a thinker, and his thought rarely penetrates to any significant level beneath the commonplace. When he does attempt discursive thought, outside his personae at any rate, it is often puerile, and even in the fiction what he *shows* sometimes subverts what he *says*. For he is a marvelous observer and prodigious inventor, working by instinct and feeling towards his singular vision; and that vision cannot be reduced to mere ideas. I do not know of any other American writer who has created vivid, memorable scenes in the quantity Himes has, scenes which are hard-edged and durable like a footprint in cement, and with an astounding economy of dialogue and language.

A passage from the second volume of autobiography, *My Life of Absurdity,* now seems to me emblematic of Himes' work, his description "of a painting I had seen in my youth of black soldiers clad in Union Army uniforms down on their hands and knees viciously biting the dogs the Southern rebels had turned on them, their big white dangerous teeth sinking into the dogs' throats while the dogs yelped futilely." The terrible ambivalence of the black's place in society, Himes' own bitterness and paradoxical rage, elements of graphic violence and *opera bouffe,* the contradictory, enigmatic and finally irreducible "message," the clarity of scene: the painting is a virtual mirror image of Himes' work.

He was born July 29, 1909, in Jefferson City, Missouri, and grew up chiefly there and in Cleveland, Ohio. His parents were middle-class, his mother a woman of dignity and iron will, his father a college instructor whose own will seems to have broken over the years, so that he wound up working distractedly at carpentry. Himes attended Ohio State University for a time but was asked to leave following a fight in a speakeasy. He then worked as a busboy for Cleveland hotels, becoming involved with the hustling life, drinking, gambling. After two suspended sentences for burglary and bad checks, he was finally sentenced in 1928 to 20–25 years hard labor at the Ohio State Penitentiary for armed robbery, serving seven years, five months of that sentence before parole.

It was in prison that Himes began to write. His first stories were picked up for publication rather promptly by black weekly newspapers and magazines such as the Atlanta *World,* the Pittsburgh *Courier,* and *Abbott's Monthly.* Then in 1934 a short story titled "Crazy in the Stir," with a prison number as its only byline, appeared in *Esquire.* Two more of Himes' stories were accepted by *Esquire* before his parole in 1936, and another six appeared there in following years. A few were published also in *Coronet.*

The years following parole were difficult ones. Even with the sponsorship of Pulitzer Prize winner Louis Bromfield, Himes was unable to find a publisher for his novel *Black Sheep;* and though he found an amenable spot writing a history of Cleveland for the Ohio Writers' Project, with the encroachment of American involvement in World War II all such WPA programs ended. Eventually he joined the river of blacks flowing towards Los Angeles and the wartime defense industry there, his work in the L.A. shipyards providing the setting (and no small part of the rancor) for his first published novel, *If He Hollers let Him Go,* published in 1945.

The alarm went off again; I knew then that it had been the alarm that had awakened me. I groped for it blindly, shut it off; I kept my eyes shut tight. But I began feeling scared in spite of hiding from the day. It came along with consciousness. It came into my head first, somewhere back of my closed eyes, moved slowly underneath my skull to the base of my brain, cold and hollow. It seeped down my spine, into my arms, spread through my groin with an almost sexual torture, settled in my stomach like butterfly wings. For a moment I felt torn all loose inside, shriveled, paralyzed, as if after a while I'd have to get up and die.

During the course of the novel, Bob Jones loses his girl, is demoted at the shipyard, suffers endless humiliation and insult, becomes entangled in a brawl and falsely accused of rape—finally having to enlist to avoid imprisonment. The story is told first-person in hardboiled prose. There's little real movement to it; structured around Bob Jones' enigmatic, terrifying dreams, the book simply moves him through a train of situations and events reinforcing the sense of him and his destiny we find in that early scene. "I'm still here," he says at the end: hope and a man's life have been thus attenuated.

Himes' next novel, *Lonely Crusade* (1947), concerned fledgling Negro union organizer Lee Gordon, a man whose marriage is dissolving and who takes illusory refuge with a white mistress. The book is uneven, with lengthy discursive passages, a some-what muddled plot, and a questionable upbeat ending typical of contemporary proletarian novels (Lee Gordon decides he cannot blame race for everything and finds his identity with struggling workingmen both black and white). But the book traces relentlessly the emasculating, the unmanning, effects of racism and, written in an omniscient point of view, is more than any other of Himes' novels, a novel of ideas. Lee Gordon is in many ways an extension of Bob Jones, but where Bob was paralyzed by the ubiquity of his enemy, Lee Gordon, among Himes' finest characterizations, is adamant in finding ground that allows struggle, and in learning *how* to fight. This hopeful (or existential) posture is one we will not see again.

Upon publication *Lonely Crusade* encountered misunderstanding and condemnation so nearly universal that Himes fell back into bitterness, gradually losing all confidence in himself. "The manuscripts of both *The Third Generation* and *Black Sheep* were making the rounds of the publishing houses at that time," he recalled in *The Quality of Hurt*, "but I had almost lost interest. That summer I had convinced myself I was a failure as a writer, and poverty and loneliness and our enforced separation had convinced me I was a failure as a husband. After fourteen years of love and marriage we had lost each other."

Himes worked various jobs, first as caretaker at resorts, country clubs and estates, then again as a porter and bellhop, over the next several years. In 1948 he gave an impassioned, brilliant address on "The Dilemma of the Negro Writer" at the University of Chicago. For the next five years he was for the most part unable to write, and in 1953, following publication of his novel *Cast the First Stone* (written sixteen years earlier as *Black Sheep*) and widespread attacks on it, Chester Himes fled to Europe.

Cast the First Stone had been written during and just after his prison experience (some of the material was adapted from *Esquire* stories) and was "the outcome of my personal hurts ... and did not contain any reference to my racial hurts." The novel as published in fact substituted a white Mississippian for the original black protagonist. It combines a graphic depiction of prison life with a remarkably sensitive story of the love between two men, Jim Monroe and Duke Dido. *The Third Generation* followed in 1954 and, a year later, *The Primitive.* Each of Himes' novels had been brought out by a different publisher.

Directly autobiographical in inception, *The Third Generation* focuses more on dissension within Negro families than on confrontation with white society, in this regard prefiguring the preoccupation of Himes' detective novels with "the infinite forms of violence perpetrated on blacks by blacks" (to borrow H. Bruce Franklin's words). The novel recounts the coming to manhood of Charles Taylor, son of educated, decorous Southern blacks, and the parallel disintegration of his family under the pressures of modern urban life and insidious racism. The parents are patently modeled on Himes' own: the father a dark-skinned trade teacher at Negro schools, gradually descending to manual work because of his wife's inability to accommodate colleagues and neighbors; the mother light-skinned and of genteel background, endlessly spurning her husband and showering her whole affection on their son. Sharing the melodramatic plot turns, sometimes diffuse theme and acute psychological portraiture of the preceding novels, *The Third Generation* represents Himes' most direct assault on the Negro middle class, a group the writer always views with suspicion. "The American Negro, we must remember, is an American," Himes said in his address at the University of Chicago; "the face may be the face of Africa, but the heart has the beat of Wall Street." One also is forced to remember Grave Digger and Coffin Ed with their comfortable homes and families out on Long Island, coming in to Harlem each day to commit mayhem against fellow (but far less advantaged) blacks in their enforcement of white men's laws.

Of the characters from *The Third Generation,* Edward Margolies has written in *Native Sons:* "On the surface, rank bigotry seldom intrudes as the direct cause of their sufferings; they appear to be defeated by their own incapacities, weaknesses, blindness, and obsessions. But Himes makes clear that in order to understand them, one must understand the generations that preceded them, black and white: they are doomed not simply by their own psychic drives but by the history that created them and forced them into self-destructive channels. They are as much the victims of a value system they implicitly accept (and which indeed flows in their bloodstreams) as are men like Bigger Thomas who rebel against the social order." With this restatement of Himes' determinism, the palpable beat of cataclysm and specific focus on black community, we are moving close to the Harlem novels. The book's title presumably derives from *Exodus* ("for I the Lord thy God am a jealous God, visiting the iniquity of the fathers upon the children unto the third and fourth generation of them that hate me"), but one remembers also that Himes chose to end his autobiography with these words: "that's my life—the third generation out of slavery."

Just as the Harlem novels culminate in *Blind Man With a Pistol,* the earlier phase of Himes' career climaxes with *The Primitive,* published the same year (1955) he began writing the first of the detective books. In the story of Jesse and Kriss, a failed black novelist and a woman whose own wounds are just as mortal, Himes found a channel for his feelings about his rejection as a writer, and for an investigation of his obsession with the white woman and all she represented to him. *The Primitive* is easily the most closely structured and artistic of Himes' novels. In it, too, we find the first exercise of the Rabelaisian humor which becomes central to the Harlem novels; prior books had been unrelievedly serious.

The narrative here, though, is anything but comic. Jesse and Kriss circle each other like ritual dancers, first simply using one another to satisfy their own needs, then increasingly turning their feelings of failure and defeat upon one another, each in truth seeking his own destruction: the book ends with Jesse calling the police, having just killed Kriss. Himes' presentation is almost theatrical, with a marvelously sustained mood, a new intensity of characterization and physical detail, and fine, impassioned writing. This is a bleak book, one in which the external world and perceptions of it are increasingly bent to the shape of the characters' own doom. In that bleakness, and with similar pervading tone, flashes of detail and inchoate bursts of energy or motion, *The Primitive* (as, for me, does much of Himes' work) recalls Nathaniel West.

Pinktoes, published in Paris in 1961 by Olympia Press, and in the U.S. in 1965, is something of a sport. Though it introduces the boisterous comedy that became a signature of the Harlem novels and takes up yet again the author's disdain for the black middle class and fascination with interracial sex, there is nothing else like it in Himes' work. The success of *Candy* and other sexual farces somewhat earlier probably accounts both for this book's existence and considerable popularity. Centered around the activities of Harlem "hostess" Mamie Mason, who believes race relations (and her own social pretensions) best served in bed, *Pinktoes* is a scattergun that misses very few targets.

Most of the novel concerns one of Mamie's parties and its aftermath for two men there, black leader Wallace Wright and Art Wills, soon to become (white) editor for a Negro picture magazine. Plot turns and scenes grow ever more grotesque and outrageous. When Mamie, because Art will not feature her in his first issue, tells his wife that he has proposed to a black woman named Brown Sugar, the wife goes home to mother. Word quickly gets around that white liberal husbands are fleeing their wives for brownskin girls and there's a panicked run on suntan lotion and ultraviolet lights. A company that had been producing a skin lightener called "Black Nomore" prospers with its new product "Blackamoor." White women rush to kink their hair, dye their gums blue, redden their eyes.

The attacks are savage ones, true—and unrelenting—yet in the conscious self-parody of his own obsession with interracial sex, and in the unbridled lampoonery of all he held in contempt, Chester Himes seems to have found a kind of deliverance from the pervasive bitterness and gravity of previous work. Without *Pinktoes,* there could have been no Harlem novels, and possibly no more writing at all.

It seems clear now that the Harlem detective novels are not the anomalies they were first believed to be and rather than breaking the line of Himes' development, significantly extended it. With them, recurrent themes fell into place and perspective, joining the dark vision of the earlier books to the turbulent comedy that surfaced in *Pinktoes*. Released from the twin burdens of autobiography and social significance (at least in any programmatic sense), Himes found the ideal vehicle for his particular gifts. The climate of suspicion, fear and violence so much at the heart of the detective story mirrored Himes' own feelings about the black in American society and allowed him a kind of privileged expression. Grave Digger and Coffin Ed, men of ruthless action, supplanted the passivity of earlier protagonists, and Himes fully embraced life's fundamental absurdity. His Harlem is a Harlem of the mind, a total realization of feeling, thought and instinct America's black heartland. He had moved from finding to making, from the purely' representational to a kind of epic poetry.

Yet the books began quite by chance. On a visit to Gallimard to drop off the manuscript for *Pinktoes*, desperate for money, Himes ran into Marcel Duhamel, who had translated *If He Hollers Let Him Go* into French and was then director of Gallimard's La Série Noire. Duhamel asked Himes to write a detective story for the series and to Himes' protests that he wouldn't know how responded:

Get an idea. Start with action, somebody does something—a man reaches out a hand and opens a door, light shines in his eyes, a body lies on the floor, he turns, looks up and down time hall.... Always action in detail. Make pictures. Like motion pictures. Always the scenes are visible. No stream of consciousness at all. We don't give a damn who's thinking what—only what they're doing. Always doing something. From one scene to another. Don't worry about it making sense. That's for the end. Give me 220 typed pages.

Gradually, from an old confidence game called "the Blow" Himes had heard of, the book built itself, pure improvisation. After eighty pages he returned to Duhamel for his opinion and more money. He got both. Duhamel loved the book and told him: "Just add another hundred and twenty pages and you've got it.... Keep the suspense going. Don't let your people talk too much. Use the dialogue for narration, like Hammett. Have your people see the description. You stay out of it." It was not to Hammett or Chandler that Himes turned, however, but to Faulkner, reading *Sanctuary* again and again in what became a virtual rite of preparation for the detective novels. The first was published in 1957 as *La Reine des Pommes* with jacket blurbs from Jean Cocteau, Jean Giono and Jean Cau, winning the Grand Prix Policier the following year. There have been nine others.

Chester Himes now lives in Spain, in poor health, and does not write. And while his books continue into new editions abroad, no American publisher seems interested in retrieving these remarkable visions. For make no mistake of it: the Harlem novels are a singular achievement. There is nothing else like them in our literature, and their author rightly deserves the same approbation given another American original, Raymond Chandler. But America has never had much room for Chester Himes.

"It is very sad," his agent, Roslyn Targ, told me in a recent telephone conversation. "There is no interest in this country despite all my efforts—none. Yet the publishers every day buy, publish and promote books with not a trace of Himes' power or originality." Money, she told me, trickles in from European editions. As we ended our conversation she asked that I send a letter care of her office, so that Chester Himes will know, despite publishers' stupidity, that he does remain admired *and read* by many people.

After speaking with Targ I walked to a nearby bookstore, a supermarket really, with bright lines of new covers receding down the aisles like Burma-Shave signs. The weather, as so often in Dallas, was uncertain, sunny one moment, then over-cast. I had been reading Graham Greene's autobiography, and as I walked, recalling his references to what critics had called "Greeneland," I realized that there is, just as clearly, and for much the same reasons, a Himesland—a coherent world apart, born from its creator's whole spirit: the Harlem of his detective novels.

It is not sad, I thought, but incomprehensible, that these books remain out of print. This is something a writer lives with, of course, often watching his best work disappear beneath the waves; he *learns* to live with it. Yet it unmans him in ways nothing else ever can—in ways that Chester Himes, author of *If He Hollers Let Him Go* and *The Primitive,* knows all too well. "Very little is needed to destroy a man," Artaud wrote; "he needs only the conviction that his work is useless."

I walked home in rain. Each day my wife goes off to work in Parkland's emergency room and brings back communiques from *this* inner city. Some weeks ago a man injected himself with novocaine and, using a hacksaw, removed his own arm. Once asked to notify a wife that her husband was shot, the police informed my wife that they could not do so; the house was under surveillance by the sheriff's office, with a drug raid planned for that same night. The wife found out anyway and soon arrived, furious because her husband was still alive and she wouldn't get her $20,000 insurance.

"We are suffering," Henry Miller wrote in *The Wisdom of the Heart*, "from a plethora of art. We are art-ridden. Which is to say that instead of a truly personal, truly creative vision of things, we have merely an *aesthetic* view."

Chester Himes has no aesthetic view. He really is, to use the title of *Life's* 1970 profile, a "Hard-Bitten Old Pro," a man who always got the work out, who always saw, if not clearly, then sharply. All he has written bears an unmistakably personal vision, and the Harlem novels are *sui generis*, almost a literary form to themselves. Seventy-four years old, in poor health and living in exile, Chester Himes remains, as he has always been, a man alone. Again and again he has held a mirror to this country, hoping the monster would see itself and feel shame, know what it was. But the monster breaks all mirrors that show true, and its madness finally drives the man from it. He stands far away, on a cliff perhaps, looking down as the monster breaks its baubles one by one, stuffs itself, fouls its nest, steeps in its hatred. Until one day the monster has nothing left, nothing, and desperately it turns its eyes to that cliff. But the man is gone.

Western Humanities Review, 37:3 (Autumn 1983), 191–206.

Postscript: *A Case of Rape*
Calvin Hernton

Chester Himes was born and reared in the United States. But since the early 1950s, he has traveled and lived outside of his native land, in Scandinavia, London, and Paris. He eventually established permanent residence in Spain. Although Himes has lived outside the United States for over thirty years, one of the remarkable things about his writing is that virtually everything he writes concerning black people in America still retains an accuracy that is downright uncanny. It is as though he never left. Since he was first published during the early 1930s, Chester Himes has been a prolific writer of short stories, articles and poems, some twenty-odd novels and two volumes of autobiography. Several of his novels have made the bestseller lists in foreign countries as well as in America. Nothing short of the realism and extraordinary brilliance of his writing can account for Himes's appeal.

Yet, today the name and works of Chester Himes are known and appreciated in the United States by only a handful of black literature enthusiasts, close friends, and fellow writers. As is true with all but a few black writers, Chester Himes is not to be found in standard white anthologies, literature texts, or books of criticism.

Because Himes writes in a framework of *social reality in* which characters and incidents are easily recognizable in everyday American life, reviewers, publicity people, and publishers as well have reacted in very mean and unethical ways, even when the books are initially well received by the reading public. More often than not, dirty deals have constituted his lot from the publishing world. He has been consistently robbed of revenues, everybody seemed to have gotten the money but him.

Strange and hurtful as it may seem, books by Himes have been printed and reprinted, sold and resold among publishers over the past thirty years—and *Himes has gotten virtually none of the money!* According to an interview with John A. Williams in *Amistad 1,* Chester Himes often does not know when his books are being published and republished in America. Having been broke most of his career, and in very ill health of late, he has been easy prey for the exploitive advance. Such was the situation with several of the Harlem series of detective novels. He wrote them quickly and sold them (or gave them away) just as quickly, because he badly needed whatever money he could get. "I got a thousand dollar advance for each of my last three books," Himes told Williams.[1]

Another painful truth surrounding Himes's career is that, with rare exception, it has always been difficult to obtain any of Himes's books the first few months after their publication. Even the books that make the bestseller list—the hilariously satirical *Pinktoes* (1961), for example—are hard to come by. They go "out-of-stock, out-of-print," although they may still be on the bestseller list. I have been teaching courses in black literature for more than ten years. Every year when I order books by Chester Himes, I receive "out-of-stock, out-of-print" notices from the publishers. Similar to books by other black writers, one must too often search for Himes's books in stores that deal in rare books.

The fate of *If He Hollers Let Him Go* (1945) and *Lonely Crusade* (1947), foretold the fate of *Cast The First Stone* (1952), *The Third Generation* (1954) and *The Primitive* (1955). When *If He Hollers Let Him Go* was surging toward the bestseller list, a stop-print directive was issued by a female employee in the office of his own publisher. People were trying to buy the novel and could not get it because the bookstore orders were not being filled.

In his autobiography, *The Quality of Hurt,* Himes tells of another malignant act deliberately perpetrated against the book.

[*If He Hollers Let Him Go*] was considered by the editorial committee for Doubleday Doran's *George Washington Carver Memorial Award* of twenty-five hundred dollars, but it was rejected because one of the women editors said it nauseated her. Instead, a novel called *Mrs. Palmer's Honey* was given the award. To add insult to injury, the advertising copy that appeared in the *Saturday Review of Literature* for *Mrs. Palmer's Honey* referred to my novel, *If He Hollers Let Him Go,* as a "series of epithets punctuated with spit."[2]

Obviously, to me at any rate, what enrages white people against Himes's books, particularly the woman who reacted so violently against *If He Hollers Let Him Go,* is the realistic manner in which black and white characters and relations are portrayed. In *If He Hollers,* a white woman who falsely accuses the black hero of raping her is depicted as she is—a racist white woman frustrated by her forbidden sexual desire for the black hero.

Malevolent deeds have also been perpetrated against books of Himes having nothing to do with black and white sex. A case in point is his second novel, *Lonely Crusade,* which centers around Lee Gordon, a black trade union organizer. Several promotional appearances scheduled for Himes in New York were canceled at the last minute, without explanation, and the author and his work were harassed and maligned by various political factions in America, white and black.

In *The Quality of Hurt,* he reports on the manner in which *Lonely Crusade* was received.

The communist review, *The New Masses,* hit the stands with a vitriolic three-page attack by a black communist, headed by a silhouette of a black man carrying a white flag above a streamer saying "Himes carries the White Flag." *Ebony* magazine ran an editorial entitled "It Is Time To Count Your Blessings," to which it said: "The character Lee Gordon is psychotic, as is the author, Chester Himes." *The Atlantic Monthly* said: "Hate runs through this book like a streak of yellow bile." *Commentary*, a Jewish journal, ran a long diatribe ... in which my book was compared to the "graffito on the walls of public toilets." ... Willard Motley wrote a vicious personal attack charging me personally with statements taken from the dialogues of my characters.... The Communist Party had launched [a campaign] against bookstores that sold the book, by buying copies, damaging them, and taking them back to the stores and demanding their money back on the ground the book was trash.... The left hated it, the right hated it, Jews hated it, blacks hated it.... I think that what the great body of Americans most disliked was the fact I came too close to the truth.[3]

In addition to problems with the distribution of his works and receipt of adequate compensation from publishers, Himes has also been plagued perennially by ill health, some of which could be due to his own mistakes and excesses, but a large measure of which could well be the result of damaging controversy persistently aimed at him and his works. Toward the end of chapter two in *The Quality of Hurt,* he writes:

One will make more enemies by trying to be fair than by trying to tell the truth—no one believes it possible to tell the truth anyway—but it is just possible that you might be fair.[4]

An important source of controversy worth mentioning is the resentful attitudes that many black Americans, like their white counterparts, are prone to feel toward any black person who has lived outside of the United States for a length of time. When Himes returned from abroad to promote the publication of his autobiography, some blacks wanted to know if he was back "home" to stay for good. When he departed for Europe, disgruntled feelings were expressed throughout the rumor network of the black literary world. The fanfare and enthusiasm over him and the publication of his autobiography died instantly, like a candle flame exposed to sudden wind.

Despite experiencing more than his share of deliberate evil and just plain old bad luck, Himes was published extensively in this country in the 1960s and early 1970s. Some of his literary creations made a tremendous popular impact that far outstripped the accomplishments of most novelists.

The nine Harlem detective novels—all of which are classed as "thrillers," featuring the colorful black detectives, Coffin Ed Johnson and Grave Digger Jones—include such American publication titles as: *A Rage In Harlem* (1964), *The Real Cool Killers* (1966), *Run, Man, Run* (1968), *All Shot Up* (1966),

The Heat's On (1967), and *Blind Man With A Pistol* (1969). *(Blind Man* is the only one in the series originally published by an American publisher.)

When two of the detective novels were made into movies—"Cotton Comes to Harlem" and "Come Back Charleston Blue"—the works of Chester Himes gained popularity among the masses of movie-goers, and, consequently, among a wider variety of readers. It was during the windfall popularity from the movies (latter 1960s and early 1970s) that several of Himes's more "serious" works were reissued, notably *The Primitive, The Third Generation,* and *Pinktoes.* The two volumes of autobiography, *The Quality of Hurt* and *My Life of Absurdity,* were also published by American publishers in original hard-back editions. Again, the reissued books, and the detective novels, plus the newly published autobiographies, went out-of-stock, out-of-print within a very short period of time. The present work, however, was not a part of what turned out to be a rather tumultuous but short-lived interest in Chester Himes.

A Case of Rape was written during 1956–57. It was first published in Paris in 1963 and entitled, *Une Affaire de Viol.* A second edition, *Affaire de Viol,* was issued in 1979. Both were produced by small French presses, Les Yeux Ouverts and Editions des Autres, respectively. It was not until 1980 that an American edition of the work was brought out by Targ Editions, a New York rare book publisher. The publication was limited, and the following statement appears on the last page:

This first edition in English is limited to 350 copies, each signed by the author.

Obviously, the Targ Edition books are consigned to that great book fair in the sky known as "'collector's items."

The Howard University Press publication of *A Case of Rape* marks the first time the book has been available in America on a large scale. Its publication is long overdue. It is not only a judicious service to Chester Himes but a great service to students and the general public, because it singularly represents all of the elements constituting the quintessence of a theme that Himes has been hammering away at in a majority of his writings. It is a theme that is at once so historically rooted in race relations and yet so emotionally inflammable that we, both whites and blacks, have gone to maddening lengths to deny it as a fact of our lives and have made its acceptance a monumental taboo, seeking thereby to insulate ourselves against its existence. The fact is interracial love, occurring specifically and particularly between white women and black men. I call this fact, which appears as a major theme in the writings of Chester Himes, and all of the machinations surrounding it, *the scarlet equation.*

In other writings, but especially in several major works of fiction including, *If He Hollers Let Him Go, The Primitive,* and *Pinktoes,* Himes has laboriously dealt with this equation. His heavily autobiographical novel, *The Third Generation,* may also be considered a work in which the major portion deals with interracial love, in that Himes's real parents correspond to the mother and father in the novel. The mother is light-complexioned enough to be repeatedly mistaken for a white woman, and she "acts" like a white woman, while the father has pure Negroid features and "acts" like a Negro, all of which provoke many problems. Indeed, I have heard some readers express the feeling that

Himes has been inordinately preoccupied with this theme. Chester Himes is a black man married to a white woman, and he has been privy to other black men/white women relationships. It seems altogether reasonable that he has been forced to deal with his more intimate knowledge of the scarlet equation, rather than with the white man/black woman equation.

Those of us who harbor a thoroughly ingrained repulsion toward interracial love, and we all are socialized in this way to some degree, find works dealing with this subject either mildly irritating or utterly disgusting. In large part, it has been Himes's apparent preoccupation with this theme that has figured in the controversial and often condemnatory reactions toward him. Some reactions have been so severe that it has been imputed that there is something "pathological" about Himes himself as a black man.

My view is that Himes's works constitute the most thoroughly illuminating "fictional" treatment available on one of the cardinal issues of our times: the tangled web of societal, institutional, and personal insanities surrounding the black man and the white woman. I submit that it is the existence of these insanities, so gothically depicted by Chester Himes, which we recognize within ourselves, that make us retaliate against Himes for daring to uncover them. These insanities, moreover, may very well lay at the bottom of the "nauseating" feelings and destructive behavior toward Himes's books by certain whites in the publishing industry, as well as by some black people too.

The insanities may be collectively identified by two categories: the insanity of racism, and the insanity of sexism. According to the tenets of racism, the purpose of white people is to rule the world and blacks are here to serve whatever wishes whites might have. According to the tenets of sexism, the male mandate is to give guidance to, provide for, protect and dominate females. As racism applies to black people both male and female, sexism applies to women both white and black. It is my contention that in environments where racism and sexism are integral factors in the mores of a people, all associations between men and women of different races tend to suffer the entangled influences of both factors.

Whether by rape, subtle coercion, or mutual agreement, white men and black women have historically engaged in sexual relations with each other. Although these relationships have gone on and are going on, it is as if such relations are invisible. They are invisible because nobody seems to *want* to know about them.

On the other hand, the sensational publicity given to black man/white woman relationships suggests that inter-racial sex occurs in no other combination. Anyone can cite any number of contemporary black man/white woman marriages. But how many people can name five black women who are married to white men? Why this is so, in the face of abundant evidence that such marriages exist, is a mystery, the unraveling of which might reveal more than anyone cares to deal with.

Whenever BLACK MAN/WHITE WOMAN is seen, mentioned or thought of, a red light flashes in our minds: The mere idea of sex between black men and white women is loaded with hot controversy. Black man/white woman association ignites emotions of pornography, nausea and repulsion; therefore, we are forced to deal with this association as the main priority. This is why, I call black man/white woman relations the scarlet equation.

In most literature dealing with the scarlet equation the emphasis is placed on the impact of racism in these relationships, to the exclusion of sexism. Several works of Richard Wright—*Native Son, The Outsider* and *The Long Dream*—are cardinal examples. Other examples are *Night Song* by John A. Williams, *Soul on Ice* by Eldridge Cleaver, and *Another Country* by James Baldwin. But when sexism is so obviously a salient ingredient of the subject under consideration, to ignore it or misname it is to short-change our understanding. Even though Himes does not employ the word sexism in the narrative of *A Case of Rape,* in describing the forces that have victimized Elizabeth Hancock he uses the term *inverted racism.* Before she met Scott Hamilton, Elizabeth had not been victimized because of her race. She had been victimized because of her sex.

To wit, in *A Case of Rape,* Himes explores the *racism* and *sexism* of interracial love and shows that when they occur together, the two factors mask each other and are virtually inseparable. In Scott Hamilton's personality, there are effects of the insanities he experienced from having lived in a racist and sexist society. Likewise, Elizabeth's personal history attests to her victimization by the sexist insanities of her cultural background and by her husband. In fact, all of the black men in the novel, as well as the white woman, are victims of the racism and sexism of Western society.

The accused men and Elizabeth's husband, are in possession of information that cold have mitigated the conviction of the men and could possibly have exonerated them. The central question, then, becomes why and how were the four men convicted when there was evidence that could have supported their innocence? What made their conviction possible?

After the opening overview, the majority of *A Case of Rape* is devoted to unraveling the details leading to the rape-murder conviction of innocent men following the strange death of Elizabeth Hancock. Since there is no eyewitness to the alleged crime, the details consist of circumstantial evidence surrounding four black men associating with a white woman. The men then are convicted by the circumstantial evidence for being black and associating with a white woman. While black men associating with a white woman is not a legal offense, it is a social taboo. To break it carries social disapprobation equaling that reserved for the crime with which they are charged. In the minds of whites, black men/white women friendships constitute an extra-legal (or supra-legal) crime of implied sexual intercourse and therefore of rape. Notice how the rape charge is stressed throughout the trial rather than the murder question. Ironically, this emphasis is not only normal in a racist society but is perpetuated by the irrational animosities arising from the mere thought of an affair between a white woman and four black men. Indeed, the opening chapters of the book serve to set the stage for Himes to depict and expound throughout the remainder on the deranging effects of racism and sexism, both on the level of individual personality and on the societal level, as writ large in black man/white woman relationships.

The choice of setting in Paris functions as a sort of clinical laboratory for Himes's meticulous study. Both the romantic aura of desperate love between Scott and Elizabeth and the uncanny effects of racism on their relationship are intensified and heightened against the backdrop of the supposedly liberal Parisian environment. The Parisian setting also highlights the fugitive stigmata that all racist societies stamp upon interracial lovers. Almost universally, black men/white women associating together are seen as "fugitives" from both the white world and the black world. For example, in extremely racist environments, interracial couples actually hide from other people. In less bigoted situations they are nevertheless fearful and tend to engage in certain avoidance tactics. They appear to be forever in flight—psychological flight and geographical flight as well.

Moreover, the fugitive motif—the motif of exile and alienation—invades the individual lives and personalities of Elizabeth Hancock and her four alleged rapists. All had left America, their native home, and are residing in a foreign land, or rather, they are "floating around" in a foreign land, wearing the label of the "expatriate." They have departed from the mores of their culture, since those mores have oppressed and demeaned them, but at the same time they still bear the scars of their degradation. Both collectively and individually, they are haunted by the sense of guilt their native culture has imposed upon them, and they are irritated by their sure knowledge of being oddities in a foreign culture. Borne in their own consciousnesses, these stigmata—of being fugitives, of being "renegades" from society—bring the fivesome together as kindred souls, as wounded people seeking healing and desiring love and companionship far more than merely sex. Paradoxically, and yet quite naturally, the situation brings about their condemnation. Condemnation? Yes, because no matter what the circumstances, above all else, the supreme taboo of the world is that black men and white women are not supposed to associate with, let alone love one another. If they do, it's an automatic crime.

Himes spends considerable time delineating the backgrounds of Elizabeth and each of the four men in terms of the formative ingredients of their personalities, their genealogies, how they happened to end up in Paris, and what they were like before coming to know each other. Himes does this to show that once we have been victimized, we carry the effects in our psyches. Once we are poisoned by the venom of sexism and racism, it becomes almost impossible for us to relate to one another as healthy persons, even in an environment relatively free of the poison.[5] Every situation involving blacks and whites, especially where male and female are concerned, is liable to be misperceived, stereotyped, and misconstrued.

Scott and Elizabeth wanted so desperately to love each other, perhaps *too* desperately. The healing that both Scott and Elizabeth sought in and through their relationship was affected by the very sexist and racist mythologies surrounding relationships between black men and white women that, first and foremost, they had to overcome in themselves. Because while they thought they knew each other, what they saw were but socially inflicted distortions of their true selves.

The tangled web of sexual racism involves a tragic irony and a cruel dialectic. Here, the four black men's show of deference to Elizabeth was not rooted in solid ground. It sprang from their bad feelings about being outcasts of humanity, and from their internalization of the white man's own "chivalrous" idolatry of the "lily white lady." Himes writes, "They all were Negroes who revered cultured American white women, desired them, perhaps, in a dreamlike manner." It was for these reasons, these feelings, that in the emotional eyes of the four men, Elizabeth was not a mere woman but was a kind of magical object whose friendship the men believed would conjure up in them a sense of pride and self-worth as men.

Elsewhere I have written that the denial of the black man's humanity is in large measure predicated by the existence of the white world's racist perspective. By this anomalous standard, the black world is described as dirty, savage, sinful. The white world is supposed to be virtuous, holy, chaste, at the center of which stands the white woman. According to the mythology of white supremacy, it is the white woman who is the "immaculate conception" of Western civilization; the possession of her is therefore perceived as a sort of ontological affirmation of the black man's self-worth. On a deeper level, however, if not consciously then subconsciously, the black man is aware of his devalued humanity compared to the overblown valuation of white women. Mixed up with his desire to possess her, and his adoration for her, there is often an irritating bitterness, guilt, and even hatred. Of Shelly Russell and Ted Elkins, Himes writes: "Deep inside of Shelly's reverence for this type of white woman, there was an animosity as deep as Ted's own."

To further explain their behavior, Himes notes that all the men, except for Caesar Gee, showed signs of having complexes regarding the white ancestry in their genealogies. Ted Elkins, for example, hated his white grandfather and felt ashamed of his mother's illegitimacy. Yet he dated and married white women. Shelly Russell maintained reverence for all the attributes of upper class, cultured Americans that his white wife possessed. "Consequently," writes Himes, "he had a sort of reverence for all women who were her prototypes." Even Caesar Gee, whose heritage was pure African, and who did not like white American women, nevertheless engaged in relations with French and, presumably, other European white women; his paintings showed an inordinate preoccupation with black and white sex of a "pornographic" nature. The great Roger Garrison himself "felt inferior to and ill at ease in the presence of American white women of Mrs. Hancock's heritage." Altogether, the men were similarly affected by the insanities inherent in the racist and sexist societies in which they were born and had lived.

The four black men brought these feelings and experiences to their encounter with the "cultured" white woman. Thus, the reverence they all held for her was fraught with the desperation and misconceptions of rejected men, and had very little basis in reality. For, as Himes tells us, they did not know, and perhaps were incapable of knowing, the real Elizabeth.

On the other hand, A Case of Rape shows that the perspective from which Elizabeth viewed these men, which was a human one, was, nevertheless, also blind. Elizabeth's background and upbringing had sheltered her not only from the realities of her own world but from those of the black world as well. Elizabeth believed that all black men were kind to white women without any knowledge of the emotional brew of love-and-hate simmering beneath that show of kindness. She truly thought, for example, that Scott was a "complete person." She even thought her husband was a complete person! She knew nothing of Scott's deep-seated insecurities and knew nothing of the thin-skinned pettiness to which he and the others, including Roger Garrison, were all susceptible. As Chester Himes tells the reader, Elizabeth was a "casualty of white Christian society," reared according to the self-flagellating ethics of Puritanism, and socialized to be "feminine"—to be soft, weak, dependent, and therefore easily victimized. Thus, she had been kept ignorant of the dehumanizing forces of both sexism and racism even as she floated back and forth between the reality of her own world and that of her black lover.

In specific references to Scott and Elizabeth, Himes writes that they "were not too far apart in race, upbringing, or religion. They had the same traditions, the same moral outlook, the same disappointments by goodness and God." Thus, although classified as a Negro, the inner fiber of Scott Hamilton, similar to that of Elizabeth, was ridden with insecurity, ignorance, and blindness. Himes tells the reader that it never occurred to Scott that Elizabeth "was as much a casualty of racism as himself," but it was "an inverted sort of racism that perpetuates the dominance of the male." Indeed, Scott puts on the garb of the "knight in shining armor to rescue his "lady in distress." "As a consequence," writes Himes, "from the first to the last, his love for her was but a dream, acting itself out in his mind. The real Elizabeth he never saw and never knew."

Collectively, the four defendants, as well as Roger Garrison, show that they are held hostage by the interplay of the racist and sexist elements within themselves. Tragically, they are not aware of this. The men harbor all kinds of petty grudges and jealousies toward each other, apart from any reference to their appreciation for the white woman who became a symbol of their alter-egos. Further, the friendship of the men is based largely on the artificiality of race, since they come together as expatriates who are all subject to racist victimization. Their bonding, therefore, easily turns into manhood rivalry and conflict. The emotional fibers of the men are so thin and insecure that the most insignificant thing becomes of the utmost importance to them. This is also true in America, where daily we hear of black men killing each other following some petty argument. For the most part, the male characters in Himes's story do indeed unconsciously—and often as a socially induced pattern of relating between males—victimize each other. This tendency may also be heightened by the effects of racism on the masculine psychology, which is a competitive, "I'm-a-better-man-than-you" psychology.

To those who are unaware of the customs of men especially men in sexist and racist environments, the notion of fooling around with the Spanish Fly occurs in the lifetime of nearly every male in Western society, usually during adolescence. Stories about the mythological effects of Spanish Fly on women become a part of the ideal masculine sexual fantasy—you give it to females and it makes them do wild things. In *A Case of Rape,* we learn that Elizabeth's husband customarily used Spanish Fly to prepare her for a night of sex. An analogy can be made between the reference to "The Great American Myth"—the notion that black men can fuck, white women in particular, longer, harder, and better than any other men—and Spanish Fly. Remember, it was a white American reporter who gave the substance to Scott in the first place and who remarked about the great myth. Both of them, black men and Spanish Fly, can drive women crazy. Also recall it was Ted Elkins who secretly wished to give the bottle of Spanish Fly to Elizabeth and steer her in the direction of Caesar Gee, whom Elkins fancied she thought of as an ape. Elkins "wanted to see how she, in a state of sexual excitement, would respond to an ape."

In other works, *If He Hollers Let Him Go* for example, Himes also dwelled on the theme of black men being falsely accused of rape. This is true of Richard Wright's classic novel, *Native Son,* and John O. Killens's *Youngblood.* It is also definitely addressed in Angela Davis's study, *Women, Race and Class.* In black literature in general this theme is a central one. This is why the title of *A Case of Rape* is loaded with significance. In fact, *A Case of Rape* is not about an actual rape. Rather, it is about the mythology of rape as associated with the historical stereotype of black men being rapists of white women. The mythology of rape is another one of the sexist-racist insanities that grew out of slavery to justify keeping black men and women in bondage. I am not saying that black men do not rape. But the mythology of black men as rapists of white women serves to incite all white people against the entire black struggle for equality by charging that all black men really want is to sleep with the daughters of white men. Moreover, since white civilization has made the white woman a goddess, all attempts by blacks to gain any rights whatever are viewed as "rape attacks" against the white supremacist world. I have termed this phenomenon the sexualization of racism. The definition of all black men as rapists also serves as a distraction from the white man's crime and guilt of rape committed against black and white women, both during and since slavery. It also projects the blame onto black men for these crimes.

Thus, the four black men were convicted of the "crime" of associating with a fetish of the white racist-sexist world. In the twisted minds and emotions of white racists, any "nigger" associating with the "precious" woman is automatically guilty of rape, whether he actually commits it or not. This—the symbolic, circumstantially imaginary rape, which is altogether real to the racist—is what *A Case of Rape* is about.

Yet, the book most certainly concerns actual rape. It concerns the white man's rape of Elizabeth Hancock, and the white world's sexist victimization of women, in general. Elizabeth, moreover, had been "raped" all of her life by Christian hypocrisy and Puritan degradation of the female sex. She had been socialized in the belief that sex was pleasurable for men only. She had never experienced an orgasm and was ignorant of the most rudimentary knowledge relating to sex, her own sexuality in particular.

Himes writes that Elizabeth was "one of those unfortunate victims of a code of ethics promulgated by the white race as its own private doctrine for the elevation of whites only; a code of ethics which the white race has been the only race to reject." Like women in general, she was cast in the traditional role of an object to be dominated and exploited by men. Her husband, for example, performed "surgery" on her for sexual purposes; he actually felt that she enjoyed having pain inflicted on her. She produced babies and remained loyal for a time to her puritanical indoctrination.

The husband, André Brissaud, raped and mutilated Elizabeth in mind and soul, as well. He drove her to a nervous breakdown and carted her off to an asylum. He pimped Elizabeth, took her inheritance and purchased himself a plush dental practice. The clincher is the way in which he regarded her: "He felt her to be a possession, and he was never any more tender toward her than toward any of his other possessions, his dog or his car."

At this juncture, it is important to point out how Stella Browning, the one black woman in *A Case of Rape,* is presented in contrast to the saintly image of Elizabeth Hancock. Himes describes her as a "black haired piece of red hot sex, rotten to the core. [She was] working as an amateur whore and sleeping free with three men." Her only saving trait is that "she had a voice." Scott married her (she was seventeen!) because she was a "challenge" or perhaps as "revenge against his white ancestors." Scott never loved or respected her. He was ashamed of her background and viewed her with contempt. On the other hand, Scott instantly falls in love with the white paragon of virtue, whom he calls "Lisbeth," and to whom he declares, "I knew you were the one person in the world for me." He even uses the money Stella sends him to finance his love affair with "Lisbeth."

Though she is never brought to life as a person or a character, in my view Stella Browning is a dynamite and wholesome woman. Unlike Scott and the rest of the characters, including Elizabeth, Stella has her feet on the solid ground of reality. She is free of the personality hangups and middle-class pretentiousness of Scott and his cronies. In a society that is doubly hard on black women, Stella's independence has been earned through what ordinary black people call "the school of hard knocks." But she is given no credit. Stella Browning is not only relegated to the proverbial "back burner" by Scott's insane, angelic perception of Elizabeth. The black woman's denigration is implied by the hyperbolic significance attributed to the black man/white woman relationship—a significance fueled by the myth of the black man's alleged desire to rape white women. Unfortunately, it is this myth which motivates Roger Garrison in his misguided investigation.

It takes no microscope to see that Roger seems more afflicted with the same disease of racist victimization and the resultant paranoia that is the anguish of the four black men he seeks to exonerate. He carries an added burden of being the one and only American Negro who is recognized on a world scale as a literary genius, a sort of overblown "Native Son" living in exile. So bloated is he with his own sense of importance that petty, even silly emotionalisms prevent him from solving the case, and cause him to contribute to the demise of his four compatriots and to that of Elizabeth as well, by sending that letter to her publisher!

Notice the role that spite and malice assume in the lives of all the "victims." Sheldon Russell married his first white wife in retaliation against the racism he experienced at Harvard University. Scott Hamilton married Stella, a black *cafe au lait*-complexioned woman, as revenge against his own white ancestry. Ted Elkins gave the bottle of poisonous sherry to Elizabeth out of "unpremeditated, racially-inspired spite"; and Roger Garrison had sent the letter also out of "racially-inspired" spite. When Elizabeth learned of the letter that was sent to her publisher, she was shattered to know she had such spiteful enemies.

It is significant that Chester Himes, in nearly all his works, writes from his own experience, basing many of his fictional characters on the lives of real people. Although I have not found any case having occurred in France such as that described in *A Case of Rape,* I have no doubt that the book is based more on reality than make-believe. In fact, a significant portion of Chester Himes's autobiography deals with his European affair with an aristocratic white woman, Alva Trent Van Olden Barneveldt. The details of this affair are strikingly recognizable as those depicted in *A Case of Rape.*

Likewise, the character Roger Garrison is reminiscent of the writer Richard Wright, who figures importantly in the autobiography. Wright occupied a place of unprecedented eminence in the minds of both blacks and whites the world over, although self-exiled in Paris for almost two decades until his death in 1960.

Even as far-fetched as the story might seem, the Spanish Fly incident is not purely fictional. According to Michel Fabre, who translated the 1979 French edition of *A Case of Rape,* Himes authenticated the existence of such a case as having occurred in Columbus, Ohio, in 1929, involving a professor at Ohio State University and a student who died as a result of having been given Spanish Fly.[6] Himes also employed a variation on the same theme in one of his earlier novels, *Cast the First Stone* (1952). "Ergo," as Fabre noted, "Chester Himes has a great facility for "transforming historical events into imaginary episodes; he is masterful at basing fictional situations on everyday happenings."

A Case of Rape reads like a blend of a case study, a court clerk's report, a journalist's report, a thriller-mystery novel, an essay, and a moral tract. Accordingly, students of literature might experience some confusion in determining the genre of the book. The matter may be cleared up when we take into account that Himes had intended to compose a much longer, more thorough work. According to Fabre, Himes referred to the book we have here as his synopsis of *A Case of Rape,* in a letter to his friend and translator, Yves Malartic. The book Himes planned was to be a "Dostoievskian work several volumes." This, no doubt, would have been an incredible project. But the full-scale narrative was never written.

The reader should be glad to know that the present work is typical Chester Himes, even though it only sketches a much larger concept. It bears the Himesian trademark for exact detail, quick wit, and an astute ability for presenting complex elements in a thriller-mystery narrative. Most of all, there is within these pages the aesthetics of a profound moral conscience. It says that Truth, no matter how unpleasant or taboo, is the ultimate beauty of a work of art. This, of course, leads to the controversy that is nearly always generated by Himes's works.

Specifically, in *A Case of Rape,* Himes deals daringly, bluntly, with the forbidden, red-light subject of the scarlet equation. While he unravels the racist and sexist elements in the social backgrounds and personalities of the men and the woman, and deals forthrightly with the motives leading to their involvement, he equally tackles the inhumanity and downright insanity of a morally and sexually degenerate world where a white woman senselessly loses her life and four black men are wrongly condemned.

It is significant that Himes portrays André Brissaud both as an individual and as a representative of the entire decadence of white civilization. Personally and symbolically, he is depicted as the epitome of the white man's inhumanity to women and to men. On page 76, Himes writes:

He was imbued with an ingrown, refined evil of generations of decadence; an evil distilled form the dark superstitions of countless centuries of Christian expedience and aged in the slowly rotting *bien faite* culture of blasé and jaded city. His was an ungodly evil that was all the more terrible because he didn't know it was evil. An evil that had been in existence for so long it had attained another status, termed by the Americans as *continental.*

The depth and scope of Brissaud's evil is brought home by his collaboration with the Nazi Wehrmacht regime.

When it comes to Brissaud's role in the condemnation of the four men, I am reminded of the novel, *Sport of The Gods,* by Paul Laurence Dunbar, America's foremost "controversial" nineteenth century black poet. In the novel, a northern white man comes south to visit the plantation of his aristocratic, slave-holding brother. Pretending to be a financial success, the man is actually penniless. While visiting his brother, he steals a sum of his brother's money. Of course, the black handyman is accused, tried, and sentenced to a long term in prison. The white man, who is of the Christian faith, could have exonerated the Negro with little consequence to himself. But he refused to do so, letting the black man take the rap for his crime, which leads to the demise of the black man's family, to say nothing of his own imprisonment.

Similarly, Brissaud represents not only white civilization's practice of blaming its crimes on black people. He also is a psychological reflection of white people's inability to extend fairness to black men and women. How can you be fair to those you seek to oppress, exploit, and vilify? When Brissaud finds out that his wife has been lover to a black man during their separation, Brissaud became more excited about possessing her sexually than he was about reconciling the broken marriage. At the same time he felt it would blemish his character as a white man to come to the defense of Negroes accused of the rape-murder of his wife. What would people think of him as a white man? What would he think of himself? If he told the truth to save the black men, revealing that his former wife and mother of his daughters had been intimate with a black man, it would cause intolerable shame on himself and his daughters as well. What white man or woman would blame him for his silence?

But if the psychology of white men as oppressors is insanely weird, so is the psychology that has been wrought in black men over three centuries of oppression. Black men are afflicted with the mentality of victims, they have the feelings and emotions of the damned. Therefore, although the defendants were intelligent, even intellectual men, they had the emotional and mental reflex of all true victims—paranoia! Or, as Himes phrases it, "pure, unadulterated fear."

Automatically, the men understood that no matter what they said or did, they would not be believed, especially because they were innocent. But how could they have been innocent? They were black. Were they not guilty of breaking the most sacrosanct of taboos—being with a white woman? Even black people themselves would feel a conscientiousness to condemn them: "Niggers shouldn't have been hanging out with that white bitch, no way." Their crime was their color and their sex. Their crime was also their oppression. Since oppressors strive to make their victims feel responsible for their predicament, and since blackness is viewed by whites as a crime, the men felt guilty indeed, and were presumed guilty by everyone.

The unfairness Chester Himes has experienced throughout his life, specifically from the publishing world and from critics and readers, is the same injustice experienced by Elizabeth and the four men, which altogether belongs to the terrible category of "man's inhumanity to man" that Himes addresses on the final page of the book. After all, Shelly and Ted conspired to give the bottle containing the Spanish Fly to Elizabeth as Scott's back was turned. Envy, jealousy, and a feeling of having been wronged by Scott and Elizabeth were the sources of their racially inspired, spiteful feelings toward Elizabeth and Scott, particularly because they were lovers. Even more revealing is that Scott Hamilton could not face having it known that his former lover, Elizabeth, had informed him of having been sexually exhausted by her former husband a few hours prior to her and Scott's rendezvous. Scott feared what people would think of him. What role had he played in the whole affair? Would he be thought a homosexual? Anyway, he feared, and knew, that people would not believe Elizabeth had visited her former husband, and he could not prove it. Who, moreover, would believe the truth of why Elizabeth was in the room with four black men? What could black men and white women possibly have in common except lust? What, anyway, would possess these men to desire to prove their dignity and honesty to this white woman, and reassure her that none of them had sent the damaging letter? Who would believe that Elizabeth found in these black men a kindred spirit, trusted them implicitly, and felt infinitely safe with them? No one. The prosecutor himself found these claims "childish and insincere," mere excuses to lure the woman into an orgy.

The men "could not conceive of a white jury believing their innocence," and rightly so. Herein lies the ultimate import of the title: A Case of Rape reveals a tragically ironic metaphor of rape. For the minds and emotions of the four black men were raped—just as the bodies and minds and emotions of all black people have been raped by centuries of "man's inhumanity to man." The ultimate effect of oppression is to have the victims collaborate in their own oppression. This is why Scott and his buddies could not come forward with the truth. The men, "had been [utterly] conditioned by their culture, by the preconceptions and generalizations of the white race which always attributes the crimes of one Negro to the entire Negro race," until they simply had been rendered incapable of believing that anyone would believe the truth. If they testified that Ted had given Elizabeth the Spanish Fly out of spite, it would have been tantamount to confessing they all were accomplices. "No one," writes Himes, "would believe they had not actually raped her." In the last line of the book, Himes lays the blame where it ultimately belongs: "We are all guilty."

Himes's masterful writing, and especially his indomitable sense of the morality of truth and fairness, reveal the integrity and frailty of the human being beneath all of the artificial trappings of society, which form the insightful substructure of this work. Because of these attributes, A Case of Rape will be relevant for as long as human life is relevant.

NOTES

1. John A. Williams and Charles F. Harris, eds., *Amistad 1: Writings on Black History and Culture* (New York: Vintage Books, 1970), 30.
2. Chester Himes, *The Quality of Hurt*, vol. 1 of *The Autobiography of Chester Himes* (Garden City, New York: Doubleday & Company. Inc., 1972), 77.
3. Ibid., 100–101.
4. Ibid., 102.
5. For a more elaborate explanation of this assertion, see Calvin Hernton, *Sex and Racism in America* (New York: Grove Press, Inc., 1965). See especially chapters two and three.
6. Michel Fabre, "Dissecting Western Pathology. A *Critique—A Case of Rape*," *Black World* (March, 1972). Other Fabre quotes and references are from the same article.

"The Postscript," from *A Case of Rape* by Chester Himes. Washington, D.C.: Howard University Press, 1984. Pp. 107–140.

Topographies of Violence: Chester Himes' Harlem Domestic Novels

Michael Denning

The detective story originally in the plain narrative form—straightforward violence—is an American product'.... It's just plain and simple violence in narrative form, you know. 'Cause no one, no one, writes about violence the way that Americans do.... that's one of the reasons I began writing the detective stories. I wanted to introduce the idea of violence.... American violence is public life, it's a public way of life, it became a form, a detective story form.
            —Chester Himes (Williams 49, 75)

Violence permeates the detective novels of Chester Himes: violence of action, violence of images, violence of language. And it is evident from his comments in interviews and in his autobiography that a particular ideology of violence informs his writing. One might see this as the characteristic concern for violence of American writers: recall Lawrence's famous comment on Cooper's heroes: "hard, isolate, stoic, and a killer" (62), a formula inherited by the hard-boiled school who created the genre Himes is reworking. Indeed Himes himself claims that "I was just imitating all the other American detective story writers.... So I haven't created anything whatsoever; I just made the faces black" (Williams 49). Despite his disclaimers, however, something happens to the detective story, the hard-boiled novel, when it reaches his pen; the forms and ideology of its violence change. And it is Himes' particular topography of violence that I will look at in this essay.

Between 1957 and 1961 Chester Himes published seven detective novels; two more appeared in 1964 and 1969.[1] All but the last two were published in France before being published in the United States. They were initially written for quick money: Himes had had five "serious" naturalist novels published when, while living in France, he was asked by Marcel Duhamel to write a detective story. Duhamel was the director of La Série Noire, which published translations of American hard-boiled thrillers by Raymond Chandler, Dashiell

Hammett and James Cain, among others. In his autobiography, Himes reconstructs Duhamel's offer:

"Get an idea," Marcel said. "Start with action, somebody does something—a man reaches out a hand down the hall.... Always action in detail. Make pictures. Like motion pictures. Always the scenes are visible. No stream of consciousness at all. We don't give a damn who's thinking what—only what they're doing. Always doing something. From one scene to another. Don't worry about it making sense. That's for the end. Give me 220 typed pages."
    "I can't write like that," I said, feeling a strange sense of stage fright. (102)

But he could and did.

Yet it would be wrong to see Himes' career as a simple turn from "serious" fiction to potboilers; he had had a long-standing interest in the detective story form, having subscribed to *Black Mask* magazine while in prison in the 1930s when he was first beginning to publish stories (Margolies 10). And he took on the rigors of the form seriously. The first of his detective novels, *La reine des pommes* (*For Love of Imabelle*), won *le Prix du Roman Policier* in 1958, and Himes had a contract to write eight more, at the rate of one every two months (*Autobiography* 123). It was twelve years before the eight were finished but by then Himes had established himself as one of the masters of the genre.

In large part, the stories follow the conventions that Duhamel spelled out. They are fast-moving, with terse sentences arid short paragraphs. There is a heavy proportion of dialogue, spiced with the tough-guy wise-cracking of the genre, Characters are sketched caricatures, allegorical shadows with emblematic names: Sweet Prophet Brown, Snake Hips, the undertaker H. Exodus Clay. And someone is always doing something; these are stories of perpetual motion. As far as their "making sense," well, that often doesn't happen even at the end.

In one respect, however, Himes' stories break radically from the genre; they are not, fundamentally, detective stories. Despite the advertising of the lurid paperback covers—"a pair of pistol-packing black supercops who make Shaft look soft"—the two cops, Grave Digger Jones and Coffin Ed Johnson, though they appear in all are not the central figures, and to compare them with Philip Marlowe or Mike Hammer seems incongruous. For in the main tradition of the hard-boiled detective story, the figure of the vulnerable but tough, wise-cracking but sentimental private eye is the consciousness that holds the characteristically first-person narrative together. As Herbert Ruhm writes, "he is slugged, shot out, choked, doped, yet he survives because it is his nature to survive. Single, poor, and lonely, he stays so by choice, guarding his incorruptibility by this aloneness, which is also a measure of his uniqueness" (xiv).

Coffin Ed Johnson and Grave Digger Jones are not this sort of hero, as both their doubling and their names indicate. The misunderstanding of the paperback jackets was repeated when Hollywood came to make a film from them. Himes says of the screen play of *Cotton Comes to Harlem*: "what I dislike most about the screenplay ... it's a good story, but it's a story about Deke, and the main purpose of Goldwyn [the producer] is to make a series of movies of Coffin Ed Smith [sic][2] and Grave Digger Jones" (Williams 55). In his autobiography Himes quotes a letter from Goldwyn saying that the "problem is that the two characters are not contrasted sharply enough. In fact, I still cannot point to any one scene in the script where their actions are so different and individual that they complement each other by them" (361). And this is true of the books as well. The two characters are not "individuals," nor does their relationship fit any of the conventional pairings of sleuth and sidekick.

Given this decentered detective, perhaps we should read these stories not as detective novels but as what Himes himself called them, his Harlem domestic series. For surely the central character in the stories is Harlem itself, whose topography and character-system they map. But before we fall into seeing these as naturalistic accounts of Harlem, it is well to recall what Himes has said of this Harlem: "I didn't know what it was like to be a citizen of Harlem; I had never worked there, raised children there, been hungry, sick or poor there. I had been as much of a tourist as a white man from downtown changing his luck.... *The Harlem of my books was never meant to be real; I never called it real: I just wanted to take it away from the white man if only in my books"* (Autobiography 126).

The stories are topographies of this unreal city, a mapping of its symbolic landscape. The major breaks from the incessant dialogue come in the simple incantatory recital of street numbers:

They kept on down to 119th street, turned back to Eighth Avenue, went uptown again and parked before a dilapidated tenement house between 126th and 127th Streets (*The Crazy Kill* 11)—

or in passages like this:

On the south side, Harlem is bounded by 110th Street. It extends west to the foot of Morningside Heights, on which Columbia University stands. Manhattan Avenue, a block to the east of Morningside Drive, is one of the corner streets that screen the Harlem slums from view. The slum tenements give way suddenly to trees and well-kept apartment buildings, where the big cars of the Harlem underworld are parked bumper to bumper. Only crime and vice can pay the high rents charged in such borderline areas. That's where Rufus lived (*The Big Gold Dream* 4)

Much is made of borderlines and frontiers in these stories for the boundaries of Harlem are the boundaries, at times claustrophobic, of this world. In a fine chase scene in *For Love of Imabelle*, Jackson, fleeing in a hearse, having smashed through a market, scattering fruit and people, comes as far as 95th and 5th Avenue, realizes he's out of Harlem and turns back towards his pursuers: "He was down in the white world with no place to go, no place to hide his woman's gold ore, and no place to hide himself" (20).

Within these limits, Himes draws his symbolic landscape with detailed but stylized descriptions of food, clothing, and social life:

It was eleven o'clock Sunday morning, and the good colored people of Harlem were on their way to church.
    It was a gloomy, overcast day, miserable enough to make the most hardened sinner think twice about the hot, sunshiny streets of heaven before turning over and going back to sleep....

Old white-haired sisters bundled up like bales of cotton against the bitter cold; their equally white-haired men, stumbling along in oversize galoshes like the last herd of Uncle Toms, toddling the last mile toward salvation on half-frozen feet.

Middle-aged couples and their broods, products of the post-war generation, the prosperous generation, looking sanctimonious in their good warm clothes, going to promise the Lord for the white folks' blessing....

From all over town they came.

To all over town they went....

To Baptist churches and African Methodist Episcopal churches and African Methodist Episcopal Zionist churches; to Holy Roller churches and Father Divine churches and Daddy Grace churches, Burning Bush churches, and churches of God and Christ.

To listen to their preachers preach the word of God: fat black preachers and tall yellow preachers, family preachers and playboy preachers, men preachers and lady preachers and children preachers.

To listen to any sermon their preacher cared to preach. But on the cold day it had better be hot. (*All Shot Up* 13)

I think we can get a better sense of this topography if we outline its organization, and one can begin with the binary opposition that orients all of the novels—the law vs. crime. As A. J. Greimas has shown,[3] however, any binary opposition logically implies a number of other terms, beginning with the simple negations of the two contraries. Using his convenient semantic rectangle, we can get a preliminary mapping of the character "Harlem" that looks like this:

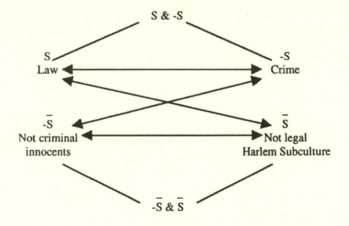

If the plot of these books is essentially the pursuit of the criminals by the law, the interest of the plot comes from the other positions. What I call the Harlem sub-culture is that quasi-legal set of institutions that Coffin Ed and Grave Digger distinguish from crime itself: "they had their own personal interpretation of law enforcement. Some people they never touched—such as madames of orderly houses of prostitution, operators of orderly gambling games, people connected with the numbers racket, streetwalkers who stayed in their district. But they were rough on criminals of violence and confidence men" (*The Big Gold Dream* 10). This world also includes evangelists, the homosexual subculture, the back-to-Africa movement, shady politicians and the Syndicate. Raymond Nelson points out that each story could be seen as dealing with one or two of these institutions: *The Crazy Kill* with gambling, *The Big Gold Dream* with evangelism and numbers, *All Shot Up* with politics and the homosexual world, and so on (260–267).

At the other corner of this semantic topography are not so much the everyday law-abiding citizens, who don't make much of an appearance, but the innocents, the suckers, the victims of the confidence games. Here we have Jackson, the dutiful hearse chauffeur, Roman Hill the sailor, and Alberta Wright the pious convert. These characters appear in the strikingly absurd beginnings to the books. In *For Love of Imabelle*, Jackson, the Southern college boy, is conned out of his money by Hank, who claims to be able to chemically raise the denominations of bills, to turn tens into hundreds, in a stove. The stove explodes, Hank splits, and Jackson is left to be arrested and blackmailed by a phoney policeman. Other openings are as surreal—the Rev. Short falls out of a window into a bread basket; Alberta Wright dies at a revival meeting when she drinks the holy water. The plots then consist of the police investigating the series of actions, including murders, triggered by this catastrophe.

Having thus mapped the basic positions, we may fill in the mediating positions:

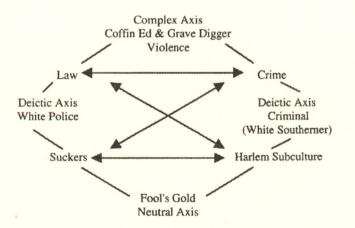

First a brief look at the two "deictic axes." Clearly the white police are a combination of the law and the suckers; as the narrator says of Goldy, the junkie disguised as a Sister of Mercy, "He knew the best way to confuse a white cop in Harlem was to quote foolishly from the Bible." (*For Love of*

Imabelle 11). Until the last three books, which, as we shall see, mark a major change, the white cops are generally totally confused and wait for Coffin Ed and Grave Digger to interpret the action to them (and take advantage of their gullibility), as in this interrogation scene:

Grave Digger saw that Brody didn't get it, so he explained. "It's a Holy Roller church. When the members get happy they roll about on the floor."
    "With one another's wives," Coffin Ed added.
    Brody's face went sort of slack, and the police reporter stopped writing to stare open-mouthed.
    "They keep their clothes on," Grave Digger amended. "They just roll about on the floor and have convulsions, singly and in pairs."
    The reporter looked disappointed. (*The Crazy Kill* 6)

The other "deictic axis," the criminal himself, is distinguished from the "crime" pole because, despite Jones and Johnson's distinction between the quasi-legitimate subcultures and the criminals of violence, the mysteries of these stories lead to the intersection of the two, and, as we shall see, outside of Harlem itself. But the mystery will be kept for the last, and we will turn now to the two terms that Greimas finds the most interesting, the complex and the neutral.[4]

The "complex term" is the one that mediates the two contraries, and it is here that Coffin Ed and Grave Digger stand; their relatively central role comes not, as we have seen, from their position as heroes or centers of consciousness, but as mediators, between black and white, life and death, law and crime. Lévi-Strauss writes that the mediator, the trickster, "occupies a position halfway between two polar terms," and that "he must retain something of that duality—namely an ambiguous and equivocal character" (223). The two detectives have this ambiguous character, at once enforcers of the law and figures of violence and death: "Coffin Ed had killed a man for breaking wind. Grave Digger had shot both eyes out of a man who was holding a loaded automatic. The story was in Harlem that these two black detectives would kill a dead man in his coffin if he so much as moved" (*All Shot Up* 4). Their "long-barreled, nickel-plated .38 revolvers" quiet crowds, elicit information, and, with their phosphorescent tracer bullets, light up night skies and dark churches: "Colored folks didn't respect colored cops. But they respected his big shiny pistols and sudden death" (*For Love of Imabelle* 8). "Don't make graves" is their advice when entering crowded bars. Nor are they invulnerable to violence; in the first book, acid is thrown in Coffin Ed's face, leaving a scar that "looked like the mask of an African witch doctor," and leaving Ed a little trigger-happy, continually having to be restrained by his partner. In *The Heat's On*, the sixth book of the series, Grave Digger is nearly killed, and after that they are equally on edge, breaking heads and pistol-whipping suspects at the least provocation.

But lest things seem too grim, it is important to note that these are not the sadistic fantasies that mark, for example, Mickey Spillane, of whom Hall and Whannel have written, "It would be an understatement to say that Mike Hammer [Spillane's protagonist] enjoys killing and violence. He is pathologically committed to it" (144). Himes' violence, on the other hand, is funny, surreal, as he himself recognizes in his autobiography: "I was writing some strange shit. Sometime before, I didn't know when, my mind had rejected all reality as I had known it and I had begun to see the world as a cesspool of buffoonery. Even the violence was funny. A man gets his throat cut. He shakes his head to say you missed me and it falls off. Damn reality, I thought. All of reality was absurd, contradictory, violent and hurting. It was funny really. If I could just get the handle to joke. And I had got the handle, by some miracle" (126).

Two scenes in this mode stand out, and I'll quote at some length. One is from *All Shot Up*: Grave Digger and Coffin Ed are following a lead within the main line of the story. They see a motorcyclist: "They didn't recognize the vehicle; they knew nothing of its history, its use or its owner. But they knew that anyone out on a night like that in an open vehicle bore investigation." Mutual suspicion leads to a chase:

One block ahead, a refrigerator truck was flashing its yellow passing lights as it pulled to the inner lane to pass an open truck carrying sheet metal.

The motorcycle rider had time to pass on the inside, but he hung back, riding the rear of the refrigerator truck until it had pulled clear over to the left, blocking both sides of the street.

"Get a tire now," Grave Digger said.

Coffin Ed leaned out of his window, took careful aim over his left wrist and let go his last two bullets. He missed the motorcycle tire with both shots, but the fifth and last one in his revolver was always a tracer bullet, since one night he had been caught shooting in the dark. They followed its white phosphorescent trajectory as it went past the rear tire, hit a manhole cover in the street, ricocheted in a slight upward angle and buried itself in the outside tire of the open truck carrying sheet metal. The tire exploded with a bang. The driver felt the truck lurch and hit the brakes.... [the motorcycle driver] was pulling up fast behind the truck carrying sheet metal when the tire burst and the driver stamped the brakes. He wheeled sharply to the left, but not quickly enough.

The three thin sheets of stainless steel, six feet in width, with red flags flying from both corners, formed a blade less than a quarter of an inch thick. This blade caught the rider above his woolen lined jacket, on the exposed part of his neck, which was stretched and taut from his physical exertion, as the motorcycle went underneath. He was hitting more than fifty-five miles an hour, and the blade severed his head from his body as though he had been guillotined.

... The truck driver glanced from his window to watch the passing truck as he kept braking to stop. But instead he saw a man without a head passing on a motorcycle with a sidecar and a stream of steaming red blood flowing back in the wind.

He gasped and passed out....

The motorcycle, ridden by a man without a head, surged forward at a rapid clip. (11)

The other scene is in *The Heat's On*: Uncle Saint, after 25 years of being a flunky for Sister Heavenly and her heroin trade, decides to rob her safe and leave. After a comic battle with a nanny goat, he gets out the nitroglycerin he has carefully saved and blows her safe:

Strangely enough the house disintegrated in only three directions—forward, backward and upward. The front went out across the street, and such items as the bed, tables, chest of drawers and a handpainted enamel chamber pot crashed into the front of the neighbor's house. Sister Heavenly's clothes, some of which dated back to the 1920s, were strewn over the street like a weird coverlet of many colors....

It was hard to determine afterwards which way Uncle Saint and the nanny goat went, but whichever way they went, they went together, because the two assistants from the Medical Examiner's Office of Bronx County couldn't distinguish the bits of goat meat from the bits of Uncle Saint's meat, which was all there was left for them to work on. (12)

In both of these cases, and throughout Himes' stories, bodies become objects, and the attacks of violence on that body are little different than the destruction of buildings or automobiles, all of which are described in patient, material detail (and both of these passages are longer than I have quoted; in the ellipsis of the second passage, we learn the entire contents of Sister Heavenly's house).

Given that one of the major narrative paradigms of black literature has been the movement from being an object, a thing, a slave, to being a person, to move, as H. L. Gates has shown, from nature to culture, it is as if Himes has reversed the plot and shown the reduction of people to objects, not for the purpose of protest but for the absurd and comic incongruity. Violence does not signify oppression in Himes, nor the myth of the stoic American killer, nor "the myth of regeneration through violence" that Richard Slotkin argues "became the structuring metaphor of the American experience" (5). Rather, violence in Himes signifies nothing but its own arbitrariness, its random intrusion on everyday life. And as such it becomes comic.

If there is a certain arbitrary nature to the books' violence, the same is true of the books' quests; and here I turn to the "neutral term" of the rectangle, the term which mediates the sucker and the underworld, and which I call "fool's gold." This is the object that got the sucker in trouble in the first place, but which in the course of the story involves people of the underworld in the same scramble or quest. For everyone is searching for the same thing, they all think that someone else has it, and they are all convinced of its great value. It circulates from one unwitting character to another, but invariably it proves to be worthless, or, if there is something valuable, it turns out to have been removed from circulation very early. As this may seem somewhat confusing (and it is confusing in the stories), I will list a few examples. In *For Love of Imabelle*, everyone is chasing a trunk full of gold which is being used to sell shares in a gold mine. It turns out to be, literally, fool's gold. In *The Big Gold Dream*, everyone is chasing a large amount of money that Alberta won in the numbers. After the smoke has cleared and the corpses are laid out, we discover that the money they were all chasing is Confederate bills; the real money had been given away before the book began. In *The Heat's On*, everyone is after a shipment of heroin, and they kill one another (and a dog) trying to find it. Once again the bag of heroin is phoney; the real heroin, hidden in some eels, had been burned mistakenly by a junkie. And in *Cotton Comes to Harlem*, a bale of cotton, supposedly filled with stolen money, passes from one character to another, all of whom think it strange to find cotton in Harlem, until someone who knows about the money buys it. Then it is discovered that a junk man had found the money and gone back to Africa himself.

These are the most striking examples of the violent, yet often unconscious circulation of worthless currency of various sorts, the confidence game in which everyone is conned. Signifiers have no signifieds, one might say, and this is true not only of the funny violence and the funny money but of the worlds of gambling, evangelical religion, and politics in general. The arbitrariness of seemingly natural signs is figured most dramatically when Pinky, the albino Negro, escapes by coloring his skin black.

If it is the work of a detective to uncover the meaning of signs, to unravel the motivations of signs, one sees why these are such unconvincing detective stories. Even though most of the early books do "solve" the original murder, most of the plot is left unexplained. Mere coincidence is often allowed as an explanation: two different crimes involving an interlocking set of people do not signify a broader conspiracy; they just happened to occur next to each other (see, for example, *All Shot Up*). This becomes more pronounced in the later books, until finally, in *Blind Man with a Pistol*, nothing is solved, and the genre appears to break down.

Nevertheless, even if Himes does not always resolve his plots, if the violence is often left unmotivated, the currency worthless, and the disguises never fully unmasked, one could argue that he has not left the genre, that he is just playing with the conventions, writing post-modernist detective stories. The detective story seems at first to be a form so conventional, so stylized, as to be without any ideological content, and so open to a purely formal reversal or disruption. And though it is tempting to treat the problem of the change in the last three stories of the Harlem domestic stories as a heightened formal permutation of the detective convention, it seems to me that the ideological determinations upon form interfere.

For, as Bruce Franklin has provocatively argued, the development of the novel moves from its origins in the picaresque lives of criminals told from the point of view of the criminal to the detective story told from the point of view of the law (222–24). So the detective story, as a form looked at in its relation to other forms, has an ideological content, related to the hegemony of capitalist law. What is particularly interesting is that the development of Himes' career as a writer is a microcosm of this larger development, as he moves from his partly autobiographical, naturalistic stories and novel about prison life to detective stories about policemen (not even stopping at the private eye, who is on the boundary of the law). In this shift there remains a profound ambivalence about the law and violence that eventually disrupts the detective stories.

I think that this ambivalence can best be uncovered by turning to Frantz Fanon's theory of colonial violence. I don't mean to demonstrate the "truth" of Himes' stories by measuring them against Fanon's theory. Nor do I think that Himes was trying to "illustrate" the theory in his books. Rather, Fanon provides a valuable hermeneutic, a way of recoding the early novels (1957–1961), and, I would argue, the way Himes himself recoded the early novels In producing the books of 1964 and 1969.

The use of Fanon as a hermeneutic first gives an ideological content to the violence of the books, a violence which I have argued is formally arbitrary and therefore largely comic. Fanon analyzes the official description and explanation of Algerian criminality, and repositions that description not as "fact," the static and unchanging nature of Algerians, but as a moment within a developing social and historical situation. So he goes over the "facts": "The Algerian frequently kills other men.... The Algerian kills savagely.... The Algerian kills for no reason." Thus the Algerian is "a violent person, of a hereditary violence" (296–98). All of these "facts" Fanon reinserts into the historical world of colonialism: the split between the settler town and the native town, and the projection of violence and amorality onto the native society ("the native is declared insensible to ethics; he represents not only the absence of values, but also the negation of values.... He of whom they have never stopped saying that the only language he understands is that of force, decides to give utterance by force.... To the theory of the 'absolute evil of the native' the theory of the "absolute evil of the settler replies" [41, 84, 93].

Perhaps the most relevant reversal Fanon accomplishes is his reinterpretation of the "fact" that Algerian violence is aimed at other Algerians, not at the settlers. Fanon takes this "fact" and places it as a moment in the development of colonial consciousness: "The colonial man will first manifest this aggressiveness which has been deposited in his bones against his own people. This is the period when the niggers beat each other up, and the police and magistrates do not know which way to turn when faced with the astonishing waves of crime in North Africa" (52).

One can see how this could be a powerful interpretive tool to approach Himes' early detective stories. Harlem is clearly portrayed as a "native town," confined within limits, its arbitrary violence and its chases for counterfeit money and fool's gold comprising a self-contained economy. Himes seems to have accepted as *imaginative* fact the clichés that blacks kill each other for no reason, that they are beyond "normal," that is white, motivation. Think of Grave Digger's analysis of the triviality of motives of Harlem violence: "This is Harlem. Ain't no other place like it in the world. You've got to start from scratch here, because these folks in Harlem do things for reasons nobody else in the world would think of. Listen, there were two hard-working colored jokers, both with families, got to fighting in a bar over on Fifth Avenue near a hundred-eighteenth Street and cut each other to death about whether Paris was in France or France was in Paris" (*The Crazy Kill* 7). The effect of this analysis of Harlem's "reason" is very much like the effect of the reduction of people to objects in Himes' violence, that is, a comic absurdity. But one of the difficulties with comedy is its basis in socially constructed types, stereotypes, and Himes often seems to be walking on the brink of a sort of violent minstrel show.

At this point a major shift occurs in Himes' work. He employs Fanon's hermeneutic to re-understand his early work and re-orient his writing. One piece of evidence for this is to be found in Himes' interview with John A. Williams when he says: "By the way [Fanon] wrote a long article on my 'Treatment of Violence' which his wife still has, and which I've thought I might get and have published. Because he had the same feeling, of course, that I have" (87). This "same feeling" is the belief that, in Fanon's words, "the colonized man finds his freedom in and through violence ... as the level of individuals, violence is a cleansing force. It frees the native from his inferiority complex and from his despair and inaction; it makes him fearless and restores his self-respect" (86, 94). Himes picks up this ideology explicitly, if somewhat more crudely: "in order for a revolution to be effective, one of the things that it has to be, is violent, it has to be massively violent.... I think the only way a Negro will ever get accepted as an equal is if he kills whites" (Williams 45, 60).

I am not concerned here with a critique of Himes' ideology of violence, but with the way it inflects his later writings. First of all, he writes his one detective novel without Coffin Ed and Grave Digger, *Run Man Run*. This is explicitly about a black-white encounter, as a drunken white cop shoots two black restaurant workers for no reason, and then pursues a third, Jimmy, who accuses him of the murders. No one believes Jimmy, and the story becomes Jimmy's attempts to stay alive while convincing everyone, including his girlfriend, that the cop is the murderer. This is not in the least comic and is very different from the Grave Digger/Coffin Ed series. It becomes a sort of belated version of *Native Son* and, without the naturalistic detail, is largely unsuccessful. The arbitrary violence here signifies oppression, which moves the novel to a very different tonality (one of tragedy or revolt; Himes' weak happy ending is neither) than the Grave Digger/Coffin Ed novels where arbitrary violence signifies arbitrariness and yields the absurd. But it does reveal some of Himes' troubles with the detective form; as he writes in his autobiography of his first "serious" novel: "I had started out to write a detective story when I wrote that novel, but I couldn't name the white man who was guilty because all white men were guilty" (102).

Second, there is a major change in Himes' attitude toward his early Grave Digger/Coffin Ed stories, and toward the characters of Grave Digger and Coffin Ed. For if he does recode them in terms of the Fanon dialectic, it becomes apparent that he has been writing about the first *stage* of colonial consciousness, and that there is a movement that would direct him away from figuring intra-Harlem violence toward figuring the violence between Harlem and the outside white world, or at least toward giving the external causes of intra-Harlem violence. But this disrupts the economy of his stories and of the genre—with the following results.

First, Jones and Johnson become more and more human; they develop into "realistic" characters. In the first novels they had no non-professional life; beginning with *The Heat's On*, however, we meet wives and children, discover that they don't live in Harlem but on Long Island, and that their children go to summer camp in the Catskills. Whereas earlier violence against them had been as object-like as the rest—"Coffin Ed went headfirst into the safety glass windshield and battered out a hole. But his hard head saved him from serious injury" (*All Shot Up* 11)—in the later stories we are in the hospital with Grave Digger's wife sweating out his recovery from gunshot wounds.

The two cops also become more honest, as Raymond Nelson has noted. In the first book we are told that "they took their tribute, like all real cops, from the established underworld" (*For Love of Imabelle* 8), but by the time of the final book, written twelve years later, we discover that "they hadn't taken a dime in bribes" (*Blind Man with a Pistol* 11).

In one way, however, this sets up a productive tension that *Run Man Run* and Himes' "political" statements lack. For in the later novels there is a clear distinction between unorganized criminal violence and organized, purposeful violence. And the two cops get caught in the middle. On the one hand, they are clearly opposed to certain sorts of violence—the awkward sermons against drug dealers and violent predators in *The Heat's On* are all too evident. Nonetheless, they are beginning to question the law they are enforcing, as young blacks in the stories challenge them on the grounds that they are serving the oppressor. No sooner is this established than it is undercut, as justifications for Grave Digger and Coffin Ed's police brutality (not conceivable in the world of the early novels) begin to appear. Jones and Johnson are suspended from the police force in both *The Heat's On* and *Cotton Comes to Harlem* for brutality. And Coffin Ed ends *The Heat's On* with a moral:

What hurts me most about this business is the attitude of the public toward cops like me and Digger. Folks just don't want to believe that what we're trying to do is make a decent peaceful city for people to live in, and we're going about it in the best way we know how. People think we enjoy being tough, shooting people and knocking them in the head. (24)

But the final turn of the screw comes when their suspension, on grounds of brutality, is revealed to be the desire of the power structure not to solve the crime, so that Grave Digger and Coffin Ed become private eyes working against the police force. The real world is erupting into Himes' unreal Harlem, straining its violent symmetries.

As the two detectives move to the foreground and become real characters with moral and social dilemmas, the solutions to the novels become more and more problematic. And here I will return finally to our semantic topography of Harlem and look at the last axis of the rectangle, the criminal, and, in particular, the white Southerner. In the early books the criminal had been revealed as someone who was part of a particular subculture but was breaking its rules. This is the case, for example, with Sweet Prophet Brown, the evangelist, and Slick, the numbers man, in *The Big Gold Dream*.

But beginning with *All Shot Up*, there is a growing sense that the real criminals have gotten away, that the end of the chain of incrimination is outside Harlem and that it has been arbitrarily cut, so as not to lead into the white world. In *All Shot Up* and *Cotton Comes to Harlem*, this is figured by the appearance of a white Southerner, not fully explained and yet somehow connected. In *All Shot Up* the Harlem politician Caspar Holmes shoots the Southerner at the end to prevent him from talking, leaving Grave Digger and Coffin Ed infuriated, unable to pursue the case further because of Holmes' political power. And in *Cotton Comes to Harlem*, the real criminal, Colonel Calhoun, the organizer of the bizarre Back-to-the-Southland movement, an attempt to recruit cotton pickers in Harlem, manages to escape at the end to the South.

This tendency comes to a conclusion in *Blind Man with a Pistol*. At this point Himes has largely worked through the awkwardnesses of his transitional books. Here the original comic absurdity is joined to his social vision, and the detective genre is twisted to a postmodernist experimentation that makes this a just contemporary of Ishmael Reed. Here nothing is solved. The police department wants them to forget about solving the murders, which are leading out of Harlem to political bosses and the Syndicate; instead, the police want Grave Digger and Coffin Ed to find out who is "behind" the riots. The book becomes a broad social satire, with a memorable scene of the convergence of three marches: the Brotherhood march, the Lynched Black Jesus march, and the Black Power march, a confrontation that Grave Digger and Coffin Ed can't stop in their usual way by drawing pistols and yelling "Don 't make graves." Instead they are as confused as anyone, including the reader, as several plots disintegrate into the riot.

The conclusion, a rewriting of Baraka's play *Dutchman*, is a subway encounter between blacks and whites which leads to a blind man firing off a pistol, creating a panic and then a riot. When asked by their bosses whether they have discovered who incited the riot, Jones and Johnson answer, "a blind man with a pistol." Despite the patness of Himes' moral—he says in the preface to the book that "I thought of some of our loudmouthed leaders urging our vulnerable soul brothers on to getting themselves killed, and thought further that all organized violence is like a blind man with a pistol"—what is striking about the image is its allusion to the first of the books, when Coffin Ed is blinded by acid and then fires his pistol at random, and eventually slugs his own partner. As so often in Himes, the grotesque overwhelms both the conventional action and the moral of the genre, leaving us with emblems of absurd and comic violence.

And these emblems, produced by Himes' forms and ideologies of violence, themselves do violence to the forms and ideologies he employs. For, far from having "just made the faces black," Himes has created a topography of Harlem that violates the conventions of the hard-boiled detective story, decentering its sentimental tough-guy hero, refusing to resolve its murders, and mocking its "realism." And the Harlem of his topography assaults the imaginary Harlems of the stories of white America.

NOTES

1. Since there are a number of editions of Himes' novels, I refer to quotes by chapter rather than page in the parentheses that follow.

2. Either this is a misprint or Himes has forgotten his character's name, Coffin Ed Johnson.

3. See A. J. Greimas and F. Rastier, "The Interaction of Semiotic Constraints" *Yale French Studies* 41 (1968): 86–105; and A. J. Greimas, "Elements of a Narrative Grammar" *Diacritics* 7 (Spring 1977). The use of the semiotic rectangle in the analysis of fiction, both literary and popular has been developed by Fredric Jameson. See his *Fables of Aggression* (University of California Press, 1979): "The rectangle is the representation of a binary opposition (two contraries) [S and -S], along with the simple negations (or contradictories) of both terms (the so-called sub-contraries) [S and -S], plus the various possible combinations of these terms, most notably the 'complex term' (ideal synthesis of the two contraries) [S and -S] and the "neutral term" (ideal synthesis of the two sub-contraries) [S and -S]" (99). Jameson points out elsewhere that this device forces us to see "that concepts do not

exist in isolation but are defined in opposition to each other in relatively organized clusters." See "After Armageddon: Character Systems in *Dr. Bloodmoney*," *Science Fiction Studies* 2 (1975): 42

4. At this point I should remark that this rectangle is not intended to be a complete mapping of the stories: to pretend such completion would be a sort of positivist utopia. Rather, this is merely one thematic articulation; others could be imagined beginning with other binary oppositions in the stories. This particular "decoding device" helps articulate the positions of law and violence in the stories. For another version of the use of the binary opposition, see H. L. Gates, "Binary Oppositions in Chapter One of *Narrative of the Life of Frederick Douglass*."

WORKS CITED

Fanon, Frantz. *The Wretched of the Earth*. New York: Grove, 1968.

Franklin, H. Bruce. *The Victim as Criminal and Artist*. New York and Oxford: Oxford Univ. Press, 1978

Gates, H. L. "Binary Oppositions in Chapter One of *Narrative of the Life of Frederick Douglass*." *Afro-American Literature*. Ed. D. Fisher and R. Stepto. Modern Language Association, 1979. 212–32.

Hall, Stuart and Paddy Whannel. *The Popular Arts*. Pantheon, 1965.

Himes, Chester. *My Life of Absurdity: The Autobiography*. Vol 2. New York: Doubleday, 1976.

Lawrence, D. H. *Studies in Classic American Literature*. New York: Viking, 1961.

Lévi-Strauss, Claude. *Structural Anthropology*. New York: Anchor, 1967.

Margolies, Edward. "The Thrillers of Chester Himes." *Studies in Black Literature* 2.1 (1970).

Nelson, Raymond. "Domestic Harlem." *Virginia Quarterly Review* 48 (1972): 260–76.

Ruhm, Herbert. Introduction. *The Hard-Boiled Detective*. New York: Vintage, 1977.

Slotkin, Richard. *Regeneration Through Violence*. Middletown, CT: Wesleyan Univ. Press, 1973.

Williams, John A. "My Man Himes: An Interview with Chester Himes." *Amistad* I. New York: Random, House, 1970.

Critical Texts, 5 (1986), 10–18.

Space and Civil Rights Ideology: The Example of Chester Himes's *The Third Generation*

Claude Julien

This paper makes no claim to theorizing, so it is best to identify a few theoretical beliefs at the outset.[1] The literary game calls for ideology to be kept out of sight in the name of art, but ideas naturally find many a hideout in the text they inform. And space, the novel's imagined world, is their privileged medium because reading boils down to conjuring from words. Man can turn the world around him into words, can proceed from words to ideas. But he cannot leave the ground for long, as imagination needs solid props to thrive on. The reader's most available solid prop is his own mental image of the fictional world. I believe this explains why readers first sense ideas through space. Places, things, animals, plants and people (to name only a few obvious spatial elements), even when they are only imagined, hold some of the tangibility needed to built meaning from: they are beacons that help the reader find his bearings, signposts that direct his feelings and induce his thinking almost against his will.

Some spatial elements speak more openly than others because they carry more meaningful visual, situational or emotional charges. Spatial layouts offer themselves for creators to pick or reject, to alter or disfigure. For instance, color coding is always ready at hand for Afro-American writers. Nothing is more glaring than two contrasting and symbolically coded colors like black and white that have the alluring potential (in fiction) to make the visible invisible[2], or, as in Chester Himes's *The Third Generation,* to merge into each other when black becomes white within the same family.

* * *

The Third Generation is a challenging story that does not follow any of the standard recipes for ethnic protest one has come to expect of a black novel. After the racially clear-cut naturalistic protest of the forties loosely called the Wrightian school, black novels of the fifties have been interpreted as a sign of the community's changing mood. Where the protest contents of the fiction of the preceding decade had been spurred by the despair of the Depression, the new outlook resulted from economic gains and, mostly, hopefulness. So stands the popular view, more or less inspired by the white liberal perspective.

This widespread theory is upheld by *The Negro Novel in America* (published in 1958 and still widely read today) in which Robert Bone speaks of an emerging "raceless" novel. For evidence, he points out the books of newcomers like James Baldwin, Paule Marshall, Owen Dodson and William Demby. *Go Tell it on the Mountain* (1953), *Brown Girl, Brownstones* (1959) and *Boy at the Window* (1951) all show black people fighting against heavy odds but racial conflict is not part of the driving machinery. Unlike the above novels, *Beetlecreek* (1950) is not confined to the black community. But it delves deep into racial small town malaise and hinges on a situation of tragic black racial bigotry.

Robert Bone finds more evidence in the evolution of such already confirmed novelists as Ann Petry and Chester Himes. He points out that Ann Petry's *Country Place* (1952) is mostly set in white society, thus differing widely from *The Street* (1946). The same applies to Chester Himes's militant *If He Hollers Let Him Go* (1945) and *Lonely Crusade* (1947), blasting the white-directed union movement, as compared to *Cast the First Stone* (1952), with an all-white cast of characters, and *The Third Generation* (1954) whose action is mostly circumscribed to the black community.

Chester Himes apparently came to share this viewpoint. At least, he expressed his dislike of his novel, when, as if finding its militancy wanting, he pronounced it "the most dishonest book [he had] ever written."[3]

In fact, if one is willing to decipher the language of its space, *The Third Generation* turns out to hinge entirely on racial strife and to propose a militant ideology such as inspired the Civil Rights campaign. But the novel presents a challenge to the reader. Not that it is opaque or impenetrable. But it offers no facile indictment of oppressors or celebration of victims. Instead, there is plenty of soul searching. An attempt at self-understanding through an emphasis on community and culture. To put it another way, *The Third Generation* tries to sound the complexity of the racial situation. A bildungsroman the books starts at the level of the individual within the family circle, moves on to the community and ultimately reaches the level of the nation.

*   *   *

Publicity captions have described *The Third Generation* as an autobiographical novel. The facts of life as described in *The Quality of Hurt*[4] (but how far is an autobiography truthful?) show that the Taylors are indeed fictional characters, totally remodeled by racial ideology and only *very* loosely connected to their real life counterparts, the more peaceful and harmonious family Himes grew up in.

Let us first sum up the plot outline to make the tracking of ideology through space easier. The novel relates the downfall of the Taylors, a middle class black (and, symbolically, white) family. The father, William Taylor, teaches arts and crafts in a Southern Negro college. Professor Taylor is competent, amiable and respected. The whites also like him because he "knows his place", as the phrase goes. Although he is certainly no Uncle Tom, Mr. Taylor feels at home in the South. He frequently quotes Booker T. Washington's famous "Cast down your bucket where you are", and is proud of his work as an educator.

The mother, Lillian, is all but a photographic negative of her husband. She is proud of her white blood and has made up for herself a line of "aristocratic" ancestors. She is light-colored enough to pass and extremely hot-tempered. A fighter, she is always ready to stand for her rights, or what she thinks her rights to be, because she is the kind of person that grows all the more opinionated as she is in the wrong. Mrs. Taylor dislikes the South, to her an inhospitable land peopled with oppressors, dangerous "red necks" and uncouth fawning blacks— "chitterlings" eaters as she sometimes calls them deprecatingly. Her dream is therefore to wrench her family from their Southern roots to go North where "civilization" is to be found. When she finally succeeds in getting her way, in an attempt to get better medical treatment for her partly blinded son, the Taylors' strained family life begins deteriorating. The adaptation to city life in Saint Louis is hard, but Professor Taylor succeeds in becoming a prosperous carpenter. The second step, in Cleveland, spells disaster. Mr. Taylor can find no suitable employment; William still cannot regain his eyesight; and Charles, Mrs. Taylors favorite son, becomes a juvenile delinquent leading a perverted sex life.

This brief synopsis brings out two basic elements: first an opposition between the parents, second a presentation of urbanization as utterly negative. Beginning with the family, I will study these components to show how American themes and social situations invested themselves into the novel to transform real life events into a fiction[5] informed by the ideology of the budding Civil Rights campaign.

*   *   *

The ill assorted Taylor couple and their children read like a microcosm of American society in which the father represents black people while the domineering mother stands for white people. There are many leads to this reading, beginning with *Lillian*, a name which connotes a white flower. When she is crossed, Lillian's face "whitens" or "blanches" (forceful terms as compared to banal phrases like "turn pale"), and she is frequently reported as falling into a "white rage".[6] Lillian Taylor is indeed a literary incarnation of the *white problem* as defined by Lerone Bennett, Jr., in the August 1965 issue of *Ebony*. Whether as a wife or as a mother, she is characterized by a need to dominate reminiscent of the plantation *Big Missy*. The mother/mistress demands obedience and respect, especially in a scene where Charles, massaging her feet and brushing her hair, looks like a body servant.[7] Besides, her frequent admonition when the children disobey her is "God doesn't like ugly", a phrase that harks back to the slaveholders' use of religion to keep the slaves in line and contributes to the web of converging elements that link the story, through group consciousness, to the black experience, past and present, in white America.

Ethnic consciousness is nowhere more manifest than in sexual matters, as racist stereotypes represent black men as hyper sexed and naturally attracted to white women. As Jesse says in *The Primitive*, "... it's below the waist the color problem lies."[8] Indeed, the antagonism between husband and wife takes on a racial hue, with a wedding night smacking of rape. The couple's engagement had been based on inequality. The romantic bride-to-be, self-provided with aristocratic ancestors, is pictured as pleased by the young man's "homage".[9] Mothers with marriageable daughters in town looked upon Professor Taylor as a good catch. Lillian was only an inexperienced school teacher but her suitor's higher social status was erased in her mind by the superiority her light-colored skin conferred upon her. During the train trip and the cab ride to the colored hotel, the honeymooning couple are described as a "woman with a white face" and a "short black man" who almost waits on her. The text plays with the bridegroom's alleged inferiority by stressing his shortness and by keeping him in the second place in most descriptions. Lillian finds the hotel's bridal suite squalid. The surrounding darkness stresses the color difference and sex turns sour as the frightened young woman twists her husband's clumsy eagerness into rape. The racial syndrome is clearly at the heart of their warped relationship. Lillian, in bed with her husband, has a vision of her father's white face, almost Christ-like with its long silky beard; an image of kindness and purity in sharp contrast with her husband's evil repulsiveness, "darker than the night."[10] The wording and the symbolical situation provide signposts to two complementary readings, a white one and a black one. The bride perceives herself as sacrificed to her husband's lust. But a black ironic comment underlies this racist fanaticism: the white woman lying on the bed in the posture of crucifixion can also be seen as the cross the black bridegroom is only too eager to bear.[11]

The children's appearances are Lillian's nightmare, a detail that allows the voice of black militancy to enter the novel and criticize blacks who cannot accept themselves as they are, dark-skinned and kinky-haired. Lillian's first two babies, Tom and William, favor their father. Tom is seen but little as he leaves the family circle to go to school. William's given name is that of his father. He has inherited his dark skin, flat nose and kinky hair, as well as his genial and amiable disposition. The third son, Charles, is his mother's last hope. She has given him her own father's first name. His tan skin is her pride. His auburn baby's hair receives all her motherly attention, as well as his nose she pinches from time to time to prevent it from becoming flat.

Lillian's partiality associates Charles with the white world. But Charles himself naturally claims his black heritage. Charles's being half-white half-black, an ambiguity also symbolically transcribed as a struggle between good and evil, reads like a fictional statement of the complexity of the racial scene in the United States, as well as the blacks' claim that they belong in America. The "new ethnicity" wave of the sixties and seventies fueled the questioning of self in contemporary black fiction[12] makes this racial stand in *The Third Generation* sound commonplace. But this is only a superficial judgment. *The Third*

Generation's racial discourse is inherited from the past and has been passed on to the more recent novels. Fictional forms change along with fashions; racial ideology results from a more permanent social discrimination and is more enduring.

* * *

The second element to come out of the plot outline is a negative presentation of urbanization—a well-worn American theme. Country vs. city, or purity and health vs. corruption and disease, provide another dichotomy that invests itself into the novel and doubles with the opposition between black and white to support its ideology.

The city never enjoyed a good name in a country that produced Thomas Jefferson's dream of a nation of farmers, and where so-called "urban crisis" is perpetually on. Black novels mirror this general bent and give a sorry picture of urban blight. One thinks of the moment when, in *Go Tell It on the Mountain,* the Grimes family leave the church after Johnny's conversion. The town is lying in wait for the sinner in the gray light of the early morning: the wail of an ambulance tears the air, and people bump into overflowing dustbins that obstruct the sidewalks and behind which cats are on the prowl. Another illustration of this widespread idea comes up in Hal Bennett's *The Black Wine* (1968) when young David, up from his native Virginia, is assailed by an offensive smell on emerging from the Newark bus station. Besides, the first city dwellers he sees are hoboes and drunkards lining up before the center where they sell their blood.

The opposition between country and city is different in Himes's novel in so far as it assumes racial overtones through associations with the Taylor parents.

Many Northern blacks refer to the South as "home" or "down home", and that is precisely the line along which the novel's spatial geography is split. The rural South is made out to be the black's homeland while the Northern city is the white world. As illustrated by the beginning of chapter IV that shows the Taylors moving down to a new location deep into rural Mississippi, the identification with the South is almost sexual. The season is spring and the trip from the ramshackle railroad station to the college takes place during a pitch-black night that holds many fears for Lillian Taylor as the protruding roots of trees along the way assume monstrous reptilian shapes. A symbolical return to the maternal womb is suggested as the wagon, rolling between corn fields down a sunken road, becomes enclosed in a tunnel or darkness. The children feel safe and go to sleep on the smooth sandy road. But their mother is impervious to the mules' sure-footed tread, to the serenity of the countryside and to the promise of fertility held in the smell of rotting underbrush. She is vastly relieved when the wagon crawls up from this dark tunnel to flat land where the moonlight holds no threatening shadows of naked roots.

Lillian Taylor sees rural Mississippi as a wilderness holding many dangers. These dangers never materialize into actual harm, but her stubborn belief never gives way, insensitive as she is to this lush land.

On the contrary, rural Mississippi means freedom for the children who are represented as joyfully involved in the growing-up process. They, too, "filled with energy like bursting seeds", or, in their father's words, impatient as if "the sap had just come into them"[13] seem to draw their stamina from the bountiful black soil. Mother nature provides for them. In spite of their mother's fears, the children never eat poisonous berries in the woods and do not drown in the marshes. When Charles is bitten by a moccasin, a tramp cuts the wound open with his pocket knife to suck the venom out and asepticizes the gash with tobacco juice. The cure works and Charles heals fast.

Lillian Taylor sees rural life as ridden with evil and vice, which mostly assume the form of free-going sex. Once again, the novel denies her ungrounded fears when an older summer school student declines to go on a date with Charles. The text identifies this girl as a rural Southerner by her accent, and her brown skin that drives Charles all aflutter has "the ripeness of the South."[14] The same point is made later when young Charles takes a long walk in the night with a nice girl his age that gives him a pure kiss on parting, an image of the innocence of first love:

> Then awkwardly they groped together, clumsy from inexperience. But there was a young sweet poetry in their clumsy hands and awkward motions (...). Finally their lips were meeting, softly pressing in a clear, cool kiss. The queerest sort of feeling surged from deep inside him; an overwhelming sense of love and purity gathered in his heart. He was flooded with the impulse to defend her. Wordlessly they broke apart and looked straight into each other's eyes. There was no shame; only the bright, luminous quality of their love. Her long dark hair, worn in loose curls down on her shoulders, made a soft, delicate cameo of her thin, fragile face.[15]

City life leads the maturing teen-ager Charles has become into active sexual involvement. The Saint Louis experiences, or rather *missed* experiences, are presented as harmlessly funny, although city girls are definitely quite forthright in their sexual games. Charles is too shy to lose his virginity with one of his girl friends and finally goes to a brothel. Again, the episode is hilarious. The prostitute he goes to almost kicks him out (so displeased she is with his performance) until she realizes her frightened customer is a virgin—which makes him, for some reason, worth the trouble. Charles sinks into evil only when the Taylors move further North to Cleveland. There, after jilting his pregnant girlfriend who is too dark-skinned to please his mother, he falls under the degrading influence of a black prostitute, Veeny, in the back room of a sordid ghetto café.

*   *   *

Charles's involvement with Veeny means lapsing into what Lillian Taylor regards as "black vice", a point hammered in by the somewhat ponderous nightmare sequence that culminates in his participation to his mother's rape and murder.

Again, the novel's sexual imaginary belies Mrs. Taylor's biases and fanaticism. Black vice does not flourish close to a congenial mother nature, but in the Northern urban ghetto, which suggests that urbanization leads to a degradation of black morals. Here again a widespread American view is embedded into the novel's space, a mythical representation traceable to E. Franklin Fraziers's 1939 thesis. In *The Negro Family in the United States,* which dominated American liberal (as well as racist) thinking and minority policies over three decades, Frazier contends that urbanization and unemployment played havoc with a non-institutionalized black family which has been reasonably stable within its former rural environment.[16]

The process of urban degradation through sex in which Charles is involved refutes Mrs. Taylor anti black biases, but the space of *The Third Generation* also invites a discussion of blackness that avoids the simplifications of ethnic fiction resting on the positive hero.

There are clearly two victims of white prejudice and wrongheadedness, William and his father. Professor Taylor is destroyed as a man, but also as a husband and a father, through the loss of his social position. William becomes almost blind due to his mother's obstinate wish to punish Charles by denying him the pleasure to assist his brother in a chemistry experiment.

But the Taylors are a family, a context under which the white branch inevitably stumbles over the obstacles it has set up to bring the black branch into line, and thus becomes the victim of its own stubborn hostility. Mrs. Taylor also suffers socially when the family falls from middle class affluence. She suffers in her flesh, too. First from William's accident; then when Charles, the son she would have liked to be (white) like herself, lapses into petty crime and, ultimately, "black" vice. But, unlike his mother, Charles never stands for a symbol of the white world. He shares his mother's fiery temperament but, opinionated and hot-tempered as he may be, he remains in between the two worlds.

The movement of the plot first brings out numerous clues about white guilt through Mrs. Taylor's disingenuity and domineering hardheadedness. However, this strong conviction of white guilt soon erodes as Charles's own guilt starts growing. Charles's guilty feelings begin with responsibility in William's eye accident. The two brothers had planned to demonstrate explosives during commencement week. But, Charles having been impertinent, his adamant mother forbade him to participate in the event. Perhaps out of a sense of duty to the college community, William decides to go ahead on his own. Anyway, cock-sure and anxious to show off on the stage, the young student mismanipulates the chemicals under his helpless brother's eyes. William is pictured in the posture of crucifixion when the explosion occurs, an unlikely analogy (as the natural gesture rather calls for shielding his eyes) that points him out as a willing victim. But, in spite of the mother's prediction, "God is going to punish [Charles]", his guilt is not endowed with any racial overtones. Instead, it is invested with the more general background of original sin: "Afraid to breath lest God discover him", Charles is associated with Adam and Eve hiding in the garden of Eden.[17]

Later on, Charles's guilt toward his brother is side-staged by his deepening involvement in "black" guilt through sex. At the point where he reaches the nadir of depravation, utterly defeating his mother's hopes, the latter symbolically regains her discarded blackness through her son's clearly recollecting a childhood episode, a rhyming game rooted in black folk

consciousness that involves Brother Fox, Brother Bear as well as the enigmatic
shadow of Tar Baby:

> ... "I'm a bear," she said. "Be-ware."
> They laughed uproariously.
> "I'm a fox—I'm sly."
> "I'm a weasel—I steal chickens."
> "I'm a rabbit—catch me."
> She laughed delightedly. "In case you've never cooked a rabbit here is a recipe
> for rabbit fricassee."[18]

The effect of this scene at so crucial a moment (Charles is about to pass out,
stupefied with drink) is to blur Mrs. Taylor's self-attributed whiteness into
blackness. This does not suggest sameness, but *unity*—an idea also contained
in the use of the family to embody the American racial scene. Indeed, Lillian
comes to plead for her husband's help to tear Charles away from the degradation
he has sunk into. Once again, as in every severe family trial, the text repeats its
insistence on the need for unity when it says with moving simplicity that
"neither could go it alone."[19] Professor Taylor later dies, stabbed by Veeny's
pimp while protecting his wife[20] and his last words are a call to serenity and
reconciliation.

Mrs. Taylor remains with her dead husband in the hospital. On leaving
them, Charles takes with him the image of his mother's

... small white hand with its swollen red knuckles resting atop the dark lifeless hand
of his father which she had drawn from beneath the sheet.[21]

Such a situation is a clear call for intra-family solidarity. But the space of the
novel, symbolically split along racial lines, invites an extension to intra-
communal solidarity tantamount to a call on blacks of all shades to unite.
Beyond that, the novel can ultimately be read as a call to national solidarity.

*   *   *

National unity is a plea blacks fighting in the war or working to help the
war effort at home had heard a great deal not so long before. It does not seem
strange to see it surface again, adapted to the needs of militant ethnic fiction.

The Third Generation is no facile indictment of white America. To be sure,
most of the blame for family strife and disintegration is placed on Mrs. Taylor.
But, as her husband says before dying, both sides have made mistakes.
Historical evidence of black guilt in the context of American slavery and racism
is hard to come by. There is not any solid evidence of black guilt in the novel
either and Professor Taylor's last words should therefore be understood as a
conciliatory stance reaching beyond the Taylor's situation: a fiction written as
the Civil Rights campaign was gathering momentum signals the black
community's readiness to hold out its hand, to forget and forgive.

Such is the ideology that clearly informs the space of *The Third Generation*.
The textual evidence outlined above is corroborated by an outside element
suggesting that the novel must have been commanded by some movement in

black public opinion. Chester Himes's book has three companion novels, also published during the fifties, whose protest strategies rely on symbolically racially split families: Go *Tell It on the Mountain, Brown Girl, Brownstones* and *My Main Mother*.[22] None of these novels is naïvely hopeful. They all plead for a place within the family (which translates as the nation) for blacks; but they also know right from wrong. Himes's first idea of a title for his manuscript was *The Cord*. Had he adopted this first choice, reading would have been oriented more exclusively toward Charles's relationship with his mother. But Himes finally decided for a passage from Exodus (XX, 5) that orients readers toward a protest contents, thanks to a coding that anchors the novel in the shadows of slavery and racism as white America's sin.[23] As we know, the curse upon the children of those that hate God is to last until the *fourth* generation: the end of the curse (that possibly doubles as the coming of racial justice) is in sight—but the times for harmony have not come yet. Civil Rights workers, who advocated the ideology that informed Himes's novel, said precisely what the title *The Third Generation* says. For instance, one can sense behind the dream motif in Martin Luther King's March on Washington speech a realistic appraisal of the situation such as had already been present in Himes's choice of a title a decade or so before.

But Chester Himes's soon discarded the Civil Rights ideology that has shaped *The Third Generation*. *The Primitive* (1956) has no use for Professor Taylor's generous last words, or for Lillian Taylor's unspoken regrets as she holds her husband's lifeless hand. By the time he was writing *The Primitive* as an expatriate in France he was already lending ear to the revenge ideology that was to spread through the last few years of the troubled sixties, the militant mood that found its way into *Blind Man With a Pistol*.

NOTES

1. See U. Eisenzweig, "L'espace imaginaire du texte et l'idéologie," in Claude Duchet, *Sociocritique*. Paris, Nathan, 1979, pp. 183–187. I also found Claude Hagège, *L'Homme de Paroles,* Paris, Fayard, 1985 (especially Chap. VI, "La langue, le réel et la logique") extremely helpful: as well as Philippe Hamon, "Pour un statut sémiologique du personnage", in *Littérature*, 6, 1972; and "Un discours contraint", in *Poetique*, 16, 1973.

2. Ralph Ellison's metaphor of invisibility naturally finds its way into *The Third Generation*: "William had entered the state school for the blind and Charles went with him on Saturdays. Unlike the city schools, here Negroes weren't segregated. Charles wondered if it was because the students couldn't see," C. Himes, *Op. Cit.,* New York, Signet, 1956, p. 145.

3. John A. Williams, "My Man Himes", in *Amistad 1,* New York, Vintage, 1970, p. 74.

4. This is the first volume of C. Himes's autobiography, New York, Doubleday, 1972. It deals with the period the novelist used as a basis to build his fiction from.

5. According to *The Quality of Hurt*, the disagreement leading to the divorce of Chester Himes's parents resulted from the wear and tear of two decades of married life. The event was thus fairly banal, at least void of any racial contents.

6. C. Himes, *Op. Cit.,* p. 180.

7. *Ibid.*, p. 73 and mentioned again p. 149. Mother/Big Missy is also possessive. She makes a scene and uses racist slurs against her sister in law ("You black devil!") for sending Charles on an errand, which in her distorted view becomes using her son as a "lackey". This episode is pp. 180–181.

8. C. Himes, *Op. Cit.,* New York, Signet, 1955, p. 69.

9. C. Himes, *The Third Generation*, p. 18.

10. *Ibid.*, 23–24.

11. This situation cuts two ways. It pokes fun at the racist stereotype of the black rapist. It may also be read as a criticism of blacks trying to associate with white women.

12. One thinks of Alice Walker's collection of short stories *In Love & Trouble*; Toni Morrison's *Tar Baby*; and Gloria Naylor's *The Women of Brewster Place*, to mention only a few significant titles.

13. C. Himes, *The Third Generation*, pp. 48–49.

14. *Ibid.*, p. 136.

15. *Ibid.*, p. 140. This passage holds many a stereotyped grand chivalrous feeling in the image of the fragile girl to be protected and loved. Such a wording opens the way to irony: protecting one's loved one(s) is a role denied to Professor Taylor, and to the black man in general in the traditional view.

Charles's courteous love emotions are certainly far removed from Mrs Taylor's view of sordid mating in the South. However, to be fair, one must admit Charles and William are involved in unsavory sexual games when an older student takes them behind the women's latrine to watch. But nothing really unhealthy is attached to an episode that ends farcically. The boys are surprised by Prof. Saunders who has been assigned to the duty of keeping male students away from the whitemen's toilets. Prof. Saunders tries to exploit this opportunity to humiliate Mrs. Taylor against whom he harbors an old grudge. But Lillian does not lose her mettle and adds to the dust he raises while fleeing away: she fires her husband's shotgun in the air.

16. The unreliability of E. F. Frazier's thesis is now recognized after the publication of H. G. Guttman's *The Black Family in Slavery and Freedom* (New York, Vintage, 1977). Back in the fifties, however, Frazier's ideas were practically an institution, the law of the land concerning the black family. Even in the mid-sixties, the *Moynihan Report* was inspired directly from Frazier's work. It is only fair to say that Frazier's socio-historical work was commanded by a prevailing view, among both racial communities. For instance, one finds it expressed, as early as 1902, in Paul L. Dunbar's *The Sport of the Gods* that represents New York as a dangerous Babylon. The derelict so-called "matriarchal" urban family as well as the picturing of a degraded ghetto morality have found their way into many a fiction. One thinks of *Native Son* in the first case. A fine instance of the second one is George Henderson's *Jule* (1946) whose hero finds city women too fickle and sluttish for his taste and comes home to marry the sweetheart of his late teens, with whom sex had been natural and pure.

17. The incident occupies the whole of chapter XIV. The quotations are to be found on pp. 128 and 130.

18. C. Himes, The *Third Generation*, pp. 300–301.

There are other moments when the mother is made to lose her whiteness and turn suddenly into a black woman. Among the most prominent instances is the episode when she confronts, gun in hand, a racist white farmer that refuses her right to using the road because the Taylor's automobile may disturb the mules hitched to the wagon he is napping in the shade. (p. 91) In another instance, she recommends Tom (the eldest brother) to marry a girl named Maud:

"If you ask me I think Maud is the best one of the lot, she volunteered.

He gave her a startled look. "Maud? Why, mother, you don't think anything of the sort. She's dark and her hair isn't four inches long and you know you wouldn't want her for a daughter-in-law."

"It's not what's on the surface, it's what's beneath," she said sententiously. "Many a golden crust holds a sour pie." (p. 152).

19. One could add to this statement the parents' joint prayers when the children almost die from small pox; as well as their repressed need for each other, for instance on the family's first night in their new Mississippi home:

"He went after the luggage. And then he had to return the hack and team to the college stable and walk the mile home in the dark. (...)

Professor Taylor returned to the darkened house to find all of them in bed. He was disappointed. He had hoped for a moment to talk with his wife and reach some kind of reconciliation. For a long time he stood in the darkness of the living room before the dying fire. (...) Finally he went upstairs and entered the empty room. His wife could have her own room if that was the way she wanted it. At least he had his sons.

In her own room down the hall she heard him moving about. She was frightened and lonely. Had he come to her then she would have welcomed him. She needed him then. Her spirit was at its lowest ebb. She needed a husband to give her strength." (*Ibid.*, p. 43).

20. The parents' names are open to an onomastic game. "Lillian" has been analysed p. 4. I do not know whether Himes knew that "William" means "the will to protect". However, Prof. Taylor dies shielding his wife from a drunken pimp's rage. Himes's father's real name was Joseph, a fact which invests Mr. Taylor's becoming a carpenter in Saint Louis with intriguing religious overtones.

21. C. Himes, *The Third Generation*, p. 315.

22. See Michel Fabre, "Pères et Fils dans *Go Tell It on the Mountain* de James Baldwin". *Etudes Anglaises*, T. XVIII, n° 1 Jan–Mar 1970, Paris Didier. About the other two novels, see Claude Julien, *L'Enfance et l'Adolescence chez les Romanciers Afro-Américains,* 1853–1969. Unpublished dissertation, Univ. de Paris VIII, 1981, pp. 498–499.

23. This theme is widely used by William Faulkner, for example in *Requiem for a Nun. The Third Generation* makes the sin seem more Northern than Southern.

Sociocriticism, Nos. 4–5 (1986–1987), 143–152.

Toni Morrison's Variations on Chester Himes

Aribert Schroeder

Among writers and critics of black literature, there seems to have developed a tendency to regard Afro-American women writers as a separate group with traditions of its own which can be traced back to Zora Neale Hurston in linear fashion.[1] Due to such views, the possibility that black male writers may also have influenced their female counterparts is, of necessity, precluded. It is the present writer's intention, in this comparative analysis, to establish such a relationship between Chester Himes and Toni Morrison by showing that, with regard to certain characters, themes, and episodes, there exists a great similarity between Chester Himes's novel *The Third Generation*, first published in 1953, and Toni Morrison's novels *The Bluest Eye*, *Sula*, and *Song of Solomon*, which appeared in 1971, 1973, and 1977 respectively.[2] The present critic believes that without detracting from Morrison's merits, which are certainly due to her as an accomplished writer of black fiction, it is possible to study her variations on Chester Himes's novel with as much legitimacy in literature as those of Franz Schubert's, for example, which were discovered in his Second Symphony, could be analyzed as adaptations from Ludwig van Beethoven's *Prometheus* overture.[3] It is hoped that this analysis will not only throw new light at Morrison's novels discussed here, which have already been widely acclaimed, but that it will draw attention to Chester Himes too, whose own achievement and influence on other black writers, including Toni Morrison, with a few exceptions,[4] seem to have been highly underrated by most critics of black literature.

If one bears in mind that Morrison, as well as Himes, present black characters in interaction with other blacks mainly in black settings, this common narrative point of view assumed by both authors can be penetrated only, if special attention is given to repetition of detail in Morrison's novels. On the basis of this approach, one might say that individual characters of Morrison's have direct counterparts in Himes's *Third Generation*, whereas others turn out to be combinations of characters created by Himes. Where differences do occur, they are largely due to Morrison's basic writing strategy in which she gives special emphasis to stereotyping by blacks and whites, but also to self-destructive thought and behavior patters among Afro-Americans, which arise from white racism.

Cholly Breedlove of *The Bluest Eye*, for example, is externally the exact counterpart of Professor William Taylor of *The Third Generation*. The latter has a short "simean" muscular body with "the bowed legs and pigeon-toed stance of a negro athlete" (TG 10, 22). Breedlove, like the rest of his family, is called "ugly" outright (BE 38). His arm muscles are "like great big peach stones sanded down," and on his chest, there are "two big swells his muscles make" (BE 120). Characteristic of Taylor's features are "a large hooked nose and flaring nostrils" which make them seem "Arabic" (TG 10). Breedlove, on the other hand, like his wife and children, has ears turned forward, high cheekbones, a crooked nose with insolent nostrils, and shapely lips (BE 28). As one can see, Morrison, in order to give special emphasis to the Breedloves' ugliness, has endowed all of them with the traits of the stereotyped Jew of cartoons.

Though Pauline Breedlove is black, and not light-skinned like Mrs. Taylor, she has several details in common with the later too. Both women are small in size. Mrs. Taylor is once described as "a tiny woman" (TG 22). They have high cheekbones (TG 197), and share a foot problem. Once proud of her tiny feet, Mrs. Taylor is now ashamed of them because she has developed bunions. Soon afterwards, the reader is informed that her son Charles has accidentally cut one of his Achilles tendons. Despite a successful operation performed on him, he has to limp for some time (TG 73, 74). In the figure of Mrs. Breedlove, these details have apparently been combined. As a child, Pauline Breedlove steps on a rusty nail which penetrates one of her feet (BE 102). She retains her subsequent limp in her adolescence and her adult life in which she needs it for implementation of her roles as a martyr and ideal servant in the black and white worlds (BE 41, 117). It also seems remarkable that a special form of address occurs in connection with these two female figures. Lillian Taylor, for example, in order to show resentment towards her husband, calls him "Mr. Taylor" (TG 35). Pauline Breedlove, on the other hand, is addressed in this way by the members of her own family, which is perhaps due to a shift of this form of address from husband to wife. And Mrs. Breedlove's white employers and their child take the liberty of simply calling her "Polly" (BE 43, 119, cf. 100). These brief examples are proof of Pauline Breedlove's "holier-than-thou" attitude in the black world and of her subservient attitude in the white one. As one can see, Morrison's special contribution here is not only that she develops certain details borrowed from Himes into thematic strains, but that she also adds a social-psychological dimension to them.

Though less impressive, perhaps, similarities between Himes's and Morrison's child figures can be pointed out too. In *The Third Generation*, for example, William and Charles Taylor are called "pigmeat" by their older fellow students (TG 255). The same term is employed by Ajax when he wants to gain Nel and Sula's attention (S 51). Charles Taylor's limp, mentioned above, reappears in "Milkman" Dead of *Song of Solomon*. As in the case of Mrs. Breedlove, Morrison has given this phenomenon a psychological dimension. "Milkman" does not originally limp, but acquires it as a habit when he starts to interact with other black teenagers (SoS 65). And he abandons the limp when he has grown to spiritual maturity (SoS 281). At the age of seventeen, Charles Taylor of *The Third Generation* tries to get sexually involved with a twenty-two-year-old woman (TG 137). Similarly, "Milkman" Dead makes sexual advances to his cousin Hagar, who is five years older than himself (SoS 98 passim). Charles Taylor accidentally relieves himself on other blacks during a train trip in the South (TG 99). Urinating becomes an important thematic strain in *Song of Solomon* involving Porter and "Milkman." The latter, for example, literally and metaphorically speaking, urinates on his sister Lena (SoS 40, 214ff.). Charles Taylor once fights with his father in a family dispute when he believes for a moment that his mother is in danger of losing her life (TG 266). "Milkman" Dead does the same in a similar situation (SoS 71).

There exist numerous thematic parallels between Himes's novel and Morrison's fiction discussed here, e.g. themes like the social-psychological impact of white racism on blacks, the internalization of white values and standards of beauty by blacks, the impact of the black colour code on black life in combination with social strata, or the social descent of a black family due to self-destruction and disintegration of an initially promising marriage relationship. Due to the fact that other black writers, employing a black narrative point of view, discuss such themes too, it may be difficult to demonstrate Morrison's indebtedness regarding them, though the similarities existing between *The Third Generation* on one hand and *The Bluest Eye* and *Sula* on the other, seem particularly striking. Still, some light can be thrown on this problem, if special attention is again given to analysis of detail, because it still seems legitimate to ask why certain items do recur in a number of themes developed by Morrison, even if the latter may be rather common.

Both, Himes and Morrison, for example, add a few happy touches to a picture of deteriorating marriage relations between the Taylors and the Breedloves, otherwise drawn rather drearily. Both fictional narrators, for example, hold Mrs. Taylor and Mrs. Breedlove highly responsible for their husbands' downfall (TG 143; 117ff.). Due to an unhappy experience on their wedding night, Mrs. Taylor, for example, hates her husband and tries to destroy him, which she eventually succeeds in doing (TG 24, 269). Though Mrs. Breedlove's hatred for her husband develops gradually, she needs him in the end as a negative contrast figure. In order to cope with her bleak life in the black community in ways that are meaningful to herself as well as her neighbours, she eventually casts herself as a martyr (BE 41, 117). Cholly duly fills the role intended for him by tumbling from one depraved act into the other, so that he becomes an "old dog," a stereotype, for the other members of the community too (BE 21). In *The Third Generation*, Mrs. Taylor's love for her son Charles becomes "intensive" when the boy massages his mother's feet (TG 107). Cholly Breedlove, on the other hand, awakens in Pauline feelings of love for him when in their first encounter he tickles her "broken foot" and kisses her leg (BE 107). Unlike Himes, however, Morrison also has Mrs. Breedlove discuss a moment of happy lovemaking with her husband at a time when they have already become problematic (BE 100). But this tale suffers from lack of credibility because it must be measured against Morrison's stereotyped casting of Mrs. Breedlove as a "bitch," martyr, and ideal servant, and of Cholly Breedlove as a "bad nigger" and an "old dog."

Thematic parallels on one hand, and a social-psychological dimension added to the text can also be demonstrated with regard to certain child characters. Thus the children of the Taylors and Breedlove families cannot help watching the parental disputes. However whereas Himes gives examples of several unrelated fighting scenes (e.g. TG 37, 42), Morrison concentrates on a single, vicious one, in which she pays special attention to Sam's hatred of his father and to Pecola's suffering regarding her parents' fight. Completely misreading his mother's cues in the situation before him, Sam screams: "Kill him! Kill him!" And Pecula hides her head under a quilt hoping to God that she will become invisible: "Please make me disappear" (BE 44).

The sexual initiation of black adolescents is handled by both writers in similar ways too. In *The Third Generation*, a black teenager tried to entice Charles Taylor into making love to her during a picnic (TG 124). In *The Bluest Eye*, Cholly Breedlove has his first sexual experience during a funeral banquet commemorating his aunt (BE 116). Instead of hating the white men for what they have done to him, Cholly in his powerless state first directs his hatred at his teenage partner Darlene and later at his wife Pauline. Morrison thus employs the so-called scapegoat syndrome in order to obtain a monocausal, but hardly convincing, explanation for Cholly's bad behavior towards his wife (BE 42). Toni Morrison's attempt to unite a number of themes under a few social-psychological aspects, does not seem to have been very successful regarding the examples discussed above.

For reasons of demonstrating in which way Morrison availed herself of episodes borrowed from Himes, several brief examples will be given, and an episode consisting of two parts will be discussed more fully. Some of the episodes for which Morrison seems indebted to Himes, can be seen as developments of nuclear scenes, like Cholly Breedlove's sexual initiation in *The Bluest Eye*, for example. In *Sula*, there is a scene in which a voodoo-like ritual is enacted by Sula and her friend Nel in their play (S. 57f.). It recalls a minstrel song of *The Third Generation*, which is charged with sexual overtones too (TG 09). And in *Song of Solomon*, "Milkman" Dead's acts of urinating on his sister Lena and Porter's urinating on other blacks can be seen as expansions of a scene in which Charles Taylor relieves himself from a carriage window inconveniencing other black passengers on the train (TG 98). In all these instances, Morrison has reached out beyond Himes by charging the materials borrowed from him with additional levels of meaning, e.g. social-psychological or symbolic ones.

For both writers, Himes and Morrison, the exposure of white racism and its impact on blacks is a major concern. But when Himes gives examples of "Jim Crow" conditions existing for blacks in the South, he employs several episodes that have been scattered throughout the novel. He even allows for a certain degree of humour in such situations. Morrison, on the other hand, excludes any humorous elements when she deals with this theme in a single passage of *Sula*. In its two parts, the reader can follow Mrs. Wright's gradual psychological and physical adjustment to conditions from which she tried to remove herself as a young wife by going north with her husband (S 25 passim).

In the first sub-episode, Helene Wright, contrary to her behaviour in the black community of Medallion, becomes a female "Uncle Tom."[5] Thus she tries to ingratiate herself with a white conductor cast as a "redneck," when the latter accuses Mrs. Wright of having boarded the carriage intended for whites only (S 25). It is interesting to note that in *The Third Generation* it is not Mrs. Taylor but her husband, who shows this type of behaviour (TG 6). To the disgust of his wife, Professor Taylor even behaves like a "clown" in a similar situation (TG 11). Lillian Taylor, on the other hand, stands up and fights whenever she is exposed to discriminatory practices. When she feels unjustly treated by a white conductor, for example, her dispute with him has to be settled by a sheriff (TG 100). By allowing certain negative behaviour patterns for Mrs. Wright only, Toni Morrison succinctly points an accusing finger to Mrs. Wright's wrong state of mind.

The second sub-episode underlines Mrs. Wright's adjustment to the "Jim Crow" conditions of the South. As there are no public toilets available for blacks in the train stations, black women are forced to relieve themselves in the bushes along the railroad tracks, where they can be watched by white men standing on the station platform. Himes depicts such a group of white people in vocabulary drawn from sculpting (TG 40):

They sat slumped in an indolent mobility, their faces rock red in the strange yellow light, still eyes staring balefully at the resting train, like figures of a long forgotten race carved by a demented sculptor in bas-relief.

Toni Morrison, on the other hand, has Mrs. Wright pass "the muddy eyes of men who stood like wrecked Dorics under the station in these towns" (S 29). Both writers, incidentally, mention "Meridian" as one of the Southern towns through which their travelers pass, and in *The Third Generation* as well as in *Sula*, this name marks the beginning of a new sub-episode (TG 97; S 28f.).

Before one tackles the issue of where this comparative analysis has taken its readers, two observations ought to be made. One is that the sum of what Toni Morrison has produced in her novels discussed here is doubtlessly larger than what she seems to have adapted from Chester Himes' *Third Generation*. The stones she broke from her literary quarry were certainly polished in such a way that they received a lustre of their own. But one should not fail to note either that Himes's materials were already unique and beautiful in themselves too. It would therefore be unfair to both writers to suggest that Morrison rewrote parts of Himes's novel and in doing this improved on his work.

If one attempts a comparison of Toni Morrison and Chester Himes on the basis of the variations isolated in this analysis, the former has certainly given more emphasis than Himes to highlighting the impact of white racism on black figures. But it can hardly be overlooked, particularly with regard to her novels *The Bluest Eye* and *Sula*, that Morrison, in an attempt to provide her characters with psychological dimensions by drawing on the problem of stereotyping, has sometimes limited her narrative options somewhat unnecessarily. Whereas Himes's figures are complex and contradictory in their behaviour, like the Taylors, for example, Morrison's characters, in particular the Breedloves and the Wrights, often run the risk of becoming abstractions. This means, in E. M. Forster's terms, that Himes's figures in the examples analyzed above appear to be "round", whereas Morrison's characters occasionally seem rather "flat,"[6] Thematically, Morrison's contributions can be seen in the addition of social-psychological and symbolic levels to her narratives. The main difference seems to be in this matter that Himes enlightens his readers about white racism and its impact on blacks by "showing," whereas Morrison seems to prefer to "show" and "teach" to them. Both writers essentially employ the same narrative technique. They sketch vignettes, which are loosely structured in *The Third Generation*, and rarely densely in *The Bluest Eye*, *Sula*, and *Song of Solomon*. Due to this, Himes in his episodes comes across as a storyteller who has been able to retain "a sense of lived reality"[7] in his novel. Morrison, on the other hand, creates quite a different impression by means of her thematic focusing and compact structuring of episodes in the novels discussed here. She seems to function as an educator about racism for her black and white readers.

The findings presented here strongly suggest, I hope, that Toni Morrison as well as Chester Himes ought to be approached from fresh perspectives by critics of black literature.

NOTES

1. Faith Pullin, "Landscapes of Reality: The Fiction of Contemporary Afro-American Women," *Black Fiction: New Studies in the Afro-American Novel Since 1945*, ed. Robert A. Lee, London 1980, 173.

2. Chester Himes, *The Third Generation* [TG], Signet, New York 1956. Toni Morrison, *The Bluest Eye* [BE], Triad/Granada, 1981 [1970]; Morrison, *Sula* [S], Triad/Granada, 1982 [1974]; Morrison, *Song of Solomon* [SoS], Triad Panther, Frogmore, St. Albans, 1980 [1977]. Further references to these editions will be given in the text.

3. *The Symphony*, ed. Robert Simpson, Vol. I, Harmondsworth, repr. 1969, 189.

4. E.g. A. Robert Lee, "Making New: Styles of Innovation in the Contemporary Black American Novel," *Black Fiction*, ed. A. Robert Lee, 230 passim.

5. Such type of woman is sometimes called an "Aunt Jemima," cf. Morrison, *Song of Solomon*, 205 passim, 210.

6. Edward M. Forster, *Aspects of the Novel*, New York 1927.

7. Robert P. Smith, "Chester Himes in France and the Legacy of the *Roman Policier*," *College Language Association Journal*, xxv (1981), 22.

AFRAM Newsletter, No. 29 (July 1989), 20–25.

The Black Man in the Literature of Labor: The Early Novels of Chester Himes

Robert Skinner

It is doubtful that many struggles in the history of the United States have been as turbulent or as dramatic as those having to do with labor. Both the nineteenth and twentieth centuries are shot with fiercely contested strikes and hard-fought negotiations between labor and business leaders.

Because of the often conflictive nature of American labor, it was inevitable that labor struggles would become the subject of many literary and dramatic presentations. For example, in 1970, a motion picture entitled *The Molly Maguires* chronicled the efforts of a Pinkerton detective to infiltrate a gang of Irish miners who were terrorizing coal mine owners in nineteenth century Pennsylvania. An early twentieth century labor dispute was the subject of the recently released motion picture, *Matewan*. James Lee Burke, a distinguished Southern novelist, wrote a moving coming-of-age novel entitled *To the Bright and Shining Sun*, which was set against the backdrop of labor unrest in the Kentucky coal mine country. The tension in Dashiell Hammett's first novel, *Red Harvest*, is derived from the conflict between a ruthless industrialist, crooked city officials, gangsters and union organizers.[1]

An aspect of labor history that has received scant attention in fiction is the experience of the Negro in industry. Because of this, the early works of Chester Himes are particularly important to the scholar who is interested in the experience of the black worker. In his first novel, entitled *If He Hollers Let Him Go*,[2] Himes starkly portrayed working conditions in a California shipyard during the early years of World War II and the tragic decline of hero Bob Jones as he fights against bigotry and his own self-destructive tendencies.

In Himes' second work, *The Lonely Crusade*,[3] we see the efforts of a labor union to unionize black aircraft workers through the eyes of Lee Gordon, a black union organizer. Both works are searing proletarian novels that point up the social stresses under which the protagonists suffer and the turbulent atmosphere brought about by the constant tension between industry, laborers and unions.

Himes was born in Jefferson City, Missouri, in 1909 to Joseph Sandy and Estelle Bomar Himes. The younger Himes had an unusually hopeful start in life for an American Negro in the early part of this century. His father was a college professor who surrounded his family with opportunities for cultural enrichment that were uncommon for people of either race in those days. Himes was in many ways fortunate that he had an ambitious mother who pushed all three of her sons to better themselves. Possibly she realized that the only chance for a black man to improve his standing in life was to get the best education possible. Her ambitions bore fruit in all her children, as each one went on to distinguish himself in his chosen field of endeavor. Eddie Himes, the eldest, became an official of the waiters' union in New York. Joseph Himes, Jr., became an internationally famous sociologist who is still active today.[4]

The family's fortunes began to take a downward turn during Chester's childhood. Estelle Himes was a combative personality who kept her husband in trouble with his colleagues and also with white residents of the semi-rural areas in which they lived. Eventually, Joseph, Sr., was unable to get work as a college instructor and was forced into a series of low-paying menial jobs. When Joseph, Jr., was blinded during a school chemistry accident, their meager resources were stretched even further and tension between the husband and wife began to build toward the breaking point.

By the time the family moved to Cleveland, Ohio, in the early 1920s, Chester had become a teenager and was having a great deal of trouble adapting socially. An especially shy and sensitive boy with a loner instinct, he was often sullen and hostile in school.

In 1926, while working as a busboy at Wade Park Manor, an exclusive hotel in Cleveland, he inadvertently stepped into an open elevator shaft. The resulting fall broke several bones, injured his back, and shattered all of his teeth. He found himself treated with extreme generosity on all sides. The Ohio State Industrial Commission awarded him a pension and arranged for all of his hospitalization and subsequent treatment.

Himes' employer agreed to continue his salary throughout the course of his treatment. This settlement appealed to his father, who preferred not to make waves where disputes with white persons were concerned. With his father's encouragement, he signed a waiver by which, in return for the award, he gave up rights to additional claims.

Unfortunately, his mother believed that he had been cheated of the opportunity to sue the hotel for a much more substantial award. She got into a fight with the hotel management, as a consequence of which the hotel withdrew its offer to pay Chester's salary. He eventually recovered from his injuries, although he was to be plagued by back troubles for the rest of his life.

Chester Himes enrolled at Ohio State University in 1926. Like many another youngster his age, he was immature enough to be more interested in having fun than in working on his studies. This was complicated by his feelings of inferiority which were accentuated by his entry into a predominantly white world for the first time. He was also resentful of the proper, light-skinned middle-class black youngsters he met in school. He began searching for a place where he fit in, making friends with prostitutes and gamblers, and spending much of his time in the tough part of Columbus.

His college education ended rather abruptly when a prank went awry. In an effort to embarrass some of the middle-class black students whom he felt had rejected him socially, he took a group of them to visit some of his seedy friends. A sojourn at a brothel climaxed in a brawl that upset a number of the young women in the group. When word of his prank got back to the dean of men, Himes was forced to withdraw from the university.

Free to follow his own desires, he left the world of respectability and entered one where he felt more at home. He began working for a gambler and learned all of the tricks of the trade, associated with bootleggers and prostitutes, carried a gun and was easily provoked into using it. Before a year had gone by he had already been arrested for stealing guns from a National Guard Armory and for passing bad checks.

Himes finally stepped too far over the line when he robbed a wealthy Cleveland family of a large sum of money and jewelry and attempted to escape the country. Ironically enough, he was arrested by Chicago police for a crime that he did not commit. During a brutal interrogation, he was forced to admit to the Cleveland crime in order to keep the detectives from beating him to death.

In December of 1928, an unforgiving judge sentenced the young man to the Ohio State Penitentiary for a term of twenty to twenty-five years. For almost anyone else, this would have been the beginning of the end. During his confinement, however, Himes began to write. His early educational experience was a thorough one and it had instilled in him a love of language and literature.

Himes claimed in his autobiography that he turned to writing in prison because it protected him from abuse by both guards and hostile prisoners. His brother, Dr. Joseph S. Himes, Jr., in a letter to the author of this article dated September 23, 1988, explained:

I, too, have speculated about Chester's seemingly mysterious going into writing. I think there is no single factor, but a cluster of experiences, influences, and his own internal drive. First, I think Chester was shocked into maturity by his succession of disasters.... I think, at this point, Chester took himself in hand and decided that he had to do something with his life. The alternative was too ghastly to consider. Even at this time he may have thought of writing as what he would like to do.

The ever-faithful Estelle Himes knew that writing was a way for her son to cope with his imprisonment. She pleaded with prison officials to excuse him from hard labor because of his back injuries and persuaded them to assign him a place where he could develop his talent. Supplied with a typewriter, paper and endless time, the young man set to work.

In 1932 his hard work began to pay off. He published numerous short stories and one book-length work in the pages of Negro periodicals such as *Abbott's Monthly* and the *Atlanta Daily World*[5]. By 1934 he was selling stories to

Esquire. Most of the stories are vivid, sharply worded pieces with vibrant, colorful characters. Since the underworld was the thing that he knew best, it is perhaps not surprising that most of them concern criminals and convicts.

His hard work paid off in other ways as well. In April of 1936, after serving seven and a half years of his sentence, Himes was paroled from prison. A year later he married Jean Johnson, the sweetheart who had waited for him, and began trying to support her with any work he could find. His first job was digging ditches with the Works Progress Administration in Cleveland. Anxious to escape this demanding and exhausting work, he applied for and got a job as a WPA research assistant.

He began by writing vocational bulletins for the Cleveland Public Library. At the same time he became active in the Congress of Industrial Organizations[6] and worked with the union newspaper, the *Union Leader*.[7] He is also supposed to have written a brief history of the CIO during this period. A historical pamphlet entitled *CIO: What It Is ... And How It Came To Be* (October 1937) may be the history that Himes wrote; it bears a marked similarity in style to essays on racism in World War II that Himes wrote for magazines such as *The Crisis* in the 1940s.

In 1940 Himes was introduced to Louis Bromfield, a Pulitzer-prize-winning white writer who wrote numerous novels, short stories and screenplays during the 1930s and 1940s. Bromfield liked Himes and his wife and tried to help Chester get a book published. He also took both of them to Los Angeles in the fall of 1941 when he went there to write the screen adaptation of Ernest Hemingway's *For Whom the Bell Tolls*.[8] Subsequent introductions to politically active blacks such as Loren Miller and Welford Wilson gained for the young writer a firsthand view of the intellectual communist life in Southern California but did little to help him find any remunerative work.

Eventually Chester and Jean moved to San Francisco where he worked for a time at the Henry J. Kaiser-owned Richmond Shipyards. At various times he also worked at an aircraft company and at several other institutions in the Bay Area. Later they moved back to Los Angeles where Chester found work as a shipfitter at the San Pedro Harbor Shipyard.

This was a particularly depressing time for Himes because, with the war in full swing, he found himself working side-by-side with Southern whites who had moved to California to take advantage of the war production boom. Nothing in the experience of these uneducated rural workers had prepared them for working with blacks and consequently racial tensions ran high. Himes' natural sensitivity to racial injustice only tended to make the experience excruciating for him.

Probably in an attempt to resolve the frustration and bitterness he felt at living in such a world, in 1944 Himes began writing *If He Hollers Let Him Go*. He received a fellowship from the Rosenwald Fund, an organization whose stated concern was "the betterment of the condition of Negroes with a view of their full participation in American life." The fellowships were granted to blacks and white Southerners each year who showed "exceptional promise," and they included support for academic study, music, literature, the arts, labor, business, the ministry "or any other field in which the individual gives promise of some special contribution to American life." According to the Fund review for 1942–1944, Himes was granted his fellowship for the production of a "sociological novel about Negro life."[9] It allowed him to finish the book and it was published in 1945 by Doubleday, Doran and Company.

Labor history substantiates the grim realities of Negro labor that Himes depicts in the story. Negroes had been prevented from entering the shipbuilding industry prior to World War II because the powerful unions in the shipbuilding trades had systematically excluded them from their ranks. During World War II, Negroes were usually placed in deadend, unskilled jobs which prevented them from learning anything that they could use in another craft. This also minimized the number who could move from one department to another. Even where blacks could make the move to another department, they would lose the accumulated seniority that they had gained within their original department. In such cases, they would be victimized the first time that it became necessary to fire or lay off employees. These barriers prevented blacks from taking any real advantage of the shipbuilding war boom prior to the intensification of labor shortages in 1943, when the war was half over.[10]

The same spirit that condoned unfairness in labor was easily found abroad in Los Angeles during the war years. One of the most dramatic and tragic events on the home front in the early days of the war were the Zoot Suit Riots, where an altercation between servicemen and Hispanic youths who wore the flamboyant "zoot suits" erupted into full scale violence. On the night of June 7, 1943, a mob of several thousand servicemen and civilians attacked, stripped and beat every Mexican, Filipino and black youth that they could find in the downtown area wearing a zoot suit. The police ignored or joined in the violence with the tacit approval of city officials. Although military police eventually broke up the downtown riots, the violence spread to the suburbs and continued for two more days.[11]

Himes' story is set in Los Angeles around 1943 and covers four days in the life of protagonist Bob Jones, a leaderman of sheetmetal workers at the Atlas Shipyard. The story is primarily concerned with Jones' preoccupation with the racism he encounters at every level of his existence, but Himes draws heavily on his own wartime experience to provide a realistic and dramatic backdrop. For example, early in the story we see Bob come on the job and enter the Navy floating drydock on which he and his crew are working:

The compartment I entered was the machine shop; forward was the carpenter shop; aft were the various lockers, toolrooms, storerooms, and such, and finally the third-deck showers and latrine—all part of the ship itself—where my gang was working.

The decks were low, and the tools and equipment of the workers, the thousand and one lines of the welders, the chippers, the blowers, the burners, the light lines, the wooden staging, combined with the equipment of the ship.... I had to pick every stop to find a foot-size clearance of deck space.... Every two or three steps I'd bump into another worker. The only time anybody ever apologized was when the knocked you down.[12]

As he directs his crew in the installation of ventilation in the shower compartments and heads of the floating drydock, it is obvious that he is intelligent, hardworking, and knows his job. He remarks at one point that "the fellows in my gang looked up to me; whenever they had trouble with the white workers they looked to me to straighten it out."[13]

Bob, however, finds it increasingly difficult to contend with the racism that he experiences at every turn in his personal and professional life. He tells us that when he came from Cleveland a couple of years earlier, he was proud and carried himself with confidence. After a while, though, the increased race hatred that was released by the bombing of Pearl Harbor has worn away his ability to carry himself like a man and planted the worm of fear in his heart. The removal of the Japanese-Americans from their homes and their subsequent internment has destroyed any complacency that he may have felt. "It was like taking a man up by the roots and locking him up without a chance," he observes.[14]

In working his background into shape, Himes also does a credible job of showing the undisguised racism that was so much a part of that era. From the time he enters the plant, Bob is continually subjected to racial slurs and other insults by everyone with whom he comes into contact. The white girl who supervises the blueprints subjects him to subtle discrimination when she hesitates to let him see the print for his area of responsibility. Later, a white leaderman refuses to lend him someone to help complete a job. The refusal is made in spite of the fact that a number of white crewmen and women are idling nearby.

A sympathetic white supervisor finally lends Bob a female tacker from his crew, a kindly act that ultimately leads to Bob's downfall. Madge, a voluptuous peroxide blond from Texas, refuses to work with Bob's crew and calls him a "nigger." Momentarily overcome with humiliation and hatred, Bob calls her a "cracker bitch." MacDougal, the department supervisor, refuses to recognize the insult to Bob or to discipline Madge for it. To compound the injustice, MacDougal demotes Bob for having insulted a white woman.

Later Bob goes to see Herbie Frieberger, the union shop steward, in the hopes of getting some help. Bob feels that it is the union's duty to tell Madge that she must work with Negro crews or lose her job. Predictably, Frieberger refuses to admit that Bob has been dealt an injustice:

"Jesus Christ, Bob you know the union can't do that ... this is dynamite. If we tried that, half the workers in the year would walk out."

Angered by this pusillanimity, Bob exclaims:

" ... to hell with you and this lousy Jim Crow union too! ... When I came to this lousy city in '41 all I did was bump my head against Jim Crow shops that were organized by your union ... this lousy local never fought for Negroes to be hired—probably fought against it—"[15]

Bob's personal life provides him with no relief from the daily anguish he experiences. He is engaged to be married to Alice Harrison, a wealthy, light-skinned woman whose life has been one of privilege. She cannot understand Bob's resentment and his inability to accept a second-class status. Later in the story her complacency is badly shaken when she and Bob are humiliated first by the waiters in an exclusive night club and then by a white policeman. Bob comforts her ironically by saying "Don't let it get you down, baby. You're not just finding out you're a nigger?" But even these experiences fail to convince Alice that the forces destroying Bob are real. She counsels him to accept his lot and strive to improve the system from within.

Bob's life is eventually destroyed by Madge, a venomous "cracker" woman. She plays a strange game with Bob, attempting to seduce him while she pretends to fear and hate him. Eventually she traps him into a circumstance where he is accused of rape. In spite of his frantic efforts to explain the truth and then escape his pursuers, Bob is arrested and badly beaten by police. Brought before a judge without any time to prepare a defense, Bob is given the choice of going to prison or joining the army. Robbed of his job, his girlfriend, his self-respect and even his future, Bob decides to join the army and the curtain falls on his tragic story.

In some ways *If He Hollers Let Him Go* is reminiscent of Richard Wright's *Native Son*.[16] Probably the first black novel to gain the widespread interest of the white literary establishment in the twentieth century, *Native Son* examined the effects of racism on Bigger Thomas, a lower-class black youth living in Chicago. Both Bigger and Bob Jones are subjected to widespread racism that frightens, maddens and brutalizes them. They become trapped in a web of hatred and misunderstanding which ultimately destroys both protagonists.

Himes' story is actually more tragic than Wright's because Bigger Thomas is a lost cause when his story opens. He is already a borderline criminal whose ability to believe in his own future or work towards any personal redemption is nonexistent.

Bob Jones, on the other hand, is a man with a future. He owns an expensive new car and is engaged to a beautiful woman with wealth and position. It is clear that he is a cut above the average because he has already achieved supervisory status at the shipyard and is in charge of a crew of fifteen people.

Jones has been working within the system to improve his life, but the system fails him badly. Circumstances have conspired against him to destroy the future he has worked for. The Japanese attack on Pearl Harbor has taken the casual bigotry that already existed in Southern California and charged it with a dense hatred directed at all people of color. The war industries have attracted scores of undereducated rural whites to the area, and the heightened racism brought on by the war has legitimized the race hatred that Himes believes is natural to the "cracker." The Japanese attack on Pearl Harbor and the subsequent fears that the West Coast would be invaded has exacerbated existing racism and resulted in the disenfranchisement and internment of Japanese-American citizens and the attacks upon blacks and Hispanics in the Zoot Suit Riots.

Trade unions, as Himes depicts them, have been tainted by racism from their earliest days. Unions have attempted to thwart full membership by blacks because of accusations that such membership represents Bolshevism (the fact that the radical Industrial Workers of the World afforded blacks full membership would lend credence to such a claim). At the same time, since blacks have been so often used as strike breakers, they are not popular with unions anyway.[17]

Thus the already compromised unions find their ranks being swelled by rural Southerners and the racism becomes two-edged. In order to keep the strength gained by the huge influx of Southern white workers, the unions will not want to alienate these new members by making concessions to Negro workers. Facing all of these historical factors, it is clear from the beginning that Bob cannot overcome the odds against him.

If He Hollers is a powerful proletarian story which benefits from Himes' intimate knowledge of the wartime shipbuilding industry and the policies of the trade unions that were involved. His descriptions of the crowded, foul-smelling compartments and of the language and attitudes of the "working-stiffs" of both races produce an accurate and believable picture of a time and a place.

Himes' second work of fiction, *Lonely Crusade* (1947), is also set against the backdrop of California war industries. His main focus in this story is on unionism and the struggle to unionize black workers in a defense plant. His protagonist is Lee Gordon, a college-educated black man just beginning a job as a union organizer at the Comstock Aircraft Corporation. Himes stresses that this low-paying union job is not considered much to the average white worker:

But to Lee Gordon it meant a new lease on life. Not only did it mean the end of a long and bitter search for dignified employment, but also vindication of his conviction that a man did not have to accept employment beneath his qualifications because his skin was black.[18]

Like Bob Jones before him, Lee Gordon is being suffocated by the racism that he finds at every turn. Also like Bob Jones, Lee has discovered that the Japanese attack on Pearl Harbor has heightened racial tensions. As he lays awake the night before he is to start his new job, he realizes that he is frightened because "he had once again crossed into the competitive white world where he would be subjected to every abuse concocted in the minds of white people to harass and intimidate Negroes."[19]

His fears are compounded by the frustration he has felt at being unable to support his wife, Ruth. Worse yet, she has been supporting him. She has a job as a counselor at another war industry in the city. She has everything Lee does not: prestige, respect, even a white secretary. His frustration has made him impotent and brutal with Ruth.

On his first day on the job, Lee realizes that by becoming a union organizer, he has thrust himself into a war between the union and the war industries. When he is picked up on his first morning by Smitty, a white organizer, Smitty asks him:

"Have you ever stopped to think, Lee, that ninety percent of the people are workers? ... Any person who does not own the business from which he derives his income is a worker."

"That sounds like Marx," Lee commented.

"I don't give a damn what it sounds like.... Unionism is the only answer," Smitty declared dogmatically. "All the rest is so much crap."[20]

When Lee arrives at the union's office outside the aircraft factory, he finds more problems waiting for him. He is subjected to prejudice by Marvin Todd, acting chairman of the local union. Then he is taken aside by Joe Ptak, the professional organizer from the national union headquarters. Ptak is a hard-bitten former worker with an immigrant's accent and two fingers missing from his left hand. He greets Lee matter-of-factly and lays things out for him:

"This is how it is. We got mostly new workers here—new to industry, that is. Most of 'em are from the South, against the union on general principles. They been taught the union is part of Russia; they believe what they read in the papers. On top of that, they're making more money than they ever made. And they're working under better conditions. The company keeps 'em hopped up on patriotism. Some of them are so ignorant they believe it's treason to join the union. They got recreation rooms in the joint, bands to play while they eat; and they even have dances.... They don't even have to buy newspapers anymore; the company gives 'em one free.... You read it and you'll learn what a son of a bitch I am.[21]

Joe explains to Lee that his specific job is to work on the "colored" workers at the plant. He does not give Lee a great deal of hope about the job:

"There's about three thousand colored workers.... Most of 'em are new workers, hired after the others.... Just enough been upgraded to prove there ain't no discrimination. From what I know about the colored workers, discrimination is most of what you got to work on. On a job like this, the union can't show any special interest in your people or we antagonize the Southern whites. Don't look for none."[22]

Joe's final word of advice to Lee is to watch out for communists. They will try to recruit him in order to use the union for their own purposes. Joe warns Lee that they will be sending someone to see him soon, most likely another Negro or a white woman.

Joe's warning is a timely one because Lee is soon joined by Luther McGregor, a brutal, profane black man whom Lee eventually begins to suspect is a communist pawn. During their acquaintanceship, Luther subtly attempts to win Lee over to the communist cause as the pair ride all over the city of Los Angeles trying to recruit Negro workers and enlist their help in convincing others to join them.

Lee finds little enthusiasm for the union among his fellow blacks. Some believe that unions are connected with communists and that if Negroes become part of that, the wealthy whites who have championed black equality will turn against them. Others are fearful that white unionists will cause trouble if they attempt to join. All are suspicious of Lee, whom they see as a "'black Greek' bearing 'white Greek' gifts."[23]

Eventually Joe Ptak holds a meeting and both black and white prospective members attend. The workers segregate themselves according to color and the room is filled with tension. This disappoints Smitty who does not understand why the blacks segregated themselves or why they remain skeptical of the union's ability to help them better their lives.

In an important passage, Lee patiently explains to the white man that the average Negro accepts discrimination as a way of life. Unionism will not help them that much because they will still be subjected to discrimination after the plant is organized. The lack of Negro supervisors will be attributed to seniority.

In such a system, white workers will be promoted to the higher paying jobs and blacks will be hired to fill their places in the lower paying jobs.

Since the basis of unionism is seniority, unionization will ultimately defeat them. Blacks as a group will continue to be the last hired and, in bad times, the first fired. Prejudice, combined with lack of experience, will continue to insure that the black worker never achieves any large degree of success. Lee points out that "under the company merit system Negroes could at least hope that by application and hard work, superior acumen and Uncle-Toming, they might get a better job than they would by the process of seniority."[24]

Worse yet, the union is misleading the black worker with promises of equality. Lee argues that the black man has no hope of equality under any circumstances. For the union to argue that unionization will bring equality is to promise something that cannot ever be delivered. Smitty, who is a particularly naive and obtuse man, fails to understand Lee's thesis and insists that the Negro worker is no different than anyone else. Smitty's inability to understand that a real difference does exist completely defeats Lee.

At the same time, the reader sees that Lee is defeating himself. While his education helps him to analyze and understand the situation of the black worker, he lacks what Himes depicts as the average Negro's ability to numb himself to the realities of life and therefore survive them.

To further complicate Lee's life, he suddenly finds himself invited to Sunday dinner at the home of Foster, general manager of the aircraft plant, as well as vice-president of the board of directors and a major stockholder in the corporation. Foster embodies every trait of the Republican businessman of this period. Handsome and dynamic, he radiates confidence. He is an "American Firster," and an anti-Roosevelt man to the core. Foster articulates the opinion that Franklin Roosevelt is Joseph Stalin's tool and that his leftist policies have endangered the entire fabric of American life.

Foster attempts to manipulate Lee by having his personal secretary engage Lee in a conversation about the union. The secretary is bitterly anti-union, contending that all unions are run by communists and criminals. After he believes that Lee has been softened up by his denigration of the union, the secretary leaves. Foster attempts to soft-soap Lee by insisting that he has no bias against the union. He points out that Negro workers always have gotten a fair shake at Comstock Aircraft. Finally he expresses deep admiration for Lee's integrity and fortitude and offers him a $5,000 job in Comstock's personnel department. He also promises, "I'll see that you get the breaks."

Lee is overwhelmed by the offer and momentarily considers taking it. The integrity that Foster has praised, however, takes over and Lee refuses because of his loyalty to the union. Foster is overcome with rage. He calls Lee a "black bastard" and threatens to get even with him. To compound the misery of the moment, Ruth's momentary pride in Lee gives way to anger at what she sees as his selfishness in not taking the job and freeing them from their penury.

Emotionally distraught over the experience and his wife's inability to understand his motives, Lee is propelled into an affair with Jackie Forks, a white woman whom the communists are using to compromise him. This affair sends Lee into a nightmarish downward spiral. The vindictive Foster spreads rumors among the black factory workers that Lee has sold out to the company.

Soon after that, Lee and Luther McGregor are waylaid by sadistic sheriff's deputies in Foster's employ. They first attempt to bribe Lee away from the union and then brutally pistol whip him when he refuses to be bought.

After he recovers from the beating, Lee learns that Luther has been playing both ends against the middle. Besides working for the communists, Luther also has been in Foster's employ, taking money regularly for his betrayals. Defeated by the duplicity he sees on all sides, Lee quits the union and goes with Luther to receive a payoff from one of the policemen who had beaten him. During the meeting, however, Luther gets into an argument with the deputy and murders him.

When Luther is later killed resisting arrest, Lee finds himself accused of complicity in the crime and Jackie Forks betrays him to the police. The police also take Ruth into custody as a material witness and attempt to trick her into giving testimony that will confirm Lee's guilt.

Joe Ptak and others in the union do not want to help Lee since he resigned. They see him as a turncoat. But Smitty still believes in Lee and engages a lawyer to help him fight the case. Smitty also uses his influence to get a number of other union people to swear that Lee was with them during the time of the murder and gets him temporarily off the hook with the police.

Smitty then explains to Lee that the organization of the black workers at the Comstock plant is not going well. Both Smitty and the union feel that Lee is partly to blame for this. He offers Lee a proposition; they have six days until the National Labor Relations Board holds an election to decide whether or not the union will represent the workers at Comstock. They need the Negro vote to win. Smitty promises Lee that if he can organize the Negro workers in time to win the election, the union will back him up against Foster and any trouble that the industrialist may throw his way. Smitty lays it on the line for Lee, telling him that when he decided to sell out the union, he lost the goodwill of most union people. This is his only chance to redeem himself from Foster's hatred.

In the six days he has left, Lee works steadily to gain the support of black leaders and citizens' groups. He realizes in this interim that his fear of white people and their bigotry has robbed him of the dignity of his manhood and he strives to win it back. During this period he finds his love for his wife renewed and begins to rebuild his relationship with her.

On the day of the election, feeling none too hopeful about the results of his efforts, Lee goes to the plant and finds that Foster has blocked the entrance with thugs and sheriff's deputies. Worse yet, Smitty tells him that a warrant has been issued for his arrest. Many workers and union people are lined up, ready to march on the plant, but most of them fear the violence they know will come.

Smitty attempts to exhort them forward from a sound truck as Joe Ptak goes out and tries to get lines of workers moving by main force. Joe eventually marches alone towards the line of deputies carrying a union banner. He is brutally beaten to the ground for his efforts. The sight of this combined with the recognition of Ruth's anguished face on the sidelines energizes Lee. Heedless of his own safety, Lee grabs the fallen banner and breaks the line alone, opening it to the other workers' advance.

Chester Himes never wrote a more demanding novel than *Lonely Crusade*, nor a more ambitious one. In this one book he treated the multiple themes of race hatred, black anti-Semitism, interracial sex, and communist manipulations of the Negro.

If the book is noteworthy for anything, it is in Himes' depiction of the precarious balancing act that the union must perform. The union's primary interest is, of course, to unionize the aircraft plant. To do that, it needs the full support of the white workers, most of whom are transplanted Southerners, and also the black workers. Each group is hostile towards or suspicious of the other. The union organizers must successfully court both without giving the impression to the whites that blacks are receiving special consideration.

To complicate matters, the union must negotiate a tricky path around the communists. The communists support the union, but only insofar as it will advance their own cause. They support Negro rights for the same reason. The union is faced with the necessity of steering clear of any direct association with the party because both white and black workers are suspicious or fearful of being associated with it.

Himes' experiences among the intellectual communist elite of Southern California in the 1940s enabled him to get a first-hand look at how the party operated.[25] Himes is skillful in his depiction of their ruthless manipulations, showing how the leaders systematically utilize anyone who will further their ends and then dispose of them as a calculated sacrifice or when they become inconvenient.

Himes' portrait of Foster, the plant manager, is particularly fine-drawn. Foster is as ruthless as the communists. He calculatingly gives his workers, white or black, just enough to make them feel fortunate. He realizes that having come from disadvantaged backgrounds, their loyalties can easily be gained with token concessions.

Foster also recognizes the connection between the union and the communists and skillfully plays the connection up to his workers to keep the union on the defensive. Like a chess player, Foster constantly surveys the playing area for threats and attempts to neutralize them. Recognizing Lee's potential to hurt him, Foster shows a willingness to use both bribery and physical violence.

Even though this was not a popular book in the 1940s, the very virulence with which it was attacked by critics on all sides suggests how close to home it came to its various audiences. Arna Bontemps, for instance, writing in the *New York Herald Tribune*, described Lee Gordon as a negative character with nonproductive attitudes who experiences minimal growth during the course of the novel. Milton Klonsky delivered a stinging rebuke in *Commentary* in which he criticized not only Himes' skill as a writer but virtually every aspect of the book. He concluded by comparing *Lonely Crusade* with the graffiti on a bathroom wall. In the *Atlantic Monthly*, Christowe Stoyan called the story too melodramatic and said that it was over-ambitious, over-generalized and over-simplified.[26] Communists, in particular, were stung by Himes' depiction of their ruthless machinations. Himes quoted a review in the communist paper *The Daily Worker* as comparing the book to the "foul words that came from the cankerous mouth of Bilbo."[27]

Chester Himes did not write again about the Negro in labor after *Lonely Crusade*. He followed this book with *Cast the First Stone*, a novel based on his prison experiences, and two protest novels, *The Third Generation* and *The Primitive*.[28]

Like several other American Negro writers and intellectuals, Himes exiled himself to France in the early 1950s in an attempt to escape the racism which he felt made it impossible for him to realize his ambitions. While in France he began writing a series of innovative crime novels set in Harlem, of which *Cotton Comes to Harlem*, published in 1965[29] is the best known. Combining the elements of the protest style with the traditions of the American hard-boiled crime story, Himes became an instant sensation and finally achieved the success that had deluded him in his own country.

In the light of changing attitudes, many critics believe that *If He Hollers Let Him Go* and *Lonely Crusade* are among Himes' finest works. In each novel he skillfully portrayed the forces in labor and industry that were arrayed against black workers and brutally exposed the racism that stood in the way of economic progress for the Negro. Both novels deserve to be considered in the front rank of the literature of labor.

NOTES

1. *The Molly Maguires* (1970, produced by Martin Ritt for Paramount Pictures, suggested by a book by Arthur H. Lewis); *Matewan* (1987, produced by Peggy Rajski and Maggie Renzi, from a story by John Sayles); James Lee Burke, *To the Bright and Shining Sun* (New York: Scribners, 1970); Dashiell Hammett, *Red Harvest* (New York: Alfred A. Knopf, 1929).

2. Chester Himes, *If He Hollers Let Him Go* (Garden City, New York: Doubleday, Doran and Company, 1945).

3. Chester Himes, *Lonely Crusade* (New York: Alfred A. Knopf, 1947).

4. Chester Himes, *The Quality of Hurt: The Autobiography of Chester Himes*, Vol. I (Garden City, New York: Doubleday, 1973), is the source of information on Himes' early life.

5. For example, Chester Himes, "His Last Day," *Abbott's Monthly* 5 (Nov. 1932): 32–33, 60–63; Chester Himes, "Prison Mass," *Abbott's Monthly* 6 (Mar. 1933): 36–37, 61, 64; 6 (April 1933): 20–21, 48–56; and 6 (May 1933): 37, 61–62 (a book-length serial); and Chester Himes, "A Modern Marriage, *Atlanta Daily World*, 2 Aug. 1933.

6. Chester Himes to John A. Williams, 31 Oct. 1962, in possession of Michel Fabre.

7. Information provided by Michel Fabre.

8. Ernest Hemingway, *For Whom the Bell Tolls* (New York: Scribners, 1940).

9. Edwin R. Embree, *Julius Rosenwald Fund Review for the Two-Year Period 1942–1944* (Chicago: The Julius Rosenwald Fund, 1944), p. 23.

10. Lester Rubin, William S. Swift and Herbert R. Northrup, *Negro Employment in the Maritime Industries: A Study of Racial Policies in the Shipbuilding, Longshore, and Offshore Maritime Industries* (Philadelphia: Industrial Research Unit, Wharton School, University of Pennsylvania, 1975), p. 21.

11. For more information on the riots consult: Carey McWilliams, *North from Mexico* (Philadelphia: J. P. Lippincott, 1949); Chester Himes, "Zoot Suit Riots Are Race Riots!" *The Crisis 50* (July 1943), 200–01, 222; Mauricio Mazon, *The Zoot Suit Riots: The Psychology of Symbolic Annihilation* (Austin: University of Texas Press, 1984). The riots have also been fictionally depicted in James Ellroy's *The Black Dahlia* (New York:

Mysterious Press, 1987) and in the motion picture *Zoot Suit* (Universal, 1981), which was based on a play by Luis Valdez.

12. Himes, *If He Hollers*, p. 16.

13. *Ibid.*, p. 24.

14. *Ibid.*, p. 3.

15. *Ibid.*, pp. 113–14.

16. Richard Wright, *Native Son* (New York, Harper & Brothers, 1940).

17. See Herman Feldman, *Racial Factors in American Industry* (New York: Harper & Brothers, 1931), pp. 27–34.

18. Himes, *Lonely Crusade*, p. 3.

19. *Ibid.*, p. 4.

20. *Ibid.*, p. 16–17.

21. *Ibid.*, p. 23.

22. *Ibid.*, p. 24.

23. *Ibid.*, p. 61.

24. *Ibid.*, p. 139.

25. Himes to Williams, 31 Oct. 1962, *op. cit.*

26. Arna Bontemps, *New York Herald-Tribune*, 7 Sept. 1947; Milton Klonsky, *Commentary 5* (Feb. 1948): 189–90; Christowe Stoyan, *Atlantic Monthly*, 180 (Oct. 1947): 138.

27. The reference is to Senator Theodore Bilbo, the Mississippi Democrat who was a notorious opponent of civil rights during the 1940s. See John A. Williams, "My Man Himes," in John A. Williams and Charles F. Harris, eds., *Amistad I* (New York: Vintage Books, 1970), p. 37.

28. Chester Himes, *Cast the First Stone* (New York: Coward-McCann, 1952); Chester Himes, *The Third Generation* (Cleveland: World Publishing Company, 1954); Chester Himes, *The Primitive* (New York: New American Library, 1955).

The term "protest novel" is used to describe a particular genre of fiction. The type was really created by Richard Wright when he wrote *Uncle Tom's Children* (New York: Harper & Brothers, 1938) and *Native Son* and was carried on by the likes of Himes, Ralph Ellison, Ann Petry, and other black writers. Such fiction was labeled "protest" because it was written with an eye towards confronting and denouncing racism within the context of a fictional presentation.

29. Chester Himes, *Cotton Comes to Harlem* (New York: G. P. Putnam's Sons, 1965).

Labor's Heritage, 1 (July 1989), 51–65.

Limited Options: Strategic Maneuverings in Himes's Harlem

Wendy W. Walters

Chester Himes, an American author who in his lifetime never found a "place" in the American literary scene, set his novels written during French expatriation in the nostalgic milieu of a Harlem he half-created in his imagination. In fiction he was able to exercise a control over U.S. racial politics which he (like most people) could never exercise in life. Himes explained the pleasure of his nostalgic literary act to John A. Williams:

I was very happy writing these detective stories, especially the first one, when I began it. I wrote those stories with more pleasure than I wrote any of the other stories. And then when I got to the end and started my detectives shooting at some white people, I was the happiest. (qtd. in Williams 315)

Himes's detective novels allow him to control the site of nostalgia, briefly to imagine refashioning U.S. race relations and law enforcement practices. His own experiences as a black convict in Ohio State Prison inform his authorial imagination in these novels.[1] An emphasis present in the detective fiction, and Himes's other writings as well, is the necessity of physical safety for African Americans. Himes's two detectives, Coffin Ed Johnson and Grave Digger Jones, emerge as "the cops who should have been;" the cops who could offer protection to the African American urban community. By analyzing two of Himes's detective novels, published in 1959 and 1969, we can chart the progress of these proposed heroes. In 1959 in *The Real Cool Killers* Himes constructs Coffin Ed and Grave Digger as viable folk heroes for the urban community.[2] But by *Blind Man with a Pistol* (1969) their effectiveness as heroes is undercut by the altered socio-political landscape of U.S. race relations.

The Real Cool Killers:
Coffin Ed and Grave Digger as Folk Heroes

Himes's second detective novel, *The Real Cool Killers*, opens with the blues lines "I'm gwine down to de river, / Set down on de ground. / If de blues overtake me, / I'll jump overboard and drown" (5). As a vernacular inscription, this epigram is well-suited to the themes of Himes's novel, which can be read as the ghetto's answer to white power. But the words of the blues lines imply a different and more pessimistic response to life in a racist society than the response suggested by the novel. My contention is that the characters in *The Real Cool Killers* employ specifically community-based, folk-heroic strategies of self-defense and solidarity in the face of intrusive, dominating power structures embodied by white cops. In all of his detective novels, Himes sets up Harlem as particularly unreadable and mystifying, not only to white "visitors" and cops, but also to his two heroes, Coffin Ed and Grave Digger, and even local inhabitants. What varies is the degree to which Harlem mystifies the various characters, and it is the community insiders' special skill both in reading Harlem *and* in manipulating its unreadability which allows for their self-protecting solidarity. Most governmental systems of ordering and labeling urban reality are not applicable in Himes's Harlem. When Grave Digger questions a suspect to find out an address, the evasive response he gets is, " 'You don't never think 'bout where a gal lives in Harlem, 'les you goin' home with her. What do anybody's address mean up here?'" (115). The breakdown of the ability to rely on official locating practices functions in several ways in the novel. First, it completely baffles the white cops (especially chiefs and lieutenants) and renders them ineffectual. It allows Himes to project Coffin Ed and Grave Digger as powerful inside readers of an otherwise inscrutable milieu. And it enables the residents of Harlem to manipulate the particular codes which confound white cops, in the interest of self-protection. In *The Real Cool Killers* the white cops continually express their frustration in being unable to pin down a systematic way to decipher their surroundings. Their inability to make sense of their environment is directly linked to their preconceived racist stereotypes, as is seen in the exasperated statement of one white cop to another: "'What's a name to these coons? They're always changing about.'"

The context which makes strategies of manipulation both necessary and successful is the historical presence of white law enforcement in black urban communities and the way this white presence has been seen by the residents of these communities. John W. Roberts explains that "the tremendous amount of power vested in white law enforcement officers in the late nineteenth century caused many African Americans to view them as the embodiment of the 'law' and, by extension, white power (197). Because these law officers were not community insiders, and only entered black neighborhoods for work, their knowledge of the territory was limited, and African Americans soon developed strategies for exploiting this white ignorance, ways of manipulating codes.

These strategies of evasion should be seen as subversive power exercised by the black Harlem residents of Himes's novels, in their manipulation of codes. This relative power is based in the underclass's superior knowledge of the minds of their oppressors. It should be readily apparent that this knowledge, coupled with behavior subversive of dominant power, calls to mind the qualities of the trickster hero of black folklore. Roberts explains that the trickster has the ability to step adeptly "inside his dupe's sense of reality and manipulate it through wit, guile, and deception to secure material rewards" (185). It is possible in a more current context to replace *material rewards* with *personal safety*. In the context of the black ghetto, safety from abusive white law enforcement becomes a most valued commodity. Sheikh, the leader of the teenage gang The Real Cool Moslems, becomes the trickster turned bad man, outlaw hero. Sheikh's skill in reading white stereotypical assumptions about black behavior enables him to baffle the cops. When his gang members question the believability of the behavioral disguise Sheikh tells them to adopt, he answers,

"Hell, these is white cops. They believe spooks are crazy anyway. You and Sonny just act kind of simple-minded. They gonna swallow it like it's chocolate ice cream. They ain't going to do nothing but kick you in the ass and laugh like hell about how crazy spooks are. They gonna go home and tell their old ladies and everybody they see about two simpleminded spooks up on the roof teaching pigeons how to fly at night all during the biggest dragnet they ever had in Harlem. You see if they don't." (52)

Sheikh banks on white inability to understand black behavior in addition to white racist assumptions about black intelligence. In this analysis he shows himself to be the more skilled reader of minds. In fact the cops who do confront the gang members on the roof are immediately unable to decipher even the physical scene, see only blackness and two "tarbabies," and the sergeant even reads the scene as a "voodoo" rite in a way that specifically emphasizes an intensely mystified othering of the African American subject. It is probably not irrelevant, however, that voodoo has been seen historically by the white community not only as mystifying or inexplicable but, by extension, *powerful.*[3] Roberts adds conjure to the trickster repertoire of means of deceiving and fooling those in power (206). The subversive power of this behavior can be seen in the white cops baffled reaction and (correct) fear that they're being duped:

   "Do you think all these colored people in this neighborhood know who Pickens and the Moslems are?"
   "Sure they know. Every last one of them. Unless some other colored person turns Pickens in he'll never be found. They're laughing at us." (119)

Recalling the novel's epigram, the blues emerge again in an analogue with roots in folk sayings: "Got one mind for the white folks see, another mind I know is me."
   If Sheikh and his quasi-criminal teenage gang of Real Cool Moslems are the trickster heroes of the novel's milieu, what role is played by Coffin Ed and Grave Digger, the two black police detectives on the Harlem beat? Indeed their position as black enforcers of white police domination has caused them to be misread as excessively violent towards "their own people" and in many ways more unapologetically complicit with the white power structure than I see them as being.

I would contest a common, and reductive, view of Grave Digger and Coffin Ed as expressed by Jay R. Berry in "Chester Himes and the Hard-Boiled Tradition": "Their cultural antecedents give them the moral authority that they exercise—from folk culture they are the 'bad niggers' in the tradition of Stackalee" (40).[4] Central to any consideration of whether this is an accurate description of Coffin Ed and Grave Digger would be a study of the particular socio-cultural bases of the uses of the term *bad nigger*. Roberts's chapter "The Badman as Outlaw Hero" is a thorough, Afrocentric revision of previous folklore scholarship on black heroic figures, and Roberts criticizes the faulty equation made by many scholars between *bad nigger* and *badman*.[5] During slavery, "bad niggers," originally a label given by whites, "sought through open defiance, violence, and confrontation to improve their lot in slavery regardless of the consequences of their actions for their own or the slave community's welfare" (Roberts 176). The "bad nigger" does *not* have moral authority either from the black community or the white power structure; he is viewed by both as dangerous. Roberts explains the Afrocentric view of the "bad nigger": "To African Americans, individuals who acted as 'bad niggers' in their communities were not heroes, but rather individuals whose characteristic behavior threatened their abilities to maintain the value that they placed on harmony and solidarity as a form of protection against the power of the law" (179). Coffin Ed and Grave Digger clearly do not fit this characterization, both because they care not for personal acquisitiveness and because their ultimate motivating force is based in community self-protection from an invading, threatening outside force—namely, white law enforcement. Contrary to the "bad nigger" stereotype, Coffin Ed and Grave Digger see the values of the black community as binding. In fact, Stackolee is a *badman,* celebrated by African American folk heroic balladry, not a *bad nigger,* which Roberts points out was *not* the focus for heroic folk-tales. Roberts explains that the bad men celebrated by balladry were outlaw folk heroes "whose characteristic behaviors were perceived as justifiable retaliatory actions" against the white power structure (205). While Coffin Ed and Grave Digger possess some similarities to badmen heroes of legend, they are ultimately a different modern figuration of heroism in Himes's conceptualization of their role in *The Real Cool Killers.*

Grave Digger and Coffin Ed possess some badmen-like qualities, such as their often violent and unpredictable behavior. Their guns, like those of many badmen heroes, are extremely formidable symbolic images and very real instruments of destruction known by the whole community. At least one scene in each of Himes's detective novels introduces these guns. Here is a representative example from *The Real Cool Killers:*

Coffin Ed drew his pistol from its shoulder sling and spun the cylinder. Passing street light glinted from the long nickel-plated barrel of the special .38 revolver, and the five brass-jacketed bullets looked deadly in the six chambers. (13)

Here the gun literally reflects the street, the life of the ghetto, and the gun's image repeats its power in the ghetto imagination when Choo-Choo, one of Sheikh's gang members, fantasizes, "'What I'd rather have me is one of those hard-shooting long-barreled thirty-eights like Grave Digger and Coffin Ed have got. Them heaters can kill a rock'" (49). Choo-Choo's hyperbolic description of the guns' power is tied to similarly legend-infused tales of Coffin Ed's and Grave Digger's own power, based on their quickness to use these infamous weapons. But Coffin Ed and Grave Digger play a very complex and multi-layered role in their negotiation of the city's white power structure and their relationship to the black community, and there is less ambivalence in their behavior than there is conscious manipulation and folk heroic maneuvering in a very tight space of operation. Traditional badmen are outlaws, and Coffin Ed and Grave Digger operate within the law and attempt to control outlaws. Thus, they cannot correctly be seen only as badmen heroes.

It is necessary to acknowledge their brutality, but not without also seeing it as a "natural" part of the general, cartoon-like excessive violence of Himes's detective fiction as a whole. For Coffin Ed and Grave Digger, violence, or its threat (which is effective due to community knowledge of the pair's capacity to do actual violence), is what enables them to get informants to talk. As cops, Coffin Ed and Grave Digger have official *sanction* from the white police department to be excessively brutal. This caveat removes the traditional prohibition against police brutality, which in many cases is only nominal anyway. But this particular nod from their white superiors functions differently for the white cops than it does for Coffin Ed and Grave Digger. For as the chief says to Grave Digger, "'You know Harlem, you know where you have to go, who to see.... I don't give a goddamn how many heads you crack; I'll back you up'" (44). Thus, their license for brutality is based on the police department's utter reliance on them as skilled readers of Harlem's behavioral and linguistic codes.

This reliance is very much like that placed on black slave drivers during slavery. Roberts tells us that, "in the black slave driver, the masters, from *their point of view,* had an individual who could be held responsible when enslaved Africans violated the rules of the system and whose loyalty could be counted on" (50; italics added). While this is what plantation owners (and the white police force) *think* they are getting in a black slave driver, the actual allegiance of the black cops is elsewhere. Hence, during slavery a body of folklore emerged celebrating the driver as trickster hero, portraying "John as a talented and skillful exploiter of his exploitation by Old Master, his dupe or foil in most of the tales" (53). The split between white perceptions of black behavior and black loyalty and the realities of that behavior and loyalty is central to an understanding of the ways that Coffin Ed and Grave Digger function as *protectors* within their community. I draw these parallels to folk culture both to locate Coffin Ed and Grave Digger within this tradition of African American folk-heroic creation, and to mark out their differences from existing or previous heroes. I see them as neither the *bad niggers* nor the *badmen* of folklore, but instead embodiments of a complex yet idealistic image of protection in the ghetto.

The Real Cool Killers opens with the murder of a white man, a "visitor" to Harlem. This fact brings the white cops to Harlem in full racist force: "'Rope off this whole goddamned area,' the sergeant said. 'Don't let anybody out. We want a Harlem-dressed Zulu. Killed a white man.... Pick up all suspicious persons'" (22). When white power in the form of armed white police officers invades the ghetto, every black person becomes a potential suspect, a potential scapegoat. And because the crime is the murder of a white man, every black person becomes a potential victim of lynching by the white mob. Himes specifically suggests this potential, again in his return to the blues, when he describes the white cops' intrusive presence swarming over the neighborhood:

[The white chief of police] turned and pointed toward a tenement building across the street. It looked indescribably ugly in the glare of a dozen powerful spotlights. Uniformed police stood on the roof, others were coming and going through the entrance; still others stuck their heads out of front windows to shout to other cops in the street. The other front windows were jammed with colored faces, looking like clusters of strange purple fruit in the stark white light. (41)

It is essential here to relate Himes's imagery of "colored faces" to its vernacular and literary black antecedents, specifically Billie Holiday and Jean Toomer, in contrast to previous critical interpretations which have aligned Himes's imagery with European painters and writers.[6] When we look to Jean Toomer's "Song of the Son" as a precursor for Himes's language we open up Himes's writing to the powerful allusions to slavery which enrich his meaning.[7] Toomer's poem from *Cane* refers to slaves as "dark purple ripened plums/squeezed, and bursting." Toomer's imagery suggests the violence of slavery, the pressure of exploitation; and these images resonate with the condition of impoverished blacks in modern U.S. urban ghettos.

Billie Holiday's famous blues song "Strange Fruit" articulates the image of lynching even more overtly, in a way that is crucial to Himes's own description of the relationship of white law enforcement to the black community. Her musical version of a poem by Lewis Allan, recorded 20 April 1939, has potent resonance in black culture, as we recall its imagery of lynched bodies as "strange fruit ranging from the poplar trees."

When seen in the context of politicized African American poetic antecedents, Himes's linguistic imagery is allowed to signify upon this verbal tradition. Singing to an urban New York audience at Cafe Society in Greenwich Village in 1939 Billie Holiday contextualizes Southern racism and oppression for the Northern audience as relevant to them. Himes uses the same metaphors for lynching as the pine-scented, squeezed-plum imagery of "Song of the Son," but substitutes for the pastoral vision of "Strange Fruit" the modern, signally urban, decaying tenement flooded with police spotlights and surrounded by uniformed white cops—perhaps urban equivalents of hooded Southern embodiments of white power. Allowing Himes's voice to resonate among Holiday's and Toomer's historicizes a critique of Southern racism by bringing it to a Northern urban context and showing the way that lynch mob "law enforcement" is replicated in the modern ghetto when a white is presumed murdered by a black.

True to the lynch mob mentality, the white cops are looking for *any* "Harlem-dressed Zulu" who can "hang" for the crime. But no criminal appears apprehendable, and the police chief is in danger of losing face before the white press. The master has been duped; he's caught unable to read the signs, solve the mystery, and appease the mob with a lynching. So he must get his hands on a black body quickly. Sonny Pickens becomes the scapegoat for the chief, who says, "'We haven't got anybody to work on but him and it's just his black ass'" (43). Obviously here Pickens's black ass is much less valuable in the cops' mentality than the white ass of Galen, the murdered man. And this essential unequivalence cannot be balanced. In the racial economy of 1959 one dead black ass does not equal one dead white ass—an unequal economy of bodies that becomes the central issue of Himes's detective fiction.

The Harlem milieu in which Coffin Ed and Grave Digger operate as detectives is one marked by the proliferation of (what they consider) minor vices like prostitution, the numbers racket, other forms of gambling, and small-scale robbery. For the most part Coffin Ed and Grave Digger allow these activities to flourish, and even develop a somewhat symbiotic relationship with their participants, who become key informers for them, people who will talk because they desire to continue operating without hassles from the law. In this way Harlem's underworld becomes part of the inner network which enables Ed's and Digger's investigative work. Historically, as institutionalized economic oppression became a more dominant factor of impoverished black urban life, such illegal activities were often a necessary part of the system by which the ghetto could continue to exist (in both the positive and the negative senses implied by such an existence). Roberts explains that

... the relative absence of the [white] "law" in black neighborhoods allowed for the creation of a socio-cultural environment in which certain types of illegal activities involved relatively little risk to personal well-being from the "law while enhancing the potential for extraordinary economic gain at its expense. In addition the pervasiveness of destructive material and physical conditions in the black community attributed to the power of the law over the lives of African Americans created an atmosphere in which social restraints against certain types of actions which violated the law greatly diminished. (198)

But Roberts also importantly acknowledges that such behaviors were only accepted until they "threatened the solidarity and harmony of communal life in ways that created the *potential of external intervention"* (199; italics added). The danger of external intervention is the propelling force behind Coffin Ed's and Grave Digger's protective strategies.

The two detectives' roles are made complex when white people come to Harlem to support its vices, buy its citizens' bodies. When some white people in a Harlem bar question Grave Digger's "tough" police language, his response is, "'I'm just a cop, if you white people insist on coming up to Harlem where you force colored people to live in vice-and-crime ridden slums, it's my job to see that you are safe'" (65). Digger's comment here is essential in several ways, the most obvious of which being that it names the invidious complicity of white socioeconomic oppression and white participation in exploitative vice. Additionally, his comment, and others like it throughout the detective novels, implies that his job is to protect *white people.* But Digger and Ed are much more skillful readers of the particular politics of violence and law enforcement in the black ghetto, and their ultimate aim is the protection of *black people,* and especially black community security. In fact, their success in meeting this goal can be measured in part by the fact that their deeper motives are not recognized by the police force. They know that the best way to ensure the security of black bodies is by keeping the lynch mobs at bay, a goal they seek to accomplish by what may seem like a circuitous means—protecting the singular white body in Harlem. As we have seen, *one* white death in Harlem brings the cops *en masse* to the area, with unquenchable lynching fervor; one white stiff ends up equaling four black corpses and one maimed black body.

If Coffin Ed and Grave Digger use violence in their questioning procedures, their goal is to solve crimes so that white cops stay out. The complexity of Coffin Ed and Grave Digger as heroes rests in this double-edged quality of their behavior: Their violence is both directed at members of their community and used as a force to prevent the more uncontrollable violence of lynch mobs. John Cawelti, writing on "hard-boiled" detective fiction, considers that "the action of legitimized violence ... resolves tensions between the anarchy of individualistic impulses and the communal ideas of law and order by making the individual's violent action an ultimate defense of the community against the threat of anarchy" (142). In their protection of the community against the anarchic forces of white law enforcement, Coffin Ed and Grave Digger are complex black heroic figures. Possessing some of the traits of the trickster, a man, and slave driver, they stand apart from all these.

Asked in a 1970 interview in *Le Monde* by Michel Fabre whether his black detectives are traitors to their race, Himes brought out an important issue which has special bearing on *The Real Cool Killers:*

Cerceuil et Fossoyeur seraient des traîtres à leur race s'ils étaient les personnages réalistes. Ce qui n'est pas le cas: ils représentent le type de policier qui *devrait* exister, celui qui vit dans la communauté, la connait bien et fait respecter la loi de façon humaine. Je crois en eux. Je les ai créés: deux personnages qui seraient les ennemis des Noirs dans la réalité, mais que j'ai voulu sympathique. (20)[8]

(Coffin Ed and Grave Digger would be traitors to their race if they were realistic characters. This is not the case: They represent the type of cop who *should* exist, who lives in the community, knows it well, and enforces respect for the law in a humane way. I believe in them. I created them: two people who would be enemies of Blacks in reality, but whom I intended to be sympathetic.)

Himes's statement is confusing in that it champions yet denies realism. When Fabre asks whether Coffin Ed and Grave Digger are traitors, he is speaking of their characters, not "real" black cops in general. Yet Himes does not respond *directly* to this question to discuss his *portrayal* of the cops, but instead hypothesizes that "real" black cops would be traitors. I take Himes to mean that Coffin Ed and Grave Digger are ideal types, that "real" cops who are black are necessarily traitors to their race, but that these two are sympathetic, that their allegiance is above all to their community.

In his 1963 article written for *Présence Africaine* entitled "Harlem ou le cancer de l'Amérique," Himes identifies the social milieu which grounds the necessity for heroes like Coffin Ed and Grave Digger. He outlines the series of American race riots in ghettos around the country, especially Harlem and Detroit. The result of a Detroit riot in which many blacks are killed by white police is that, "en consequence, Harlem fut submergée de policiers blancs qui portaient de lourdes matraques et patrouillaient dans les rues à cheval ou à motocyclette. Les incidents succédèrent aux incidents" (55). ("Consequently, Harlem was flooded with white policemen who carried heavy bludgeons and patrolled the streets on horseback or motorcycles. There was one incident after another.") Coffin Ed and Grave Digger, then, are created in the hope of preventing this abusive presence from invading black neighborhoods. They can be seen as artful strategizers of legal politics whose perhaps imperfect methodology of protecting one white body (their overt, white-perceived purpose) has as its goal the effective prevention of a general lynching of black bodies. While such a goal was possible to *articulate* in the U.S. racial environment of 1959, it was not possible to *realize*. Coffin Ed and Grave Digger cannot fully prevent the lynching, and innocent black citizens are killed. Ten years later, with the publication of *Blind Man With a Pistol,* Coffin Ed's and Grave Digger's strategic methodology is much less plausible even to articulate and becomes, in fact, absurd.

Blind Man with a Pistol: Riots and Revolutions

A friend of mine, Phil Lomax, told me this story about a blind man with a pistol shooting at a man who had slapped him on a subway train and killing an innocent bystander peacefully reading his newspaper across the aisle and I thought, damn right, sounds just like today's news, riots in the ghettos, war in Vietnam, masochistic doings in the Middle East. And then I thought of some of our loudmouthed leaders urging our vulnerable soul brothers on to getting themselves killed, and thought further that all unorganized violence is like a blind man with a pistol (Himes, Preface to *Blind Man With a Pistol*)

In the ten-year span between the publication of *The Real Cool Killers* and *Blind Man With a Pistol* race relations in the U.S. had become even more volatile as white power cemented itself further. The assassinations of Martin Luther King, Jr., and Malcolm X had violently demonstrated U.S. institutional response to powerful black heroes. In his chapter "Sixties' Social Movements, the Literary Establishment, and the Production of the Afro-American Text," W. Lawrence Hogue explains that the increasing economic disparity between blacks and whites led to riots and rebellions across the nation, and the civil rights and black power struggles which "continued to undermine and bring into question the authority and legitimacy of the dominant ideological apparatus" (50). Coffin Ed and Grave Digger, by virtue (or fault) of their connection to this apparatus, would also meet with challenges to their previously unquestioned authority. The nationalist impulse in the black community in the 1960s saw white power as centralized and therefore fightable. Thus, in any conceptualization of two distinct sides, Coffin Ed and Grave Digger were now seen as on the wrong one.

As his preface shows, during his expatriation in Europe, Himes remained closely aware of both internal and international U.S. politics and ideology. Given the social circumstances outlined by Hogue, the creation and function of Coffin Ed and Grave Digger as ideal heroic solutions and community protectors become entirely implausible for Himes. White power and white law enforcement domination is so entrenched, and its control over the ghetto so pervasive, that the smaller scale heroism of a Coffin Ed or Grave Digger becomes ineffectual. *Blind Man,* as Himes's last completed detective novel set in Harlem, charts this landscape and demonstrates this collapse. The removal of a protective capacity in turn leads to widespread random violence throughout Harlem, a situation which allows Himes to bring forth his long-held criticisms of unorganized violence.

While *Blind Man* is less a detective story than any of Himes's previous detective fiction, there is the premise of a mystery within the novel. Like *The Real Cool Killers,* it involves a white man who lives outside Harlem, comes there to buy a black body for sex, and ends up dead on the street. As *Blind Man* progresses it becomes obvious that, if Ed's and Digger's former heroic strategies were ever viable ones, they can no longer succeed, for in 1969 the urban scene is very different from that in 1959. The corruption of the police force, previously alluded to, now works to circumscribe Ed's and Digger's behavior. Predictably, the dead white man on the street brings on the white cops in full force, and Grave Digger and Coffin Ed try futilely to protect the citizens from the ensuing lynch mob. At the scene of the crime Grave Digger says to Coffin Ed,

> "I just wish these mother-rapers wouldn't come up here and get themselves killed, for whatever reason.
> ... Coffin Ed turned on [the crowd of black onlookers] and shouted suddenly, "You people better get the hell away from here before the white cops come in, or they'll run all your asses in."
> There was a sound of nervous movement, like frightened cattle in the dark, then a voice said belligerently, "Run whose ass in? I lives here!"
> "All right." Coffin Ed said resignedly. "Don't say I didn't warn you." (35)

While Coffin Ed and Grave Digger are still following their earlier strategy of protecting Harlem citizens from the anarchic wrath of white law enforcement, the scene has changed. The unidentified belligerent voice who contests Coffin Ed's demands and who asserts his rights as a resident is the voice of a new generation which does not automatically respect either Ed's and Digger's authority or the intimidating practices of the white cops. Ed's answer back to the voice is "resigned," a new way to describe Ed's and Digger's behavior in a crowd.

The breakdown of Ed's and Digger's uncontestable heroic authority originates from two different directions. Primarily, their behavior is curtailed by the white cops who run the force. But also, this new, more militant generation of Harlem citizens has no respect for "the law" in any form. Confronting some young kids threatening another kid with violence because he is too chicken to stone the white cops, Coffin Ed and Grave Digger are neither automatically recognized nor feared. One kid challenges the once formidably terrifying Coffin Ed:

> "You scared of whitey. You ain't nothing but shit."
> "When I was your age I'da got slapped in the mouth for telling a grown man that."
> "You slap us, we waste you."...

"We're the law," Coffin Ed said to forestall any more argument. Six pairs of round white-rimmed eyes stared at them *accusingly*.

"Then you on whitey's side."...

"Go on home," Grave Digger said, pushing them away, ignoring flashing knife blades. "Go home and grow up. You'll find out there ain't any other side." (140; italics added)

Here Coffin Ed and Grave Digger express their recognition of the pervasiveness of white power. Whitey's side is the ruling paradigm, and they do not see the nationalist moment as viable, the opponent as fightable. The younger generation of Harlem citizens, however, represents a popularized version of nationalism, which Himes's novel will ultimately critique. They at this point possess the impulse of anger toward white power, the refusal to tolerate further oppression, but they lack the organization of purpose which Himes sees as essential to revolutionary efficacy.

Himes now depicts his former heroes as laughable. Throughout the novel they are frequently described in clown-like imagery: "They looked like two idiots standing in the glare of the blazing car, one in his coat, shirt and tie, and purple shorts above gartered sox and big feet, and the other in shirt-sleeves and empty shoulder holster with his pistol stuck in his belt" (141–142). Their former possibly heroic stance, Himes's ideal creation of the cops who "*devrait exister*," is no longer even a viable part of the cultural imagination. Their role has been fully obviated.

Harlem, however, is still a mystified space of illogic to the white cops and to outsiders. The confused anger on the part of whites who can't understand black Harlem linguistic play ends up leading to violence in more than one scene in the novel. Toward the absurdly random end of the novel, a misunderstanding between subway riders is exacerbated by this phenomenon: "The big white man thought they were talking about him in a secret language known only to soul people. He reddened with rage" (183). Because the white cops also fear this "secret language" they still rely on Coffin Ed's and Grave Digger's interpretive police skills, however cursory this reliance may be.

In one scene the white cops who maybe have basically taken care of the investigation of the white man's murder are accompanied by Ed and Digger, following the blood trail to a tenement's basement room:

The blood trail ended at the green door.

"Come out of there," the sergeant said.

No one answered

He turned the knob and pushed the door and it opened inward so silently and easily he almost fell into the opening before he could train his light. Inside was a black dark void.

Grave Digger and Coffin Ed flattened themselves against the walls on each side of the alley and their big long-barreled .38 revolvers came glinting into their hands.

"What the hell!" the sergeant exclaimed, startled.

His assistants ducked.

"This is Harlem," Coffin Ed grated and Grave Digger elaborated:

"We don't trust doors that open." (60)

Here Ed and Digger are their old selves, acting in tandem, keenly reading the visual clues of the environment they know by heart. But despite their obviously superior knowledge they are not allowed to act alone, they are not allowed to *investigate*. Coffin Ed's and Grave Digger's skills in interpreting the Harlem environment lead them too close to uncovering embarrassing connections to Harlem's vice industry on the part of the white power structure and the deeper levels of corruption and complicity within the police force. Therefore Captain Brice and Lieutenant Anderson curtail their activity.

As Brice tells them to leave the investigation to the D.A.'s homicide bureau he asks,

> "What do you think you two precinct detectives can uncover that they can't?"
> "That very reason. It's our precinct. We might learn something that wouldn't mean a damn thing to them." (95)

This fact, Ed's and Digger's heightened ability to decode their environment, is what makes them successful investigators and therefore what now makes them threatening to the white police force with something to hide. Ed and Digger, over a twelve-year development as characters, have lost any earlier optimistic idealism:

The two black detectives looked at one another. Their short-cropped hair was salted with gray and they were thicker around their middles. Their faces bore the lumps and scars they had collected in the enforcement of law in Harlem. Now after twelve years as first-grade precinct detectives they hadn't been promoted. Their raises in salaries hadn't kept up with the rise of the cost of living. They hadn't finished paying for their houses. Their private cars had been bought on credit. And yet they hadn't taken a dime in bribes. Their entire careers as cops had been one long period of turmoil. When they weren't taking lumps from the thugs, they were taking lumps from the commissioners. Now they were curtailed in their own duties. And they didn't expect it to change. (97)

Thus, while Coffin Ed and Grave Digger may have begun the series with the heroic potential of ideal figures, the further institutionalization of discrimination throughout U.S. society has rendered them ineffectual. Not only has white power cemented its position, but it also acts to prevent any public discovery of its complicitous actions.

Coffin Ed's and Crave Digger's previously folk-heroic strategies for maintaining community security have become absurd. Even as they attempt to pursue their original investigation of the white man's death, they are now aware of this absurdity and identify its racial basis. Astute readers of police force ideology, Ed and Digger clearly see, and state, the racial politics behind the restraint placed on them. When Anderson denies them access to what they know is a key suspect, Grave Digger responds,

> "Listen, Lieutenant. This mother-raping white man gets himself killed on our beat chasing black sissies and you want us to whitewash the investigation."
> Anderson's face got pink. "No, I don't want you to whitewash the investigation," he denied. "I just don't want you raking up manure for the stink."

"We got you; white men don't stink." (111)

Coffin Ed's and Grave Digger's initial strategies fail as their political consciousness rises. The more they know about the inner workings of the white-run police force, the more clearly they realize that the premise of their role as detectives or investigators is flawed and ineffectual at its base.

As increasingly politically conscious readers of their racist U.S. environment, Coffin Ed and Grave Digger are quite able to *name* the culprit. What they cannot do is apprehend "him." During the course of *Blind Man* Harlem has been the scene of several riots, and the white cops have given Grave Digger and Coffin Ed the task of finding out who is the cause of these seemingly inexplicable riots—a particularly conservative and palliative version of law enforcement so commonly practiced by the white cops. In a crucial confrontation with Lieutenant Anderson toward the end of Blind *Man*, Ed and Digger point the blame at the unapprehendable criminal they have been chasing their whole careers. In this key scene they are so mentally attuned to one another they speak in a close call-and-response pattern that frustrates Anderson, who exclaims,

"All right, all right! I take it you know who started the riot."
"Some folks call him by one name, some another," Coffin Ed said.
"Some call him lack of respect for law and order, some lack of opportunity, some the teachings of the Bible, some the sins of their fathers," Grave Digger expounded. "Some call him ignorance, some poverty, some rebellion. Me and Ed look at him with compassion. We're victims."
"Victims of what?" Anderson asked foolishly.
"Victims of your skin," Coffin Ed shouted brutally, his own patchwork of grafted black skin twitching with passion.
Anderson's skin turned blood red. (153–54)

Ed and Digger are quite clear here on the balance of law and order on their beat: While the rioters may be black citizens, the instigator, the criminal responsible, is the white racism which causes poverty, ignorance, the hypocrisy of religion, etc. Their own alignment is clearly, as it has ever been, on the side of the victims.

Himes's writing here is at its resonant best as he focuses on the twitching patchwork of Ed's grafted skin. As any reader of the detective novels knows, Ed's face was scarred early in the series by an acid-throwing hoodlum. It is thus a sort of narrative reflection of the violence borne by these two would-be protectors and defenders against white lynch mob law enforcement, as are the other scars and marks which attest to Ed's and Digger's life work. But the pastiche of skin on Ed's face can also be seen as an aspect of the arbitrariness and absurdity of race as a determining category, of blackness as a social construct. By calling attention to the "grafted on" nature of Ed's blackness, and juxtaposing it to Anderson's white, then red face, Himes implicitly questions the absoluteness of race as a category, especially as so obviously resorted to by the white police force. In his 1969 interview with John A. Williams Himes historicizes this discussion of the "cause" of U.S. race riots:

... this whole problem in America, as I see it, developed from the fact that the slaves were freed and that there was no legislation of any sort to make it possible for them to live.... What is it that they have in heaven—milk and honey? That some poor nigger could go and live on nothing. Just to proclaim emancipation was not enough. You can't eat it; it doesn't keep the cold weather out. (346)

Himes makes a similar statement in an italicized "Interlude" in *Blind Man*, where Grave Digger and Coffin Ed name Lincoln as the instigator of the riots: "*He hadn't ought to have freed us if he didn't want to make provisions to feed us*" (135). Here Ed and Digger clearly provide Anderson with the singular culprit so doggedly desired by the police force, but of course he cannot be apprehended, and further, if he were, he couldn't be convicted—because he's white. Says Coffin Ed, "'Never was a white man convicted as long as he plead good intentions'" (135).

Blind Man ends with less resolution than any of Himes's previous detective novels, a point noted by many critics as Himes's ultimate stretching of detective fiction's generic limits. A. Robert Lee writes, *"Blind Man With a Pistol,* especially, approaches antic nightmare, a pageant of violence and unresolved plot-ends which, true to the illogic of a dream, careens into a last chapter of senseless riot" (103). Coffin Ed and Grave Digger are reduced to the inanity of shooting at rats fleeing a burning tenement. These are crucial aspects of Himes's own longstanding political philosophies about both "senseless riot" and the absurdity of racism. Himes would write in *The Crisis* as early as 1944,

The first step backward is riots. Riots are not revolutions.... Riots are tumultuous disturbances of the public peace by unlawful assemblies of three or more persons in the execution of private objects—such as race hatreds.... Riots between white and black occur for only one reason: *Negro Americans are firmly convinced that they have no access to any physical protection which they do not provide for themselves.* It is a well-known and established fact that this conviction is rooted in history: *Negroes in fact do not have any protection from physical injury inflicted by whites other than that which they provide for themselves.* It is a rather deadly joke among Negroes (especially since the Detroit riots) that the first thing to do in case of a race riot is not to call the police but to shoot them.... "Man, what you mean call the police; them the people gonna kill you." (174)

Fourteen years before the publication of *The Real Cool Killers* Himes stated the relationship of white law enforcement to the black community. It is important to see the discourse of *protection* running throughout Himes's writings, even at this early stage.

Himes, who throughout his life was against random violence (as opposed to planned revolution), critiques the chaotic, riotous violence which erupts in Harlem at the end of *Blind Man*. In his 1970 *Le Monde* interview with Michel Fabre, Himes explains the genesis of *Blind Man:*

Il y a plusieurs années, de nombreuses émeutes ont éclaté en Amérique, suivies d'émeutes spontanées après l'assassinat de Martin Luther King et de batailles entre les Pantheres noires et la police. J'ai pensé que toute cette violence inorganisée que les Noirs déchainent en Amérique n'était rien d'autre que des coups de feu tirés à l'aveuglette, et j'ai intitulé mon roman *Blind Man with a Pistol.* Tel était mon commmentaire sur l'inefficacité de ce type de violence. (21)

(Several years ago, numerous riots erupted in America followed by spontaneous riots after the assassination of Martin Luther King and battles between the Black Panthers and the police. I thought that all this unorganized violence that the Blacks unleashed in America was nothing other than shots fired blindly, and I titled my novel *Blind Man With a Pistol.* Such was my commentary on the inefficacy of this type of violence.)

While Himes had since at least 1944 seen unorganized, riotous violence as ineffective, it is important to trace out his "call" for successful planned revolution.[9] Edward Margolies, in his article "Experiences of the Black Expatriate Writer: Chester Himes," quotes from the English transcript of Himes's *Le Monde* interview:

I realized that subconsciously that was the point I had been trying to make in [*Blind Man*].... I think there should be violence ... because I do not believe that anything else is ever going to improve the situation of the black man in America except violence. I don't think it would have to be great shattering and shocking violence. If the blacks were organized and if they could resist and fight injustice in an organized fashion in America, I think that might be enough. Yes, I believe this sincerely. (427)

In his representation of chaos and the inefficacies of splintered popular nationalisms at the novel's close, Himes maintains a consistency with his views about the need for a more systematic form of revolution as a means of opposing white power. This need for violent revolution is a common line of thought in Himes's writings, not only occasioned by particular events of the Sixties, but present within his political ideology since (or before) his 1944 *Crisis* article "Negro Martyrs Are Needed." The title of the article points us toward the role of a single martyr in the revolutionary cause, and Himes's short story "Prediction" (1969)—as well as the prefigurings of his final detective novel set in the U.S., *Plan B*.[10]

It is possible to see Himes's philosophies about the need for organized violence as in some ways an inverted economy of bodies, bearing in mind his earlier idealized construction of Coffin Ed and Grave Digger as protectors of one white body in order ultimately to protect many black bodies. What happens in the economy of "Prediction" and "Negro Martyrs Are Needed" is an ideologically revolutionary inversion: One black body is martyred in the interest of creating more white corpses. In his 1944 article Himes states, "The first and fundamental convictions of the political tactician fighting for the human rights of the people are: (1) Progress can be brought about only by revolution; (2) Revolutions can be started only by incidents; (3) incidents can be created only by Martyrs" (159). Himes specifically counterposes this idea of a *planned* incident by a martyr to what he sees as more random, spontaneous rioting, which he condemns as ineffectual and based in self-interest, as opposed to race betterment. Twenty-five years later he would tell John A. Williams,

Even individually, if you give one black one high-powered repeating rifle and he wanted to shoot it into a mob of twenty thousand or more white people, there are a number of people he could destroy. Now, in my book [the uncompleted *Plan B*], all of these blacks who shoot are destroyed. They not only are destroyed, they're blown apart; even the buildings they're shooting from are destroyed, and quite often the white community suffers fifty or more deaths itself by destroying one black man. (311)

There is a distinct contrast, which we should not ignore, between Himes's comments to John A. Williams, fellow black American writer, and Michel Fabre, white French literary critic. Though both interviews were given at about the same time, Himes's divergent expressions of revolutionary ideology reveal both ambiguities in his own thought as well as alterations for his perceived audiences. To Fabre he states (assures?) that "great shattering and shocking violence" is not necessary. Blacks should just use violence "to resist and fight injustice in an organized fashion" (427). His words here seem like platitudes, as he implies a specific and localized enemy who could be systematically resisted. The author of *Blind Man,* however, knows that there is no such singular enemy. The act of shooting a repeating rifle into a crowd of twenty thousand, as Himes describes to Williams, is fairly "shattering and shocking violence." And the portrayal of this act in "Prediction" emphasizes the graphic nature of the violence. While the philosophy of limited black deaths in order to produce larger numbers of white deaths seems a reversal of the economy of bodies in the discourse of *protection* articulated in the detective novels, the ideological basis understands white behavioral motivation in the same way. The white reaction to black violence against whites is one that crushes anything in its path. This is simply a more advanced stage of the lynch mob reactiveness of law enforcement behavior as seen throughout the detective novels. In Himes's 1969 short story, appropriately titled "Prediction," this crushing white reaction is disembodied in the form of a tank with a brain.

The story, which would become chapter 21 of *Plan B*, opens with an all-white police parade "headed north up the main street of the big city" (281). Instead of the precisely locatable, named Harlem geography of the detective novels, the incidents of "Prediction" and *Plan B* could theoretically occur in any U.S. city. The story describes an all-white scene: white cops, white crowds, white workers, etc. "There was only one black man along the entire length of the street at the time, and he wasn't in sight" (281). This unnamed man, hidden in a church with an automatic rifle, is Himes's martyr for the cause of black liberation: "Subjectively, he had waited four hundred years for this moment and he was not in a hurry" (282). Just as Lincoln was the criminal responsible for the riots in *Blind Man*, historical racial oppression since slavery is clearly the instigator of the revolution which will follow this triggering incident. The martyr knows, however, the nature of white reaction to his planned crime—he is aware of the lynch-like fervor to follow: "He knew his black people would suffer severely for this moment of his triumph. He was not an ignorant man" (282). The man is "consoled only by the hope that it would make life *safer* for blacks in the future. He would have to believe that the children of the blacks who would suffer now would benefit later" (282–83; italics added). Note here the presence again of the discourse of safety and protection running throughout Himes's depictions of black life in the U.S. This language exists in dialogic relationship with the language of equality, with greater emphasis on safety as the most important condition of freedom for African Americans.

When the police parade reaches a key position on the street, the black gunman opens fire and begins mowing down rows of officers. Himes's depiction of this carnage shows his writing at its maximally grotesque:

[The commissioner] wore no hat to catch his brains and fragments of skull, and they exploded through the sunny atmosphere and splattered the spectators with goo, tufts of gray hair and splinters of bone. One skull fragment, larger than the others, struck a tall, well-dressed man on the cheek, cutting the skin and splashing brains against his face like a custard pie in a Mack Sennett comedy. (284)

Combined with the more obvious political reasons, this level of grotesque description of white deaths caused by blacks is something Himes knew the U.S. publishing establishment—and, by extension, reading public—would reject. Discussing *Plan B* with John A. Williams he says, "I don't know what the American publishers will do about this book. But one thing I do know, Johnny, they will hesitate, and it will cause them a great amount of revulsion" (312).

The slaughter causes general pandemonium in the crowd, with police officers firing at each other, at civilians, etc., in their frustrated confusion and inability to find the sniper. The lynch mob mentality takes hold, and

all were decided, police and spectators alike, that the sniper was a black man for no one else would slaughter whites so wantonly.... in view of the history of all the assassinations and mass murders in the U.S., it was extraordinarily enlightening that all the thousands of whites caught in a deadly gunfire from an unseen assassin, white police and white civilians alike, would automatically agree that he must be black. (285)

In an apocalyptic climax, the lynch mob itself takes the form of a technologically developed war machine, a riot tank, endowed with a brain and an eye searching, at first futilely, for the hidden sniper:

Its telescoped eye at the muzzle of the 20-mm. cannon stared right and left, looking over the heads and among the white spectators. over the living white policemen hopping about the dead, up and down the rich main street with its impressive stores, and in its frustration at not seeing a black face to shoot at it rained explosive 2O mm. shells on the black plaster of Paris mannequins displaying a line of beachwear in a department store window. (286)

The lynch mob law enforcement behavior has here reached its apocalyptic level of absurdity, shooting at plaster images of black bodies when it cannot find a human black body. This destructive action in turn triggers further mass hysteria and killing of vast numbers of innocent bystanders, until finally the tank demolishes the church with the sniper inside.

Even this last act, however, is not conclusive for the white mob, since it does not produce the desired black *body:* "It did not take long for the cannon to reduce the stone face of the cathedral to a pile of rubbish. But it took all of the following day to unearth the twisted rifle and a few scraps of bloody black flesh to prove the black killer had existed" (287). When whites are killed, only a black body will appease the lynching mob, and the capturing, dead or alive, whole or in pieces, of this body becomes the all-important aim. In the breakdown of criminal apprehendability which characterizes the cementing of white hegemonic power as represented in the socio-cultural milieu of *Blind Man,* blackness is made to function as redundancy in white power relations. It is as if, after Lincoln, after four hundred years of oppression, after the ghetto, white power is still, *redundantly,* emptying its bullets into an already beaten black "opponent."

For the martyr, because of the number of whites he has killed, the exchange of his body for their deaths seems fair:

He was ready to die. By then he had killed seventy-three whites, forty-seven policemen and twenty-six men, women and children civilians, and had wounded an additional seventy-five, and although he was never to know this figure, he was satisfied. He felt like a gambler who had broken the bank. (286).

Himes specifically envisions this kind of murderous gamble as the key move to trigger more widespread planned violence by blacks "which will mobilize the forces of justice and carry us forward from the pivot of change to a way of existence where everyone is free" ("Negro Martyrs" 159).[11]

In 1972, Himes explained his long-held belief in the necessity of violence to Hoyt Fuller: "I have always believed—and this was from the time that *If He Hollers* ... was published—that the Black man in America should mount a serious revolution and this revolution should employ a massive, extreme violence" (18). Again, notice that to a black interviewer, for a piece published in *Black World,* Himes calls for "massive, extreme violence." Himes's political philosophizing moves from an assertion of defensive violence to an aggressive violence, yet all within the construct of making the U.S. ultimately a *safer* place for blacks.

Himes's literary expression of black revolutionary ideologies should be seen within a tradition—his voice obviously is not the first, nor does it stand alone. Hoyt Fuller, in his *Black World* interview, calls Himes's attention to his literary company in Sam Greenlee's *The Spook Who Sat By the Door* (1969) and another novel whose author is unnamed, *Black Commandoes.* I would historicize this revolutionary discourse further and add Sutton Griggs's *Imperium in Imperio* (1899) to the list. Griggs's novel exists as an interesting precursor for *Plan B,* since it too involves two heroes, long-time companions who disagree over particular revolutionary ideologies, with death as the result. Coffin Ed and Grave Digger play a minor role in *Plan B.* Himes states, "I began writing a book called Plan *B*, about a real black revolution in which my two black detectives split up and eventually Grave Digger kills Coffin Ed to save the cause" (*My Life* 360). Grave Digger is then killed by Tomsson Black (*Plan*

B 209). Thus, in *Plan B* we see the final role and ultimate demise of Himes's two heroes.

For Himes, then, white law enforcement represents the greatest threat to personal safety for impoverished African American urban dwellers. In an environment pervaded by racial oppression the first requirement of freedom is protection from lynch mobs, and the feeling that one's body is not endangered. But over the course of Himes's writing we see this first requirement become less and less attainable. We reach what Himes always considered the absurdity of U.S. race relations.

NOTES

1. Both H. Bruce Franklin (223–24) and Edward Margolies (*Which Way* 59) also discuss Himes's prison experiences as influential on his detective story writing.

2. John Roberts, in the Introduction to his excellent study *From Trickster to Badman*, expresses the need for an analysis of African American folk heroes "as symbols of black cultural identity" (2). He emphasizes that "African American folk heroic creation is a normative cultural activity linked to black culture-building in America" (4). This is the sense in which I use the term *folk heroic creation* as well.

3. See Senter for a discussion of white responses to voodoo.

4. Ten years earlier than Berry's article, Raymond Nelson, in "Domestic Harlem: The Detective Fiction of Chester Himes," uses nearly identical phrasing to delineate the two cops as 'bad niggers' (266).

5. Levine also discusses "Badmen and Bandits" (407–20).

6. Gilbert Muller invokes Marc Chagall and Hogarth (83–84). Nelson cites Bosch (274). Margolies names Hogarth *(Which Way* 66). Dy finds scenes of *Blind Man* Rabelaisian (20). René Micha calls Himes's Harlem Dickensian (1507). Such analogies strip away the redolent meanings and complexity of Himes's vision and obscure his particularly African American literary voice in the same way that critical appraisal of him in terms of a previously all-white genre of detective fiction does.

7. I am grateful to Sherley Anne Williams for reminding me of Toomer's poem.

8. Himes did not speak French; Michel Fabre translated his responses for publication in this French magazine. The French-to-English translation is my own.

9. What does it mean to "call" for revolution from an expatriate stance of non-participation? In Himes's discussions of what "the black man in America" should do, he stands outside the implied group of actors whom he refers to as "they." This self-positioning certainly raises questions for revolutionary political polemicizing, it not for literary analysis.

10. *Plan B* was published in the U.S. in 1993 (by the UP of Mississippi).

11. It is interesting to note that in 1944, when Himes was still living in the U.S., his revolutionary proclamations were expressed in terms that include *him:* He uses the pronoun *us* instead of *them.*

WORKS

Berry, Jay R. "Chester Himes and the Hard-Boiled Tradition." *Armchair Detective* 15.1 (1982): 38–43.

Cawelti, John. "The Study of Literary Formulas." *Detective Fiction: A Collection of Critical Essays.* Ed. Robin Winks. Englewood Cliffs: Prentice, 1980. 121–43.

Dy, J. M. "Étude." *Le Monde* 13 Nov. 1970: 20.

Fabre, Michel. "Écrire: une tentative poor réveler l'absurdité de la vie." *Le Monde* 13 Nov. 1970: 20.

_____. *La Rive Noire: De Harlem àl a Seine*. Paris: Lieu Commun, 1985.

Franklin, H. Bruce. *Prison Literature in America: The Victim as Criminal and Artist*. Westport: Lawrence Hill, 1978.

Fuller, Hoyt. "Chester Himes: Traveler on the Long, Rough, Lonely Old Road." *Black World 21* (Mar. 1972): 4–22, 87–98.

Greenlee, Sam. *The Spook Who Sat By the Door*. 1969. New York: Bantam, 1976.

Griggs, Sutton. *Imperium in Imperio*. 1899. New York: Amo, 1969.

Himes, Chester. *Blind Man With a Pistol*. 1969. New York: Vintage, 1989.

_____. "Harlem ou le cancer d'Amérique." *Présence Africaine* 45 (Spring 1963): 46–81.

_____. *My Life of Absurdity: The Later Years*. 1976. New York: Paragon, 1990.

_____. "Negro Martyrs Are Needed." *Crisis* 51 (May 1944): 159, 174.

_____. *Plan B*. Paris: Lieu Commun, 1983.

_____. *The Real Cool Killers*. 1959. New York: Vintage, 1988.

Hogue, W. Lawrence. *Discourse and the Other: The Production of the Afro-American Text*. Durham: Duke UP, 1986.

Holiday, Billie. "Strange Fruit." Rec. 20 April 1939. *Billie Holiday: Strange Fruit*. Atlantic Records, SD 1614.

Lee, A. Robert. "Hurts, Absurdities and Violence: The Contrary Dimensions of Chester Himes." *Journal of American Studies* 12.1 (1978): 99–114.

Levine, Lawrence. *Black Culture and Black Consciousness: Afro-American Folk Thought from Slavery to Freedom*. Oxford: Oxford UP, 1977.

Margolies, Edward. "Experiences of the Black Expatriate Writer. Chester Himes." *CLA Journal* 15.4 (1972): 421–27.

_____. *Which Way Did He Go?" The Private Eye in Dashiell Hammett, Raymond Chandler, Chester Himes, and Ross Macdonald* New York: Holmes and Meier, 1982.

Micha, René. "Les Paroissiens de Chester Himes." *Les Temps Modernes* 20 (Feb. 1965): 1507–23.

Muller, Gilbert H. *Chester Himes*. Boston: Twayne, 1989.

Nelson, Raymond. "Domestic Harlem: The Detective Fiction of Chester Himes." *Virginia Quarterly Review* 48.2 (1972): 260–76.

Reilly, John M. "Chester Himes' Harlem Tough Guys." *Journal of Popular Culture* 9.4 (1976): 935–47.

Roberts, John W. *From Trickster to Badman: The Black Folk Hero in Slavery and Freedom*. Philadelphia: U of Pennsylvania P, 1989.

Senter, Caroline. "Beware of Premature Autopsies: Hoodoo in New Orleans Literature." Thesis, UC San Diego, 1991.

Toomer, Jean. *Cane*. 1923. New York: Harper, 1969.

Williams, John A. "Chester Himes—My Man Himes." *Flashbacks: A Twenty-Year Diary of Article Writing*. Garden City. Anchor, 1973. 292–352.

African American Review, 28:4 (1994), 615–631.

African American Anti-Semitism and Himes's *Lonely Crusade*

Steven J. Rosen

Most critics have considered Chester Himes's second novel about racial conflict at a Los Angeles war industry plant, *Lonely Crusade* (1947), to be his most ambitious and substantial work.[1] However, the novel has attracted little notice since its reissue (1986), having long been unavailable after its initial publication.[2] Were it known as it deserves, *Lonely Crusade* would still stir controversy.

Himes maintained that the Communist party—excoriated in *Lonely Crusade*—had effectively suppressed it.[3] However, as he also acknowledged, "Everyone hated it.… The left hated it, the right hated it, Jews hated it, blacks hated it" *(Quality of Hurt* 100).[4] According to Himes, black reviewers (such as James Baldwin) had been offended by his hero's discovery that "the black man in America … needed special consideration because he was so far behind" (Williams 38). As Himes insisted, this argument for what he provocatively called "special privileges" long preceded demands for "affirmative action" (Williams 38–39). *Lonely Crusade* also anticipated the controversy, occasioned nearly twenty years later by the Moynihan Report (1965), about African American matriarchy (61). Additionally, Himes's hero, Lee Gordon, finds black workers resistant to integration and has to explain this to a baffled white liberal (138–40); such self-segregating tendencies (as in recent proposals for all-male African American high schools) still surprise liberals.

But perhaps the most controversial topic Himes pioneered in *Lonely Crusade* was black anti-Semitism. "The conflict between Blacks and Jews," as Addison Gayle asserted in his history of the African American novel, had been "previously ignored by other black writers" (225).[5] In light of more recent black-Jewish conflict, Himes's treatment has proven to be very prescient.

As Himes acknowledged, *Lonely Crusade* did offend Jews, such as the *Commentary* reviewer Milton Klonsky, discussed below. Is the novel anti-Semitic? I argue that it is, but the subject is highly complicated. Himes ventured to mediate between Jewish leftists and blacks whose hostilities to Jews he thought partly irrational and partly justified. In *Lonely Crusade,* the hero explains black anti-Semitism to a sympathetic Jew puzzled and troubled by its increase. Lee Gordon cites various black complaints against Jews, which no doubt were more widespread at that time than most black leaders or Jewish liberals cared to acknowledge. But Gordon dissociates himself from some of these charges, such as ignorant exaggeration of Jewish economic power. And Himes further distances himself from black anti-Semitism by noting, in his narrative voice, his hero Lee Gordon's irrational hostility to Jews. In a talk delivered at the University of Chicago one year after *Lonely Crusade's* disappointing reception, Himes complained of having been "reviled" for his rare "integrity" in revealing such "realities" as "paradoxical anti-Semitism" among the effects of black oppression ("The Dilemma of the Negro Novelist in the United States" 75).

In my view, *Lonely Crusade* not only, as Himes claims, depicts and deplores black anti-Semitism, it also ventilates an anti-Semitic streak that recurs in Himes's work in tandem with anxiety to assert masculinity. Himes tended to disparage Jews in order to construct his manhood—differentiating himself from those (Jews) who imputedly lacked masculinity or disrespected its significations. To locate this and other anti-Semitic tendencies in Himes means neither that he was always unsympathetic to Jews, nor that his criticisms of Jews were wholly unjustified. In my opinion, two other Himes novels that deal with Jewish characters much more incidentally *(If He Hollers Let Him Go* and especially *The Primitive)* deftly criticize a Jewish ethnocentricity that for Himes, perhaps, epitomized racism's absurdity.[6] Dreading to seem unfair to Himes, whose early novels remain unjustly unappreciated, I focus on *Lonely Crusade,* where his critique of Jews is both most fully and rather objectionably developed. Its anticipation of current black-Jewish hostilities, together with a misleading discussion of "the question of anti-Semitism" in the foreword to the novel's 1986 edition, make the subject irresistible (ix).[7]

Actually, the foreword, by Graham Hodges, minimizes both sides of the issue's embarrassment: (I) the novel's irreducibly unreasonable anti-Semitism and (2) the possible justification for some African American hostility to Jews. According to Hodges,

the portraits Himes draws of Jewish paternalism and black anti-Semitism are unflinchingly honest. Most tellingly, it is Abe Rosenberg, Ruth, and Smitty, another union organizer, that are [the main character, the African American Lee] Gordon's only true allies. At one crucial point, Lee and Rosenberg, a highly sympathetic character, engage in a fierce debate over these historic racial tensions in American history, hurling insults and stereotypes at one another until finally, like exhausted fighters, they come to recognize their ignorance and hatred by confronting them in honest discussion.... We come to see Lee Gordon as far less anti-Semitic than Maud, the Communist secretary. (ix)

Lonely Crusade does have an air of honesty; the main Jewish character, Rosenberg, does act benevolently. However, the confrontation Hodges describes as a mutual combat is rather a black intellectual's tirade against Jews, occasionally interrupted by a Jew who makes not one criticism of blacks (except that he is beginning to notice anti-Semitism among them [151–62]). Were he tactless, Rosenberg might have answered Gordon's charges against Jews by simply reversing them—i.e., countering gouging Jewish landlords and merchants with irresponsible black tenants and debtors, or opposing the charge that Jews pamper their children by asserting that blacks brutalize theirs. However, as Stephen Milliken observed, Rosenberg unrealistically "listens to Lee's anti-Semitic diatribes with smiling patience, responds with eager, warm understanding, indeed almost with cloying sweetness" (130). Why did their confrontation remain more monologue than dialogue? Apparently, Himes did not want Gordon's charges against Jews effectively opposed. His hero complains about Jews, not so much to exemplify the problem of black anti-Semitism, as Himes sometimes implied, but to air Himes's own hostility. Indeed, Himes substantially reiterated his hero's complaints against Jews more than twenty years later, when interviewed by John A. Williams (53–54, 83–85).[8]

Besides misrepresenting a barely qualified attack on Jews as a "debate," Hodges ignores the novel's malicious caricature of Jewish characters. He cites one minor figure, Maud, a Communist secretary and a "self-hating" Jew, as someone whose anti-Semitism exceeds and thereby condones that of Himes's hero. But Himes significantly links her self-hatred to her typically ugly Jewish looks and mannerisms:

She hated all Jews and all things Jewish with an uncontrollable passion as an escape from which she had become a Communist. And yet she was as Jewish in appearance as the Jewish stereotype. (272)

Maud, a grotesque, speaks in a "usually rasping voice," and when provoked, "the stub of her missing arm jerk[s] spasmodically" (271). Lee Gordon perceives the main Jewish character, Abe Rosenberg, similarly:

Hearing the delayed cadence ending on a question mark, he thought "Jew," before he jerked a look down at Abe Rosenberg's bald head in the sunshine. Sitting on a disbanded wooden casing, feet dangling and his froglike body wrapped in a wrinkled tan cotton slack suit, Rosie looked the picture of the historic Semite. (151)

Even when Gordon comes to feel "grateful" to Rosenberg, who defends him to his own cost, the Jewish Communist remains a "frog-shaped" and "grotesque little man" (375, 383). While gentile grotesques (such as the murderous black Communist Luther MacGregor) also inhabit the novel, only its Jewish characters consistently alienate by moving and speaking oddly—Maud twitches and rasps, Abe dangles and sing-songs, and another Jewish character, Benny Stone, scampers and effuses.

The first time a Jewish character, Benny Stone, saunters into view, an omniscient voice narrates: "Benny's effusive greeting brought a recurrence of the old troubling question. On what side did the Jew actually play?" (19). This instances a third aspect of the novel's anti-Semitism. Although Himes's narrative voice sometimes dissociates itself from his hero's hostility to Jews, for instance, by calling it a "tendency to anti-Semitism," it participates in that tendency as well (162). Similarly, Gordon's assertions that other blacks, rightly or not, blame Jews more than he does work to substantiate and normalize his diatribe (156–59).

Altogether, the main character's tirade, the physical repulsiveness of all the Jewish characters, and the narrator's complicity in the hero's anti-Semitism establish, at the least, that Himes wanted to disabuse Jews of any presumptions upon the high regard of blacks and, more generally, to wound them in their self-esteem.

One probable reason for the novel's articulation of black anti-Semitism was Himes's desire to overcome the fear of "writing the unthinkable and unprintable" *(My Life of Absurdity* 69). When Gordon tells Rosenberg that "the Jew ... [has] cornered us off into squalid ghettos and beaten us out of our money," Rosenberg retorts, "Such nonsense should never be spoken" (153). The very prohibition placed on such expressions by the Jews who comprised most of Himes's white friends and benefactors might well have conferred an allure upon them. Yet the likeliest reason that *Lonely Crusade* voiced hostility to Jews is simply that Himes felt some himself. And we can begin to locate his grievances in the complaint his protagonist produces, charges including: (1) betrayals, exploitations, and manipulations of African American causes by Communists, at a time when many Communists were Jews; (2) a Jewish tendency to ridicule blacks for gentiles (e.g., as humorists); (3) the exploitative practices of Jewish businessmen, with whom blacks had been obliged to deal preponderantly; (4) Jewish prejudice against blacks, which Gordon claims exceeds that of other whites, despite the sympathy Jews ought to feel for other oppressed people; (5) miscellaneous Jewish "manners and personal habits" the character finds "repulsive"—aside from discourtesy in money matters—chiefly mothers spoiling their sons (158–59).

Though space limits here (among other factors) preclude an adequate analysis of these complaints, it would be unfair to ignore them. So I will briefly consider the context of Gordon's charges against Jews, assess how Himes apparently felt about them, and note where they seem partially justified and where disturbingly objectionable. Significantly, one common component emerges: the (supposed) Jewish insult to black masculinity.

Communists. Like his friends Richard Wright and Ralph Ellison, Himes criticized the Communist party, chiefly for cultivating a ruthless disregard of truth and decency in its members and also for subjecting the personal and national interests of African Americans to a shifting party line, humiliating in its inconsistencies and emanating, absurdly, from the Soviet Union (249).[9] At that time, though few Jews were Communists, many American Communists were Jews (Naison 321). Still, African American contemporaries of Himes who criticized the Party did *not* tend to fault its Jewish representation.[10] Wright's *American Hunger* focuses on the oppressive anti-intellectualism of *black* Communists; they even expel "a talented Jew" along with Wright from a theater company (114). Likewise, Ellison's notably unrealistic treatment of the

Communist party (obscured as The Brotherhood in *Invisible Man)* may have been motivated in part by his unwillingness to seem anti-Semitic.[11] Not without anguish, Himes overcame that inhibition. Though the most venal Communist in *Lonely Crusade* (Luther McGregor) is African American, and the most idealistic one (Rosenberg) is Jewish, Himes does relate at least some objections to Communist party culture to its heavily Jewish membership. These offenses are the Communists' inappropriate internationalism (which may mask specifically Jewish interests and sympathies); their humiliating imposition of alien discourse and values on African American members; and, most crucially, their insufficient appreciation of specifically *masculine* dignity.

Himes had already connected a tactless preoccupation with an international agenda to a putative Communist's Jewishness in his first novel, *If He Hollers Let Him Go* (1945). When a union steward with a "big hooked nose" asks the black hero to subordinate his racial grievance for the unified fight against fascism, the latter calls the steward both "Comrade" and "Jew boy" (106–08). Likewise, in *Lonely Crusade,* Lee Gordon "felt vindicated in his stand against the Communists, whose insidious urging that he become a laborer to help defeat fascism had become obnoxious" (88).[12] Why "insidious"? "At a party of Jewish Communists" (121), he interprets their fervent internationalism as a covert Jewish nationalism: Another Jew joined in the conversation. "Russia must be saved!" "For who? You Jews?" Lee asked harshly (89).

The prolonged, preponderant, inevitably resented influence of Jews, however benevolently motivated, not only on African American policies in the American Communist Party, but as executives in civil rights organizations such as the NAACP and the Urban League, helps explain Himes's associated hostilities to Jews and Communists.[13] As Harold Cruse was to contend in *The Crisis of the Negro Intellectual* (1967), it must have been galling for African American Communists to have their situation defined for them by others (many of them Jews) and to be made by the Party to speak a language of leftist jargon that alienated other African Americans. Even Mark Naison, who defends the sincere dedication of Jewish Communists to African American causes and culture, acknowledges that the party's "language and ideology, and above all its interracialism" alienated African Americans (xv). From this perspective, one might understand the appeal of anti-Semitic language for Himes; it might seem an exquisitely iconoclastic declaration of independence, potent in its populistic appeal. (Likewise, Jesse Jackson "on one occasion" characterized his later renounced "anti-Semitic discourse" as "talking Black" [Reed 101].)

Perhaps the chief cultural differences between Jewish Communists and black populists involved constructions of gender. In *Lonely Crusade,* a benevolent Jewish Communist, obtuse to their cultural difference, provokes one of Lee Gordon's most visceral revulsions: The "small, elderly Jewish man with a tired, seamed face and kindly eyes" takes Gordon into a bedroom at the party and shows him "a picture of a naked Negro" which Gordon mistakes for a "ballet dancer" until the Jew identifies him as a lynching victim (90–91). Shocked, nauseated, enraged, reminded that such crimes go unavenged, and confronted perhaps with a mutilated black figure of uncertain gender, Gordon's masculinity has been insulted. Significantly, he directly hears "someone ... saying: 'There are no such things as male and female personalities. There is only one personality'" (91). In reaction, Gordon promptly asserts his traditionally construed masculinity:

I like women who are women.... I like to sleep with them and take care of them. I don't want any woman taking care of me or even competing with me. (91)

In *My Life of Absurdity,* Himes remarks that to enjoy his detective novels as they enjoyed their folk culture "American Blacks had to get all the protest out of their minds that the communists had filled them with" (158). That is they had to stop regarding themselves as suffering victims, with the attendant implication of unmanliness. Rather than "just victims," as "protest writer[s]" portrayed them, Himes wished to present black Americans as absurd"—i.e., as capable perpetrators as well as victims of violence, humorous, extroverted, and full of *joie de vivre (My Life of Absurdity* 36). In contrast, he felt that Jewish Communists sought to politically organize African Americans through pooled self-pity, and that they demeaned black masculinity by making the lynch victim a protest logo.

Humorists. Lee Gordon complains that, to similarly demeaning effect, "the Jew will hold Negroes up for ridicule by the gentile—that in instances where the gentile is not thinking of the Negro, the Jew will call attention to the Negro as an object of scorn" (157). Apparently, Himes felt this way himself because twenty-three years later he reiterated the charge in his Williams interview, claiming that Jews, paradoxically because of their somewhat similar status, are most likely to offend blacks. He said, "You know, some of the Jewish writers, because of the fact that they belong to a minority too, can get more offensive than the other writers do" (Williams 54). Himes more pointedly told *Black World* editor Hoyt Fuller that a Jewish screenwriter's rejected treatment of *Cotton Comes to Harlem* was "a smart Jew-boy angle, especially of the racial scene, because he figured the Jews had a right to do so" (Fuller 87). Likewise, a Jewish fence in Himes's detective novel *The Big Gold Dream* (1960), having through prolonged familiarity assumed the speech style of blacks, also indulges in offensive racial humor (19–21). And a Jewish junk dealer in Himes's *Cotton Comes to Harlem* (1965) tries some tactless ethnic humor while bargaining with blacks (64).

Himes told John Williams he once walked out of a Hollywood script conference on a film about George Washington Carver beginning with Carver ironing a shirt in his kitchen—i.e., feminized by tool and workplace. He understandably resented the traditional movie treatment of blacks as comical servants and menials, and he may have held the predominantly Jewish studio heads accountable (Williams 57–60).[14] Likewise, while praising *Lonely Crusade's* treatment of black-Jewish relations, Himes's admirer Ishmael Reed complained of "Jewish playwrights, cartoonists, film-makers, novelists, magazine editors and television writers [who] depict Blacks in such an unfavorable light as if to say to whites, 'we'll supply the effigy, you bring the torch'" (29–30). (Reed compared David Susskind, for "defending the troopers' actions at Attica," to Hitler.) Jews are liable to be blamed—as recently and controversially by City College professor Leonard Jeffries—for unflattering references to African Americans in the news or entertainment media. Of course, anti-Semitic exaggerations of their offenses do not absolve Jews from whatever blame their conduct may merit. However, I regard the claim that Jews have been especially prone to racist ridicule as dubious, and that gentiles have needed Jewish incitements to "scorn" African Americans as preposterous.[15]

Businessmen. Lee Gordon's complaints about the exploitative control of black commercial life by Jewish businessmen, while not unjustified, also contain disturbing exaggerations and dangerous implications. Again, Himes later reasserted these complaints in his own voice, and again anxiety about masculine dignity attaches to the issue.

Speaking of the 1940s, Lee Gordon chiefly justifies growing African American hostility to Jews by real economic grievances:

Most of the Negro contact with the business world is with the Jew. He buys from the Jew, rents from the Jew, most of his earnings wind up, it seems, in the Jew's pocket. He doesn't see where he's getting value in return. He pays too much rent, too much for food, and in return can't do anything for the Jew but work as a domestic or the like. (156)

His Jewish interlocutor acknowledges that "many [Jewish businessmen] exploit Negroes" (156) but counters that at least they give blacks commercial opportunities others deny them; Rosenberg adds that their own exclusion from gentile-dominated industry forced Jews to deal with blacks (159). Gordon grants that most blacks exaggerate Jewish economic power, but he insists that "many [other] Negroes [wrongly] ... think that Jews control all the money to the world" (159).

By sometimes differentiating his narrator's views from his hero's, as well as his hero's from those of less sophisticated African Americans (whose ideas he nonetheless needs to convey), Himes lends an interesting ambiguity to the novel's anti-Semitic expressions; and he protects himself through undermining their authority. However, since he insists on conveying (while denying) an irrational anti-Semitism he imputes to a segment of the black population less able than he to propagate their views, those views take on the pathos of suppressed thoughts struggling for expression. And, indeed, a recurrent, fundamental association of Jews with money—both as benefactors and as exploiters—functioned importantly for Himes himself.

In his Williams interview, Himes again attributed then current (1969) black hostility to Jews to economic factors. He claimed, like his character Gordon, that the real basis of black animosity to Jews was that they were formerly the only, and currently the primary, dealers of goods and services to blacks, and that they took advantage of that position. He also granted, as his character Rosenberg had asserted, that Jews had been relegated to servicing blacks by an anti-Semitic society. But Himes himself used emphatic and exaggerated language in asserting that, given the commercial ignorance of blacks,

Jewish landlords and merchants misused them All businesses in the ghettoes were owned by Jews.... The black had an ingrown suspicion and resentment of the Jew. He realized that he was being used in certain ways by all Jewish landlords and merchants. Even today a Jew will make a fortune out of the race problem, and this builds up a subconscious resentment—although most of the white people I do business with, who help me, whom I love and respect, are Jews. But that doesn't negate the fact that the Jews are the ones who had contact with the blacks and took advantage of them. (Williams 83–84)

Some hyperbolical and mystifying aspects of Himes's language here indicate a disturbing willingness to cultivate an irrational approach to this topic. Surely Jews cannot have owned "all" the ghetto businesses. Can "all" the Jewish "landlords and merchants" have "misused" blacks? Describing black resentment of Jewish economic exploitation as "ingrown" and "subconscious" means that its existence cannot and need not be demonstrated; that it can thrive without concrete occasion; yet that releasing such resentments might constitute the African American's most essential liberation.

The degree to which Jews had controlled ghetto commerce was hotly debated in the sixties. The most widely accredited writer to deal with the topic, James Baldwin, both condemned and condoned black rage against Jewish landlords and businesses.[16] Jewish writers commonly argued that banks, universities, market forces and other impersonal institutions and conditions actually controlled the ghetto economy.[17] Of course, Jews were conspicuously engaged in ghetto commerce (in part because they had lived there before blacks did). Some certainly cheated blacks, and even if they did constitute a small percentage of Jewish businessmen, it does not take many instances of victimization (as with criminal violence) to stigmatize a perpetrator's group if it already carries signs of otherness. Certainly most major Jewish businesses in ghettoes were slow to employ blacks in responsible positions. And nobody likes landlords, whatever their ethnicity. So when Himes wrote *Lonely Crusade* (and later when he discussed the issue with Williams), black resentment of Jewish businessmen was both widely felt and understandable, if often disproportionate to real offenses. Hence, Himes's treatment of this conflict cannot be dismissed as unrepresentative, though its representativeness does not excuse it from criticism.

Himes's complaints about the behavior of Jewish businessmen might especially typify resentments among black creative artists. Himes hoped for work as a writer in Hollywood, but reported that Jewish employers jim-crowed and insulted him there (Williams 53–60). Today, mistrust of Jewish employers is commonly voiced among black jazz musicians and rap artists. In Spike Lee's film, *Mo' Better Blues,* graceless, greedy Jewish nightclub owners apparently exploit black performers; their caricaturization provoked a controversy in which the Anti-Defamation League, Nat Hentoff, and other Jewish writers attacked Lee, who defended his Jewish characters as realistic.[18]

In Himes's *Lonely Crusade,* unlike Lee's less complex film, the major Jewish character, the Communist Rosenberg, behaves very generously to his black friend, Gordon. And Himes himself readily acknowledged many Jewish friends and supporters.[19] He wrote his first novel on a Rosenwald Fellowship. An element of ambivalence on this subject—i.e., a tendency to regard Jews not only as exploiters but as benefactors—might help explain why Himes describes the general black hatred of Jewish businessmen as "subconscious." The fiercely independent Himes might have resented Jewish philanthropists as much as Jewish businessmen, but also felt that it was wrong to do so.[20]

Himes's convoluted economic connections with Jews may have predated his birth. He claimed that his "father's father was the slave blacksmith of a Jewish slaveowner, probably named Heinz, whose name he took when he was freed. That's how [he] came by the name of Himes" *(The Quality of Hurt 5).* However, Himes scholar Edward Margolies told me that Himes's brothers did not corroborate this claim and that both blacks and whites named Himes—none of them apparently Jewish—occupied the region of his father's forbears. From an early age, Himes seems to have found Jews risky sources of substantial funds. In 1928, having heard a chauffeur "bragging about the large sums of money his boss always kept in his house," Himes held up the boss (named Miller) and his wife in their home (47). (Margolies opines that the couple were Jewish.) Himes fled to Chicago, where he approached "a notorious fence called Jew Sam" (56). Sam turned him over to the cops. Then the police "sent to Cleveland for someone to identify the jewelry, and one of the executives of the firm that insured it arrived. His name was Frieberg. Later he became a friend" (57). Near the conclusion of his autobiography, Himes described some traveling and dining that he and his second wife, moderately prosperous at last, enjoyed in the company of his good friend and "excellent agent," Roslyn Targ, and her husband. The Targs are Jews. At the end of their trip, as both couples sat together in Himes's home,

Roslyn began crying and said, "Chester, at last you've got your own house. I congratulate you both." We all began crying, thinking that after all these years at last I had a house when I was sixty-one years old. *(My Life of Absurdity* 377)

My point is that Himes, who consistently associated Jews with money, blamed them when financially frustrated and bonded with them when successful.

Himes was willing to exploit, even to inculcate, a very reductive association of Jews with money in his Harlem thriller *The Big Gold Dream* (1970). The Jewish fence, whose offensively familiar humor was cited above, is reduced to a mere stereotype through constant reference to him simply as "the Jew." Such images as "his face lit slowly with an expression of uncontainable avarice ... saliva trickled from the corners of his mouth" (30) make "the Jew" grotesquely greedy—but so are many of Himes's black characters. What bothers me here is that Himes's black detectives, who always speak with authority, simply reduce the Jew's meaning to money with several statements such as "in order to bring the Jew into it, there had to be money" (66). This disturbs because the dehumanizing equation of Jews with money prompts people to take out their economic frustration on innocent Jewish scapegoats. Thus, for instance, the Nobel Prize winner Elias Canetti in *Crowds and Power* (1960) explained the Nazi persecution as a reaction to catastrophic inflation; Germans associated Jews with money and passed on the sting to them when their currency became worthless (187). Likewise, according to one analysis, an outburst of black anti-Semitism occurred when African Americans did not get the economic parity some expected after the achievement of civil rights legislation—not because Jews exploited blacks but because disappointment and envy required an outlet.

Himes's tendency to associate Jews with money also ramified into his gender anxiety. His very first published story, "His Last Day," reciprocally relates

Jewish money and black masculinity. A condemned convict, Spats, aims to walk to his death so coolly that fellow convicts will say "what a man," and he spends his last day recalling the "frightened eyes of the little Jew ... a little tyke," i.e., *kike,* whom he had robbed *(Collected Stories* 292–94). He also blames himself for trembling "just like that tyke" he had threatened with his gun (296). Note how the euphemistic substitution of "little tyke" for "kike" insults both the Jew's ethnicity and his masculinity.[21] Later, Spats frightens and gyps his lawyer, a "lousy tyke fixer who [inadvertently] gave his services for nothing," by refusing to locate his cache for the lawyer's payment (298). Despite his bravado, Himes's convict only barely masks his "utter fear" (303) before electrocution. And, of course, the story does not propose that blacks ought to assert their masculinity by robbing and intimidating Jews. Still, Spats's lack of remorse, his toughness, his candid irreligion—among other qualities Himes, then imprisoned for robbery, presumably admired—suggest at least some identification with the convict.

Lee Gordon also resembles Spats, Himes's first protagonist: he expresses hostility to Jews, is benefited by one he verbally abuses (rather than robs), and manfully walks to his probable death at the plot's conclusion. Gordon's characterization also reflects Himes's financial-marital crisis when he wrote *Lonely Crusade:* His promising connections with Jewish leftists in Hollywood having proven fruitless, Himes later wrote that his intense inner hurt only became consciously racial when he found he could not support his wife, i.e., fulfill his traditional economic role as a man *(The Quality of Hurt* 776). She "had a better job than [he] did and ... that was the beginning of the dissolution of [their] marriage" (75). As Himes put it, he "was no longer a husband to [his] wife; [he] was her pimp. She didn't mind, and that hurt all the more" (75). Furthermore, it was through a relative of his wife that he got a fellowship from the Rosenwald Foundation. When Himes was broke and embarrassed before his wife, she enjoyed both a better job and better relations with Jews than he did, all of which threatened his masculinity.

Conspirators. In *Lonely Crusade,* Lee Gordon claims that Jewish prejudice against blacks exceeds that of other whites. He also insists that he "believe[s], like other Negroes, that Jews fight, and underhandedly [the African American] struggle for equality" (159). Charges of secretive, conspiratorial opposition can hardly be disproven. But clearly, by their former substantial involvement in civil rights organizations (however disparaged as conscience money) and their still quite similar voting records (despite divergent economic interests), Jews have demonstrated far less hostility to blacks than other whites.[22]

Here Himes might be distinguished from his character, whose paranoia on this point might be what the narrator means when he refers to Gordon's sentiments as "anti-Semitism" (162). As noted above, a Jew, Rosenberg, proves Gordon's most devoted friend. However, Gordon also recalls an incident when a white gentile had warned him "that the Jewish people ... were trying to get the white people to drive them from their neighborhood," lest "the property would go down" (125). There the narrative does intimate at least one Jewish anti-black conspiracy.[23]

Perhaps the most important aspect of Lee Gordon's charge that Jews fight blacks "underhandedly" is that such contention is unmasculine. Unlike open hostility—"fighting like a man"—secretive opposition affords no opportunity to affirm masculinity, even if defeated, through combat. This links the charge of conspiracy to Gordon's other complaints against Jews by their common insult to black manhood. Jewish Communists emasculate blacks by publicizing their victimization in lynchings. Jewish producers and entertainers present or joke about unthreatening, submissive black men. Jewish businessmen make black husbands look bad before wives they find difficult to support, lacking a Jew's economic opportunities.

Mothers. Gordon's final, apparently incidental but psychologically crucial complaint against Jews explicitly concerns gender: Jewish mothers pamper their sons. He deplores "the repulsive manner in which Jewish mothers worship their sons, making little beasts of them. I've sat on a streetcar and seen Jewish tots beat their mothers in the face ..." (159). But significantly, Gordon is the novel's only character who beats an unprotesting woman, his wife, in part because she plays an excessively maternal role. In other words, the defense mechanism of projection appears to be operating in this instance of his anti-Semitism.

Himes's resentment of women clarifies his parallel resentment of Jews. As his most autobiographical novel, *The Third Generation,* reveals, Himes disastrously overidentified with his mother, a very light-skinned woman of color highly contemptuous of blacks. She both doted upon and beat him, and photos show that she kept him, her youngest child, overlong in girlish attire.[24] Perhaps another source of gender anxiety might have been Himes's prison experience. Because he wore a back brace, he was housed with "crippled" inmates. In *Cast the First Stone,* his prison novel, the hyper-masculine hero's homoerotic love object is embittered, disabled, and effeminate.

Himes's intense identification with his mother and perhaps his prison experience disposed him to differentiate himself from women violently. His autobiographical novels, *The Primitive* and *The Third Generation,* reflect their author's woman-beating tendencies, justified as follows in *The Quality of Hurt:* "the only way to make a white woman listen is to pop her in the eye, or any woman for that matter" (137).

The marital relationship in *Lonely Crusade* closely parallels Himes's account of his own domestic circumstances when he wrote the novel. Ruth Gordon has a better job than her husband, resulting in a sexual "impotency, that was ... trampling down his every endowment of manhood" though he beats and rapes her. The narrator states that Gordon's wife

had not minded absorbing his brutality, allowing him to assert his manhood in this queer, perverted way, because all of the rest of the world denied it. But at so great a price, for it had given to her that beaten, whorish look of so many other Negro women, who no doubt did the same. (7)

Gordon knows that it is wrong to beat his wife, but reflects, "Lord God, a man had to stand on somebody, because this was the way it was" (143). Gordon reflects that his wife had formerly, at her first job, worked for Jewish Communists who had "wooed" her, so that he "felt that the [Jewish] Communists were taking her away from him" (47). These Jews may pose a sexual threat, indirectly, through their ability to offer her salary and flattery. However, the Jew is feared here, not so much as a wife-seducer but as someone likely to conspire with her against her husband's desire to affirm masculinity with other men, including white men, if only through open combat against them.[25]

Gordon is a union organizer, and when the company's WASP tycoon offers to buy him off with a high-paying job, his wife wants him to take it. But that would be "without honor." And

he had reached the point in life where if he could not have the respect of men he did not want the rest. And if this entailed her having to work for what he would not give her in dishonor, she should at least understand that there was nothing noble in her doing so; it was only the white man's desire to deride the Negro man that had started all the lies and propaganda about the nobility and sacrifices of Negro women in the first place. (188)

Eventually, Ruth Gordon does quit her job to repair her husband's masculine ego. But she can never bond with him in violent heroism. Nor can the Jewish Communist Rosenberg, despite pronouncing Gordon "a Negro of revolutionary potential" (381) who will "not be afraid to die" (383). As Gordon marches into suicidal combat against union-busting cops at the book's conclusion, his wife screams in terror, while the equally self-sacrificing and protective "Rosie" stands at her side and yells: "No, Lee! No!" (398).

Gordon finds his wife financially superior and physically inferior. Her very supportiveness unmans him; the Jewish analogy (in Hodges's) is to "paternalism." (383) "Little Rosie" likewise treats Gordon to lunch and absorbs his (verbal) abuse. When Gordon hides out, hunted and sick, Rosenberg comes to nurse him, undressing him, putting him to bed and feeding him—functions more readily associated with wives and mothers than with buddies (374–83). In short, the novel's chief Jewish character resembles the hero's wife as an oddly maternal figure. But Gordon resents their motherings. One of his pet peeves is the theory that African American society is matriarchal, which he won't accept "even if it is true," because "in a white society where the family unit of the dominant group is patriarchal, doesn't that make us something less?" (61).

This line of thought reflects Himes's personal need to establish a masculine identity by cutting himself away from his overbearing mother. But the associated anti-Semitism and anti-feminism he sometimes expressed may not be explained so well by his personal psychology as by his intuition of how African American cultural authority would have to be communicated to a broader audience.

Himes determined that African Americans would only be respected in America by emphatically (if "absurdly") brandishing their masculinity, and that this entailed the sacrifice of their special relationship with Jews and the world view of leftist Jewish intellectuals. Blacks could bond with Jews through political argument, as Rosenberg and Gordon do in *Lonely Crusade*. But they could more readily and authoritatively bond with gentile white Americans in drinking, fast driving, brawling, shooting, and gambling—i.e., through the rituals of mainstream, masculinity-proving American culture.[26]

Underlying the connection between Lee Gordon's hostility to Jews and to women is his attraction to a masculinity-proving ethos—a violent, straight-dealing culture shared with most American black and white men, but he felt neither with his wife nor with American Jews. Hence, Himes characterized the model of *Lonely Crusade's* Rosenberg, his friend Dan Levin, as the author of a novel "in a way a forerunner of the Jewish writer's treatment of the war theme.... Jewish writers never glorified war" (*The Quality of Hurt* 141). Contrastingly, in *Lonely Crusade,* war *is* glorified in a speech by a Southern white army officer who trains black pilots; it tells them that World War II requires their fighting heroism, though formerly they have been encouraged to suffer misfortune patiently. This call to arms includes such phrases as "all of us must prove first of all that we are capable of the dignity and nobility of manhood" (106). To Gordon, this means that "whenever a Negro came to believe that full equality was his just due, then he would have to die for it, as would any other man" (139).

Clearly, a political rhetoric that prioritizes proving manhood poses problems. For one thing, it is dangerous. Note that it is a socially privileged male, a white Southern army officer, who asserts the need to "prove first of all that we are capable of the dignity and nobility of manhood." It was by courageously fighting for the unjust cause of slavery that Southern army officers established their iconic masculinity in American culture. Indeed, *unjust* occasions for combat (e.g. gang warfare) may facilitate proving masculinity even better than just ones. The rhetoric is also unrealistic. Himes himself lived a good long seventy-five years, rather than dying for "full ... equality as would any other man." It is also problematic that these values exclude women and, with them, (Diaspora) Jews—not Israelis, whose combativeness Himes admired and thought American blacks should emulate (Williams 61–62).[27] Both women and (Diaspora) Jews have generally felt—as Himes's Southern colonel said of traditional African Americans—that their group would be more harmed than helped by displays of heroic violence.

Unsurprisingly, one of *Lonely Crusade's* most negative reviews did come from the Jewish journal *Commentary.* The review and Himes's response to it together illuminate the black/Jewish *kulturkampf* brewing then and yet to come. Both the black novelist and the Jewish reviewer (Milton Klonsky) misrepresented each other's texts and seemed most obtuse to each other when dealing with the touchy gender issue.

Complaining in *The Quality of Hurt* about the biased reception of *Lonely Crusade,* Himes said that "the writing might well have been bad, but the writing was not criticized by one review I had read" (101). He also said the *Commentary* review most objected to his depiction of a "Christ-like Jew" (101). Both accounts are mistaken.

The *Commentary* reviewer, who was not the only one to do so, did attack what he (wrongly) called Himes's "shabby style" and "clumsily written" novel (Klonsky 190). He found especially ludicrous Himes writing of lovers going to bed "to consummate their gender." (Might this refusal to consider the sexual act as an signification of gender typify a difference in the sexual sensibilities of Jewish and black writers?) Not above delivering a gender insult in a patronizing racial tone, Klonsky wrote that "although the author is himself a Negro, his book is so deracinated, without any of the lively qualities of the imagination peculiar to his people, that it might easily have been composed by any clever college *girl"* (190; emphasis added).[28]

The reviewer also objected, not to Himes's treatment of his main Jewish character as "Christ-like," but to Rosenberg being stereotyped as a Communist and caricatured as physically repulsive. He also objected to the black and Jewish characters' discussion of "why Jews love money." (But their discussion of the domination of ghetto commerce by Jewish businessmen makes no such claim; it is hardly that crude.) While conceding that Himes might have been well-intentioned, Klonsky concluded that his "treatment here reveals a bias which is almost incredible in a book of its pretentions." That is, Himes's evident hostility to Jews was oddly incongruous with his intention to analyze and warn of black anti-Semitism.

Himes considered himself a mediator between worried Jews and blacks more anti-Semitic than he, all of whom required compassionate attention. His response to the *Commentary* review attributed Klonsky's hostility to "subconscious disturbances within the individual" and denied its "calumny"—that the book was anti-Semitic. He asserted that his hero's "self-destructive ... anti-Semitism" resulted from "oppression." But Himes's attribution of his hero's anti-Semitism to "oppression" too thoroughly condones it. Rather than substantiate such an analysis, the novel ventilates an anti-Semitic tirade, then qualifies it (e.g., in Rosenberg's kindness and "wisdom of five thousand years" [154]). Though this ambivalence is one of the book's many sources of interest, it does not erase its anti-Semitism.

Himes's reply to *Commentary* twice insisted that his novel's main theme was the universal one of "searching for manhood" even, implausibly, that "this story could have been written about a Jew, a Gentile, a Chinese.... And he concluded his response by repeating his Southern officer's call to masculinity-proving heroism.[29] By insisting upon the masculinity-proving theme and its universality, Himes both assertively countered the charge of ethnic bias and, implicitly, blamed Jews like Klonsky, because they lack authority and manifest obtuseness in masculinist discourse. Indeed, most American Jews have felt proving manhood by violence to be inimical to their culture and potentially dangerous to them.

Klonsky's reply to Himes boasted of his review's having stuck it to the novelist—"It seemed to have stuck in his throat but barely grazed his mind" (474). He otherwise refused to perpetuate the dialogue. *Commentary's* reviewer was understandably disturbed and offended by *Lonely Crusade*. However, he grossly underestimated Himes's extremely well-written and prescient novel.

Himes's prescience consists essentially in having realized, in the heyday of Ernest Hemingway and Humphrey Bogart [30] (and just before Jackie Robinson), that African Americans would most effectively enter the mainstream of American culture through a display of hyper-masculine endeavor: that is, in sports, in the military, in hard-driving music, perhaps in the police (like his Harlem detectives), and in other potentially heroic roles, which men (perhaps especially Southern, even racist white men) cannot help but admire. It is too bad that Himes sometimes employed Jewish characters or formulated Jewish traits as a foil to the black American masculinity he endeavored to invoke. This made Himes a disturbing exponent of African American anti-Semitism—though he remains one of its more penetrating analysts. Certainly, in encouraging discussion of this touchy and offensive topic, few set a bolder example than Chester Himes.[31]

NOTES

1. These include Margolies (1968), who imputed "a certain intrinsic value" to the novel's treatment of "anti-Semitism among Negroes" (92); Milliken (1976), who praised the novel's often "brilliant" prose (97) and its penetrating psychology: the Dostoevskian analyses of its profoundly paradoxical black male characters—whose bitter rages, according to Gayle (1976), were to serve as models for black writers yet to come (231); Lundquist (1976), who stressed the positive, inclusive aspect of the novel's generally unappreciated conclusion; and perhaps Muller (1989), though he regards Himes's detective fiction as his most artistically realized work.

2. Luc Sante's recent retrospective of Himes's career treats *Lonely Crusade* and the other early, confessional fictions respectfully but Himes's later, detective fiction enthusiastically. This judgment accords with Muller's, in the most recent book on Himes. I prefer the more complex, realistic, ideologically richer earlier works.

3. Cf. Himes, *The Quality of Hurt* (98–102) and Williams (36–38).

4. Actually, Himes exaggerated the totality of his book's initial rejection. *Lonely Crusade* got all kinds of reviews—good, mixed, and bad. While the Communist press understandably trashed it, the far more widely circulated *New York Times* review (by Nash Burger) was wholly positive. *Book Review Digest* (1947) classified most of the reviews as mixed. It certainly deserved a better reception.

5. Gayle exaggerated the novelty of Himes's treatment. Four years before the publication of *Lonely Crusade*, Roi Ottley, in *'New World A-Coming': Inside Black America* (1943), produced a very similar analysis of "anti-Semitism among Negroes" (122), based on the latter's frequent "contact" (123) in disadvantaged economic situations with Jews. Ottley cited black complaints against Jewish merchants (who sold inferior goods on exploitative installment plans), landlords and rental agents (who "herd [ed]" African Americans into "BlackBelts" [126]), and employers of domestic workers (who harried and humiliated them). Like Himes, Ottley said that blacks especially resented mistreatment by Jews because Jews were "a persecuted people" themselves (129). Contrasting his views from those of other African Americans, he said the latter neither realized that Jews behaved no differently from other white businessmen, nor knew that many Jews had worked with distinction and at personal cost for civil rights. He criticized the assumption common among blacks that Jews act cohesively. Ottley noted earlier attacks on "Jewish control" of "the Negro's economic life" (122) by Marcus Garvey and Claude McKay (132).

6. Herbie, the shop steward in *If He Hollers,* is discussed above under *Communists.* Dave Levine, a handsome, gentlemanly Jew in *The Primitive,* sponges off, then leaves his gentile girlfriend because his ethnocentric mother controls him financially. In both novels these minor Jewish characters enrage Himes's protagonists by contradictions between their pretensions to universalism and their residual ethnocentricity, their real decency yet inability to resist bargaining and legalism.

7. Similarly, Muller misleadingly ascribes all of the novel's anti-Semitic sentiment to its protagonist. Observing that "Lee must overcome a penchant for

Semitic stereotyping," he cites an unflattering picture of "'Rosie' [as] the picture of the historic Semite"—but the description is the narrator's (35).

8. In a letter to Williams, Himes wrote, "of course I was Lee Gordon" (Muller 30).

9. Mark Naison, who carefully defends the performance of Communists and specifically Jewish ones, regarding African Americans, acknowledges that "by 1941 ... Communists ... had lost much of their moral credibility" among black (as among white) intellectuals, by preoccupation with a foreign policy unscrupulously determined by Soviet national interests (xix).

10. Naison (323) cites McKay as representative of African Americans who criticized the Communist party but not the Jewishness of its membership; however, Cruse cites McKay's disputes with Mike Gold as symptomatic and predictive of black-Jewish tension on the left. "Indeed, on one occasion, Gold challenged McKay to box outside a village restaurant" (Cruse 49).

11. The famous critical controversy between Irving Howe and Ellison over the latter's rejection of New York leftism for a kind of African American cultural nationalism may likewise reflect an underlying, unacknowledged black-Jewish *kulturkampf* Cf. Ellison's "The World and the Jug" (in 1963 and 1964) in *Shadow and Act* and Howe's "Black Boys and Native Sons" (1963) in *Decline of the New*.

12. The letter to Williams cited above in note 8 says rather that "the communists ... used [Himes] to prove a point. So they would send me out practically every day to apply for work in various firms which did not employ Negroes" (30).

13. Jewish participation in black civil rights organizations is analyzed in Reed, Jr. (88–105). Of course, former Jewish Communists have their own perspective on these matters, and some have complained of humiliation by black Communists, whom they felt to be favored in the party (Gornick 137, 165).

14. Himes suffered frustrated aspirations to write for the movies; he claimed that movie magnate Jack Warner told someone who had ventured to hire Himes, "I don't want no niggers on this lot" (Williams 60).

15. Compare the Jewish David 0. Selznick's undoubtedly offensive *Gone With the Wind* (1939) to the gentile D. W. Griffith's dangerously inflammatory *The Birth of a Nation* (1915). But no doubt some Jewish entertainers have overestimated the license an ethnic persona affords them. Al Jolson, a Jewish entertainer hugely remunerated for singing "Mammy" in blackface—at once appropriating African American culture, matriarchalizing it, and making a lot of money—might be cited as a performer likely to provoke several of Himes's resentments. The Jewish dialect comedian Jackie Mason claims a special fondness for the black doo-wop music he often hears performed by fellow night club entertainers, but caused a scandal by calling David Dinkins a "fancy *schvarze*" in the last New York mayoral election.

16. Baldwin "resign[ed] in protest" from the black nationalist magazine *Liberator* after it published a series of articles called "Semitism in the Black Ghetto" (Hentoff 1970, unnumbered page 3). However, Baldwin's subsequent article "Negroes Are Anti-Semitic Because They Are Anti-White" condemns his family's Jewish landlords and grocer and "the [Jewish] merchants along 125th street," because "all of them were exploiting us and that was why we hated them."

17. Arthur A. Cohen made this defense (Katz 8) in *Negro and Jew* (1967), an anthology of articles from the Jewish magazine *Midstream* consisting primarily of responses by Jews to black resentment of Jewish economic conduct. Some writers defended Jewish businessmen as traditionally more accommodating to black customers than other white businessmen, e.g., likely to allow black customers to try on clothes (Golden, in Katz 63; see also Williams 83 and Davis 12, 19–20); Harry Golden observed that "Southern black slum housing, often more scandalously sub-standard and under-serviced than that of northern urban ghettoes, was primarily

owned by white Protestants" (63). Floyd McKissick, former chairman of CORE, wrote "that Jews are disproportionately represented in the ownership of low-cost [ghetto] housing and ... retail establishments ... [but that] Black Americans ... are exploited by a small number of these Jews" (97; emphasis added).

18. See Nat Hentoff, "The Bigotry of Spike Lee," *Village Voice*, September 4, 1990, 2, 21; Matthew Flamm, "ADL Gives Spike Mo' Blues," *New York Post*, August 8, 1990, 21. The jazz vocalist Babs Gonzales disparaged Jewish night club owners in his autobiography, *I Paid My Dues* (1967).

19. Two of Himes's Jewish friends, Edward Margolies and Dan Levin, told me of their respect and affection for him and reported no indications of anti-Semitic animus in Himes's personal dealings with them or with other Jews.

20. To account for the recent rise in anti-Semitism among African American intellectuals, Henry Louis Gates, Jr. cited the "inordinate" involvement of Jews in the civil rights movement and the aphorism, "We can rarely bring ourselves to forgive those who have helped us" (A1).

21. A like diminishment of an exploitative Jew's masculinity is effected by Himes's character Jake Kubansky, a drug-dealing (presumably Jewish) dwarf, who dies after a beating by Grave Digger Johnson and Coffin Ed Jones in *The Heat's On*.

22. Baldwin characterized these contributions as mere "conscience money" (Hentoff 6). For studies demonstrating less Jewish (than other white) hostility to African Americans, see Katz 43.

23. Ishmael Reed takes this intimation as a certainty (29).

24. Cf. *My Life of Absurdity* photos #4 and #6 on unnumbered pages, between 88–89. The correspondingly hyper-masculine Hemingway also suffered prolonged cross-dressing by his overbearing mother.

25. *The Primitive* hints at a black-Jewish sexual rivalry (over white gentile women) in the left-wing world Himes inhabited before his expatriation. The philo-Semitism of Kriss, the hero's lover and murder victim, exceeds her Negrophilia. "Most of the people whom she had ever deeply admired had been Jews and a few Negroes" (16). She carries a torch for a gentlemanly Jew and curses the black hero, closely modeled on Himes, when his phone call makes her miss "'The Goldberg Family' ... her favorite program" (51).

26. While Himes disparaged Hemingway, to whom he has been compared, he could alternatively find these motifs of masculinist style in the writer he claimed most consistently inspired him—Faulkner. One Faulknerian masculinist ritual that the urbane Himes would seem to have eschewed is hunting; however, in Europe he took pride in his pet dogs' tendencies to savage his neighbors' poultry (*My Life of Absurdity* 330–31).

27. Unlike many African Americans, who identify with the Arab grievance against Israel, Himes associated Moslems with slave traders and disputed Malcolm X about Islam (*My Life of Absurdity* 292).

28. Ironically, Himes's successful detective novels, three of which have been made into Hollywood films, would fulfill Klonsky's prescription for lively, imaginative and peculiarly African American expression—no "college girl" stuff. Himes claimed that these thrillers (e.g., *Cotton Comes to Harlem*) came from "the American black's secret mind itself" (*My Life of Absurdity* 158). Their carnivalistic violence is consistently inventive; the two tough cop heroes, virtually indistinguishable in manner and frequently synchronized in movement, perform prodigies of male-bonding.

29. Twenty-three years after writing *Lonely Crusade,* in the Williams interview, Himes was still approvingly citing that speech—an actual, historical address (47).

30. Himes was a Bogart fan (*My Life of Absurdity* 288).

31. I thank Graham Hodges, Edward Margolies, Dan Levin, and John A. Williams for their help and encouragement in treating this touchy topic. They bear no responsibility for statements in the essay except those attributed to them.

WORKS CITED

Baldwin, James. "Negroes Are Anti-Semitic Because They Are Anti-White." *Black Anti-Semitism and Jewish Racism*. Ed. Nat Hentoff. New York: Schocken, 1970.

Burger, Nash K. "Fear in Our Midst." *New York Times* 14 September 1947: 20.

Canetti, Elias. *Crowds and Power*. Trans. Jerome Neugroschel. New York: Seabury, 1960.

Cruse, Harold. The *Crisis of the Negro Intellectual: From Its Origins to the Present*. New York: Morrow, 1967.

_____. "My Jewish Problem and Theirs." *Black-Anti-Semitism and Jewish Racism*. Ed. Nat Hentoff. New York: Schocken, 1970.

Davis, Lenwood G. *Black-Jewish Relations in the United States, 1752–1984: A Selected Bibliography*. Westport, CT: Greenwood, 1984.

Ellison, Ralph. *Shadow and Act*. New York: New American Library, 1964.

Flamm, Matthew. "ADL Gives Spike Mo' Blues." *New York Post* 8 August 1990: 21.

Fuller, Hoyt W. "Traveller on the Long, Rough, Lonely Old Road: An Interview with Chester Himes." *Black World* 21 (March 1972): 4–22, 87–98.

Gates, Henry Louis, Jr. "Black Demagogues and Pseudo-Scholars." *New York Times* 20 July 1992: A1.

Gayle, Addison, Jr. *The Way of the New World: The Black Novel in America*. New York: Anchor, 1976.

Gonzales, Babs. *I Paid My Dues*. East Orange, NJ: Expubidence, 1967.

Gornick, Vivian. *The Romance of American Communism*. New York: Basic, 1977.

Hentoff, Nat, Ed. *Black Anti-Semitism and Jewish Racism*. New York: Schocken, 1970.

_____. "The Bigotry of Spike Lee." *Village Voice* 4 September 1990: 20–21.

Himes, Chester. *A Case of Rape*. Washington, DC: Howard UP, 1980.

_____. "Author's Protest." *Commentary* May 1948: 474–75.

_____. *The Big Gold Dream*. New York: Avon, 1970.

_____. *Cast the First Stone*. New York: Coward-McCann, 1952.

_____. *Collected Stories*. New York: Thunder's Mouth, 1990.

_____. *Cotton Comes to Harlem*. New York: Vintage, 1988.

_____. "The Dilemma of the Negro Novelist in the United States." *Beyond the Angry Black*. Ed. John A. Williams. New York: NAL, 1966.

_____. *If He Hollers Let Him Go*. New York: Doubleday, 1945.

_____. *The Heat's On*. New York: Vintage, 1988.

_____. *Lonely Crusade* New York: Thunder's Mouth, 1986.

_____. *My Life of Absurdity*. New York: Doubleday, 1976.

_____. *The Primitive*. New York: NAL, 1955.

_____. *The Quality of Hurt*. New York, Doubleday, 1972.

_____. *The Third Generation*. New York: NAL, 1956.

Hodges, Graham. Foreword. *Lonely Crusade*. By Himes. New York: Thunder's Mouth, 1986.

Howe, Irving. "Black Boys and Native Sons." *Decline of the New*. New York: Harcourt, Brace, 1970.

Katz, Shiomo Ed. *Negro and Jew: An Encounter in America.* New York: Macmillan, 1967.

Klonsky, Milton. "The Writing on the Wall." *Commentary* February 1948: 190–91.

Lundquist, James. *Chester Himes.* New York: Ungar, 1976.

Margolies, Edward. *Native Sons: A Critical Study of Twentieth-Century Negro American Authors.* Philadelphia: Lippincott, 1968.

Milliken, Stephen F. *Chester Himes: A Critical Appraisal.* Missouri: U of Missouri P, 1976.

Muller, Gilbert. *Chester Himes.* New York: Twayne, 1989.

Naison, Mark. *Communists in Harlem During the Depression.* Urbana: U of Illinois P, 1983.

Ottley, Roi. *'New World A-Coming': Inside Black America.* 1943. New York: Arno, 1969. Reed, Adolph L., Jr. *The Jesse Jackson Phenomenon: The Crisis of Purpose in Afro-American Politics.* New Haven: Yale UP, 1986.

Reed, Ishmael. "The Author and His Works, Chester Himes: Writer." *Black World* March 1972: 23–38.

Sante, Luc. "An American Abroad." *New York Review of Books* January 16, 1992: 8–12.

Williams, John A. "My Man Himes." *Amistad I: Writings on Black History and Culture.* Ed. John A. Williams and Charles F. Harris. New York: Vintage, 1970.

Wright, Richard. *American Hunger.* New York: Harper & Row, 1979.

MELUS, 20:2 (Summer 1995), 47–68.

Slaying the Fathers: The Autobiography of Chester Himes

Gary Storhoff

In a crucial moment in *The Quality of Hurt* for the history of African-American literature, Chester Himes relates the famous argument between Richard Wright and James Baldwin about Baldwin's essay "Everybody's Protest Novel." In the essay, Baldwin criticizes "protest literature," implying that Wright's work is similar in intent to Harriet Beecher Stow's *Uncle Tom's Cabin*. Wright had his opportunity to retaliate when Baldwin, wishing to borrow money, asked Wright to meet him at a restaurant, and Wright requested Himes to accompany him. Unlike Baldwin, Himes recalled the event as rancorous.[1] The argument's climax occurs when Baldwin retorts to Wright, "The sons must slay their fathers"—meaning that Baldwin's Oedipal destiny was to write in opposition to his literary forbearers, especially Wright, so as to establish himself. Himes feigns incomprehension at Baldwin's parting riposte: "At the time I thought (Baldwin) had taken leave of his senses ..." (*Quality* 201).

Himes's disingenuous comment is belied by his own entire lifetime of Oedipal revolt, both in his literature and his personal life. The Oedipal aggression Baldwin exposes describes Himes also; especially in his use of the autobiographical genre, Himes exhibits his aggression toward precursors, both literary and ancestral. The two volumes of his autobiography—*The Quality of Hurt* (1971) and *My Life of Absurdity* (1976)—reveal his life lived out in rebellion in which he imaginatively slays father figures that he confronts, either historically or literarily. The meaning of Himes's work emerges from constant and incessant repudiation of fathers, expressed not only literally and thematically against the "fathers" that appear throughout his autobiography, but formally against the autobiographical narrative itself.

Himes goes beyond assaulting parental surrogates in the plot; he so fundamentally disrupts the autobiographical form in plot, theme, and action that the reader's expectations are undermined. The white (or black) reader coming to Himes's autobiography expecting a meditation on Himes's "African-American experience" will be profoundly disappointed. Of course, Himes ferociously indicts racism, as do other African-American autobiographers; however, the emphasis of his work is rather on his own aggressiveness toward those who attempt, from his perspective, to control him. The Oedipal rebellion, which David Dudley sees as a component of all male African-American autobiographies, cuts across every dimension of Himes's life and work, dictating life choices, racial politics, and narrative design.[2] Himes's autobiography thus constitutes an assault—on authority figures, on the autobiographical form itself, and by extension, on the (white/black) reader.

"The Pure and Simple Necessity to Beat Him to the Trigger": Himes and Monolithic Masculinity

Himes's vision of himself derives from a childhood and young adulthood during which he was socialized *toward* violence, when he was taught that violence is an appropriate, even necessary, means of dealing with disagreement and disobedience. Himes seeks what Leland S. Person in a much different context terms "a monolithic masculinity" (516)[3]—a one-dimensional, overly simplified social construction of manhood that stresses brutality, dominance, and conflict. In the autobiography, Himes shows that his childhood was marked by his evolving conviction that violence was essential to maintain manhood. Born in 1909 in a middle-class family that lived in the south and in Ohio, Himes witnessed incessant conflict between his father and mother that quickly escalated into mutual spousal abuse. Although his two brothers become successful (Joseph becomes an internationally known sociologist; Edward, a union leader), Chester turns to crime in his adolescence. He chooses the role of gang-leader, writing that his most important goal was "the pure and simple necessity to beat [anyone] to the trigger" (*Quality* 42). At nineteen, he commits armed robbery in a suburban Cleveland home; captured, he serves over seven years for armed robbery at the Ohio State Penitentiary and is paroled in 1936.

Himes's career as a writer brings impersonal satisfaction and monetary reward in the celebration of violence. He begins his career as a writer in prison, describing in his short stories the brutality of prisoners and the horror of the 1930 fire at the penitentiary in "To What Red Hell" (1935). Meeting with critical rejection of his subsequent work, he decides to expatriate to Paris in 1953, never to return to America. In 1956, Himes meets Marcel Duhamel, who convinces him (with a $1,000 advance to write a detective story; his nine detective novels, beginning with *A Rage in Harlem* (1957), feature graphic violence commensurate with his own rebellion: "I was writing some strange shit.... [M]y mind had rejected all reality as I had known it and I had begun to see the world as a cesspool of buffoonery. Even the violence was funny. A man gets his throat cut. Hs shakes his head to say you missed me and it falls off. Damn reality, I thought" (*Life* 126).

The choice of violence as a life pattern emerges as his revolt both against his mother and his father. His dark-skinned father, Joseph Himes, was a professor of mechanical arts at various Southern "Negro A & M Colleges" (*Quality* 4); as Himes grew older, he felt increasingly contemptuous of his father's servility before whites. He disposes of his father precipitously, primarily because his father is submissive in his response to white racism. By putting the words of Booker T. Washington in his father's mouth, Himes economically but cynically characterizes his father's racial accommodationism: "As a child I often heard my father quote the famous saying of the great educator: 'Let down your buckets where you are'" (*Quality* 4). The minimal reference to his father implies Himes's refusal to identify with a textualized castrated father.

His light-skinned mother, Esther [sic] Bomar Himes, threatens whites with a loaded pistol (like Chester himself), one of his earliest childhood memories (*Quality* 8). It is her incipient violence against white racism that most clearly anticipates Himes's own.[4] But his mother's own internalized racism complicates his identification with her; light-skinned, he is continuously taught by his mother to despise the prominently African features of his father and of his father's family. Mrs. Himes instills her own aggressions against the white power structure *and* Africanist features.[5] To identify with her would risk his masculinity; to repudiate her would compromise his racial identity.

His relationship with her is further complicated by her identification with unreasoning authority. At a critical moment in Himes's youth, Mrs. Himes becomes the symbol of absurdist persecution and punishment that he will inevitably rebel against. This formative incident occurs when Himes was thirteen, when Chester and Joseph follow through on Chester's idea of making torpedo bombs as a chemistry experiment. Mrs. Himes, punishing Chester for minor disobedience, forbids him to assist Joseph, though Chester's help is essential. Joseph, alone on a stage conducting the experiment, is blinded in an unexpected explosion, which presumably Chester's involvement would have prevented, when ground glass particles blast into his eyes. When he finally receives treatment after being turned away from white hospitals, he has lost his vision permanently. From Chester's perspective, his mother's punishment precipitated both Joseph's tragedy and Chester's guilt. The theme that will later shape Himes's detective fiction and autobiography—the absurdity of arbitrarily harsh punishment, which will inevitably have horrifying consequences for the victim and persecutor—originates in his relationship with his mother and her punishment and its unforeseen consequences to innocent people. His mother's punishment resulted in Joseph's suffering and his own guilt; he will mete out his own punishment of his mother to the women who come into his life. Yet mixed with his desire to inflict pain and suffering on the mother-substitute is his devotion to his mother despite his repudiation of her: "I loved my mother with a strange fierce love which survived everything" (*Quality* 22).

"Complex, Intriguing, and Not Particularly Likable":
Himes's Treatment of Women

Perhaps the most troubling aspect of Himes's autobiography is his frank description of his mistreatment of women.[6] In his abuse of women, he is, in his own words, "complex, intriguing, and not particularly likable" (*Quality* 258). Himes documents his abuse intimately throughout the two volumes of his autobiography, each of which was intended to revolve around his relationship with a woman.[7] In his affairs, he seems to test the boundaries of the black masculine roles that are made available to him by a racist society; thus, from this perspective, his brutality toward women stems from his *over*conformity to a masculine code of toughness,[8] and to his unquestioning acceptance of a social construction of masculinity that enshrines the strong, autonomous, violent male. The women in his autobiography act as witnesses to (and recipients of) his ritualistic male gestures of manhood. Yet Himes, perhaps unwittingly, dramatizes the precarious nature of his violent assertions of male identity. The consequences of his objectifying women in his work turn against him, and the effect of his quest for monolithic masculinity is the alienation of his first wife, his subsequent lovers, and many of his friends. Himes's sexual life inevitably leads him into conflicts, not only with Richard Wright and other black expatriates, who (according to the autobiography) refuse to accept Himes's lovers, but with racists he continuously encounters in Europe.[9]

His sexuality becomes a weapon for him to punish women but also to expect (and perhaps welcome) punitive responses from them. His tumultuous relationships with women reveal Himes's own will to control and dominate, his own need to fulfill a code of brutal masculinity, but also his need to experience abuse and punishment in return. His typical attraction to neurotic, depressive women, in unconscious rebellion against his strong mother who plays the patriarch's role in his childhood, ironically brings him much unhappiness— women who are viciously abused and controlled by him, but who exact some emotional revenge by clinging to him unmercifully.

Himes's choices in women continually seem to invite reprisals—not only from his society, but from the women themselves.[10] The most brutalized of his white lovers is Marlene Behrens (Regine Fischer), a German actress half his age whose story constitutes the first sections of Himes's second volume, *My Life of Absurdity*. Behrens suffers terrible beatings from Himes, he admits, and she lands in the hospital from one incident of battering (these attacks were not isolated), yet he nevertheless depicts her as controlling him, as himself as *her* pawn: "'You're going to make me hurt you some day,' she said" (*Life* 60). He senses a threat in her presence: "Marlene was entirely capable of destroying me if she didn't have her way" (*Life* 195). In blaming his victim, Himes intentionally inscribes the most violent form of sexism in their limited relationship: "The final answer of any black to a white woman with whom he lives in a white society is violence" (*Quality* 137). Behrens and Himes's relationship evolves quickly into a mutually destructive affair; despite his abuse of her, he acts as he rescuer, helping her through her many neurotic periods, but Marlene apparently accepts her role as victim adroitly.

Himes's attempt to force the relationship's end is associated in his autobiography with a struggle against a father figure. In a biographical article, Michel Fabre shows that by 1960, Himes was deeply involved with a new lover, his wife-to-be, Lesley Packard (223–8), and that he wished the relationship over. In his autobiography, however, Himes contrives the ending of his relationship with Behrens over a quarrel with her father who demands of Himes that he "act humanely" (*Life* 199–200). When confronted with an ostensibly reasonable and equitable father who encourages Himes to identify with him "as a man of [his] generation," Himes refuses to be manipulated by a father surrogate. Himes is willing to accept Mr. Behren's identification with him only in his own terms: "You've never been kind to her. Neither have I" (*Life* 200). In the narrative, then, a bitter and angry conflict with the father rescues not only the daughter, but the fictive "son" from a destructive love affair.

The Behrens affair seems to solidify in Himes's imagination the trap posed not only by the white world, but by his own Oedipal rages. In an attempt to exert maximum control over a woman, he loses control of himself completely: "I was her slave because she was helpless" (*Life* 199). His statements about his own culpability are evasive; rather than confront his own explosive rage honestly, he associates his violence against her with the existential "truth" he learned during his incarceration at Ohio State Penitentiary—that "anyone could do anything" (*Quality* 65). But if the world was essentially out of control, he too was implicated in this confusion of passions: against the best advice of his friends, her parents, and of his own vague intuition, he had involved himself in a relationship with Behrens that could have been fatal to his artistic career, if not his life. Not only was Behrens in great danger, but so was he. Unwilling to acknowledge his guilt in his vicious treatment of her but also unconscious of why he needed Behrens, he evades the intimate realities of their violent relationship and of the abuse he meted out to her consistently to assert a general, anonymously absurdist conclusion about humanity: "All of reality was absurd, contradictory, violent and hurting" (*Life* 126).

Himes's involvement with women in his autobiography was intricately connected with his Oedipal resistance, a coded "slaying" of his mother, whose obsession with skin color and arbitrary punishment required, in his own mind, violent retribution through surrogate lovers he chose. Unlike his father, who married a light-skinned African American who revered white skin, Himes chooses white lovers curious about his black skin and then makes them suffer for choosing him. Like a literary character Himes knew well—Richard Wright's Bigger Thomas—Himes repudiates the image of the father by attacking women.

"One Black at a Time":
Himes and Richard Wright

Himes's compulsion to attack father surrogates extends to his own literary father, Richard Wright himself. David Dudley, who ignores Himes in his recent discussion of African-American autobiography, argues that repudiation of the male predecessor is a primary component of the black male autobiographical tradition: his purpose is to "identify among these writers a kind of Oedipal conflict wherein each rising writer faces and overcomes his predecessor in the tradition" (1). Beyond tradition, Fabre implies that Himes's repudiation of Wright is caused by Himes's envy: "Was Himes resentful of Wright's success and security?" (219). However, envy in this case is complicated by Himes's grim understanding of the economics of publishing, which may overlook him in favor of an established writer: "The powers that be have never admitted but one black at a time into the arena of fame, and to gain this coveted admission, the young writer must unseat the reigning deity. It's a pity, but a reality as well" (*Quality* 201). Perhaps too, Himes saw in Wright's *Native Son* a reflection of his own inclination toward violence, especially violence directed toward white women. Bigger Thomas is the most famous literary depiction of a black man abusing women, white and black. His rejection of Wright may stem from that fact that he sensed Wright understood his own compulsions to strike out against surrogates of parenthood all too well.

Himes's rage against Wright is consistent with his repudiation of all authority figures. He met the ultimate father figure in his benefactor, mentor, and literary paterfamilias, Richard Wright. The surprisingly few comments he makes about Wright—who assisted him in his passage to Europe, welcomed him in Paris once he arrived, arranged for his hotel accommodations, lent him money and supplies, supported his work both personally and in published reviews, and introduced him to friends, agents, and publishers—are for the most part unflattering, if not flatly disparaging.[11]

In the narrative, it is clear that Himes constructs Wright as his own foil. Where the more famous Wright sacrifices integrity for even greater fame, Himes self-consciously chooses the role of the alienated, African-American artist. He makes Wright at least partially responsible, however, for Himes's own alienation. He writes that he frankly "had never liked Dick since early 1957 when he had told [Himes] he had organized the Paris Club, an organization of brothers, and barred [Himes] from joining" (*Life* 215). Himes asserts that what he found most deplorable in Wright was his adaptation to a "white," middle class life, one which violated Himes's sense of Wright's inner self:

In trying to effect his departure from America and its way of life, Dick had become more of an American than he had ever been. But, whereas in the U.S. he could not escape his image of a *Black Boy*, in Paris he was a rich man. And he enjoyed being a rich man, he loved the bourgeois life. But he wasn't adapted to the bourgeois life. From beginning to end, deep in his soul, Dick identified with the poor and the oppressed. He was a natural-born leftist ... (*Life* 8)

The passage creates a stunning contrast of temperaments: whereas Himes has the courage of his own convictions and lives in poverty, Wright chooses affluence and surrenders his identity; whereas Himes stoically bears the existential condition of his own absurdity, Wright craves "authority ... he was rootless without an absolute" (*Life* 8); whereas Himes fulfills in his career and in his personal life the social construction of masculinity, Wright can never escape the "image of a *Black Boy*." Himes's derogation of Wright's masculinity reinforces the seriousness of Himes's commitment to the masculine mystique, but this ideology cuts him off from the potentiality of Wright's friendship, offered many times throughout their association in the autobiography. Himes portrays Wright's efforts at friendship as intimidating, threatening his own sense of sexuality that must be bolstered with Himes's aggressiveness.

Himes's repudiation of Wright centers on his repugnance of Wright's own sexuality, and on Himes's own insecurity about his readers' reading of Himes's masculinity. Unable to develop a relationship with Wright that is intimate but free of his own anxieties about possible homosexual implications, he persistently projects his concerns onto observers and his reader. He is especially apprehensive, for instance, that homophobic friends in Paris do not misconstrue his relationship with Wright and his wife Ellen: "[T]he residents in the hotel began to wonder what sort of arrangement we had—were Dick and I lovers, or Ellen and me, or did they take turns with me?" (*Quality* 188). For Himes, Wright's genuine interest in Himes and his work cannot be untainted by sexual drives. According to Himes, Wright constantly intrudes into Himes's love affairs, but Himes sees Wright's concern only as a vicarious lasciviousness and perhaps evidence of Wright's own latent homosexuality, as when Wright jokes about Himes's "secret weapon," or when he describes Wright's onanistic fascination with two lesbians: "He had a sharp curiosity about the sexual behavior of odd couples, lesbians, and prostitutes.... He was greatly stimulated by these encounters [with lesbians], and after a moment rushed away to write or to indulge in whatever else he had in mind" (*Quality* 196).

The main purpose of Himes's own construction of Wright's gender is to fashion Himes's redoubtable masculine identity by contrast. The more powerful, famous, and wealthy Wright is deployed by Himes to dramatize weakness and impotency in comparison with Himes's own virility. Once again, Himes constructs Wright as his complement—where Himes is virile, Wright is voyeuristic; while Himes's masculinity seems controlled, Wright can barely conceal his burning but passive lust; as Himes enjoys his sexual liberty, Wright seems to chafe within his monogamous but (from Himes's perspective) frustratingly bourgeois marriage. Because Himes cannot imagine a friendship with Wright, he forecloses possible friendship and intimacy.

Perhaps the most violent repudiation of Wright that Himes could contrive within the autobiography is the rejection of Wright as a literary mentor, in favor of William Faulkner, Himes's "secret mentor" (*Life* 169). Himes writes, "I had no desire to write like Dick: Faulkner had the utter influence over my writing" (217). Faulkner, Himes claimed, had a clear sense of life's absurdity, and therefore Faulkner was far closer to Himes's vision of a tormented world than Wright, who seemingly was unable to detach himself emotionally from his own characters. Racial coding in Faulkner's characters paradoxically makes Faulkner seem artistically closer to Himes. The character of Joe Christmas, in one of Himes's favorite books, led Himes to an emotional identification with Faulkner, who, he conjectured, understood the absurd situation of African Americans better than Wright himself:

I read Faulkner's *Sanctuary* and *Light in August*; I would crack up reading how the old white Southerner would taunt his grandson by telling him, "You're a nigger, you're a nigger...." I would feel like running through the street crying "I'm a nigger, I'm a nigger...." It was lunacy. (*Life* 179)

In this context, beyond the obvious privileging of the white author over Himes's direct black antecedent, one must recall Faulkner's well-known criticism of Wright and of African-American literature, made in Japan in 1955; Wright, said Faulkner, "had a great deal of talent," but

[h]e wrote one good book and then went astray, he got too concerned in the difference between the Negro man and the white man and he stopped being a writer and became a Negro.... Another one named Ellison has talent and so far he has managed to stay away from being first a Negro, he is still first a writer (185)

Himes's argument for Faulkner's preeminence is contextualized by the respect accorded to Faulkner during the 1960s and 1970s, as opposed to the dismissive attitude toward Wright's work. Himes takes sides against Wright in a critical debate that situated Wright as a distinct inferior, particularly among white literary critics. William Andrews summarizes the segregated nature of literary criticism during this time regarding Faulkner and Wright: "In Faulkner's shadow lurked Richard Wright, but Wright's perspective ... was judged parochial next to Faulkner's much-vaunted universality" (1).

Beyond his personal derogation and repudiation of a literary nexus, Himes's autobiography could be read as an encoded "slaying" of Wright's *Black Boy* and *American Hunger*—Himes's "signifyin(g)" of Wright, to use H. L. Gates's term to describe intertextual competition among African-American writers (290). More indirect than James Baldwin's distancing from Wright, Himes subverts many of Wright's most essential themes in Wright's autobiography. *The Quality of Hurt* and *My Life of Absurdity*—in their contemptuous rejection of Wright's political vision and in Himes's insistence upon his own sexuality—could be interpreted as an implicit repudiation of Wright's own politicized (and almost asexual) autobiography, *Black Boy* (1945). More important, Himes eschews the "hopeful ending" of Wright's autobiography that, as Janice Thaddeus has pointed out, was imposed on *Black Boy* by Wright's publishers.[12] If Wright (as Thaddeus argues) at first intended to write an "open" autobiography but failed because of the pressure of his editors, Himes pointedly refuses to conclude his autobiography on "a note of triumph." Unlike Wright's text, Himes's autobiography insists on a world of deprivation, unrelieved oppression, barely controlled rage, and rebellion—in Himes's favorite word, an unrelenting experience of racial "absurdity." By creating an autobiography that essentially denies the world Wright depicted in *his* autobiography, Himes's "slaying" of his literary forbearer transcends the merely personal.

The "Serious Savage":
Himes and the Autobiographical Form

Himes's repudiation of the formal expectations of the autobiography go beyond his personal relationship with Richard Wright and his intertextual combat with Wright's autobiography. This rejection extends to the conventions of the autobiographical form itself. Although some disagreement exists as to the nature of the genre, surely the controlling expectation a reader brings to an autobiography is that a completed identity will be expressed in the narrative—a rounded, thoroughly known self, encapsulated in the past tense, that the author has meditated upon. In a seminal essay on the genre of autobiography, Georges Gusdorf writes, "Autobiography ... requires a man to take a distance with regard to himself in order to reconstitute himself in the focus of his special unity and identity across time" (35). Roy Pascal argues that this quest for "special unity" is an almost formulaic feature of the genre: it "imposes a pattern on a life, constructs out of it a coherent story" (9). The autobiographer's retrospection and his or her faith in the language to construct a self, should lead to a rounded narrative with a strong sense of closure. Ross Miller writes, "The pose of the autobiographer as an experienced man is particularly effective because we expect to hear from someone who has a completed sense of his own life and is therefore in a position to tell what he has discovered" (231). In a much more dramatic tone, Roger Rosenblatt writes that "Every autobiography is an extended suicide note; both announcement and vindication of the event. The life recorded is the life complete to a specific point, and is therefore as good as dead" (178). Though the life is not ended, the reader expects the autobiographer's Aristotelian curve: a plot with a beginning, middle, and definite end; a closed narrative that relates a conceptualized "meaning" that summarizes the writer's existence.[13]

But Himes resists a reader's attempt to enfold his life within these generic criteria. He deliberately fills his autobiography with trivia to deflect the reader from other, more serious considerations that would lead to an inference of completed meaning of the self. He is especially concerned in overturning a reader's possibly complacent sense of realism in the autobiographical genre. It is as if Himes intends the reader to sense the comic absurdity of a scrupulous concern for accurate representation, given the racist system an African American must confront. For example, he gives the addresses of acquaintances, and then explains that they died or moved (e.g., *Life* 253, 388). The reader learns of bad restaurants (*Life* 319, 370, 387; *Quality* 219), the menu at a much better restaurant (*Life* 335), the illnesses of his cat (*Life* 301–5), his neighbor's obnoxious pets (*Quality* 321), and the misbehavior of his dog Mikey. He goes into inordinate detail about the various pets he owned, even dedicating *My Life* to his wife "and our cat, DEROS."

He similarly subverts the conventional inclusion of photographs in an autobiography; photography in an autobiography is supposedly a stringently realistic text, to be "read" just as the literary text itself is interpreted. Himes, however, includes photos that deny an easy assumption that life can be captured in a photo. Several of his photos (ones of his mother and of himself) are full-faced. But other photos humorously taunt the reader attempting to discover Himes. His dog Mikey, for example, is fully featured in two pictures, and two other dogs appear in two other pictures. Four pictures (one a single photo) feature his pet cats, although DEROS does not appear. Two photos depict Himes with his cars; one car is apparently malfunctioning while Himes (dressed in a suit) attempts to repair it. One of the few pictures portraying another

African-American writer, Ralph Ellison, is taken from a great distance, so it is impossible to tell which figure he is in the photo.

Himes's playful evasiveness also colors his narrative. He goes into great detail about an automobile he purchased, telling its price, its malfunctioning, its repairs, etc. Knowing that he is violating the generic convention that only "important" material be included in an autobiography, Himes writes: "If one thinks I'm writing too much of my autobiography to my secondhand Volkswagon, that is the way it was" (*Life* 157)—toying with the reader's expectation of a realistic description of significant events—"that is the way it was."

In a more conventional autobiography (e.g., Wright's), the tortured story of Himes's adolescence and childhood would be "justified" by an adult perspective characterized by a transcendent and unifying vision, acceptance, and integration. In the beginning of the narrative, Himes establishes these conventional generic expectations of autobiographers' sense of completion. That is, he seems to initiate on his first page (when he intimates his reasons for living in Paris) the generic structural movement from the utter chaos and invisibility of his childhood, adolescence, and imprisonment, to a retrospection in which he reassembles his life's fragmentation into a "special unity." There were "many reasons" he left America, he tells the reader (*Quality* 3). But Himes comically upends the reader's expectations in the text's conclusion. He ends the first volume not with his self-vindication, his affirmation of an identity as an expatriate gained through suffering and meditation, but with a letter of apology to a friend for a bounced check that he had intentionally written. The bounced check, however, is a message in itself to the reader of his autobiography. Himes is ending his autobiography by defining himself as a trickster, engaging the world in its most significantly empirical form—money—and then misrepresenting himself and his situation. Furthermore, the deliberately bounced check is itself a literary text, a sign to be interpreted within the context of Himes's generic subversion.

Himes's refusal to play strictly by the genre's rules is emphasized especially in the second volume. Critics have conjectured that the "failure" of *My Life* is the effect of Himes's illness (he suffered from Parkinson's Disease), his progressively weakening eyesight, poor editing by publishers, or simply Himes's ineptness or artistic indifference. A reading more sympathetic to his oppositional stance leads to a realization that Himes's autobiographical decisions are deliberate and calculated. "Genres," writes Frederic Jameson, "are essentially literary institutions, or social contracts between a writer and a specific public" (106). Thus, when Himes intentionally violates the conventions of the form and averts in obvious ways the reader's most elementary expectations, he voids Jameson's sense of literary conventions as the "social contract."

Comically overturning literary convention, moreover, implies his latent aggression towards his readership. Himes remarked in an interview with John A. Williams, "I want these people [his white readership] just to take me seriously. I don't care if they think I'm a barbarian, a savage, or what they think; just think I'm a serious savage" (314). Explicit in Himes's remark is a distrust, verging on hostility, of his readership; a vision of himself as an autobiographer that undermines the reader's complacencies about race and gender so that finally he or she begins to hear what he is trying to say. In *The Quality of Hurt*, Himes writes that he survived his prison experience only by rage: "I had such violent seizures of rage that I made men twice my size quake with fright. In my fits of insensate fury I would have smashed the world, crushed it in my hands, kicked down the universe" (62). He succeeds in channeling his rage into his literature: In *My Life*, he writes, "I had come to a final decision a long time ago when I was in prison that I was going to live as long as possible to aggravate the white race" (314). The aggravation he intends to inflict is produced in his manipulation of the autobiography genre, a commodity consumed by those readers eager for a considered "truth" about Himes's unique African-American experience. His "serious savagery" is subtly implied in his aggression against his reader, and his own sensibility leads him to wrench conventional forms.

How are we to assess his work? Himes is uninterested in the opportunity the genre offers to reveal his subjective experience and uncover the causal patterns of his life. For example, most of the critics who discuss Himes's autobiography are puzzled that Himes chooses to withhold from his reader why he began writing fiction in the first place.[14] Just as Frederick Douglass neglects to narrate the details of his escape, Himes never explains why he chose to begin writing in prison. But such a personal revelation is relevant to his fundamental concerns. Himes is concerned with interrogating the traditional autobiographical form of a completed, considered life. Himes challenges the authority of autobiographical conventions by refusing to comment on his most private decisions, and by "concluding" his narrative casually, with irresolution, with a sense that any presentation of a self is only provisional.[15] To determine precisely what he does is to call into question the socio-political nature of reader-response literary analysis, especially since theorists are often indirect or evasive in treating how a (white, middle-class especially) reader confronts a text written by an African American, particularly a writer so long ignored as Himes has been.

Briefly, reader-response criticism examines the effects of a text on a reader, or on "interpretive communities." In essence, the reader in this model is forced to engage with a text to shape its meaning himself or herself; no passive recipient of a predetermined meaning, the reader actively processes a text that is filled with gaps, erasures, and blanks, to construct a meaning that is his or her own. Aesthetic meaning emerges, then, from a process of interaction between the reader and the fissiparous text. The aesthetic object, which Wolfgang Iser in *The Act of Reading* identifies as the meaning of the text, varies "in accordance with the social and cultural code of each individual reader" (93).

The "social and cultural code," however, remains problematic for a writer who chooses to reject traditional Euro-American autobiographical models. Robert B. Stepto has brilliantly called into question the reader-response approach offered by Iser, Stanley Fish, Jonathan Culler, and other theorists. Stepto has proposed that African-American writers, anticipating the skepticism or even hostility of their (white) readers, have been led to "create and refine ... a discourse of distrust" (312). Stepto contends that an African-American author posits an unreliable reader who himself or herself must be assaulted:

In Afro-American storytelling texts especially, rhetoric and narrative strategy combine time and again to declare that the principal unreliable factor in the storytelling paradigm is the reader (white American readers, obviously, but blacks as well), and that acts of creative communication are fully initiated not when the text is assaulted but when the reader gets "told"—or "told off"—in such a way that he or she finally begins to hear. It is usually in this way that most written tales express their distrust not just of reader but of official literature culture in general. (318)

This is precisely what Himes is accomplishing: he is using his autobiographies to disappoint and frustrate the reader, to "tell the reader off." In challenging the formal shaping of the autobiography genre itself, Himes challenges the (white) literary establishment that endows an autobiography with meaning. He forces a re-examination of covert assumptions about literary forms. For an African American like Himes, Euro-American discourse and discursive structures have been used primarily to oppress. For Himes, racism functions in the subtlest expressions, the most obvious forms. The conventional autobiographical form—because it assumes closure, coherence, and meditative meaning—leaves Himes no space to speak with force and political power.

Himes does not merely ignore literary conventions. He defies them. He structures his work in patterns of violated expectations; he first asks us to read his text as an autobiography, but then deliberately leads us to question the critical conventions on which our readings are based. Thus, the fictive frame of his work is constantly being broken. Involuntarily, the reader of Himes's own rage—against his family, his colleagues, his women, and finally against his own readership. Describing one of his earlier books, Himes writes, "I had intended to write about the deadly venom of racial prejudice which kills both racists and their victims" (*Quality* 112). By "telling [the reader] off," Himes keeps alive in the reader's imagination his struggle against racism.

There are, presumably, many reasons for the scholarly neglect of Chester Himes. The last thirty years of his life were spent in Paris although Himes never became the internationally known figure Richard Wright was. Himes's work, including the autobiographies, has gone in and out of print in part as a consequence of his tumultuous relationship with his agents and publishers. Himes himself had a theory about critical indifference to his work: he believed that the white publishing world rewarded only "one black at a time," and he was eclipsed by the more famous Wright, and then by James Baldwin and Ralph Ellison. Yet in reading the autobiographies, one senses that a major reason for Himes's neglect may be that he deliberately creates a very unappealing self-portrait, one that virtually assaults the reader. In his autobiography, he mocks his family, commits crimes, brutalizes his women companions, and betrays his wife, his friends, and his patrons. It is as if his own rage inspires his work. Himes's aggression cuts across literary precursors to life choices and narrative structures. At the heart of his aggression is his unrelieved Oedipal revolt.

NOTES

1. For other discussions of this incident, see Charney, Fabre 362–3, and Leeming 64–5. For Baldwin's account, see his essay "Alas, Poor Richard" (156–9). Baldwin remembers a rather cordial discussion with Wright.

2. Dudley's study of the male African-American autobiography develops two themes in seven writers: the Oedipal revolt against precursorial literary models and "a three-part pattern of bondage, flight, and freedom as the prevalent pattern of men's writing" (10). Although he does not discuss Himes, Dudley's model is useful in illuminating Himes's intertextual relationship with Wright's *Black Boy*. However, my study differs from Dudley's in my attempt to demonstrate Himes's Oedipal dynamic influencing both life and narrative. For a discussion of the Oedipal Complex in Himes's fiction, see Reckley.

3. Both Person and Brod argue that "masculinity" is as much a social construct as is "femininity." As Brod writes in asserting the need for a systematic "men's studies," "[t]he most general definition of men's studies is that it is the study of masculinities and male experiences as specific and varying social-historical-cultural formations" (40).

4. Himes's mother's propensity for gun-play is recounted dramatically in his autobiographical novel *The Third Generation* (1954), when "she took a small revolver from her purse and aimed it at the white man's back" (100). His own identification with his mother's ambivalence to race, but the frustration that a black reader may experience is entirely deliberate.

5. Houston Baker, in his review of *The Quality of Hurt*, discovers an absence of "group consciousness" in the volume (90) and hypothesizes that an African-American reader, expecting African American solidarity, will be disappointed. Perhaps Himes's resistance to brotherhood begins with his tortured relationship with his mother's ambivalence to race, but the frustration that a black reader may experience is entirely deliberate.

6. A simplistic view of Himes's troubling behavior towards women would be that his violence is somehow "within him," evidence of a possible personal disturbance to explain his battering. Himes himself implies this explanation, suggesting that he was an almost passive agent of his own violence: "I discovered I had become very violent" (*Quality* 47). Possibly abuse was linked to Himes's wish to demonstrate his masculinity, a cause of violence "more frequent than realized," according to Davidson (37).

A more complex view of his violence, however, considers his violent background, his learned response to stress while in prison, black powerlessness in society, and the patriarchal structure of the world. From this perspective, violence is generated not only by the individual, but finds its origin in the interactions of systems that enmesh the individual. Giles-Sims writes: "A general systems theory of family violence assumes that violence is the outcome of the complex social interaction within the family system which exists as part of a larger social system" (19).

7. Himes planned three volumes of his autobiography. Each volume was to revolve around his relationship with a woman. The last volume was to describe the relationship with his wife.

8. In this context, consult Russell on the concept of the "virility mystique." See also Brod, esp. 51–3.

9. For a discussion of Himes within the context of the African-American expatriation to Europe in the 1940s and 1950s, see Margolies.

10. He meets the first lover, Alva Trent Van Olden Bameveldt (Willa Thompson), on the ship's passage across the Atlantic. While they live together, he completes his novel, *The End of the Primitive*; in a letter to his agent, he explains the inspiration Alva provides: "No, I have not killed Alva. I found I was able to do it with my imagination in creating the [novel's] murder scene. So she is still here" (*Life* 311). Although they collaborate on a novel, when it is rejected by publishers, she suffers a deep depression that makes life difficult for Himes; her departure for America is a relief for him.

Another white lover, Vandi Haygood, is addicted to drugs and alcohol; in a mutually abusive relationship, the two finally split up never to see each other again. She eventually dies young, perhaps of an intentional overdose of barbiturates.

11. Fabre speculates that Himes's attacks on Wright spring from a thinly veiled envy: "But Himes felt estranged from the novelist who had made it [Wright]: ... Was Himes resentful of Wright's success and security?" (219).

12. Thaddeus's thesis, that Wright was forced to submit a truncated ending to his autobiography in order to be published at all during the war years, exonerates Wright from the implication that he simply caved in to his editors. Though willing to accommodate with his publishers' requests, Wright had no clear idea of the kind of drastic changes that were to be made in his text's conclusion.

13. Olney also argues that the genre is self-consciously literary, even in earliest autobiographies (4).

14. For criticism of Himes's reticence about discussion of his own motives for writing, see Hairston, Lederer, and Skeeter.

15. Cf. Werner: "[The] insistence on the continuity of the self ... becomes a leitmotif in Afro-Modernist autobiographies" (211).

WORKS CITED

Andrews, William L. "Mark Twin, William Wells Brown, and the Problem of Authority in New South Writing." *Southern Literature and Literary Theory.* Ed. Jefferson Humphries. Athens: U of Georgia P, 1990. 1–21.

_____. *To Tell a Free Story: The First Century of Afro-American Autobiography, 1760–1865.* Urbana: U of Illinois P, 1986.

Baker, Houston A., Jr. Rev. of *The Quality of Hurt*, by Chester Himes. *Black World* 21 (July 1972): 89–91.

Baldwin, James. *Nobody Knows My Name: More Notes of a Native Son.* New York: Dell, 1961.

Braxton, Joanne M. *Black Women Writing Autobiography: A Tradition within a Tradition.* Philadelphia: Temple UP, 1989.

Brod, Harry. "The Case for Men's Studies." *The Making of Masculinities: The New Men's Studies.* Ed. Brod. Boston: Allen, 1987. 39–62.

Butterfield, Stephen. *Black Autobiography in America.* Amherst: U of Massachusetts P, 1974.

Charney, Maurice. "James Baldwin's Quarrel with Richard Wright." *American Quarterly* 15 (1963): 65–75.

Davidson, Terry. *Conjugal Crime: Understanding and Changing the Wifebeating Pattern.* New York: Hawthorn Books, 1978.

Dudley, David L. *My Father's Shadow: Intergenerational Conflict in African American Men's Autobiography.* Philadelphia: U of Pennsylvania P, 1991.

Eakin, Paul John. "Malcolm X and the Limits of Autobiography." Olney, *Autobiography* 181–93.

Fabre, Michel. *From Harlem to Paris: Black American Writers in France, 1840–1980.* Urbana: U of Illinois P, 1991.

Faulkner, William. *Lion in the Garden: Interviews with William Faulkner, 1926–62.* Eds. James B. Meriwether and Michael Millgate. New York: Random House, 1968.

Franklin, H. Bruce. *The Victim as Criminal and Artist: Literature from the American Prison.* New York: Oxford UP, 1978.

Gates, Henry Louis, Jr. *The Signifying Monkey: A Theory of African-American Criticism.* New York: Oxford UP, 1988.

Giles-Sims, Jean. *Wife Battering: A Systems Theory Approach.* New York: Guilford, 1983.

Gusdorf, Georges. "Conditions and Limits of Autobiography." Trans. James Olney. Olney, *Autobiography* 28–47.

Hairston, Loyal. "Chester Himes—An Indigenous Exile." *Freedomways* 12.2 (1973): 155–8.

Himes, Chester. *The Quality of Hurt: The Early Years.* New York: Paragon House, 1971, 1972.

———. *My Life of Absurdity.* New York: Doubleday, 1976.

———. *The Third Generation.* New York: Thunder's Mouth, 1989.

Iser, Wolfgang. *The Act of Reading: A Theory of Aesthetic Response.* Baltimore: Johns Hopkins UP, 1978.

Jameson, Fredric. *The Political Unconscious: Narrative as a Socially Symbolic Act.* Ithaca: Cornell UP, 1981.

Jelinek, Estelle C. *The Tradition of Women's Autobiography: From Antiquity to the Present.* Boston: Twayne, 1986.

Leeming, David. *James Baldwin: A Biography.* New York: Knopf, 1994.

Lederer, Norman. Rev. of *The Quality of Hurt*, by Chester Himes. *America* 15 (April 1972): 408.

Margolies, Edward. "Experiences of the Black Expatriate Writer: Chester Himes." *CLA Journal* 15 (June 1972): 221–32.

Muller, Gilbert H. *Chester Himes.* Boston: Twayne, 1989.

Olney, James. "Autobiography and the Cultural Moment: A Thematic, Historical, and Bibliographical Introduction." Olney, *Autobiography* 3–27.

———., ed. *Autobiography: Essays Theoretical and Critical.* Princeton, N.J.: Princeton UP, 1980.

Pascal, Roy. *Design and Truth in Autobiography.* Cambridge: Harvard UP, 1960.

Person, Leland S., Jr. "Henry James, George Sand, and the Suspension of Masculinity." *PMLA* 106.3 (1991): 515–28.

Reckley, Ralph. "The Oedipal Complex and Interracial Conflict in Chester Himes' *The Third Generation*," *College Language Association Journal* 21 (1977): 275–81.

Stepto, Robert B. "Distrust of the Reader in Afro–American Narratives." *Reconstructing American Literary History.* Ed. Sacvan Bercovitch. Cambridge: Harvard UP, 1986, 300–22.

———. *From Behind the Veil: A Study of Afro-American Narrative.* Urbana: U of Illinois P, 1979.

Thaddeus, Janice. "The Metamorphosis of Richard Wright's *Black Boy*." *American Literature* 57.2 (1985): 199–214.

Werner, Craig. "On the Ends of Afro-American 'Modernist' Autobiography." *Black American Literature Forum* 24.2 (1990): 203–20.

Williams, John A. "My Man Himes: An Interview with Chester Himes." *Flashbacks: A Twenty-year Diary of Article Writing.* Garden City, NY: Doubleday, 1974.

From *a/b: Auto/Biography Studies*, 11:1 (Spring 1996), 38–55.

AN INTERVIEW

Chester Himes—The Ethics of Ambiguity: An Interview with Joseph Sandy Himes, Jr.

Gwendoline Lewis Roget

The writings of Chester Bomar Himes (1909–1984) are a testament to his uncanny talent for mystification. His two volumes of autobiography, *The Quality of Hurt* (New York: Doubleday, 1972) and *My Life Of Absurdity* (New York: Doubleday, 1976), as well as his novels, are infused with biographical data that reveal the joys, sorrows, conquests, rebuffs, and rejections that were an integral part of his personal odyssey. Yet, despite his apparent propensity for self-disclosure, the authentic Chester Himes continues to elude his readers.

Between the mid-1930s and the late '70s, Himes's was one of the most poignant voices raised against racism, bigotry, intolerance, social injustice, and the victimization of black people in America. He experienced the most heinous bigotry, slights, and malicious slander because of his writings. Although he was often bitter, fundamentally Himes was never deterred from his belief in the brotherhood of man. Experience had taught him, however, that "human beings—all human beings, of whatever race or nationality or religious belief or ideology—will do anything and everything" (*Quality*, 3).

Through the circuitous and ironically liberating route of incarceration for armed robbery, Himes, scion of black middle-class parents, discovered his vocation as a writer in Ohio State Penitentiary. Commenting on the motive force that led him to commit armed robbery, Himes relates, "I wanted to leave Cleveland and Ohio and all the United States of America and go somewhere I could escape the thought of my parents and my brother, somewhere black people weren't considered the shit of the earth" (*Quality*, 48).

His adolescent defiance of the virtues and values inculcated in him by his parents can be perceived, on one level, as an attempt on his part to disassociate himself from his family and heritage. Paradoxically, his writings attest to his love for both his parents and brothers, as well as his belief in the dignity and worth of all human beings. Yet, it appears that Himes's affection for the members of his family did not exclude some ambivalence. His revelations about himself and his thoughts about the people who had an impact on his life are fraught with ambiguity, contradiction, and paradox. Himes's unique ability to bare his soul while remaining an enigma has given rise to the Chester Himes mystique.

Inconsistency and ambiguity inform Chester Himes's seventy-five years of life, which began on July 29, 1909, in Jefferson City, Missouri. The youngest of three children, all sons, born to Joseph Sandy and Estelle Bomar Himes, Chester struggled throughout his life with ambivalent feelings for his family, race, and country. His mother, on the one hand, was an octoroon, fearless and resentful of Jim-Crow laws that circumscribed her existence. She was uncomfortable in the black world and was denied free access to the white world. His father, on the other hand, was dark of hue. Differences between his parents became a source of tension for the future writer. The love-hate dichotomy that marked Chester's relationship with his parents carried over to his other affective liaisons, particularly his relationship with his brother Joseph Sandy Himes, Jr. The boys were only one year apart in age and, according to Chester, "inseparable" (*Quality*, 7).

Up to the age of twelve, Chester enjoyed a halcyon childhood. This ended in 1923, when an accident occurred during a school program before an audience of parents, teachers, and classmates. Chester was to have assisted Joseph in a demonstration of how to make torpedoes. However, on the day of the program, Chester broke one of the family's rules, and his mother refused to allow him to participate. Joseph ended up performing an experiment alone that actually required a partner. The flask he was holding exploded in his face, blinding him. For the remainder of his life, Chester would carry with him the guilt of being responsible for his brother's accident. This guilt resonates on an unconscious level in Chester's writings.

Undaunted in his push to achieve, Joseph adjusted quickly to his new situation. He graduated from high school with top honors, received a Bachelor of Arts Degree from Oberlin College and a Master of Arts and a Doctor of Philosophy in sociology from Ohio State University, and went on to lead a brilliant and distinguished career as a professor of sociology at the University of North Carolina, Durham and Greensboro. He died in September 1993. The writer conducted an interview with Joseph ten years earlier, on June 22, 1983. The writer also sought to interview Chester, but, at the time, his agent Roslyn Targ felt that that was not feasible. He was suffering from Parkinson's disease and, as it turned out, near death. The interview with Joseph produced significant findings. Among other things, Joseph repudiates the myth that Chester intended to remain for the balance of his life outside the United States. Joseph's perspective on the Himes family sometimes corroborates and at other times refutes the portrait painted by Chester in his autobiographies. He casts Chester in a human light, showing the many nuances of Chester's complex personality.

From his perspective as both son and sociologist, Joseph provides not only a personal reminiscence but also a clinical view of the factors operating in the first half of the twentieth century that contributed to the dissolution of his parent's marriage and the economic decline of his black middle-class family. Moreover, he reveals new information regarding the nature and texture of real-life relationships that served as the inspiration for the fictional relationships in Chester's early novels *The Third Generation*, *Lonely Crusade*, and *Pinktoes*. It hardly needs adding that the interview reflects a strong emotional investment on the part of the interviewee, who gave so generously of himself to share memories some of which, at least, must have been painful. By doing so, he has helped scholarship move closer to unraveling the mystery that surrounds his brother.

The writer takes this opportunity to express her gratitude to Arlette and Robert Smith, who were instrumental in arranging the dinner meeting with Dr. Himes and his charming wife Estelle. A heartfelt word of appreciation is also expressed in memory of our gracious hostess, the late Madame Edith Massiah, colleague and friend of Dr. Himes, who encouraged so many people in their creative endeavors.

The following excerpts from the original interview, with only slight editorial changes for clarity, represent about three-quarters of the whole.

Roget: Dr. Himes, both you and your brother, Chester, have distinguished yourselves in your respective fields, in spite of the prevailing racial and economic barriers of the time, which, for many of your contemporaries, were overwhelming. Do you attribute your push to achieve predominantly to parental influence? If not, to what influence?

Himes: Well, without any doubt in my judgment, to parental influence, to the family. I have just written a short personal autobiography, a thirty-page document. A Yale professor who is putting together a book of short biographies of black social scientists asked me to do it. I lay very heavily on the point that in my family there existed a strong theme of family tradition. My oldest brother, Edward, left home when he was just fifteen or sixteen. That must have been about 1917 or 1918. He went off to Atlanta University to go to school, and he never came back. So when I talk about the family, it does not include him. It is just my mother, my father, Chester, and me. The four of us lived in Mississippi, in Arkansas, in Missouri, and, for a short time, in Cleveland, a period of let's say from 1917 to 1927 or 1930, a fairly short time. During those years, we had what I like to call the Puritan ethic, a powerful driving force in our family experience. You know, "Work hard, you'll get ahead. Be honest, save," just a straight ole Puritan ethic.

Now, how does a black family get a Puritan ethic? The answer is simple. It's very simple. My mother and father went to colleges in South Carolina that were staffed by white missionaries from Massachusetts, from Connecticut, in short, from New England. They went down there, and they taught reading, writing, arithmetic, and the Puritan ethic. They taught more of the Puritan ethic than they did those other things.

My father did not talk about it as much as my mother did. She told us that she attended a school in South Carolina called Scotia Seminary, a kind of elite finishing school for black girls, during the early 1900's. The faculty consisted for the most part of maiden ladies from New England who escaped the fate of being unmarried. Do you know what I'm talking about? That was the fate worse than death. The women who escaped were most often in the missionary community.

It is just like the second and third sons of aristocratic families in England during the sixteenth and seventeenth centuries, when the rule was primogeniture and entailment. The estate went to the first son. This meant that the second son didn't have anything. So, what did these sons do? A lot of them escaped through Virginia. They escaped through the Virginia colony. Now, those fellows were as poor as Joe's turkey, but they made themselves into aristocracy, Virginia aristocracy. They invented what I call the known foreign culture, the whole racial system by the Virginia aristocracy.

Anyway, my mother and my father got the Puritan ethic from their teachers. That is what they taught us. My mother was ferocious about it. Now Chester likes wine, women, song, all that, but he has also learned you get ahead by hard work. Chester worked hard. He worked hard, there is no kidding about that.

Roget: Chester's prodigious literary output is testament to the hard work that you are speaking about. It is also illustrative of a point he likes to make: "A fighter fights, a writer writes" (*Quality*, 3). Besides the Puritan ethic, what other early instruction did Chester receive that helped to shape his ability to write?

Himes: When we went to Mississippi, at Alcorn College, Chester was five, and I was six. We lived there for seven years, from 1913 to 1920. We had not yet started school. We never went to school a single day while we lived there. Mother taught us at home. It was not until we moved to Pine Bluff, Arkansas, in 1920, that we went to school. I was thirteen, and Chester twelve. We entered high school; high school, and we burned it out! After my accident in 1923, we wound up in 1925, in Cleveland, Ohio, at the East High School, which was Cleveland College's preparatory high school. My parents, my father and my mother, managed to get us there.

Chester made a good record. I made the best record in my class. Why? Because mother taught us in Mississippi and because, when we were living in Pine Bluff, we were lucky to have an English teacher by the name of Ernestine Copeland, who taught us English for two years. She taught us what the English language is. That lady would drive us through sentences. We would parse them. We would conjugate verbs. She tread with the lash. That's the reason Chester and I are literate today, because mother and that woman drove us. They taught us an ethic, both of them. It was just oozing out of their pores, and they drove us with it. We didn't know what the hell was happening to us. They isolated us so much from the rest of the community. We didn't know whether this was good, bad, or indifferent. This was just the way the world was for us as far as we were concerned. They worked our tails off.

So, when we got to East High School, we had no trouble. I have a letter from the principal of that school. He indicated that, when I graduated, I made the highest average of anyone who ever attended East High School, which is a palpable and a factual exaggeration, but he and I agreed that we would discuss it.

He had a special medal made for me that said highest honor from high school. Now, I don't say this to brag, this is the data. This is how the people took to us. This is why we worked so hard.

Roget: Your formative years must have provided the occasion for many family anecdotes. Chester relates a few in his autobiographies. Two of them come readily to mind, the green paint incident and the saga of your mother's toting around a pistol in the car as her personal protection against affronts.[1] Do you recall either of these incidents?

Himes: I don't recall any story that involved a pistol. I don't believe there was a pistol in the house. As for the green paint, this occurred before we left Missouri, when I was six and Chester was five, and this was before then. As I recall, one day mother went off some place, and we found some green paint. We put it on the fence, and when she came home, we had paint all over us. We were so proud, we said, "Maimi, Maimi, look, we've been painting." At that time, Chester had long curls, which had to be cut off, to the despair of my mother.

Roget: Fortunately, your parents had pictures of you and Chester that pre-date the green paint incident.

Himes: May I tell you another anecdote?

Roget: Yes, please do.

Himes: One hot day there was a baseball game in town, just a few miles from the campus. We lived then in Mississippi. We asked Mother if we could go. We had to ask Mother. She said no. We wanted to go, so we snuck off. We were there having a ball, having a great time! Then mother came up with a piece of rattan. Do you know what rattan is? Rattan is a kind of palm branch that is sinuous and taut like steel. Well, my mother chased us home with the rattan. It was a case of child versus rattan. We are here today because we outran the rattan. (laughter)

Roget: Turning now to another concern, the source for Chester's writings and, more specifically, Chester's choice of subjects, one notes the presence of several people and incidents from his personal experience, particularly, family members and the women in his life. In *The Third Generation*, Chester's autobiographical novel, the maternal character Mrs. Taylor appears to bear a striking physical resemblance to the portrait of your mother that Chester gives in *The Quality of Hurt*.[2] Other than the physical similarity, to what extent does the authentic Mrs. Himes, your mother, resemble the image portrayed in the fictional character Mrs. Taylor?

Himes: Describe the image. It has been a long time since I read that. Chester disturbs me too much.

Roget: In *The Third Generation,* Mrs. Taylor fabricates her genealogy: "The resulting story was that her father was the son of [Dr. Jessie] Dr. Manning and a beautiful octoroon, the most beautiful woman in all the state, whose own father had been an English nobleman. Her mother was the daughter of a son of a United States President and an octoroon who was the daughter of a Confederate Army general.... She created the fiction of being only one thirty-second part Negro deliberately. It symbolized her contempt and disdain for all the Negroes she felt had tried to hurt her. It was her final rejection of all the people who would not recognize her innate superiority. Because regardless of how much they hated her, or tried to hurt and belittle her, none of them could possibly be her superior, and but a very, very few her equal, because she possessed the very maximum of white blood a Negro can possess and remain a Negro" (*Third*, 18). As far as personality traits and genealogy are concerned, what analogies can be drawn between Mrs. Himes and her fictional counterpart?

Himes: I don't recollect any connection with a President. One of the things I do remember—his may be a matter of selective memory—is Mother's saying that the general who was in charge of the Revolutionary forces at the Battle of King's Mountain, which was a little irrelevant skirmish on the hill side of North Carolina, was a British person who was an ancestor of some kind. I don't know where the connection was. That's the only definite connection I know of. Chester remembers some things that I don't remember. Obviously, there were some white ancestors, because mother physiologically was a Nordic. She had flaxen hair, transparent white skin, blue-gray eyes, aquiline nose, the works. Now, my father was a different character. He was very interesting. He had a sort of walnut color, with obvious Negroid features, a big flaring nose. He had a hump in his nose, a Middle-East hump. He had brilliant blue eyes which were striking in his brown face, and his features were chiseled. He was fairly short, with bowed legs, and long arms. He played football at Claffin College, one of the great, petite prestigious black colleges in the 1890s and early 1900s. He played on the line I think, in what was known as the flying wedge. It was the kind of blackness that was characteristic of black athletes in those days: long arms, bowed-legs, barrel chested, not really barrel chested but big-chested, with high broad shoulders.

Roget: Chester mentions that your father, in addition to teaching, worked as a blacksmith. This trade, he indicates, was handed down to him from his father, who had also been a blacksmith.

Himes: I don't recall my father talking about his ancestry, Chester may, but I don't. However, in my mother's family, her mother and father were house servants, in the home of their owner. This was prior to the Civil War, before they were freed. They were in the slave-servant class, among the aristocrats, if you see what I mean.

Roget: You have to be a sociologist to slice it that thin. That's nice use of "aristocrats" in the slave-servant category.

Himes: Now, Mother was a snob. Does Chester say that?

Roget: Yes, emphatically!

Himes: Mother was one heck of a snob, but she was an interesting woman. She was fierce and determined. After my accident occurred and my sight was damaged, my mother devoted the rest of her life to assuring that I should have a chance. She paid dearly for that contribution. It was a kind of fierce passion in her life, but she was a snob. She was a snob because of her awareness in the black community of her background and origin. She was a snob because she was fair. She exploited all of her resources of snobbery.

Roget: The subject of color snobbery is one of the leitmotifs in *The Third Generation*. In his autobiographical account of the parental situation, he suggests that Mrs. Himes's color snobbery helped create the fractious situation in her marriage. Was the color antagonism an invention of Chester's for the sake of art and sales?

Himes: He did fabricate some of it. I heard in New York, and I read, that Chester said that my mother hated my father because he was dark, and that may have instituted their divorce. That is absolutely wrong. It is a device that Chester used to help sell his book. Now, he has not said that to me specifically, but he has said that he used that kind of gimmick at times as a selling issue. I am not going to get into the business of their marriage. I am not sure about the texture and the quality of the relationship, but when I was old enough to be aware, to perceive, I don't think there was any degree of love, of passion and devotion between them. But it was their relationship. They were married in the sense that there was a certain religious obligation about it. There were children. There was respectability. All of this made for stability in the family.

When mother stayed in Alcorn, she hated it like sin. She hated the place. When I look back, I understand why she hated it. At that time, I was too young to recognize it. As a child, you know, life was all fun and play. She stayed through Pine Bluff. That's where the accident happened to me. In a sense, I provided her *raison d 'être*, a cause in her life. After that, the family went through a fundamental change, a destructive strain. Before that, my father had been a teacher at Jefferson City, Missouri, Alcorn, and Pine Bluff, and before I was born he taught at a college in Savannah, Georgia. That's all he had done.

Both Mother and Father were college graduates, such as colleges were when they were graduated. For them, this was important. This was the thing that saved them from being servants or laborers. That was an important achievement for black people at that time. So my father was a professor, which was a rank of high status in the black community. Throughout all of these years, Mother was the wife of a professor, except for the fact that she was the wife of a college professor in a trivial, insignificant place like Pine Bluff and Alcorn. This was irritating to her. Now, I've asked myself, why did she agree to marry him instead of any one of the other men that she could have married, for she was a good woman? I think she calculated that he represented a promise of advancement in academia, to become ultimately a president. I think she hoped for this. She worked for this. She supported him for this. She thought she could guide him. But ultimately she was too managerial. She was too bossy. When I became head of the family, she bossed me.

Anyway, after the accident, first we went to St. Louis, then to Cleveland. There were no black colleges there, and my father could not find a job in the public schools. I don't know what the problem was. I guess it was a combination of his training and hiring relevance in history and manual arts. He didn't have much of either to be useful in high school. He would have had to go back to school to study some more history and education. In fact, he didn't have any training in education. He either didn't want to do that or couldn't afford to do that or refused to do that, but, for whatever reason, he didn't do it. He tried to use his manual skills to get a job as a carpenter or as an electrician, but he couldn't do either of these very well. He tried all sorts of things.

The years in St. Louis and Cleveland were difficult years. He never made a good living. We started out with a nest egg of money to buy a nice house in a residential neighborhood. I was just a little teenager at that time. I don't know how much money it was, but when I look back, I know they owned these properties. At the time, they used time payments. The mortgage was commuted into monthly payments. Eventually they couldn't keep up with the payments on the house in Cleveland, and they lost that home. Now, how much equity they got out of it, I don't know. That was about 1927. I had gone off to college. They lost the house. The family had broken up, and my parents were separated.

The separation came, I am sure for two reasons: One, my father could not earn enough to maintain the family together, and, two, my mother was bitterly and hopelessly disillusioned in her failed aspiration for him to become a dean or college president, an academic position with high prestige which was of crucial importance in her background. Now, I don't think the problem between them was specifically because of color and her projection on him because he was not white. I don't think that is true at all. Now I am not as dark as my father, but I am not, obviously, a white person. Mother did not flinch for a moment to take me anywhere, and she got a lot of bad treatment, because many people in Cleveland presumed that she was white, and she was with this little colored boy.

Well, then, anyway, if that's Chester's hypothesis, I think that he was wrong. I guess he really didn't understand the dynamics of the family breakup, or he saw a way to utilize it in a literary way to make it pay off. He fabricated this just as he does a lot of things, as you know. He fictionalizes and fabricates and tells a lot of things which are sometimes actually untrue, but he writes fiction, not history. He is the first to admit that *The Third Generation* is not a biography of the family, it is a novel about the family. Does this deal with the point that you are raising?

Roget: Yes, it does. From your vantage point as a son, you have painstakingly recounted some very emotionally charged memories. As a sociologist, your sensitivity and understanding of family dynamics adds invaluable insight to this situation which you addressed with such candor. It certainly puts the black middle-class family during the post-World War I and Depression eras in perspective.

Himes: I perceive this to be the dynamics of family in the American situation, and this could happen to a family of any color, except to be black almost insures it. If my father bad been white, it would have been a different situation.

Roget: From a clinical viewpoint, is it possible that Chester's perception of the relationship that existed between your parents had an impact on how he would later view black male-female relations in general and, as such, delimited his perception of what these relationships could *be* from a positive perspective?

Himes: I have no way of knowing how it had an impact on him. I would guess that the impact came from another source. Chester perceived many marriages between black men and women. He saw that some women are perceptive, sensitive, and insightful and that they use their talents and resources to support their husbands and to insure that they succeed, and, thus, the whole family succeeds. There are other women who feel that they are somewhat diminished, exploited, lessened by sacrificing themselves for their husbands. They would be better off if they worked for themselves. It isn't that they are competing with their husbands. They are working for themselves. They are motivated by a self-oriented feminist drive, a drive for me. These women are willing to use their husbands to achieve their own successes, their own feelings of prestige and advancement. This happens to many women.

My guess is that Chester perceived this as he looked at the relation between many women and men. This is what he is seeing when he talks about the relation between his mother and his father. He is seeing his mother as being motivated by a self-oriented feminist drive. He is seeing her ... if her husband can't do it, she drops him and does it for herself. She stops trying to support him, because she is wasting her time and talents. Not that she is against him as a person, or as a black person. Nothing of that sort, it's "Me first."

Roget: Looking at Chester's own marriage to his first wife, Jean Johnson, to what extent do you think that the racial constraints and socio-economic pressures of the time contributed to the dissolution of that marriage, as well as his fatalistic portrayal of the black middle-class marriage in *Lonely Crusade*.

Himes: Well, I would guess—I am not sure about this, but I feel I have enough instinct to say—that Chester reached the point in the early 1950's where he had become totally disillusioned with the American society. This was after he had published *Lonely Crusade*. He had come to the conclusion that it was impossible for a black person to succeed as a writer in this country, and he needed to leave this country. I think Chester also perceived that a black wife would be a handicap in Europe.

Now, Jean is a nice girl. I know Jean very well, and I am extremely fond of her. Jean couldn't help Chester do what he wanted to do in Europe, probably anywhere. So he said pragmatically, unemotionally, "Jean has to go. I'm going forward. She can't help me, so I leave her." And, he left her. I don't think it was because he didn't like Jean, or he didn't care for Jean. It was a simple calculation, and Chester is like that on one level. Everything that comes his way within sight is legitimate to be used to advance his goals.

Roget: In his autobiography, Chester attributes the lack of money and his inability to be the breadwinner as precipitant to the dissolution of their marriage of fourteen years. He expresses his displeasure in letting Jean support him when he could not find a job. He says he resented it when Jean was given an office job with her own secretary, while he, a black man, was denied comparable employment.[3]

Himes: Perhaps it's true, but I don't think that he experienced many years of her being the major breadwinner. Jean only finished high school. She didn't attend college at all. I have no idea how she got into social work. That's what she did at the end of her career. She recently retired from a social work job as a manager of a settlement house in Chicago. Now, I am not sure, but let's put it this way: A, if Jean were at one time the major wage earner in the family, this was not for a long period of time. But I can't imagine Chester being awfully humiliated by that. That does not strike me as consistent with his orientation to use people. But people have many layers. They have a layer that is pragmatic, utilitarian, and exploitative, and they have another that is sensitive, made of guilt material. For Chester, both of these motifs may have been relevant. He may have said, "Yes, she is making more money than I. She is now supporting me. I am a lazybone depending on her. I'm not going to do a thing but write, and I can't make a living at it yet, and I am trapped by these guilt feelings. I need to escape from the United States because it's an impossible place for me here, but in Europe she's no good." He could be motivated by both of these simultaneously.

Roget: Are you saying that Chester was dependent on Jean at one level, but he wanted more recognition and fortune than he could get in the United States? However, in Europe, Jean would have been a liability?

Himes: Yes, that right. In one sense she was carrying him, and he was dependent upon her, in the sense of a dependent. I don't know how Chester feels. I know how I feel, and I think I know how, Eddie, our older brother, feels: to be dependent on people is real terrible, a real agonizing feeling. You do many things to avoid it. Maybe it's true for Chester, but I never thought of him in that way. There were so many times when he was using some woman to pay his bills and keep him while he wrote his books and lived the good life. If you look at the people who have been the basis for the characters in his stories.... You remember, in *The Quality of Hurt*, he talks about this white woman in Chicago who worked with the Rosenwald Foundation?

Roget: Yes, you are referring to Vandi Haygood.[4] In speaking about his affair with Vandi, Chester spares neither the intimate nor graphic details of their relationship, which he portrays as tempestuous and destructive, filled with lust and brutality, with obsessive jealousy on both sides.

Himes: Vicious. I wouldn't do that to my enemy. But it made a good episode for his stories. So he didn't hesitate to use her [in his fiction], to call her by name [in his autobiography]. That's why I hope he never uses me in his books, because every time he mentions me, he uses me. One of the ways he uses me, one of his great themes, is, "Joe is blind because I didn't help him that day. If I had been there to help him in that experiment, he wouldn't be blind. I am to blame." It's a wonderful cross to carry for a whole generation, publicly. I don't blame him for what happened. I am older than he. I did the experiment because I wanted to do it. It was not his fault, but he did not ask me what I thought about it. He didn't pay a bit of attention to me. It's a good gimmick for the image of Chester Himes, so he did it. There is something else I want to say about Chester. I like Chester very much. But, what the hell, he might be a hero to a lot of people, but he is just another guy where I am concerned, another guy with a lot of talent.

Roget: Through his writings, it appears that Chester derives a sardonic pleasure in his burlesques and caricatures of middle-class blacks. Is this an accurate perception?

Himes: This is true. I think that Chester has for many years had a strong feeling of—what is it?—contempt. No, that's not the word. He thought that prestigious blacks, richer blacks, were hot air, a bunch of crap. You know how they act. I think he would admit that immediately, if you faced him with it. You see it in his story *Pinktoes*.

Roget: Ah, *Pinktoes!* Chester wrote that novel in 1956 when he was living in France. Ironically, the French version was called *Mamie Mason, ou un exercice de la bonne volonté*. As we know, this book was anything but "an exercise of goodwill." It is, in fact, a burlesque of the black middle class in Harlem and the social gatherings that they had with white integrationists. Chester implies that, under the guise of coming together to hold political discussions on how to solve the "race problem," these gatherings were merely an opportunity for promoting interacial sex and orgies. Behind all the lewd scenes and the Rabelaisian conviviality, there lies the author's attack on the main character, Mamie Mason, and her coterie of friends. Chester has confessed that the character Mamie Mason was modeled after your cousin Henry Moon's wife Molly. I've read that Molly and Henry Moon were members of President Roosevelt's unofficial black Cabinet, which consisted of a few members of the black intelligentsia who had politically influential friends and contacts with powerful groups and networks.

Himes: Exactly. They [Molly and Henry Moon] were members of the Harlem social elite. Molly considered herself to be the reigning social priestess of the black elite of Harlem in Manhattan. Henry Moon was the public relations person of the NAACP. Chester had a wonderful anecdote about those people. Let's see. There was Walter White, way back in the early days when Fidel Castro came to the United Nations and rented a whole floor of the Hotel Theresa. Castro had a reception up there. He invited a lot of big shots, including, I think, Walter White. They were all eating chicken legs and so on and dropping chicken bones on the floor. Well, Castro went up to Walter White, extended his hand, stepped forward with his hand extended, slid on a chicken bone, and ended up punching Walter White in the stomach. (laughter) No one in the world could think of that but Chester. Maybe it was Walter White who punched Castro in the stomach. One of them stepped on the chicken bone. Utterly ridiculous!

Roget: According to Chester's autobiographical account, the Moons were his benefactors. They took him in, and made him welcome in their home. Molly introduced him to Richard Wright and other luminaries. It was Mrs. Moon's friendship with Vandi Haygood that served as a conduit at the Rosenwald Foundation, where he received the grant to complete his first published novel (*Quality*, 75). Given this, why did Chester sully Molly's reputation with his caricature of her in *Pinktoes?*

Himes: Sometime before he went to Europe, Chester was really having a hard time, and the Moons were not very nice to him, or at least he thought they were not. Chester thought they turned on him like a poor relation. I don't know the details, but Chester was hurt by the experience. He harbored a grudge.

Roget: So, if Chester harbored a grudge against the Moons, he satirized them in *Pinktoes* as, perhaps, a way of settling an old score with them. Assuming this to have been the case, why do you think that he chose to demean the relations between blacks and whites by suggesting that they were based on sexual exploitation and only tangentially of political significance?

Himes: I don't know, I guess it was a way of sticking the knife in and twisting it a little. My guess is that he carried the grudge for years and that he wanted to get back with a quick thrust and a twist. But I'm just guessing. People is people, you know.

Roget: In Chester's novels *If He Hollers* Let *Him Go*, *Lonely Crusade*, and *The Primitive*, the protagonists all suffer a form of alienation. Each one of these characters is, to a certain degree, modeled after the image of his creator. Chester has confessed that, whether in America or in Europe, he felt like a pariah. Now, in your comprehensive and scholarly work, *The Study of Sociology: An Introduction* (Glenview, IL: Scott, Foresman and Co., 1968), you define alienation, in part, as a sense of detachment and a loss of personal identity (374). Given this, do you perceive Chester as being alienated?

Himes: Oh, yes, from American white society, absolutely. This is a key element in his social-psychic structure and behavior. He says, I read, that "the United States is a dirty, ugly, mean society." He means white United States. That's alienation talk. You don't identify with a society that has those characteristics.

Roget: Chester has written that, after he left the United States for Paris, the label of protest writer began to grate on him. His turn to the detective genre was the change in direction that he felt he needed at the time. Nonetheless, he has confessed that he was so disgusted by some of the "trash" that he was asked to write that he discarded some of his manuscripts in spite of his desperate need for money. Since the generation of writers, represented by Richard Wright, Chester Himes, and James Baldwin, who left America to escape the racial prejudice and constraints of the 1940's and 1950's, how do you think the situation for black writers in America has changed?

Himes: My guess would be that it is relatively less stringent in 1984 than it was in 1953, when Chester left. There are still constraints limiting black writers, however. Chester has told me that he has a whole trunk full of unpublished manuscripts that he didn't get publishers for, a trunk full of them.

Roget: Do you know at what point in his life Chester may have written these unpublished works? Were these the stories and articles written during the 1930s and 1940s, when he first began to write?

Himes: Some of them may have been left over from that era, but most of them were written after he went to Paris.

Roget: Chester Himes has written many contradictory things about black Americans. He has been both champion and critic of black American expatriates. When he wrote his novel *The Primitive*, he stated that it hurt him to have blacks taken for primitive creatures, discriminated against, or accused of racial inferiority. Chester is in the vanguard of writers who have struggled against social injustice and man's inhumanity to man. Merciless in his dislikes, he made caustic remarks and incendiary diatribes that spared no racial group. Considering this and by way of conclusion, who is Chester Himes? Is he an ethnic disaffiliate, or is he the ultimate individualist?

Himes: I would say, theoretically and ideologically, that Chester likes to think of himself as a human being not limited by any ethnic restriction. He is a human being, just as human [as] in a white situation with a white skin, or an Arab skin, or a Hindu skin, still a human being. I think that Chester has never disaffiliated himself from the American Negro group. He was in this country two years ago, and he communicated to me his wishes. He wants to be accepted by American blacks. He wants to return to the United States to live and die in this country. All of this is contradictory. I have said that people are all contradictory. They go in different layers and sections. They go in different directions in those layers.

NOTES

1. "The only memory I have of my life in Jefferson City is of my brother Joseph and myself painting our hair with green paint left by the house painters" (*Quality*, 4).

"My mother used to take us for rides in the country with a student driving, but we got into so many controversies with the cracker farmers of the county by frightening their mule teams that my father was dismissed from school and driven from the state. And I must confess I find white people just the same today, everywhere I have ever been, if a black man owns a big and expensive car they will hate him for it. Of course part of that was due to my mother's attitude; she always carried a pistol on our car rides through the country, and whenever a cracker mule driver reached for his rabbit gun she beat him to the draw and made him drop it" (8).

2. "My mother was an octoroon, or perhaps whiter. I remember her as looking like a white woman who had suffered a long siege of illness; she had hazel eyes, a sallow complexion, and auburn hair" (4).

3. "It hurt me for my wife to have a better job than I did and be respected and included by her white co-workers, besides her rubbing elbows with many well-to-do blacks of the Los Angeles middle class who wouldn't touch me with a ten-foot pole. That was the beginning of the dissolution of our marriage. I found I was no longer a husband to my wife; I was her pimp. She didn't mind, and that hurt all the more" (*Quality*, 75).

4. Chester Himes met Vandi Haygood while she was acting director of fellowships for the Rosenwald Foundation, which at the time awarded him a fellowship to complete his first novel, *If He Hollers Let Him Go*. The pair engaged in an on-again, off-again relationship for nearly ten years. She was the model for Kris in *The Primitive*, a book in which he settled a lot of old scores (*Quality*, 135–138).

Xavier Review, 14:1 (Spring 1994), 1–18.

Bibliography

The following checklist includes selected reviews, articles, interviews, and books about Chester Himes in English which are not included in this volume. For a more comprehensive bibliography, including foreign language materials particularly in French, see *Chester Himes: An Annotated Primary and Secondary Bibliography*, compiled by Michel Fabre, Robert E. Skinner and Lester Sullivan (Westport, Connecticut: Greenwood Press, 1992). Additional bibliographic material is contained in the "Chronological List of the Works of Chester Himes" in *The Several Lives of Chester Himes* by Edward Margolies & Michel Fabre (Jackson: University Press of Mississippi, 1997), pp. 195–198.

Books:

Fabre, Michel and Robert E. Skinner. *Conversations with Chester Himes*. Jackson: University Press of Mississippi, 1995.

_____. Robert E. Skinner and Lester Sullivan, compilers. *Chester Himes: An Annotated Primary and Secondary Bibliography*. Westport, CT: Greenwood Press, 1992.

Lundquist, James. *Chester Himes*. New York: Frederick Ungar Publishing Co., 1976.

Margolies, Edward and Michel Fabre. *The Several Lives of Chester Himes*. Jackson: University Press of Mississippi, 1997.

Milliken, Stephen F. *Chester Himes: A Critical Appraisal*. Columbia: University of Missouri Press, 1976.

Muller, Gilbert H. *Chester Himes*. Boston: Twayne Publishers, 1989.

Skinner, Robert E. *Two Guns from Harlem: The Detective Fiction of Chester Himes*. Bowling Green, OH: Bowling Green State University Popular Press, 1989.

Wilson, M. L. *Chester Himes*. New York: Chelsea House Publishers, 1988. (Black Americans of Achievement)

Articles, Chapters in Books, and Introductions:

Bailey, Frankie Y. "Chester Himes (1909–1984)." *Out of the Woodpile: Black Characters in Crime and Detective fiction*. Westport, CT: Greenwood Press, 1991. Pp. 62–68.

Bell, Bernard W. "Ann Petry's Demythologizing of American Culture and Afro-American Culture." *Conjuring: Black Women, Fiction and Literary Tradition*. Edited by Marjorie Pryse and Hortense J. Spillers. Bloomington: Indiana University Press, 1985. Pp. [105]–115.

Bennett, Stephen B. and William W. Nichols. "Violence in Afro-American Fiction: An Hypothesis." *Modern Fiction Studies* 17 (Summer 1971), 221–228.

Bone, Robert. "The Contemporary Negro Novel" from *The Negro Novel in America*. New Haven, CT: Yale University Press, 1958. Pp. 173–176.

Bryant, Jerry H. "Politics and the Black Novel," *Nation*, December 20, 1971, pp. 660–662.

Campenni, Frank J. "Black Cops and/or Robbers: The Detective Fiction of Chester Himes," *Armchair Detective* 8 (Spring 1975), 206–209.

Chelminski, Rudolph. "The Hard-Bitten Old Pro Who Wrote 'Cotton'." *Life*, August 28, 1970, pp. 60–61.

Davis, Ursula. "Chester Himes" from *Paris Without Regret: James Baldwin, Kenny Clarke, Chester Himes, and Donald Byrd*. Iowa City: University of Iowa Press, 1986. Pp. [66]–96.

Diawara, Manthia. "Noir by Noirs: Toward a New Realism in Black Cinema" from *Shades of Noir*, edited by Joan Copjec. London: Verso, 1993. Pp. 261–278.

Fabre, Michel. "Chester Himes's Ambivalent Triumph" from *Harlem to Paris: Black American Writers in France, 1840–1980*. Urbana: University of Illinois Press, 1980. Pp. [215]–237.

_____ and Robert E. Skinner. "Introduction" to *Plan B: A Novel* by Chester Himes. Jackson: University Press of Mississippi, 1993. Pp. [vi]–xxx.

Feuser, Willfried. "Prophet of Violence: Chester Himes" from *African Literature Today, Number 9: Africa, America and the Caribbean*. Edited by Eldred Durosimi Jones. New York: African Publishing Company, 1978. Pp. 58–76.

Franklin, H. Bruce. "Two Novelists: Braly and Himes" from *The Victim as Criminal and Artist: Literature from the American Prison*. New York: Oxford University Press, 1978. Pp. 206–232.

Hodges, Graham. "Introduction" to *Lonely Crusade* by Chester Himes. New York: Thunder's Mouth Press, 1986. Pp. vii–x.

_____. "Foreword" to *If He Hollers Let Him Go* by Chester Himes. New York: Thunder's Mouth Press, 1986. Pp. vii–ix.

Hughes, Carl Milton [John Milton Charles Hughes]. *The Negro Novelist*. New York: The Citadel Press, 1953. Pp. 69 and passim.

Kane, Patricia and Doris Y. Wilkinson. "Survival Strategies: Black Women in *Ollie Miss* and *Cotton Comes to Harlem*," *Critique* 16:1 (1974), 101–109.

Lee, A. Robert. "Hurts, Absurdities and Violence: The Contrary Dimensions of Chester Himes," *Journal of American Studies* 12 (1978), 99–114.

Margolies, Edward. "Race and Sex: The Novels of Chester Himes" from *Native Sons: A Critical Study of Twentieth-Century Negro American Authors*. Philadelphia: J. B. Lippincott, 1968. Pp. 87–101.

_____. "The Thrillers of Chester Himes," *Studies in Black Fiction* 1:2 (Summer 1970), 1–11.

_____. "Experiences of the Black Expatriate Writer: Chester Himes," *CLA Journal* 15 (June 1972), 421–427.

_____. "Chester Himes's Black Comedy: The Genre Is the Message" from *The Private Eye in Dashiell Hammett, Raymond Chandler, Chester Himes and Ross Macdonald*. New York: Holmes & Meier, 1982. Pp. 53–70.

_____. "Afterword" to *Pinktoes* by Chester Himes. Jackson: University Press of Mississippi, 1996. Pp. [257]–264.

Peden, William. "The Black Explosion," *Studies in Short Fiction* 12:3 (Summer 1975), 231–241.

Rabinowitz, Peter. "Chandler Comes to Harlem: Racial Politics in the Thrillers of Chester Himes" from *The Sleuth and the Scholar: Origins, Evolution, and Current Trends in Detective Fiction*. Edited by Barbara A. Rader and Howard G. Zettler. Westport, CT: Greenwood Press, 1988. Pp. 19–29.

Reckley, Ralph. "The Oedipal Complex and Interracial Conflict in Chester Himes' *The Third Generation*," *CLA Journal* 21:3 (December 1997), 275–281.

Reilly, John M. "Chester Himes' Harlem Tough Guys," *Journal of Popular Culture* 9 (Spring 1976), 935–947.

Sallis, James. "Chester Himes: America's Black Heartland" from *Difficult Lives: Jim Thompson—David Goodis—Chester Himes*. Brooklyn, NY: Gryphon Books, 1993. Pp. 72–98.

_____. "Introduction" to *A Case of Rape* by Chester Himes. New York: Carroll & Graf Publishers, 1994. Pp. v–ix.

Sante. Luc. "An American Abroad," *New York Review of Books*, January 16, 1992, pp. 1–2, 8–12.

Sawyer-Lauçanno, Christopher. "The Legacy of Hurt: The Odyssey of Chester Himes" from *The Continual Pilgrimage: American Writers in Paris 1944–1960*. NY: Grove Press, 1992, pp. 182–211.

Schneider, Wolf. "*A Rage in Harlem*: Zakes Mokae in America," *American Film* 16 (March 1991), 58–59.

Siegel, Jeff. "Lonely Crusade: A Few Words about Chester Himes. *Armchair Detective* 29:4 (Fall 1996), [406]–409.

Smith, Robert P., Jr. "Chester Himes in France and the Legacy of the *Roman Policier*," *CLA Journal* 25 (September 1981), 18–37.

Van Pebbles, Melvin. "... His Wonders to Perform" from *Yesterday Will Make You Cry* by Chester Himes. New York: W. W. Norton (Old School Books), 1998. Pp. 11–21.

Willeford, Charles. "Chester Himes and His Novels of Absurdity," *American Visions* 3 (August 1988), 43–44.

Yarborough, Richard. "The Quest for The American Dream in Three Afro-American Novels: *If He Hollers Let Him Go, The Street*, and *Invisible Man*," *Melius* 8:4 (Winter 1981), 35–59.

Reviews:

If He Hollers Let Him Go (1945):

Anon. *Kirkus Review*, September 1, 1945, p. 378.

_____. *New Yorker*, November 3, 1945, p. 102

_____. "A Savage Novel on Racial Issue," *St. Louis Post Dispatch*, November 16, 1945, p. 2–C.

_____. *Saturday Review of Literature*, February 16, 1946, p. 13.

_____. *Kliatt Young Adult Paperback Book Guide*, 20 (Fall 1986), 14.

Beach, Joseph Warren. "The Dilemma of the Black Man in a White World," *New York Times Book Review*, December 2, 1945, p. 7.

Burns, Ben. "Off the Book Shelf," *Chicago Defender*, November 24, 1945, p. 13.

Clayton, Horace R. "Negro's Troubles," *Pittsburgh Courier*, March 2, 1946, p. 7.

Kupferburg, Herbert. *New York Herald Tribune Book Review*, November 4, 1945, p. 10.

Rosenfeld, Isaac. "With the Best Intentions," *New Republic*, December 31, 1945, p. 909.

Schuyler, Josephine. "A Hard-Hitting Novel," *Pittsburgh Courier*, March 16, 1946, p. 7.

Turner, Jenny. "Paperbacks: Be-ing and No-thingness," *New Statesman*, June 13, 1986, p. 28.

Wilkins, Roy. "Blind Revolt," *Crisis*, 52 (December 1945), 361–362.

Lonely Crusade (1947):

Anon. *Kirkus Review*, July 18, 1947, p. 372.

_____. *New Yorker*, September 13, 1947, p. 120.

Bontemps, Arna. "Some of the New Novels," *New York Herald Tribune Weekly Book Review*, September 7, 1947, p. 8.

Burger, Nash K. "Fear in Our Midst," *New York Times Book Review*, September 14, 1947, p. 20.

Burke, Arthur E. "The Pathology of Race," *Crisis*, 55 (January 1948), 27.

Farrelly, John. "Fiction Parade," *New Republic*, October 7, 1947, p. 30.

Klonsky, Milton. "The Writing on the Wall," *Commentary*, 5 (February 1948), 189–190.

McKitrick. "Through Many Eyes," *Saturday Review*, October 25, 1947, p. 25.

Streator, George. *Commonweal*, October 3, 1947, p. 604.

Cast the First Stone (1952):

Anon. *Kirkus Review*, September 15, 1952, p. 611.

Millstein, Gilbert. "Life in a Cell-Block," *New York Times Book Review*, January 18, 1953, p. 24.

Williams, John A. "Chester Himes Is Getting On." *New York Herald Tribune Book Review*, October 11, 1964, p. 2.

The Third Generation (1954):

Anon. *Kirkus Review*, November 1, 1953, p. 716.

_____. "Paperbacks: Fiction Originals," *Publishers Weekly*, April 21, 1989, p. 84.

Byam, Milton S. *Library Journal*, January 15, 1954, p. 145.

Fuller, Edmund. "A Moving Novel of Negro Life," *Chicago Sunday Tribune*, January 10, 1954, p. 5.

Hughes, Riley, "Novels Reviewed," *Catholic World*, 179 (April 1954), 72.

Jackson, Joseph Henry, ed. "Books: The Parade of New Novels—From Mississippi to British Guyana," *San Francisco Chronicle*, February 7, 1954, p. 12.

Levin, Martin. "Ill-Starred Family: Chester Himes's Latest Novel, 'The Third Generation'," *Saturday Review*, March 13, 1954, p. 51.

P., D. P. *Kliatt Young Adult Paperback Book Guide*, 23 (September 1989), 10.

The Primitive (1956):

Winslow, Henry F. *Crisis*, 63 (November 1956), 571–572.

For Love of Imabelle [*A Rage in Harlem*] (1957):

Anon. "Mysteries," *Washington Post Book World*, January 21, 1990, p. 12. [With *Blind Man with a Pistol* and *The Crazy Kill*]
Foley, Michael. "Black Thrills," *Irish Press*, March 9, 1985, p. 6. [With *The Real Cool Killers*]

The Real Cool Killers (1959):

Anon. *Book World*, 15 (November 17, 1985), 16. [With *A Rage in Harlem*]
Nichols, Lewis. "In and Out of Books: American in P—," *New York Times Book Review*, September 27, 1959, p. 8.

The Big Gold Dream (1960):

Anon. *Publishers Weekly*, June 23, 1975, p. 78.

Pinktoes (1961):

Anon. *Time*, July 30, 1965, p. 70.
_____. *Choice*, 2 (December 1965), 684.
Craig, Patricia. "Interracial Intercourse," *New Statesman and Society*, May 12, 1989, pp. 37–38.
Katz, Bill. *Library Journal*, April 1, 1965, p. 1743.
Levin, Martin. "Reader's Report," *New York Times Book Review*, August 15, 1965, p. 30.
M., F. *Observer*, April 2, 1989, p. 45.
S., J. L. *Best Sellers*, July 15, 1965, p. 171.
Willis, Ronald. "Ronald Willis on Side-Strapping," *Books and Bookmen*, 11 (February 1966), 32–33.
Woodford, John. "Books Noted," *Negro Digest*, 15 (November 1965), 49–50.

Cotton Comes to Harlem (1965):

Anon. *Kirkus Review*, January 1, 1965, p. 17.
_____. "Fiction," *Book Week*, July 28, 1985, p. 12.
_____. "Ebony Book Shelf," *Ebony*, 44 (May 1989), 22. (With *The Heat's On* and *The Real Cool Killers*).
Boucher, Anthony. "Criminals at Large," *New York Times Book Review*, February 7, 1965, p. 43.
Butler, Tony. "Was Sigmund Freud Misinterpreted After All?" *Irish Times*, October 26, 1985, p. 12. (With *Love for Imabelle* and The *Real Cool Killers*).
Brunet, Elena. "Current Paperbacks," *Los Angles Times Book Review*, December 11, 1988, p. 14.
Grant, Mary Kent. "Mystery—Detective—Suspense," *Library Journal*, February 1, 1965, p. 670.
Hariston, Loyle. "A Masterpiece of Satire," *Freedomways*, 6 (1966), 185–186,

Harris, Leo and Ronald Willis. "Crime fiction." *Books and Bookmen*, 11 (February 1966), 33–34.
Hentoff, Nat. "Making the Fuzz Fly," *New York Herald Tribune Book Week*, March 28, 1965, p. 11.

Run Man Run (1966):

Anon. "Clue Works," *Best Sellers*, December 1, 1966, p. 328.
Boucher, Anthony. "Criminals at Large," *New York Times Book Review*, November 27, 1966, p. 64.
Grant, M. K. *Library Journal*, December 1, 1966, p. 6004.

Blind Man with a Pistol (*Hot, Day, Hot, Night*) (1969):

Bolard, John. *Books and Bookmen*, 17 (October 1971), 53.
Boyd, Melba J. *Black World*, 21 (March 1972), 51–52, 68–69.
Grant, Mary Kent. *Library Journal*, February 15, 1969, p. 779.
Harris, Leo. *No Prizes Offered*," *Books and Bookmen*, 15 (October 1969), 38.
_____. "Unlawful Assembly," *Punch*, July 23, 1969, p. 158.
Keating, H. R. F. "Chester Himes: *Blind Man with a Pistol*" from *Crime & Mystery: The 100 Best Books*. New York: Carroll & Graf Publishers, 1987. Pp. 149–150.
Lawler, Daniel F., SJ. *Best Sellers*, March 15, 1969, p. 506.
McLoughlin. "Crime Novels," *Punch*, January 21, 1987, p. 67.
Mather, Bobby. "Militants: A Betrayal of Their Brothers?" *Detroit Free Press*, February 9, 1969, p. B–5.
Parley, Peter. "Fun with Guns," *Spectator*, July 12, 1969, p. 48.
Pooter, *Times Saturday Review*, June 28, 1969, p. 22.
Rhodes, Richard. "Blind Man with a Pistol," *New York Times Book Review*, February 23, 1969, p 32.

The Quality of Hurt (1972):

Anon. *Publishers Weekly*, January 17, 1972, p. 53.
_____. *New Yorker*, March 18, 1972, p. 155.
_____. "Notes on Current Books," *Virginia Quarterly Review*, 48 (Summer 1972), lxxxix.
Gingrich, Arnold. "'A Writer Writes'," *Book World*, March 26, 1972, p. 12.
Greenlee, Sam. "The Quality of Hurt," *Black Books Bulletin* 1 (Spring–Summer 1972), 52–57.
Huggins, Nathan Irvin. "The Quality of Hurt," *New York Times Book Review*, March 12, 1972, pp. 5, 32.
Lacy, Dan. "Reflections on Being Black in America," *Commonweal*, December 1, 1972, pp. 211–212.
Lederer, Norman. *America*, April 15, 1972, p. 408.
Lehmann-Haupt, Christopher. "Another Quality Not Strained," *New York Times Book Review*, March 3, 1972, p. 41.
Mok, Michael. "PW Interviews: Chester Himes," *Publishers Weekly*, April 3, 1972, pp. 20–21.
Moon, Eric. *Library Journal*, March 15, 1972, p. 1007.
Muggeridge, Malcolm. "Books," *Esquire*, 77 (May 1972), 55–56.

Owomoyela, Oyekan. "Himes on Hurt," *Prairie Schooner* 48 (Winter 1974–1975), 365–366.
Young, Al. *New York Times Book Review*, February 13, 1977, p. 24.

Black on Black (1973):

Anon. *Kirkus Reviews*, January 1, 1973, p. 18.
_____. *Virginia Quarterly Review*, 49 (Summer 1973), cv.
Curran, T. M. *America*, July 21, 1973, p. 44.
Glendinning, Victoria. "In the Swim," *New Statesman*, April 11, 1975, p. 489.

My Life of Absurdity (1976):

Anon. *Kirkus Reviews*. September 15, 1976, pp. 1066–1067.
_____. *Publishers Weekly*, October 4, 1976, p. 70.
_____. *Choice*, 14 (April 1977), 200.
Bredes, Don. "The Purgative Thoughts of Chester Himes," *Los Angeles Times Book Review*, March 20, 1977, p. 7.
Lindborg, Henry J. *Library Journal*, December 15, 1976, p. 2564.

A Case of Rape (1980):

Anon. *Los Angeles Times Book Review*, August 21, 1994, p. 7.

Plan B (1993):

Anon. *Publishers Weekly*, September 13, 1993, p. 94.
Miller, J. A. *Choice*, 31 (March 1994), 1126.
Traxel, David. "Political Parable," *New York Times Book Review*, October 31, 1993, p. 40.
Angus. *Booklist*, November 19, 1993, p. 602.

The Collected Stories of Chester Himes (1990):

Anon. *Kirkus Reviews*, April 1, 1991, p. 422–423.
_____. *Publishers Weekly*, April 5, 1991, p. 139.
_____. *Booklist*, May 1, 1991, p. 1693.
Bess, R, A. *Choice*, 29 (September 1991), 94.
R., D. P. *Kliatt Young Adult Paperback Book Guide*, 25 (September 1991), 31.

Index

About the Editor

CHARLES L. P. SILET is Professor of English at Iowa State University. He has written widely on crime and mystery fiction and his articles, reviews, and interviews have appeared in journals both in the United States and abroad. He was a Consulting Editor for *The Armchair Detective* and is presently a Consulting Editor for the new *Strand Magazine*. His most recent book is *Talking Murder: 20 Interviews with Mystery and Crime Writers*.

ISBN 0-313-29941-2

HARDCOVER BAR CODE